A View to a Death in the Morning

To b

Matt Cartmill

A VIEW TO A DEATH
IN THE MORNING

Hunting
and
Nature
through
History

HARVARD UNIVERSITY PRESS
CAMBRIDGE, MASSACHUSETTS
LONDON, ENGLAND

First Harvard University Press paperback edition, 1996

Library of Congress Cataloging-in-Publication Data

Cartmill, Matt.
A view to a death in the morning : hunting and nature through
history / Matt Cartmill.
    p.   cm.
Includes bibliographical references (p.   ) and index.
ISBN 0-674-93735-X (cloth)
ISBN 0-674-93736-8 (pbk.)
1. Nature—cultural conceptions. 2. Hunting—History.
3. Human-animal relationships. 4. Animals—Symbolic aspects.
5. Hunting stories.   I. Title.
GN388.C37   1993
304.5—dc20   92-44960
CIP

Designed by Gwen Frankfeldt

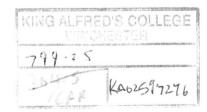

FOR KAYE

with love and thanks

CONTENTS

Illustrations

Preface

THIS BOOK is about the connections that various people have tried to draw between hunting and being human. It deals above all with the hunting hypothesis of human origins, which is the story of how some apes became human when they took up weapons and began to kill. The killer-ape story has roots in older tales, and so this book is in part a literary history. But it is also a book about science, because scientists have been the chief tellers of that story.

I have begun my history near its end, by tracing the rise and ascendancy of the hunting hypothesis in anthropological thought after the end of World War II. In Chapter 2, I describe the collapse of the hypothesis during the 1970s and ask why such a flimsy story with such unpalatable implications was accepted for so long by thoughtful scientists. Some critics argue that the vision of *Homo sapiens* as a lunatic killer ape attracts those who seek to excuse war, violence, and cruelty as inherent in human nature. But that argument cannot apply to the early versions of the hunting hypothesis, which contain some of the most vitriolic denunciations of these evils ever written. What, then, do we get out of seeing ourselves as sick, disordered animals—and why should anyone think that the origins of our sickness are somehow tied to hunting?

The central part of the book tries to answer these questions. In Chapter 3 ("Virgin Huntresses and Bleeding Feasts"), I show that hunting has been likened to warfare throughout the history of European thought. In ancient Greek myth and literature, the hunt was usually regarded as a just war, a triumph of the humane and rational over the bestial and irrational; but throughout the Christian era, hunting has been viewed in an increasingly unfavorable light. Chapter 4 ("The White Stag") tells how the meaning of hunting began to change in the later Middle Ages, when the hunt became an exclusive privilege of the aristocracy, the wild forest came to be seen as a lovely place, and the hunter's quarry took on an air of tragedy, nobility, and mystery. Chapter 5 ("The Sobbing Deer") describes the emergence of the hunt as a symbol of tyranny and an object of moral indignation in the Renaissance.

From the seventeenth century on, the growth of antihunting sentiment has been linked in various ways to the growth of science. In Chapter 6 ("The Noise of Breaking Machinery"), I show how science itself has called into question the moral foundations of man's dominion over nature by blurring the boundary between people and beasts. The Romantic reaction against science, described in Chapter 7 ("The Sorrows of Eohippus"), has taught us to think of nature as a sacred realm opposed to the spreading pollution of technology. Conversely, the opposing, Darwinian view of nature as a struggle for existence is often cited as a justification for hunting. In the Victorian era, Darwinism was also widely invoked to justify imperialism and laissez-faire capitalism. In Chapter 8 ("The Sick Animal"), I show that big-game hunting was embraced by European colonialists as a symbol of human dominion over the lower orders, and attacked as cruel and oppressive by opponents of imperialism. Chapter 9 ("The Bambi Syndrome") describes how fear of war, Romantic reverence for nature, Freudian pessimism about man's future, and the symbolic values we attach to deer entered into the making of the most influential piece of antihunting propaganda ever produced.

In Chapter 10 ("A Fatal Disease of Nature"), I return to the scientific versions of the hunting hypothesis and show that essentially the same stories that scientists embraced warmly in 1960 were coldly ignored when others proposed them in 1920. Part of this difference was due to the triumph of neo-Darwinism in the 1930s and the recovery of new fossils in the 1940s; but I argue that much of it reflects underlying cultural and historical changes, including the collapse of Nazi Germany and the European empires, the postwar rise of ecological consciousness, and the fears of scientific technology spawned by the atom bomb and the onset of the cold war. The book's concluding chapters express my doubts about the meaning and reality of the distinctions we draw between artifice and nature and between people and animals.

I could not have finished all this without a great deal of help from others. Many of them are thanked in the Acknowledgments at the end of the book. Here, at the beginning, I want to give special thanks to my wife, friend, and colleague Kaye Brown. Throughout the years of research and writing that went into this book, she listened to my ideas and helped me weed out the mistakes, contributed many keen insights, helped organize our lives and schedules so that I could stick to the job, and saw to it that I concentrated my energy and attention on the painful labor of getting the words down on paper. Like most of what I have managed to accomplish, this book is due in large measure to her thoughtful help and affectionate support. It is dedicated to her with love, gratitude, and admiration.

D'ye ken John Peel with his coat so gay?
D'ye ken John Peel at the break of day?
D'ye ken John Peel when he's far, far away,
With his hounds and his horn in the morning?

'Twas the sound of his horn brought me from my bed,
And the cry of his hounds which he oftimes led,
For Peel's "View hallo!" would awaken the dead,
Or the fox from his lair in the morning.

Yes, I ken John Peel and Ruby too!
Ranter and Ringwood, Bellman and True,
From a find to a check, from a check to a view,
From a view to a death in the morning.

—Traditional foxhunting song (attributed to
  John Woodcock Graves, c. 1820)

Note: In quoting from English sources earlier than 1700, I have modernized spellings. In the bibliography I list early authors under editors and translators, to avoid such misleading references as "Darwin, 1937." Uncredited translations are my own.

ONE

The Killer Ape

Pessimistic accounts of the human condition may be regarded
as warnings of what we may choose to avoid.

—S. A. Barnett

SOUTH AFRICA's northern province, the Transvaal, stretches four
hundred miles from east to west along the southeastern edge of the
Kalahari Desert. In 1922 the Transvaal was a dismal backwater of the
British Empire, and its capital, Johannesburg, was a dusty mining
town full of tin-roofed shanties. But there were prospects of great
things ahead on the city's cultural horizon. The old South African
School of Mines had just completed a three-year metamorphosis into
the University of the Witwatersrand, with a big new campus down-
town, thirty academic departments, and its own medical school.[1]

Unfortunately, the new university also had a nasty scandal on its
hands. The head of the medical school's department of anatomy, E. P.
Stibbe, had in his wife's absence been seen entering a cinema with a
woman. Called on the carpet for this enormity, Stibbe indignantly
told the head of the university that it was none of his business—and
was promptly fired from his job.[2]

When this news reached the celebrated neuroanatomist G. Elliot
Smith back in London, he quickly pressed forward one of his protegés
as a replacement for Stibbe. Smith's candidate, a young Australian
anatomist named Raymond Dart, was not enchanted with the prospect
of swapping his prestigious job at University College London for a
post in some jerkwater college on the remote frontiers of civilization.
He let Smith talk him into applying for the Witwatersrand opening,

and he accepted the job offer when it came; but he did so against his better judgment.[3]

At first it seemed to Dart that he had made a disastrous mistake. He arrived at the School of Medicine in Johannesburg in January 1923 to confront "an abysmal lack of equipment and literature."[4] The department of anatomy was housed in a shabby old building. Its central facility, a ramshackle dissecting hall strewn with dried-up cadaver parts, was used for tennis practice when medical classes were not in session. Most of Dart's new colleagues thought it a shame that the well-liked Stibbe had been sacked and replaced—worst of all, by an Australian. Dart's previously bright prospects as a scientist were starting to look sour and dim.

Then something happened that transformed everything: Dart's life, the university, and South Africa's place in the history of science. Eventually it was to transform the way people thought about the nature and origin of the human species.

For many years the Northern Lime Company had been quarrying limestone at a place called Taung, 250 miles east and south of Johannesburg. Miners occasionally found fossils in the limestone at Taung and kept them as curiosities. A company director who visited the site in May 1924 was shown a collection of those fossils. He picked out a nice monkey skull to use as a paperweight on his desk back home in Johannesburg. His son borrowed the fossil to show to his friends at the university—and one of those friends, a pre-med student named Josephine Salmons, borrowed it yet again to show to her anatomy professor, Dr. Dart.

Dart identified the skull as that of a new species of baboon, and noticed that a neat round chunk had been broken out of the roof of the braincase. Intrigued by the specimen, he asked Professor R. B. Young in the university's geology department to see what he could do to get more fossils from the site. Young went to Taung in November and returned with another fossil skull. The new fossil was no baboon; it looked like the skull of a baby ape.

This was an important and puzzling find. Apes today live in forests, but northern South Africa has been a grassy and semiarid country for millions of years. How could an animal like a chimpanzee or an orangutan have survived on a treeless plain? As Dart studied the skull,

2

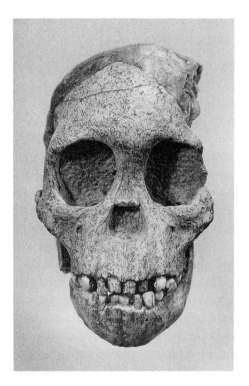

The fossil skull of the infant *Australopithecus* from Taung. (Courtesy of Professor Phillip Tobias)

he noticed that the brain seemed to have been unusually large and humanlike—and he began to wonder whether this creature might have some connection with our own ancestry. His immediate thought, when he first saw the infant's skull, was that this extinct South African ape might have made its living as a hunter:

> As I pondered the mystery of how the big-brained creature could have survived in the Transvaal without an anthropoid's natural foods my mind flashed back to Miss Salmons' baboon skull which had come from the same mine. I remembered the neat round hole on top on the right side.
> Was it possible that the opening had been made by another creature to extract its brain for food? Did this ape with the big brain catch and

eat baboons? If so it must have been very clever to catch them and kill them; and very courageous too.[5]

Dart rushed into print with amazing speed. Working night and day, he chiseled the Taung skull out of the limestone, cleaned it, made several drawings and photographs for publication, wrote up his findings and conclusions, and sent his manuscript off to the British science journal *Nature*—all in less than six weeks.[6] Dart's paper was published on February 7, 1925. In it, Dart named his big-brained anthropoid *Australopithecus africanus* (the African southern ape), hailing it as an upright biped and a human ancestor.

In a longer article published the following year, Dart offered some conclusions about the habits of his man-ape. *Australopithecus,* he thought, had been a predatory primate, an ape that "had become sufficiently weaned from its frugivorous tropical diet to vary its table with the fruits of the chase." But those first fruits of the chase looked like pretty meager pickings. After studying the collection of bony rubbish found in the Taung breccias, Dart concluded that it must represent leftovers from australopithecine meals, since it was too pathetic a collection of scraps to be the leavings of a large, effective carnivore:

> The material, which looks like the comminuted bones of turtles, birds, insectivores, rodents, baboons, and perhaps small bok, as well as birds' eggshells, indicates by its nature, its sparsity, and its searched over and exhausted character, the careful and thorough picking of an animal, which did not live to kill large animals, but killed small animals in order to live.[7]

The australopithecines, wrote Dart, had gotten started down the road to humanity precisely *because* they were eking out a marginal living in a harsh environment. The other apes, lolling about in the lush equatorial jungles, had things far too easy. ("In the luxuriant forests of the tropical belts, Nature was supplying with profligate and lavish hand an easy and sluggish solution . . . of the problem of existence."[8] But for an ape living in the Transvaal, survival "constantly and increasingly demanded the operation of choice and cunning . . . to find and subsist upon new types of food and to avoid the dangers and enemies of the open plain." Dart surmised that *Australopithecus*

4

had been forced to get up on its hind legs to escape from predators, "for sudden and swift bipedal movement, to elude capture." Its strenuous life spent dodging cheetahs and ambushing baby antelope had "evoked the thinking and planning powers of the anthropoid, and, with these powers, caused the transformation from anthropoid to man."[9]

Dart's early papers depict the ape from Taung as a skulking picker of bones and licker of eggshells, "a cave-dwelling, plains-frequenting, stream-searching, bird-nest-rifling and bone-cracking ape."[10] The australopithecines, he wrote in 1940, had managed to survive only through "exploitation of every accessible source of food." No doubt they had even "chased away the vultures and hyaenas and filled themselves with the noisome remnants of the lion's feasts."[11]

But as more fossils came to light from other sites in the Transvaal, Dart gradually abandoned his original picture of *Australopithecus* as a sort of chimpanzee studying to be a jackal. The man-ape fossils from the new Transvaal sites were commingled with the remains of wildebeest, kudu, warthog, zebra, and other big game. Dart's studies of these fossil animals convinced him that they had all been killed, butchered, and eaten by the man-apes.[12] By the 1950s, he was no longer picturing *Australopithecus* as a scavenger contending with vultures for the lion's noisome leavings. All the small animal bones and eggshells in the Taung breccias, which had once suggested to him that the man-apes were indiscriminate omnivores, he now saw as proof that *Australopithecus* "was in the process of taking dominion over every beast of the field . . . and every creeping thing that creepeth upon the earth." "The main food supply of the breccia-makers," he concluded in 1957, "was venison."[13]

Originally Dart had regarded *Australopithecus* as a desperate fruit eater that had been forced to turn to meat in order to survive in a hostile environment. By the 1950s he had come to believe that the man-apes had purposely moved out of the equatorial jungles into the grasslands looking for meat. "The ancestors of *Australopithecus*," he wrote, "left their fellows in the trees of Central Africa through a spirit of adventure and the more attractive fleshy foods that lay in the vast savannas of the southern plains."[14] It was a taste for blood, not the rigors of life in the Transvaal, that had made us human.

The South African australopithecine sites yielded thousands of bones of game animals, but far fewer stone tools. The few tools found came from the latest deposits in the caves and had probably been made by more advanced human ancestors. There was no good evidence that the australopithecines themselves had ever chipped a single pebble. Then how had they been able to slay and butcher all those animals? By using the bones themselves as weapons, Dart decided; and he brought forward specimens and statistics to show that the man-apes had utilized the bony parts of their prey as tools in killing and butchering. Hyena mandibles had been put to use as butcher knives, warthog jaws as battle axes, antelope horns as daggers, zebra thighbones as clubs, and so on.

Few archaeologists took Dart's bone tools very seriously, and scientists generally agreed that the australopithecines (like most people today) had eaten "a preponderantly vegetable diet."[15] Yet Dart's vision of our remote ancestors as killer apes was warmly embraced by his peers. From the early 1950s to the mid-1970s, the major authorities on human evolution agreed that *Australopithecus* had been a hunter and that our ancestors had become human largely as a result of taking up hunting. Kenneth Oakley's 1951 essay "A Definition of Man" sounded the keynote:

> The apes of to-day are forest creatures, subsisting almost exclusively on fruits, leaves, shoots and insects. All known races of man, on the other hand, include a substantial portion of animal flesh in their diet . . . I suggest that meat-eating is as old as man; that with the change from forest living to open country, the diet of proto-men inevitably became more varied and that they changed from being eaters largely of plants and the fruits of plants to being partly meat-eaters.

The first technology, Oakley thought, was the tool kit of a butcher. "The early hominids must often have encountered difficulty in removing skin and fur, and in dividing the flesh. In the absence of strong canine teeth [this difficulty] would have been overcome most readily by using sharp pieces of stone . . . All the main uses of stone tools were, I suggest, connected in the first place with adoption of semi-carnivorous habits."

In a much-reprinted 1953 article, the zoologist G. A. Bartholomew and the anthropologist J. B. Birdsell portrayed the australopithecines as "generalized carnivorous animals" and big-game hunters, "for which the freeing of hands and the use of simple implements enormously broadened the scale of food size." Why had the man-apes taken up hunting in the first place? Bartholomew and Birdsell related it to sex. Hunting, they suggested, had originated as an accidental side effect of fights between our apelike forefathers over sexual access to females. The biggest and most aggressive males won those fights and so got to pass on their genes to the next generation. After many generations of this, all the males would be big and aggressive. The bulk and viciousness of the new breed of males would have coincidentally suited them to taking up big-game hunting, "a secondarily-derived function related to aggressive behavior."

But hunting also forced the males to learn to cooperate with each other. Dart had shown that *Australopithecus* preyed on baboons, which travel in large, well-defended groups. Bartholomew and Birdsell reasoned that the male australopithecines must also have banded together in groups to hunt, since "a single australopithecine, even armed with a club, would not be a serious threat to a group of baboons." Coordinated group effort, like tool use and the differentiation of sex roles, was another distinctively human characteristic that had originated as a side effect of hunting.

William Etkin went on from this to develop a model of the proto-human family, in which "the male specialized as hunter, the female as domestic." The domestic economy of a killer ape, thought Etkin, would have required some such difference between the roles of the two sexes. Because baby anthropoids cling to their mothers and take a long time to grow up, a female ape or monkey "is almost continuously carrying a child. As one is weaned the next is born. The female therefore cannot be an effective hunter. The development of a hunting economy can occur in an anthropoid only if the male cooperates in feeding and care of the young."[16]

Etkin thought that this cooperation—what he called "the socialization of the male"—had been brought about by "the diffusion of sexual activity over the entire menstrual period" in the female. The female's unflagging interest in sex had acted "to tie the male and female together socially in a highly advantageous way." Sexual activity became more playful and affectionate, controlled more by the brain and less by an irresistible periodic rush of hormones. Our big brains, argued Etkin, are "thus related to sexual behavior control as well as to the intellectual functions."

"The social organization of the integrated family," Etkin suggested, "would also shift selective pressures with respect to the development of the offspring." With father furnishing most of the family's food, mother no longer need carry or herd the babies around while she foraged herself. Instead, she could stay put in a nest or home base of some sort and devote her time and attention to her offspring. Given such intensive mothering, her offspring need not grow up quickly; they could afford a longer period of dependency on their parents. This would be useful, because the young man-apes had a lot of lessons to learn. None of the things they needed to know in order to survive—how to make and use tools, cooperate in the hunt, have cortically controlled sex, and tend their own helpless offspring—came instinctively to them. Each new generation had to learn the whole list from scratch, and the list grew longer all the time. A prolonged infancy would "permit a longer period for learning on the part of the young," so that they could learn all these skills before they went off to fend for themselves and start their own families.

Intensive mothering was theoretically important for another reason: it made it possible for the infant's brain to grow bigger. "The reason that the newborn baby may commit more of its birth-weight to the human specialty, brain, and relatively less to a largely helpless body," wrote Weston La Barre, "is precisely that it enjoys this protected dependency and fostering by the mother."[17] S. L. Washburn found a connection between this and bipedalism:

> In all the apes and monkeys the baby clings to the mother; to be able to do so, the baby must be born with its central nervous system in an advanced state of development. But the brain of the fetus must be small enough so that birth may take place. In man adaptation to bipedal locomotion decreased the size of the bony birth canal at the same time that the exigencies of tool use selected for larger brains. This obstetrical dilemma was solved by delivery of the fetus at a much earlier stage of development. But this was possible only because the mother, already bipedal and with hands free of locomotor necessities, could hold the helpless, immature infant.[18]

8

All these patterns reinforced one another. Hunting demanded weapons. Weapons encouraged bipedalism. Bipedalism made it possible to carry things—not only weapons and helpless babies but also meat.[19] Bipedal males could therefore carry food to their mates, who could not hunt for themselves because they were encumbered by infants. "The slow-moving mother, carrying the baby, could not hunt," Washburn wrote, "and the combination of the woman's obligation to care for slow-developing babies and the man's occupation of hunting imposed a fundamental pattern on the social organization of the human species."[20] This fundamental social pattern was the nuclear family, consisting of a male provider, a female nurturer, and a string of more or less incompetent, slow-maturing offspring. Supported by their hunting fathers, the young man-apes could afford to stretch out their childhood years while they developed larger brains and learned more complicated skills. But supporting the females and young during this longer infancy made greater demands on the males' hunting abilities. To meet those demands, the males had to develop more effective tools, techniques, and teamwork. This in turn called for more learning, which meant still bigger brains, which meant still more dependent infants—and so on and on, round and round, onward and upward, with everything human flowing from that crucial shift to a more carnivorous diet.

"Hunting has dominated human history," wrote Washburn and Lancaster.[21] "Our intellect, interests, emotions, and basic social life—all are evolutionary products of the success of the hunting adaptation." "Man's life as a hunter supplied all the other ingredients for achieving civilization," asserted William S. Laughlin in 1968. "Hunting is the master behavior pattern of the human species."[22] And an imposing array of distinguished scholars and eminent anthropologists agreed: hunting was what had turned apes or man-apes into people, and man's need to become an ever more effective hunter had governed the whole course of human evolution until the invention of agriculture.[23]

WE CAN call this, as Robert Ardrey did, the *hunting hypothesis*.[24] As sketched above, it all sounds properly cool-headed, scientific, and objective. But from its very first appearance in Dart's papers of the early 1950s, the hunting hypothesis was colored with a wash of the darkest moral disapprobation. As Dart's opinion of the australopithe-cines' hunting ability went up, his opinion of their morals declined in proportion. "They were just as competent hunters as human beings," he wrote, "probably more competent, because they had fewer inhibitions." The Transvaal man-apes

> like Nimrod long after them, were mighty hunters. They were also callous and brutal. The most shocking specimen there was the fractured lower jaw of a 12-year-old son of a manlike ape. The lad had been killed by a violent blow delivered with calculated accuracy on the point of the chin either by a smashing fist or a club. The bludgeon blow was so vicious that it had shattered the jaw on both sides of the face and knocked out all the front teeth. That dramatic specimen impelled me in 1948 and the 7 years following to study further their murderous and cannibalistic way of life.[25]

Dart did not need all seven of those years to arrive at a verdict. In his 1953 article "The Predatory Transition from Ape to Man," he was already depicting the man-apes as "confirmed killers: carnivorous creatures, that seized living quarries by violence, battered them to death, tore apart their broken bodies, dismembered them limb from limb, slaking their ravenous thirst with the hot blood of victims and greedily devouring livid writhing flesh." *Australopithecus* was not only a predator, but a cannibal who "ruthlessly killed fellow australopithecines and fed upon them as he would upon any other beast."[26]

Poring over the cracked and battered bones from the Transvaal caves, Dart to his horror began to see that human beings are only made-over australopithecines and that we preserve all the vicious traits of our original. In his first paper announcing this discovery to the world, Dart began by quoting the seventeenth-century Calvinist divine Richard Baxter: "Of all the beasts the man-beast is the worst, / To others and himself the cruellest foe." And Dart went on to describe *Homo sapiens* in the most embittered and misanthropic language he could summon up:

> The creatures that have been slain and the atrocities that have been committed in the name of religion from Carthage to Mexico, the hecatombs of animals that have been sacrificed from the altars of antiquity to the abattoirs of every modern city, proclaim the persistently blood-

stained progress of man. He has either decimated and eradicated the earth's animals or led them as domesticated pets to his slaughterhouses. The loathsome cruelty of mankind to man is the inescapable byproduct of his blood lust; this differentiative human characteristic is explicable only in terms of man's carnivorous and cannibalistic origin.

The blood-bespattered, slaughter-gutted archives of human history from the earliest Egyptian and Sumerian records to the most recent atrocities of the Second World War accord with early universal cannibalism, with animal and human sacrificial practices or their substitutes in formalized religions and with the world-wide scalping, head-hunting, body-mutilating and necrophiliac practices of mankind in proclaiming this common bloodlust differentiator, this predaceous habit, this mark of Cain that separates man dietetically from his anthropoidal relatives and allies him rather with the deadliest of the Carnivora.[27]

The misanthropy expressed in these passages was not peculiar to Raymond Dart. Many other scientists thought they had found the roots of human murderousness in the same predatory habits that had made our ancestors human. Washburn and Avis suggested that human sadism might be a predator's instinct: "Unless careful training has hidden the natural drives, men enjoy the chase and the kill. In most cultures torture and suffering are made public spectacles for the enjoyment of all. The victims may be either animal or human. This behavior is strikingly similar to that of many carnivores."[28] The connection between hunting and warfare was explored by Washburn and Lancaster:

Men enjoy hunting and killing, and these activities are continued as sports even when they are no longer economically necessary . . . Evolution builds a relation between biology, psychology, and behavior, and, therefore, the evolutionary success of hunting exerted a profound effect on human psychology. Perhaps, this is most easily shown by the extent of the efforts devoted to maintain killing as a sport. In former times royalty and nobility maintained parks where they could enjoy the sport of killing, and today the United States government spends many millions of dollars to supply game for hunters . . . And until recently war was viewed in much the same way as hunting. Other human beings were simply the most dangerous game. War has been far too important in human history for it to be other than pleasurable for the males involved.[29]

Then why don't lions and wolves and other hunting animals murder *their* friends and relations for pleasure? Konrad Lorenz, the Nobel-laureate zoologist, was ready with an answer. Other predators had evolved their killing apparatus over millions of years. During this long process, there was heavy natural selection against those who used their weapons on their mates or offspring. As a result, "all heavily armed carnivores possess sufficiently reliable inhibitions which prevent the self-destruction of the species." Man's unique murderousness, said Lorenz,

> arises from his being a basically harmless, omnivorous creature, lacking in natural weapons with which to kill big prey, and, therefore, also devoid of the built-in safety devices which prevent "professional" carnivores from abusing their killing power to destroy fellow members of their own species . . . In human evolution, no inhibitory mechanisms preventing sudden manslaughter were necessary . . . until, all of a sudden, the invention of artificial weapons upset the equilibrium of killing potential and social inhibitions. When it did, man's position was very nearly that of a dove which, by some unnatural trick of nature, has suddenly acquired the beak of a raven.

Because our weapons were abruptly invented, not slowly evolved, we have not had time to acquire the inhibiting instincts that ought to go with our killing ability. When a defeated wolf goes belly up, the victor turns away with instinctive chivalry; when a defeated man goes belly up, the victor spears him in the belly. Using weapons also unnaturally distances us from our killing and spares us the distasteful experience of killing prey with our own hands and teeth. In Lorenz's view, the intervention of the weapon between us and the quarry is the only thing that makes sportive hunting possible: "No sane man would even go rabbit hunting for pleasure if the necessity of killing his prey with his natural weapons brought home to him the full, emotional realization of what he is actually doing."[30]

Hunting also entailed man's estrangement from nature. As Washburn and Lancaster put it:

> Hunting changed man's relations to other animals and his view of what is natural. The human notion that it is normal for animals to flee, the whole concept of animals being wild, is the result of man's habit of

hunting. In game reserves many different kinds of animals soon learn not to fear man, and they no longer flee. James Woodburn took a Hadza into the Nairobi Park, and the Hadza was amazed and excited, because although he had hunted all his life, he had never seen such a quantity and variety of animals close at hand . . . In the park the Hadza hunter saw for the first time the peace of the herbivorous world. Prior to hunting, the relations of our ancestors to other animals must have been very much like those of the other noncarnivores. They could have moved close among the other species, fed beside them, and shared the same waterholes. But with the origin of human hunting, the peaceful relationship was destroyed, and for at least half a million years man has been the enemy of even the largest mammals.[31]

"The whole human view of what is normal and natural in the relationship of man to animals," concluded Washburn and Lancaster, "is a product of hunting, and the world of flight and fear is the result of the efficiency of the hunters."

During the 1960s the hunting hypothesis and its attendant misanthropy were spread far beyond the anthropological community by science popularizers and the mass media. The hypothesis received its name and its greatest publicity from the dramatist Robert Ardrey, who snatched Dart's ideas virtually from his typewriter and worked them up into a series of bestselling books. Ardrey portrayed Dart and Lorenz and so on as the vanguard of an enlightened struggle against outworn scientific and religious myths. "The New Enlightenment" is the title of the first chapter of Ardrey's mockingly titled *African Genesis*. Its opening paragraph is memorably ominous:

> Not in innocence, and not in Asia, was mankind born. The home of our fathers was that African highland reaching north from the Cape to the Lakes of the Nile. Here we came about—slowly, ever so slowly—on a sky-swept savannah glowing with menace.

Man, argued Ardrey, "is a predator whose natural instinct is to kill with a weapon."[32] War is the natural product of the interaction between our killing instinct and our territorial instinct. It is an intrinsic part of human life, as central to our humanity as language or walking upright:

> No man can regard the way of war as good. It has simply been our way. No man can evaluate the eternal contest of weapons as anything but the

sheerest waste and the sheerest folly. It has simply been our only means of final arbitration. Any man can suggest reasonable alternatives to the judgment of arms. But we are not creatures of reason except in our own eyes.[33]

Ardrey had a journalistic talent for finding dire portent in ambiguous facts and subversive novelty in commonplaces. This talent helped make his books compelling to laymen, but it infuriated scientists, who denounced his works indignantly in their reviews.[34] Yet Ardrey's ideas were essentially those of Dart, and many of them became enshrined as facts in American textbooks of physical anthropology.[35] C. L. Brace, although long one of Ardrey's harshest critics, could nevertheless write in 1972:

> No informed person now questions the fact that the modern human condition owes much to the shaping effects of a lifeway that included hunting as a major component . . . The regularly manifest human capacity for lethal activity has no parallel among the nonhuman primates and almost certainly is an evolutionary legacy from the half-million years or more that the human line spent as the only primate who practiced hunting as a major part of its subsistence activities.[36]

During the 1960s, the central propositions of the hunting hypothesis—that hunting and its selection pressures had made men and women out of our apelike ancestors, instilled a taste for violence in them, estranged them from the animal kingdom, and excluded them from the order of nature—became familiar themes of the national culture, and the picture of *Homo sapiens* as a mentally unbalanced predator threatening an otherwise harmonious natural realm became so pervasive that it ceased to provoke comment. These themes were disseminated not only through popular-science books but also through novels, cartoons, films, and television. Millions of moviegoers in 1968 absorbed Dart's whole theory in one stunning image from Stanley Kubrick's film *2001*, in which an australopithecine who has just used a zebra femur to commit the world's first murder hurls the bone gleefully into the air—and it turns into an orbiting spacecraft.[37]

The Rich Smell of Meat and Wickedness

People have always eaten people;
What else *is* there to eat?
If the Juju had meant us not to eat people,
He wouldn't have made us of meat.

—Michael Flanders

THE hunting hypothesis paraded as fact in anthropology textbooks for two decades. But by the late 1970s scientific opinion had started to turn against it.

Dart's collection of bone and horn "tools" from the Transvaal breccias was the first part of the package to be tossed out. Those supposed tools had not been taken very seriously by many scientists in the first place,[1] and they lost all credibility when C. K. Brain showed that they look exactly like the fragments left by leopards and hyenas chewing on bones.[2] Round holes in the fossil skulls, which Dart and Ardrey thought the man-apes had made with bone daggers, turned out to match up perfectly with the fangs of a leopard.[3] Dents that Dart had thought were left by bone clubs were now reinterpreted as the impressions of rocks pressed against the buried fossils.[4] By the mid-1970s there was no reason left for believing that *Australopithecus* in South Africa had used animal bones and horns as tools.

At first the loss of the South African evidence was not keenly felt, because there seemed to be newer and better evidence for early hunting at other sites. Starting in 1959, australopithecine fossils had begun to turn up in East Africa. The East African man-apes were found not only with the remains of game animals, but also with unmistakable stone tools. Most scientists assumed that the East African australopithecines had made those tools themselves and had used them to butcher the animals.[5]

But as more and more fossils came to light, it became clear that the australopithecines were not the only hominids in those East African deposits. There were also brainier, more advanced fossil hominids who deserved to be recognized as primitive members of our own genus, *Homo.* It appears now that fossil *Homo* can be relied on to turn up sooner or later wherever stone tools are found.[6] There is no good evidence that *Australopithecus* ever made tools or weapons. It is hard to go on thinking of the australopithecines as mighty hunters and skillful butchers.

Perhaps the most serious blow to the hunting hypothesis came from E. S. Vrba's analysis of antelope bones from the Transvaal caves. In the older levels of those caves, *Australopithecus* is the only hominid, and there are no stone tools. More recent deposits, from higher levels of the same caves, contain fossil *Homo* and primitive stone tools. There are many antelope bones at both levels. But the antelopes from the *Australopithecus* deposits are mainly young animals in a few restricted size ranges, whereas the *Homo* deposits yield antelope fossils of all sizes and ages.[7]

This difference is significant. Different sorts of bones accumulate in the lairs of different sorts of meat-eating animals. Among big African carnivores today, the more skillful hunters—lions, leopards, wild dogs—are choosy about what they kill. They prefer to go after young, helpless victims, and each kind of predator concentrates on prey of one particular size. Scavengers, on the other hand, eat whatever they can get: fresh meat or carrion, young animals or old, big species or little ones. Thus, by looking at the bones in a meat eater's lair, a biologist may be able to tell whether it kills its own preferred prey or steals all sorts of mixed leftovers from more effective predators. The antelope bones from the *Australopithecus* levels of the Transvaal caves look as if they were brought in by a choosy, efficient predator. The bones from the more recent levels—where fossil *Homo* is found—are a mixed bag, which seem to have been dragged into the caves by a mere scavenger.

Was *Australopithecus,* then, a more accomplished hunter than his larger and brainier descendants in the genus *Homo?* It seems unlikely. It is easier to believe that the bones in the older deposits were brought into the caves by some four-footed meat eater. If so, then the australopithecines were not predators but prey. Those holes left by leopard teeth in man-ape skulls point to the same conclusion. The current consensus among scientists is that the man-apes, like the antelopes and baboons found with them, were killed, dragged to the caves, and eaten by big carnivores of some sort.

Later hominids found in those caves drove out the animals and took over the caves for themselves. We know this because the later deposits contain stone tools (which leopards and hyenas would not have dragged into the caves). The antelope bones found alongside the tools were presumably brought to the caves by early *Homo* too. But those bones are an unselective jumble of animals of all ages and sizes, from tiny klipspringers up to eland of 2,000 pounds. This suggests that early *Homo* was something of a scavenger, who was getting most of his meat by taking it away from various four-legged predators.[8]

If early *Homo* was nothing more than a scavenger, it seems doubtful that *Australopithecus* could have been much of a meat eater at all. Most students of human evolution today probably would agree with C. O. Lovejoy that "there is no evidence whatsoever that early hominids hunted," and that meat was probably not a significant part of the australopithecine diet.[9]

Two other facts that surfaced in the late 1960s also helped to undercut the hunting hypothesis. First, it turns out that a taste for animal flesh is not something that distinguishes human beings from the apes. Chimpanzees also prey on other animals and steal kills from other predators—and even kill and eat their own kind. If chimpanzees are predators, then predation was probably not a new departure for our own apelike ancestors. Therefore predation by itself cannot explain why our ancestors evolved into australopithecines and chimpanzees did not.[10]

Second, even among hunting peoples in the Kalahari Desert today, two-thirds of the diet consists of plants.[11] This undercuts Dart's notion that our ancestors had to turn carnivore or starve when they moved out of the forest. There is no reason to think that *Australopithecus* had to be any more carnivorous than a chimpanzee to survive on the fringes of the Kalahari.

All these new facts and interpretations contributed to the anthropological reaction against the hunting hypothesis. But that reaction had a political basis as well. Most of the brickbats hurled at the hunting hypothesis of human origins came from the direction of the left. Marxist critics disliked the Dart–Ardrey–Lorenz picture of human nature because it blamed many of our social ills on human ancestry rather than on our economic systems. Pacifists disliked the notion that an instinctive, ineradicable joy in killing is one of the causes of war. And feminists looked with understandable suspicion on the assumption that "the male specialized as hunter, the female as domestic" from the very start of human evolution. Since the early 1970s, anthropologists (who tend to be left-wing, pacifist, and feminist) have accordingly tended to dismiss the hunting model as a myth that serves reactionary interests.

The pacifist reaction against the hunting hypothesis began in the late 1960s, at the height of the Vietnam war. The prevailing suspicion among pacifist critics at the time was that the whole hypothesis had been cooked up as an excuse for cold-war militarism. "A line of argument like that of Ardrey's," wrote K. E. Boulding in 1967, "seems to legitimate our present morality . . . by reference to our biological ancestors. If the names of both antiquity and science can be drawn upon to legitimate our behavior, the moral uneasiness about napalm and the massacre of the innocent in Vietnam may be assuaged."

This analysis of the ulterior motives behind the hunting hypothesis has remained popular among students of anthropology. Ashley Montagu, for instance, thinks that books like Ardrey's are "comforting to the reader who is seeking some sort of absolution for his sins . . . If it is our 'nature' to be what we are, if we are the lineal descendants of our 'murderous' ancestors, we can hardly be blamed or blame ourselves for . . . crime, rape, murder, arson, and war."[12] Niles Eldredge and Ian Tattersall likewise call the myth of Man the Killer Ape "a cop-out—blaming our wars and violent crimes on some remote

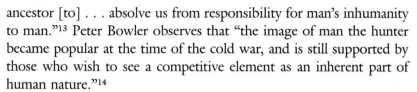

ancestor [to] . . . absolve us from responsibility for man's inhumanity to man."[13] Peter Bowler observes that "the image of man the hunter became popular at the time of the cold war, and is still supported by those who wish to see a competitive element as an inherent part of human nature."[14]

Feminist critics find a different subtext tucked away in the hunting hypothesis. Adrienne Zihlman and Nancy Tanner noted that the familiar anthropological image of Man the Hunter

> stresses the role of men almost to the exclusion of women. In that tradition men are portrayed as protectors of children and women with whom they are assumed to be attached sexually in a pair-bond relation. Men bring back meat, the presumed major food source, to the waiting dependents at camp. This view links males with technology and the provision of basic subsistence . . . It promotes the idea of male aggression as necessary for hunting and for protecting the weak and passive females and children and assumes male dominance over females inherent to the hunting way of life.[15]

Other critics see the hunting model as a vehicle for other antiquated ideologies. Timothy Perper and Carmel Schrire call the hunting hypothesis "a mixture of biological facts and evolutionary concepts entangled in the constricting threads of Western myth."[16] They dismiss the whole killer-ape story as a rehash of the old biblical tale of the forbidden fruit and Adam's fall from grace (with raw meat instead of an apple on the menu this time around). Kenneth Bock sees Ardrey and Lorenz as continuing what George Boas called the "theriophile" tradition—a tradition, extending back to Ovid and Plutarch, of comparing *Homo sapiens* unfavorably to saner and gentler beasts.[17] Bock, like many other cultural anthropologists, thinks that all such comparisons of people to animals are misleading because we are not like the beasts in any important respect. "Our curious inclination to regard ourselves as being like other animals," he writes, may provide "relief from guilt feelings about our conduct; it serves in this way as a substitute for the doctrine of original sin."[18]

Some of these criticisms seem wrong-headed. Most of the defenders of the hunting hypothesis did not try to assimilate *Homo sapiens* to the beasts. On the contrary, they depicted our species as *alienated* from the other animals and from the natural order by our habit of hunting with weapons. This motif of alienation is especially clear in the works of Dart, Washburn, and Lorenz. And the doctrine of original sin is not intended to keep us from feeling guilty, as any Calvinist can testify.

Yet the critics are surely right to think that the attractiveness of the hunting hypothesis had nothing to do with the scientific evidence. Scientific evidence furnished excuses, not grounds, for accepting the hunting story and the misanthropy that went with it. Although Ardrey pretended that Dart's gloomy assessment of human nature was a bitter pill to swallow,[19] people were in fact willing to swallow it on such flimsy pretexts that its bitter coating must have concealed an ulterior sweetness of some sort.

Dart's own writings show this clearly enough. Confronted with just two fossils from Taung, a baboon skull with a hole in it and the skull of an apelike infant, Dart at once concluded that the infant's elders were human ancestors who had killed the baboon and made the hole to eat its brains. This was not a painful conclusion to which Dart was reluctantly driven by the overwhelming weight of the evidence. It was a conclusion for which there was no evidence at all. The supposed evidence of hunting that turned up later at the other australopithecine sites—all those scraps of bone that Dart interpreted as tools and battered prey and cannibal leftovers—were almost as fanciful. The Transvaal fossils were evidently seized on as a pretext for believing something that Dart and others had prior reasons for wanting to believe.

But what can those reasons have been? Was the anthropological community of the 1950s and 1960s really conspiring to breathe new life into the biblical tale of the Fall of Adam or to cook up specious excuses for militarism and the oppression of women?

The works of two literary figures, the American poet Robinson Jeffers and the British Nobel laureate William Golding, shed some light on these questions. During the 1940s and 1950s, both writers foreshadowed Dart in finding links between hunting, human origins, and human depravity.

JEFFERS began forging those links five years before Dart did. His 1948 book *The Double Axe* contains a short poem, pointedly entitled "Original Sin," which portrays man's remote ancestors as sick animals estranged from nature by their predatory cruelty. Jeffers describes a band of ice-age apemen:

> The man-brained and man-handed ground-ape, physically
> The most repulsive of all hot-blooded animals
> Up to that time of the world: they had dug a pitfall
> And caught a mammoth, but how could their sticks and stones
> Reach the life in that hide?

Jeffers' ground-apes solve the problem by flinging wood and flaming brands from their fire into the pitfall—cooking the screaming animal slowly to death. The lines describing the kill are interlaced with a lyrical description of the surrounding beauties of nature. The poem ends on a note of misanthropy so glacially pure that it turns into lofty moral injunction:

> These are the people.
> This is the human dawn. As for me, I would rather
> Be a worm in a wild apple than a son of man.
> But we are what we are, and we might remember
> Not to hate any person, for all are vicious;
> And not be astonished at any evil, all are deserved;
> And not fear death; it is the only way to be cleansed.[20]

In "The Love and the Hate," the long narrative poem that begins Jeffers' book, the themes of hunting, human vileness, and fiery death are repeated and linked to war. The poem's hero is a soldier killed in World War II, who returns from the grave to destroy the father who sent him off to war. On the first day of deer-hunting season, he goes hunting with his father, shoots him in the back, and watches him burn to death in a brush fire. The fire is started by stolen army tracer bullets, which other hunters are firing at jacklighted deer. The dead soldier describes man as "the eventual hell of life, the animal / Toward which all evolution toiled and was damned / From the beginning."

Jeffers sounds these themes again in the short poem "The King of Beasts," which summons the suffering animals to rejoice at Hiroshima and Auschwitz:

Cattle in the slaughter-pens, laboratory dogs
Slowly tortured to death, flogged horses, trapped fur-bearers,
Agonies in the snow, splintering your needle teeth on chill steel—
    look:
Mankind, your Satans, are not very happy either. I wish you had seen
    the battle-squalor, the bombings,
The screaming fire-deaths. I wish you could watch the endless hunger,
    the cold, the moaning, the hopelessness.
I wish you could smell the Russian and German torture-camps . . .

William Golding's first two novels, written in the early 1950s, draw a cooler but equally despairing picture of Man the Hunter. In his first and best-known novel, *Lord of the Flies,* Golding depicts a troop of English schoolboys marooned by shipwreck on a tropical island. The boys' efforts to cling to some semblance of civilized behavior collapse when they begin hunting wild pigs. The chase unleashes blind, primitive impulses that soon have them hunting and killing one another, chanting "Kill the beast! Cut his throat! Spill his blood!"[21] A British naval officer suddenly appears to put a stop to the carnival of murder. But he is really only raising it to an adult level, as he takes the boys aboard a warship that will soon be hunting and killing other human prey with the same senseless ferocity.

Golding's second novel, *The Inheritors,* sketches the prehistoric origins of man's "diseased nature."[22] Again, Golding seeks the roots of human depravity in hunting. The book tells the story of the last band of Neanderthal men: stupid but gentle and intuitive folk, who feed mainly on plants. When fruits and berries cannot be found, the Neanderthals turn reluctantly to scavenging the kills of big cats. But they sense that there is something profoundly wrong about cutting up and eating dead animals:

> The doe was wrecked and scattered. Fa split open her belly, slit the complicated stomach and spilt the sour cropped grass and broken shoots on the earth. Lok beat in the skull to get at the brain and levered open the mouth to wrench away the tongue. They filled the stomach with tit-bits and twisted up the guts so that the stomach became a floppy bag.
> All the while, Lok talked between his grunts.
> "This is bad. This is very bad." . . . The air between the rocks was forbidding with violence and sweat, with the rich smell of meat and

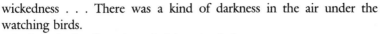

wickedness . . . There was a kind of darkness in the air under the watching birds.

Lok spoke loudly, acknowledging the darkness.

"This is very bad. Oa brought the doe out of her belly . . . But a cat killed you so there is no blame."[23]

Oa is Mother Nature, the Neanderthals' creator goddess. As the Neanderthals skulk in the shadows peeping at a band of *Homo sapiens* that has invaded their forest, they sense that there is something unnatural about the new folk. "Oa," says one of them, "did not bring them out of her belly." The new people are brilliant psychopaths—godlike, uncanny, and cruel. They do not scavenge; they kill, and they enjoy doing it. Even their sexuality is predatory and sadistic.[24] At the end of the book, with the last of the adult Neanderthals dead, their inheritors set off in canoes toward symbolic darkness, carrying one surviving Neanderthal baby—for sacrifice to the bloodthirsty demons that trouble their disordered dreams.

Although Dart, Jeffers, and Golding all depict human beings as sick animals whose sickness has its focus in a relish for hunting and its cruelties, there is no reason to think that any of the three men copied his ideas from one of the others. Golding's books appeared too late to have influenced Jeffers or Dart. Jeffers' 1948 poems might have influenced Dart or Golding, but it seems unlikely. *The Double Axe* was not widely read. In fact, it was "universally consigned to oblivion, effectively ending Jeffers' role as a creditable poetic voice during his lifetime."[25] Dart's 1953 article, in which he first linked hunting to human depravity, appeared even more obscurely in a privately published journal. It almost certainly did not attract Golding's attention-while he was writing *Lord of the Flies* (1954) or *The Inheritors* (1955). And Dart could not have borrowed the idea from either Jeffers or Golding, since aspects of it had been revolving in his mind since 1925, when Jeffers was reading proof on his first successful book and Golding was a schoolboy.

Another reason for thinking that each of the three men developed his ideas independently is that their ideas differ. Each author puts man's fall from animal grace at a different stage of human evolution—*Australopithecus* for Dart, early *Homo* for Jeffers, modern *Homo* for Golding. Dart thinks our flaw is carnivory plain and simple, but

Golding and Jeffers think that human hunting is peculiarly evil because it is contaminated by the human will. Jeffers makes that plain in his poem "Orca" from *The Double Axe,* which describes killer whales devouring a sea lion:

> Here was death, and with terror, yet it looked clean and bright, it was beautiful.
> Why? Because there was nothing human involved, suffering nor causing; no lies, no smirk and no malice;
> All strict and decent; the will of man had nothing to do here. The earth is a star, its human element
> Is what darkens it. War is evil, the peace will be evil, cruelty is evil; death is not evil. But the breed of man
> Has been queer from the start. It looks like a botched experiment that has run wild and ought to be stopped.

What prompted these three men to come up independently with such similar stories about hunting and human nature during the same postwar decade? Part of the answer is World War II itself. Golding spelled out its effect on him in a 1962 speech:

> Before the Second World War I believed in the perfectibility of social man . . . but after the war I did not because I was unable to. I had discovered what one man could do to another. I am not thinking of one man killing another with a gun, or dropping a bomb on him or blowing him up or torpedoing him. I am thinking of the vileness beyond all words that went on, year after year, in the totalitarian states . . . Anyone who moved through those years without understanding that man produces evil as a bee produces honey, must have been blind or wrong in the head.[26]

Jeffers says the same sort of thing over and over in *The Double Axe,* and Dart points to "the most recent atrocities of the Second World War" in making his case for man's inborn wickedness.[27] It seems clear that the war was one of the things that drove these men to think about the historical roots of human viciousness. The stories that all three came up with expressed a horror of our immediate past and a dread of our immediate future.[28] The killer-ape stories of the 1950s were not (as some of Dart's critics would have it) myths dreamt up to legitimize war and violence. They were intended to warn us against them.

24

But the horrors of World War II and the nightmares of the postwar years cannot explain earlier statements of the hunting hypothesis. That hypothesis goes back almost two hundred years before World War II. It was first put forward in 1773 by the Scottish aristocrat James Burnett, Lord Monboddo.

In the first volume of his massive treatise *Of the Origin and Progress of Language,* Monboddo argued that human society had originated when our ancestors came together in groups to join forces for defending themselves against other animals—and for hunting. The consequences of taking up hunting, thought Monboddo, were calamitous:

> This change of man from a frugivorous to a carnivorous animal must have produced a great change of character . . . While man continued to feed upon the fruits of the earth, he was an innocuous animal, and, like others who lived in the same way, more disposed to fly from an attack than to make one. But, as soon as he became a hunter, the wild beast, which is part of his composition, became predominant in him. He grew fierce and bold, delighting in blood and slaughter. War soon succeeded to hunting; and the necessary consequence of war was, the victors eating the vanquished, when they could kill or catch them; for, among such men, war is a kind of hunting.[29]

All this sounds remarkably like what Raymond Dart was saying two centuries later, right down to the equation of war with hunting. Monboddo anticipated not only Dart's theories but also his misanthropy. Man, averred Monboddo,

> if not tamed, or subdued by laws or manners, is the most dangerous and mischievous of all the creatures that God has made; much more so than any lion or tiger, or any other the fiercest animal that roams the forest . . . He has already almost depopulated the earth, having in many countries destroyed whole species of animals, and continuing daily to destroy those that remain, not only to gratify his luxury and vanity, but for mere sport and pastime.[30]

And Monboddo went on from this to wish what Jeffers so often wished—that the animals might soon be freed from man's oppression by man's extinction:

> What attonement, most pernicious biped . . . canst thou make for this so great abuse of thy superior faculties, and this destruction of the

25

creatures of God? None other, except to destroy thyself next, and so avenge the rest of the animal race. This thou art doing as fast as possible; and for this only can I commend thee. When this work is accomplished, then shall the true state of nature be restored, and the real golden age return . . . So shall the rest of the animal creation, freed from a tyranical and capricious master, live the life which nature has destined for them, and accomplish the end of their being.[31]

Monboddo was not driven to these gloomy conclusions by fossil finds from the Transvaal or by the carnage of World War II. Dart's critics are evidently right to think that the whole hunting hypothesis expresses some cultural theme that has been around for a long time— since the late 1700s, at any rate. But what that theme is, and what the moral of the killer-ape story is supposed to be, is not clear.

There is no obvious reason, either factual or symbolic, why anyone should look for the roots of human wickedness in hunting. Hunting is a productive and pleasurable activity, praised as a great builder of health, courage, and moral character by Western philosophers and statesmen from Plato and Xenophon down to Theodore Roosevelt.[32] If myths are supposed to affirm traditional values, then we ought to be telling stories about how brave and splendid our hunting forefathers were, not deprecating hunting as man's original sin.

There is also no clear reason why anyone should be attracted to the misanthropy that the major proponents of the hunting hypothesis have worked into their stories. Once we disabuse ourselves of the notion that Dart, Jeffers, and Golding were flacks for the Pentagon or chauvinists glorifying the male role in prehistory, we are hard pressed to explain why the outlook they shared should appeal to anybody. We ought to find it intolerably depressing to think of *Homo sapiens* as a psychopathic ape cutting a bloody swath across the face of sweet green nature. Yet that view of the world and our place in it has become more and more prevalent since Monboddo's time, and it pervades most of the versions of the hunting hypothesis.

It may be that the hunting hypothesis appeals to us because it indirectly supports some fundamental values of our culture. Perhaps, as Perper and Schrire claim, the hypothesis affirms Christian religious values by retelling the story of the Fall in scientific terms.[33] Or perhaps, as Bock's criticisms suggest, the roots of the hunting hypothesis go back into Greek antiquity. It is worth taking a look to find out.

In doing so, it is also worth remembering that not all myths are simply false stories. We should remain open to the possibility that the killer-ape myth became popular not only because it reflected the tensions of the cold war, or because it retold the familar story of Eve and Adam, but because it is—at least in some symbolic way—essentially true.

Virgin Huntresses and Bleeding Feasts

THE importance of hunting lies in its symbolism, not its economics. For a few skilled hunters in rural areas, "harvesting" wild animals with a gun may still be an efficient way of putting meat on the table; but the average U.S. deer hunter, who expends about five man-hours of labor and $20 in cash to bring home a single pound of venison, would be better off harvesting some roast beef in a good restaurant.[1] "Every box of shells I have burned up would buy a steak," confesses one experienced hunter. "The time I have spent in the field at current prices for labor would nearly build our home. If you calculate the returns in pounds of food and cash values, it is not a good business, and I might add that he who looks at these sports from this angle will never be a real sportsman."[2]

In short, hunting in the modern world is not to be understood as a practical means of latching onto some cheap protein. It is intelligible only as symbolic behavior, like a game or a religious ceremony, and the emotions that the hunt arouses can be understood only in symbolic terms.

The symbolic meaning that hunting has for us has a lot to do with our definition of the term, which is a curiously restricted one.[3] Hunting is not just a matter of going out and killing any old animal; in fact, very little animal-killing qualifies as hunting. A successful hunt ends in the killing of an animal, but it must be a special sort of animal that is killed in a specific way for a particular reason.

Above all, the quarry must be a *wild* animal. The word "wild" can mean many things; but for the hunter's purposes, a wild animal is one that is not *docile*—that is, not friendly toward people or submissive to their authority. No other criterion of wildness counts in hunting.[4] The game animals on a private hunting estate may be someone's legal chattels, but they still count as wild beasts for the hunter so long as they run from him. Even domesticated livestock can be fair game for the hunter if they have "run wild," like the pigs in *Lord of the Flies.* But walking up to an animal that does not flee—say, a tame deer in a park—putting a revolver to its ear, and pulling the trigger is not hunting. It does not even count as a defective, unsporting sort of hunting, like shooting sitting ducks, because the animal being killed is not a wild animal in the sense that is important to the hunter. Such an animal is part of the human domain, and killing it is just animal-killing, like shooting a cow in the dairy barn.

The hunted animal must also be *free*—that is, able to flee (and to strike back at) its human assailant. Shooting tigers in the zoo does not count as hunting.[5]

The methods and motives of the hunter are also important in defining hunting. Hunting has to involve *violence.*[6] (You can hunt elephants with poisoned arrows, but putting out poisoned hay for them is not hunting.) The fatal violence must be inflicted *directly,* not mediated by a snare or a trap. The hunter's assault on the quarry must be *premeditated,* which usually entails a period of chasing, stalking, or lying in ambush. (Running over wild animals on the highway does not count as hunting, even if you do it on purpose.) Finally, the killing must be undertaken at the hunter's initiative. (Shooting wolves that are chasing you is not hunting.) Animal-killing that does not meet all these criteria is not hunting but something else: fishing, trapping, slaughter, vandalism, religious sacrifice, self-defense, pest control, or a road kill.

We define hunting, then, as the deliberate, direct, violent killing of unrestrained wild animals; and we define wild animals in this context as those that shun or attack human beings. The hunt is thus by definition an armed confrontation between humanness and wildness, between culture and nature. Because it involves confrontational, pre-meditated, and violent killing, it represents something like a war waged by humanity against the wilderness.

An organized hunt, with its weapons and strategies and deployment of hunters, resembles a military campaign, and it is not surprising that many people have found parallels between hunting and warfare. Throughout history, hunting has been widely regarded as a sort of war game, the first step in a young man's combat training. "Proven ability to track down animals in the field," writes Steven Lonsdale, "is a prerequisite in many cultures for joining the ranks of warriors on the battlefield. Hunting and war require similar weapons, skills and inner qualities. A hunting spear doubles as a warring lance; the hunter's ability to plan the strategy of the hunt, to train and set his dogs on the quarry, to aim, and kill the victim, corresponds in war to the plotting of military tactics, the training and arrangement of troops on the battlefield, and the successful capture or routing of enemy forces."[7]

This sort of analogy between hunting and war, which was a key element in the hunting model of human origins, was not something invented by Raymond Dart and Sherwood Washburn. The analogy recurs throughout the history of Western literature, starting with the ancient Greeks. Warriors in the *Iliad* are likened repeatedly to hounds, hunters, predators, and prey.[8] More elaborate analogies between hunting and battle are drawn in the *Odyssey,* where Odysseus' final bloody vengeance on his wife's suitors is the climax of a metaphorical deer hunt that frames the whole story.[9] In his *Cynegeticus* (A Hunting Man), the earliest known book on hunting, the Greek soldier and historian Xenophon likened hunters to warriors fighting against the wild beasts that are man's enemies. Xenophon thought hunting "the best training for war," because it cultivates manly virtues and teaches military skills such as maneuvering and attacking.[10] Aristotle too praised the hunt as a prototype of the morally just war.[11] Similar praise of hunting as a model of, and a preparation for, warfare is a commonplace of subsequent writings on field sports, from the days of imperial Rome down to our own time.[12] "If Hitler had ever spent a fall in a New England village, watching the bucks go by on the running boards," wrote E. B. White in 1941, "he never would have dared reoccupy the Rhineland."[13]

But if the hunt is a war, it is a strange sort of war, in which the only side that can win is careful not to do so. Hunting is an end in itself for the hunter, and he wants the beasts he kills to be endlessly replaced so that his sportive battle with the wilderness can go on indefinitely. Even Xenophon, for all his military rhetoric, urged hunters to spare very young hares, so as to preserve the breeding stock.[14] Throughout European history, hunters have tended to see themselves as enemies of the individual animals but friends of the animal *kinds*— and by extension as friends of the wild, nonhuman realm that the animals inhabit.

Hunters, then, are not simply fighters on the side of humanity against the wilderness. Their loyalties are divided. Because hunting takes place at the boundary between the human domain and the wilderness, the hunter stands with one foot on each side of the boundary, and swears no perpetual allegiance to either side. He is a liminal and ambiguous figure, who can be seen either as a fighter against wildness or as a half-animal participant in it. Both these images of the hunter date back to classical antiquity. In Greek literature, they are associated respectively with Apollo, the god of reason and light, and Dionysus, the bringer of holy madness.

THE Greeks had many words for various sorts of hunting, which differed in social status and symbolic significance. The most general term, *thera* (from *theria,* wild animals), included not only what we call hunting but also fishing, trapping, and birdcatching. The chase proper was conducted with hunting dogs, and it was accordingly called *cynegia* (dog driving). *Cynegia* had higher status than other kinds of *thera*. Plato calls fishing and trapping idle amusements, in which "the slothful hunter's work is done for him" by traps and nets; and the "seductive itch for fowling" Plato thinks "hardly a taste for the free-born man." In Plato's ideal city-state, the young ruling-class males were to practice only *cynegia,* a sport in which "the strength and violence of the quarry are overpowered . . . by the triumph of an energetic soul":

> Thus the only variety of hunting left free to all, and the best variety, is the chase of a four-footed quarry in reliance upon one's horse, one's dogs, and one's own limbs, where the hunters—those, that is, who cultivate godlike courage—all hunt in their own persons and achieve all their success by running, striking and shooting.[15]

"Such hunters," Plato concluded, "are truly sacred." In Plato's utopia, "none shall hinder them from hunting *(cynegetein)* when and where they please."

This "truly sacred" *cynegia,* the hunting of large mammals with dogs, bows, and spears, is the sort of hunting that figures in Greek mythology. In ancient Greece as in our own society, the mythic importance of hunting was far out of proportion to its trivial role in the economy.[16] Several Greek gods were associated with the hunt in both myth and religious practice. Three of them—Apollo, Artemis, and Dionysus—were major deities, honored throughout the Hellenic world with innumerable temples, shrines, statues, and sacrifices.

The Greeks thought of Apollo and Artemis as brother and sister deities, with a nominal joint jurisdiction over the hunt. According to Xenophon, "Game and hounds are the invention of Apollo and Artemis," and so pious hunters should "vow to Apollo and Artemis the Huntress to give them a share of the spoil."[17] But by the time the Greeks started writing down their mythology, most of Apollo's associations with game and hounds had evaporated.[18] Whatever connection he may have had with hunting in prehistoric Greek religion was transferred early on to his sister Artemis, whom the Romans called Diana.

Artemis was not a native Greek deity; the Greeks seem to have picked her up from the Cretans to the south. The Greeks adopted her as Apollo's sister and gave her a number of Apollo's attributes.[19] Perpetually virginal herself, she was worshipped as the patron goddess

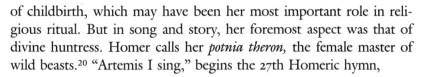

of childbirth, which may have been her most important role in religious ritual. But in song and story, her foremost aspect was that of divine huntress. Homer calls her *potnia theron,* the female master of wild beasts.[20] "Artemis I sing," begins the 27th Homeric hymn,

> of the arrow of gold and the hunting cry,
> Chaste virgin pursuing the deer, showering arrows,
> Gold-bladed Apollo's own sister, who courses
> Over the shadowy hills and wind-swept peaks
> Taking delight in the chase, and, bending her golden bow,
> Sends forth her arrows of anguish. The peaks of the high mountains
>   tremble,
> And the shady woodland screams with the cries of wild creatures.[21]

The Greeks were so captivated by Artemis that they imported her image again and again into their religion and literature. Greek mythology abounds in beautiful fleet-footed maidens who live chastely in the wild mountain forests, bringing down game with unerring arrows. Most of these mythic huntresses—Opis, Daphne, Arethusa, Syrinx, Callisto, Cyrene, Taygete, Atalanta—were originally just various local names or titles of Artemis herself.[22]

As the goddess of hunting, Artemis embodies all the ambiguities inherent in the figure of the hunter. Though she persecutes the wild animals with her "arrows of anguish," she is also their friend and protector. She killed (or contrived in the death of) the great hunter Orion because he boasted in her hearing that he would kill every wild beast alive. The wild places of the earth are sacred to her, especially mountain forests. Catullus' gorgeously alliterative lines call her "mistress of mountains and bursting forests, of secret mountain gorges and resounding rivers,"

> montium domina
> silvarumque virentium
> saltuumque reconditorum
> amniumque sonantum.[23]

The aura of holy virginity that surrounds Artemis extends to the wild places she loves, and men who too boldly invade her presence or violate her chaste remoteness are risking destruction. The story most often told about her was the myth of the hunter Actaeon, who sur-

33

prised her as she bathed naked in a forest pool. The outraged goddess splashed water on him, changing him into a stag:

> And when he saw his face and his antlers mirrored in the water,
> "Wretched me!" he thought to say; but no voice followed.
> He groaned; that was his voice. Tears flowed down lips
> Not his own. Only his mind was left intact.[24]

When Actaeon's hunting dogs caught sight of him as a deer, they gave chase, brought him down, and tore him to pieces. Other characters in Greek mythology met similar ends for similar offenses against the chastity of Artemis or her attendants.[25]

Like Artemis, Dionysus haunts the mountains and is attended by a band of huntresses. But the Bacchae, the holy madwomen who follow Dionysus on the hills, are nothing like the chaste girl archers who help Artemis keep the wild beasts in line. The Bacchae are wild beasts themselves. When they hunt (which they do frequently), they do not strike their quarry with spears or arrows as human beings do; they kill like predatory animals, using their bodies as weapons. In the *Bacchae* of Euripides, King Pentheus' spy narrowly escapes their frenzied assault:

> So we took to our heels and escaped
> being torn to pieces by the bacchants; but they attacked the grazing
> heifers, with hand that bore no steel . . .
> You could have seen ribs, or a cloven hoof,
> being hurled to and fro; and these hung
> dripping under the fir trees, all mixed with blood.
> Bulls that were arrogant before, with rage
> in their horns, stumbled to the ground,
> borne down by the countless hands of girls.
> The garments of flesh were drawn apart more quickly
> than you could close the lids over your royal eyes.[26]

In the worship of Dionysus, this tearing apart (*sparagmos* or *diasparagmos*) of a live animal was celebrated as a solemn rite; a goat or other sacrificial victim was ceremonially hunted down, pulled limb from limb, and eaten raw by the communicants.[27] The slain animal was regarded as a symbol or incarnation of the god, who had in myth likewise been dismembered and eaten—and afterwards resurrected.[28]

34

The "red and bleeding feasts" that followed these ritual hunts gave Dionysus the nickname *Omestes,* eater of raw flesh.[29]

Several myths associate Dionysus with the hunt. The most important, the story of Pentheus, tells how a long-haired, effeminate foreigner came to Thebes and lured the city's women off to wild dances and hunts in the mountains. Pentheus, the city's king, ordered the revelers jailed and their leader executed. But that leader was Dionysus himself, who magically freed himself and his imprisoned followers— and then tempted Pentheus into taking a firsthand peek at the bacchant orgies. When the Bacchae discovered Pentheus, the god caused them to see the king as a lion and tear him to bits in a mad *diasparagmos.*[30]

Euripides makes this story into an extended metaphor of the hunt. Pentheus promises that he will hunt down the orgiasts and capture them in nets. The chorus warns him of the fate of Actaeon. When the royal guards bring the captured god before the king, they announce that they have "hunted down this quarry" and found that "this beast was gentle". The roles of predator and prey are then reversed; the Bacchae become "coursing hounds" and Pentheus becomes the quarry. At the end of the play, Pentheus' own mother enters in a state of divine madness, carrying her son's severed head on a pole. "Come and see this quarry!" she exclaims; and the chorus shouts, "For our Lord is a hunter."

Although Dionysus is associated with hunting, he is in every other way the symbolic opposite of Artemis.[31] Artemis is chaste; Dionysus is dissolute. She stands for restraint; he stands for excess. She is a masculinized female (real Greek women did not hunt); he is an effeminate male. Artemis directs a troop of maiden archers in an orderly program of wildlife management; Dionysus dances at the head of a column of drunken crazies who tear beasts and men apart with their bare hands. The followers of Artemis discipline the wilderness, but the followers of Dionysus participate in it. Euripides describes the Bacchae as ecstatic quasi-animals. They clothe themselves in fawnskins and living serpents, decorate themselves with garlands of wild leaves and flowers, and nurse wild animals at their breasts. The earth in return yields milk and wine when they strike it with the sacred staff, the thyrsus. Euripides' Bacchae have crossed over from the human domain into a state of union with nature. Their choruses are exceptional in classical literature in depicting the natural world as a realm apart from human life, a separate country with its own wild beauty and freedom:[32]

> Oh, feet of a fawn to the greenwood fled,
>   Alone in the grass and the loveliness;
> Leap of the hunted, no more in dread,
>   Beyond the snares and the deadly press:
> Yet a voice still in the distance sounds,
> A voice and a fear and a haste of hounds;
> O wildly labouring, fiercely fleet,
>   Onward yet by river and glen . . .
> Is it joy or terror, ye storm-swift feet? . . .
>   To the dear lone lands untroubled of men,
> Where no voice sounds, and amid the shadowy green
> The little things of the woodland live unseen.[33]

The mirror-image opposition of Artemis to Dionysus in Greek hunting myths contrasts human discipline with animal wildness. The association of both gods with hunting makes symbolic sense, for the hunt is by definition something that happens at the boundary where the human domain confronts the wild. Artemis and Dionysus face each other across that boundary. Perhaps one of the reasons why the hunt plays a large role in Greek mythology—and in later Western thought about human origins—is that it takes place on that boundary, and thus marks the edge of the human world.

THOUGH there were no important gods of hunting among other pagan Europeans,[34] the Greeks' fascination with the hunt found parallels in the older civilizations to the east. The Egyptians and various Semitic peoples worshipped Artemis-like virgin goddesses associated with hunting and the bow.[35] The sacred literature of Hinduism is also full of mythical hunts and hunters, and it shows some suggestive correspondences to Greek hunting mythology.[36] The importance given to hunting in Greek religious imagery seems to reflect an older Middle Eastern tradition traceable from the eastern shores of the Mediterranean all the way to India.

Other aspects of that tradition have entered our own culture through the Old Testament. At first glance, the Hebrew scriptures show no obvious connections with ancient Near Eastern hunting mythology. No biblical figure recalls the Semitic goddess of the hunt (perhaps because her Palestinian version was Baal's consort). Hunting is in general proscribed by Jewish dietary laws, and it does not loom large in Old Testament stories. Nevertheless, two biblical themes with widespread Near Eastern parallels have influenced subsequent thought about hunting, wildlife, and nature.

The first is the use of deer as erotic symbols. "Rejoice with the wife of thy youth," exhorts the Book of Proverbs. "Let her be as the loving hind and pleasant roe, let her breasts satisfy thee at all times; and be thou ravished always with her love" (5:18–19). This is a curious image, which would become a ludicrous one if almost any other mammal were substituted for the loving hind and pleasant roe. We accept it because we accept the symbolic conventions that equate deer with objects of desire. The Song of Solomon goes on at length in the same vein: "Thy two breasts are like two young roes that are twins, which feed among the lilies . . . My beloved is like a roe or a young hart . . . He feedeth among the lilies. Until the day break, and the shadows flee away, turn, my beloved, and be thou like a roe or a young hart upon the mountains of Bether." This sort of simile did not occur to pagan Greek and Roman authors, for whom deer were symbols of cowardice;[37] but amorous similes involving deer are commonplaces of Indian and Semitic poetry. European writers probably picked up this habit of thought from eastern sources, especially the Old Testament. It has exerted a significant influence on Western thought about hunting ever since the late Middle Ages, when the stag became the stereotypical hunted animal and the deer hunt became a favored metaphor for sexual love in upper-class art and literature.

The other hunting-related theme that enters European thought chiefly through the Bible is the vision of a vegetarian Eden where animals and people once dwelt together in peace and harmony. According to the first chapter of Genesis, God had originally intended that all "living creatures" (that is, animals) should feed on plants:

> And God said, Behold, I have given you every herb bearing seed, which is upon the face of all the earth, and every tree, in the which is the fruit of a tree yielding seed; to you it shall be for meat. And to every beast of the earth, and to every fowl of the air, and to every thing that creepeth upon the earth, wherein there is life, I have given every green herb for meat: and it was so.

Even after Adam's disobedience brought death into the world and Adam and Eve were driven out of Eden, God expected the children of Adam to be vegetarians, content with eating "the herb of the field."[38] Noah and his descendants were given express permission to eat animal flesh, but God's chosen people were allowed to do so only with the proviso that they return the slaughtered animal's "life"—that is, its blood—to God:

> For the life of the flesh is in the blood: and I have given it to you upon the altar to make an atonement for your souls . . . And whatsoever man there be of the children of Israel, or of the strangers that sojourn among you, which hunteth and catcheth any beast or fowl that may be eaten; he shall even pour out the blood thereof, and cover it with dust. For it is the life of all flesh; the blood of it is for the life thereof: therefore I said unto the children of Israel, Ye shall eat the blood of no manner of flesh; for the life of all flesh is the blood thereof: whosoever eateth it shall be cut off. (Leviticus 17:11–14)

Returning the blood from the slaughtered animal to God exonerates the butcher from bloodshed. Conversely, if any man kills livestock without bringing them "for peace offerings unto the Lord," then "blood shall be imputed unto that man; he hath shed blood; and that man shall be cut off from among his people" (Leviticus 17:3–4).

Isaiah promises that the vegetarian harmony of Eden will be restored in the golden age to come, when the "wolf and the lamb shall feed together, and the lion shall eat straw like the bullock: and dust shall be the serpent's meat. They shall not hurt or destroy in all my holy mountain, saith the Lord" (65.25). The Christian vision of the Peaceable Kingdom derives from such Old Testament prophecies.

This vegetarian paradise was not just a Jewish notion; similar fantasies were widespread among pagan Greeks and Romans. In the long-ago age of gold, writes Ovid,

> . . . Earth herself, untouched by the hoe
> and unwounded by the plowshare, gave all things freely:
> and contented with foods produced without work,
> they gathered arbutus fruit and wild strawberries
> and dogwood berries and blackberries clinging to prickly brambles
> and whatever acorns dropped from Jove's spreading oaks.
> Spring went on forever then, and the calm zephyrs

Adam and Eve in the garden of Eden, as depicted by Albrecht Dürer in 1504. The cat and the mouse lying down together at Adam's feet symbolize both the vegetarian harmony of Eden and man's dominion over the animals. The cat, hare, ox, and stag typify the four humors (choler, blood, phlegm, and black bile), reflecting the belief that man is the sole creature in whom the elements and humors are mixed together in perfect proportion. (British Museum)

39

> with their warm breezes stroked the flowers,
> which sprung up by themselves from no seeds at all.
> The untilled earth bore fruit, the unharrowed fields
> turned white with heavy ears of wheat;
> the rivers ran with milk and nectar,
> and yellow honey dripped from the green holly.[39]

This primordial golden age, wrote Empedocles, was the reign of the Goddess of Love, when "all creatures were gentle and obedient toward men, both animals and birds, and they burned with kindly love; and trees grew with leaves and fruit ever on them . . . And (the goddess's) altar was not moistened with pure blood of bulls, but it was the greatest defilement among men to deprive animals of life and eat their goodly bodies."[40]

It was widely felt that there was something defiling about killing animals and eating their goodly bodies, though most people went right on doing it anyway. In several important religious cults—Orphism, Pythagoreanism, Isis-Osiris worship, Manichaeism—senior initiates were expected to avoid eating animal flesh.[41] Some Greek temples prided themselves on having pure *(catharos)* altars, unstained by animal sacrifices.[42] But a vegetarian diet never became the norm anywhere in the countries around the Mediterranean, and most official religions continued to center on animal sacrifices and their accompanying barbecues. Almost all ancient vegetarianism was rooted in eccentric minority doctrines about ritual pollution or reincarnation, not in any belief in the value of animal life.

No intrinsic value was attributed to the lives of beasts in ancient Greece and Rome. Ancient philosophers generally agreed that the ability to reason is the only really valuable human trait and that beasts (which lack reason) have no more innate worth or moral standing than sticks and stones. "Use animals and other things and objects with a liberal spirit," counseled Marcus Aurelius; "but towards human beings, as they have reason, behave in a social spirit."[43] Aristotle portrayed not only beasts but stupid people as "living tools" provided by nature for smart people to exploit. Dull-witted people, he argued,

> are slaves by nature, as much inferior to their fellows as the body is to
> the soul, or as the beasts are to men . . . And indeed the use made of
> slaves and domestic beasts is not very different . . . The slave is as it

40

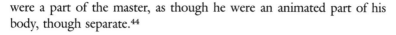

were a part of the master, as though he were an animated part of his body, though separate.[44]

In a world where philosophers could seriously argue that human slaves are only detached parts of their masters' bodies, and where grotesquely awful deaths were regularly meted out to human victims to amuse the arena-goers, few concerned themselves with the lives of beasts. Outside of places like Egypt, where certain kinds of animals were the object of superstitious reverence, animals were routinely treated with a mixture of brutal indifference and sadism. As far as I know, ancient history records only two instances of what might be called political agitation against the mistreatment of animals: the Athenians once expelled a man for flaying a ram alive,[45] and in 55 B.C. the Roman mob rose up in the arena to protest the butchery of a score of elephants in a staged hunt.

This latter incident is the first known protest against any sort of hunting, and so it deserves a closer examination. During the latter days of the Roman republic, the holders of certain political offices were expected to spend vast amounts of their own money to entertain the masses with gladiatorial shows. These entertainments usually included staged hunts called *venationes* (the source of our word "venison"). All sorts of large wild animals, from lions to deer, often numbering in the thousands, were driven into the amphitheater to fight, flee, and die for the amusement of the crowd. On this occasion, a *venatio* put on by Pompey the Great, eighteen African elephants were turned loose to be slaughtered by heavily armed men. But to Pompey's dismay,

> the crowd took pity on them, contrary to [his] intentions. They stopped fighting when they were wounded and went round holding up their trunks to heaven and lamenting bitterly. This gave rise to a story that . . . they were protesting against the violation of the oaths in which they had trusted when they had crossed over from Libya and were calling on Heaven to avenge them. For it is said that they would not set foot upon the ships until their mahouts promised under oath that they would suffer no harm.[46]

Cicero, who saw the elephant show that day, wrote to a friend about it:

> The *venationes* were . . . magnificent; nobody denies it. But what pleasure can a cultured man get in seeing a puny human torn to pieces by a powerful beast, or a noble beast run through by a hunting spear? . . . They brought in the elephants on the last day. This amazed the vulgar crowd but pleased nobody. Indeed, the whole affair was attended by a sort of pity, and a feeling that these huge animals have something in common with humankind.[47]

Cicero was not the only Roman who was indifferent to the pleasures of the chase. Hunting was not a traditional Roman pastime. The Romans of the early republic had regarded hunting as a farm chore, like slaughtering hogs or killing rats. It had none of the mythic and ceremonial importance for them that it had for the Greeks, and they did not practice it as a sport. Sportive hunting came to Rome as a rich man's affectation; Romans with pretensions to Greek culture took it up the way some American anglophiles take up fox hunting. Like many things Greek, it filtered into Roman life following Rome's victory over Macedon in 168 B.C.[48] After that victory, as Plutarch noted, "not only the grammarians and sophists and teachers of rhetoric that surrounded the young [Roman] men were Greek, but the sculptors and painters, and keepers of horses and hounds, and instructors in the art of hunting *(thera).*"[49]

Greek authors like Xenophon and Plato had praised hunting as a fine manly pursuit that builds character and courage, but early Roman writers saw it as a faintly contemptible Greek practice. Sallust dismissed hunting as a *servile officium,* a slave's job,[50] and prided himself on not having taken it up in his retirement. The Roman satirist Varro lampooned the sportive hunter as a pretentious ninny:

> There you go, chasing wild boars on the mountain with your spear, or stags (which never did any harm to you) with your javelin. What a splendid art! . . . What is the point of running round, missing your night's rest and your dinner? Do you hunt for profit or for pleasure? If for profit, sell your game; if for pleasure, watch the sport in the Circus and keep your legs whole instead of scratching them to bits as you jog through the woods.[51]

An air of unreality and play-acting hovers around depictions of hunting in Roman art and literature. The few writers of the Roman Empire who seem knowledgeable and serious about hunting are either

Greeks—Arrian, Oppian, Julius Pollux—or else semibarbarian provincial ethnics like the Spaniard Martial or the North African Nemesianus. The difference in this regard between Greece and Rome shows up in their epic poetry. Throughout the *Iliad* and the *Odyssey,* Homer evinces a cheerful, robust pleasure in the killing of animals, whether wild or domestic. When the mighty huntsman Odysseus kills a stag, Homer's description is straightforward and anatomical:

> He started from the bush and wheeled: I hit him
> square in the spine midway along his back
> and the bronze point broke through it. In the dust
> he fell and whinnied as life bled away.
> I set one foot against him, pulling hard
> to wrench my weapon from the wound, then left it,
> butt-end on the ground. I plucked some withies
> and twined a double strand into a rope—
> enough to tie the hocks of my huge trophy;
> then pickaback I lugged him to the ship . . .
> And all that day until the sun went down
> we had our fill of venison and wine.[52]

But in Virgil's Latin epic, the *Aeneid,* the hunt becomes a poetic and sentimental affair, full of self-consciousness and mixed emotions. When Aeneas goes stag hunting with Queen Dido, no bloodshed is reported, and all the emphasis falls on the rich trappings and splendid retinues. In a later scene, when one of Aeneas' band finally manages to shoot a stag, it turns out to be somebody's pet, and it runs home to *complain:* "And the animal, / wounded, fled back to his familiar roof; / moaning, he reached his stall and suppliant / and bleeding, filled the house with his lament."[53] This pathetic figure of the innocent deer pierced by a hunter's arrow recurs in Virgil's description of the love-smitten Dido:

> Burning and wretched, Dido roams the city
> Distraught, like a doe pierced by a fatal arrow—
> A careless doe, that some shepherd pursued
> Far off with idle shots through Cretan groves
> And struck unwittingly with winging steel;
> In vain she flies through Dicte's glades and forests;
> The deadly shaft still sticks in her side.[54]

Although several Roman writers show a distaste for hunting or sympathy for the sufferings of the hunter's quarry, probably the only important ancient author actually to denounce hunting as morally wrong was Plutarch, a Romanized Greek living under the rule of the empire. Plutarch's attack on hunting occurs in one of his moral dialogues, where it is put into the mouth of his father Autobulus. When the hunter Soclarus praises the chase as a harmless substitute for gladiatorial shows, Autobulus retorts that cruelty to animals is not a substitute for cruelty to men but its historical source:

> the very source, my dear Soclarus, from which they say insensibility spread among men and the sort of savagery that learned the taste of slaughter on its hunting trips, and has grown accustomed to feel no repugnance for the wounds and gore of beasts, but to take pleasure in their violent death . . . Thus the brute and the natural lust to kill in man were fortified and rendered inflexible to pity, while gentleness was for the most part deadened.[55]

This notion that hunting is the source of man's inhumanity to man is a conspicuous part of the modern hunting hypothesis. So is the image of *Homo sapiens* as the sick animal, an image that shows up elsewhere in Plutarch's dialogues. In one of them, Odysseus and Gryllus, a Greek who has been transformed into a boar by the witch Circe, debate whether people are better than beasts. Gryllus insists that he has been much improved by becoming a pig. Swine and other animals, he says, are naturally virtuous, whereas human beings are full of vices and perversions.[56]

Other classical writers also contrasted human perversity with animal sanity and innocence. "The human species," lamented Pliny the Elder, "has devised all sorts of crimes against nature—sexual perversions among the males, even abortions among the females. How much more wicked we are in this respect than the wild beasts!"[57]

Kenneth Bock points to this widespread "animalitarian" strain in classical thought as an antique superstition underlying the misanthropy of Dart, Ardrey, and Lorenz.[58] No doubt some ancient authors do furnish precedents for some aspects of the hunting hypothesis and the sour view of humanity that goes with it. But it would be a mistake to read modern notions of human depravity back into pagan antiquity.

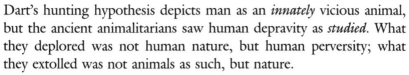

Dart's hunting hypothesis depicts man as an *innately* vicious animal, but the ancient animalitarians saw human depravity as *studied*. What they deplored was not human nature, but human perversity; what they extolled was not animals as such, but nature.

Their idea of nature was different from ours. We tend to think of nature as a sort of territory, the sum of all the pristine parts of earth not yet defiled by human use and occupation. There are hints of that vision of things here and there in classical literature, but it was not a widespread vision and it had no name attached to it. The word "nature" then usually meant what it still means in the phrase "human nature"—that is, a thing's characteristic, inherent disposition to be something, to do something, or to become something else. Fish swim, birds fly, rocks fall, flames rise, seeds sprout, because it is their nature to do so. When ancient Romans spoke of *natura,* they were talking not about wild landscapes or the unspoiled countryside, but about something more like what we call natural law.[59]

Ancient *natura* is not, however, the same thing as the modern concept of natural law. One important difference is that natural laws command our obedience, but *natura* only urges us to certain courses of action. We cannot violate laws of nature in the modern sense (if we can, they cease to count as laws), but we can ignore the promptings of *natura* in the ancient sense. We human beings are free—as rocks and flames and beasts are not—to choose what is unnatural for us.

It follows from this that only human beings have the capacity to be corrupted. Most ancient philosophers assumed that whatever is natural is good.[60] Since animals always do what is natural for them but people do not, animals are better than some people in this regard. But this does not imply that all human beings are necessarily depraved or that animal nature is better than human nature. The idea that the other animals are by their very nature better and saner than man is essentially a modern idea. It commingles classical animalitarianism with a distinctively Christian belief—the doctrine that in human beings nature herself has gone rotten.

CHRISTIANITY originated as a religious and philosophical system of pagan antiquity, and the Church Fathers agreed with their pagan contemporaries on many things. From the very first, Christian writers adopted the prevailing rationalism of classical thought, disdaining all things fleshly and intuitive and glorifying everything spiritual, intellectual, and verbal. ("In the beginning," says the Gospel of John, "was the Word, and the Word was with God, and the Word was God.") Man's likeness to God, by virtue of which he has dominion over all other creatures, lies in his reasoning intellect. Like many pagan thinkers, early Christian authors tend to equate cosmic order with social stratification. As the master is to the bondsman or the parent to the child, so is male to female, mind to body, God to man—and man to animal.[61]

Animal life meant as little to Christians as it did to pagans. In Jewish ritual and belief, the taking of animal life was a dire act, and the eating of flesh was hedged about with taboos. But the new revelation freed the Christians from kosher inhibitions about meat:

> And [Peter] saw heaven opened, and a certain vessel descending unto him, as it had been a great sheet tied at the four corners, and let down to the earth: wherein were all manner of fourfooted beasts of the earth, and wild beasts, and creeping things, and fowls of the air. And there came a voice to him, Rise, Peter; kill, and eat. (Acts 10:11–13)

To traditional Christians, the beasts are merely part of God's stage machinery for the moral drama of human life. They have no intrinsic value in God's eyes, and we owe them no duties of justice or even charity.[62] Paul, commenting on the Old Testament injunction about muzzling the ox that treads out the grain, asks rhetorically, "Does God care about oxen?" and concludes that he does not (I Corinthians 9:9–10). Both Christians and pagans saw human vices and defects as animal traits, lapses from a higher to a lower status in the hierarchy of created things. "For so excellent is a man in comparison with a beast, that man's vice is beast's nature," wrote Augustine.[63]

As the sole focus of a loving creator's concern, the human race in some ways enjoyed a higher status in Christian than in pagan belief. Later Christian thinkers often portrayed man as the unifying thread that ties together the hierarchy of creatures, the vast ladder of nature *(scala naturae)* that rises from dead matter at the bottom up through the plant and animal kingdoms to the angelic realm of pure spirits at the top. Human beings are unique in this hierarchy because they

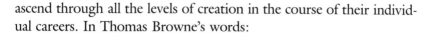

ascend through all the levels of creation in the course of their individual careers. In Thomas Browne's words:

> for first we . . . only are, and have a dull kind of being not yet privileged
> with life, or [promoted] to sense or reason; next we live the life of
> plants, the life of animals, the life of men, and at last the life of spirits,
> running on in one mysterious nature those five kinds of existences, which
> comprehend the creatures not only of the world, but of the universe;
> thus is man that great and true *amphibium,* whose nature is disposed to
> live not only like other creatures in divers elements, but in divided and
> distinguished worlds.[64]

For this reason man is in himself a microcosm, a miniature sketch of
the entire created world. Because man plays such a pivotal part in the
balance of the universe, a world without human beings is almost as
unthinkable as a world without God. Man, wrote Francis Bacon, is
the fulcrum of the balance of nature, "the thing in which the whole
world centers, with respect to final causes; so that if he were away, all
other things would stray and fluctuate, without end or intention, or
become perfectly disjointed and out of frame; for all things are made
subservient to man, and he receives use and benefit from them all . . .
so that everything in nature seems made not for itself, but for man."[65]

Most Greek and Roman philosophers would have agreed with these
words of Bacon's. Ancient writers as far apart otherwise in their beliefs
as Xenophon, Aristotle, and Augustine shared this happy confidence
that all things are made for the benefit of man. The world, concluded
Cicero, was created "for the sake of those living beings that have the
use of reason; these are the gods and mankind, who assuredly surpass
all other things in excellence, since the most excellent of all things is
reason."[66]

The Church Fathers and the pagan philosophers they supplanted
agreed in regarding man as the center of the material world. Unlike
their pagan precursors, though, Christian philosophers saw man as
inherently depraved.[67] In Christian eyes, the material world was a fruit
that had gone rotten at the core.

Few Christians today put much stress on the doctrine of man's
innate depravity. Yet that doctrine follows logically from the fundamental Christian belief that all human beings are lost and can be saved

47

only through faith in Jesus Christ. For if we could choose goodness of our own free will, then we could be saved without Christ; but we cannot, and so the human will must be innately wicked and human nature must be corrupt. Augustine put it the other way around: "If righteousness come by nature, then Christ died in vain."[68]

Christian thinkers from Paul onward have attributed our innate depravity to the Fall of Adam described in Genesis. The Genesis account tells how God placed our first parents in a garden full of friendly beasts and delicious fruits, where they could live happily forever without working. But when they ate the fruit of a forbidden tree, God angrily drove them from the garden, took away their immortality, and compelled them to till the earth for their food. For Christian purposes, this story has been taken to mean that all of Adam's descendants are cursed with an inborn taint—our so-called original sin—which dooms us to eternal punishment unless we are redeemed through faith in Christ.

The doctrine of original sin was also invoked to explain nature's imperfections. We find the world full of sickness, suffering, and death, and these evils are hard to explain as the deliberate creations of a loving and omnipotent God. Traditional Christian thought holds that when Adam fell, all nature fell to some extent. All living creatures are accordingly afflicted by disease, predators, deprivation, and other natural evils—which did not exist before the Fall. "The whole order of nature was subverted by the sin of man," wrote Calvin.[69] "The world did in her Cradle take a fall," lamented John Donne,

> And turn'd her brains, and took a general maim
> Wronging each joint of th' universal frame.
> The noblest part, man, felt it first; and than
> Both beasts and plants, curs'd in the curse of man.[70]

"Let any principal thing, as the sun, the moon, any one of the heavens or elements, but once cease or fail or swerve," argued the Elizabethan theologian Richard Hooker, and "the sequel thereof would be ruin . . . And is it possible that man, being not only the noblest creature in the world but even a very world in himself, his transgressing the law of his nature should draw no manner of harm after it? . . . Under Man, no creature in the world is capable of felicity and bliss."[71] A

48

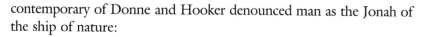

contemporary of Donne and Hooker denounced man as the Jonah of the ship of nature:

> Now in this great uproar and tumult of nature, when heaven and earth seem to threaten a final destruction, give me leave with the mariners of Jonah's ship to cast lots and search out the first occasion of this evil. Alas, alas, the lot falls upon man: man alone of all other creatures, in regard of the freedom of his will and the choice of his own actions, being only capable of the transgression, the rest of the creatures are wholly excluded from the offence; the punishment (I confess) appears in them but chiefly and principally in man.[72]

To us today, it seems unfair that the rest of the creatures have been made to suffer through no fault of their own, and some modern theologians regard the fact of animal suffering as a major theological problem.[73] Yet it was not seen as such before the eighteenth century. To earlier Christian thinkers, the suffering of beasts in this world seemed trivial by comparison with the eternal agonies to which Adam's sin had condemned the human race. Some felt that the animals were getting off easy.[74] "All beasts are happy," moans Dr. Faustus in Christopher Marlowe's play as he awaits his damnation, "For when they die / Their souls are soon dissolved in elements. / But mine must live still to be plagued in hell."

Against the backdrop of eternal bliss or torment, the pains and pleasures of the visible world seem transitory, insubstantial, and unimportant. "All sensible things are to be despised," declared Augustine flatly.[75] A thousand old hymns express the Christian contempt for fallen nature:

> My thoughts that often mount the skies,
> Go, search the world beneath,
> Where nature all in ruin lies,
> And owns her sovereign—Death![76]

Natural objects attracted the intellectual interest of ancient Christians chiefly as types—that is, natural symbols—of some eternal reality. In early Christian tradition, nature study takes the form of the bestiary, in which we learn how the peculiarities of each creature illustrate some religious doctrine or moral homily. For instance, the Alexandrian *Physiologus* of the second century tells us that otters kill crocodiles by jumping down their mouths and tearing out their guts from the inside; just so did Christ descend to hell to loose the bonds of death. The lioness brings forth her young dead, but her dead whelp is revived on the third day by the breath of her mate: just so "the God and Father of the universe wakened our Lord Jesus Christ, His Son, from the dead." When the lion copulates with an ant (!), their offspring is the ant-lion, which has the foreparts of a lion and the hind end of an ant, and soon starves because there is no food that suits both halves; just so the hypocritical sinner is doomed because of his "double spirit contrary in all its ways."[77] And so on. Whether all this was literally true was not important to the early Christian reader; if real animals did not illustrate doctrine, so much the worse for real animals. What makes things significant, said Augustine, is what they *mean,* not whether they actually exist.[78]

From this perspective, the question to be asked about animal suffering was not whether it was unjust, but what it was supposed to signify. Augustine suggested that the vast sum of animal pain was intended as a rebuke to polytheists. "We should never know what eagerness there is for (bodily) unity in the inferior animal creation," he wrote, "were it not for the pain suffered by animals. And if we did not know that, we should not be made sufficiently aware that all things are framed by the supreme, sublime, and ineffable unity of the creator."[79]

A more common interpretation was that the carnage of nature reflects the fallen condition of man. In traditional Christian thought, man is the subordinate god of this world, commanded by the creator in Genesis to "replenish the earth, and subdue it, and have dominion over the fish of the sea, and over the fowl of the air, and over every living thing that moveth upon the earth." Man, wrote Donne, is

> this World's Vice-Emperor, in whom
> All faculties, all graces are at home;
> And if in other Creatures they appear,
> They're but man's ministers, and Legates there,
> To work on their rebellions, and reduce
> Them to Civility, and to man's use.[80]

The beasts of Eden were submissive and obedient to Adam, as God had intended; but after the Fall, they grew wild, predatory, and unruly.

Throughout the history of Christianity, the wilderness has therefore been held up as typifying the creation alienated from God, and the disobedient wild beasts that live there have been viewed as symbolic demons and sinners. Christian tradition condemns the wildness of wild animals as a satanically incited rebellion against man's divinely constituted authority over nature. To quote C. S. Lewis:

> Atheists naturally regard . . . the taming of an animal by a man as a purely arbitrary interference of one species with another. The "real" or "natural" animal to them is the wild one, and the tame animal is an artificial or unnatural thing. But a Christian must not think so. Man was appointed by God to have dominion over the beasts, and . . . the tame animal is therefore, in the deepest sense, the only "natural" animal—the only one we see occupying the place it was made to occupy.[81]

Because of this doctrine, wild animals and their habitat have in Christian thought often been regarded with severe disapproval as a natural symbol of our fallen condition, "the very abstract of degenerated nature."[82] This traditional Christian image of the wilderness as a sort of terrestrial Hell, a demoniacally perverted caricature of Eden, is diametrically opposite to the familiar modern conception of wilderness as a domain of beauty, purity, and order that must be protected from defiling human incursion. Wild nature began to acquire this aura of holiness in the Middle Ages. The change emerged from pre-Christian ideas that became woven into the fabric of Christian tradition in northern Europe.

FOUR

The White Stag

Oh swift and swift comes through the forest
That white deer with the silver horns;
Who follows that unlikely quarry,
Drained of manhood he returns.

For three months of a silent winter
I chased him through the glassy wood;
And when he turned and knelt for pity,
Took out my knife and drew his blood.

The Lady of the Mountains feeds him
Among her inaccessible rocks;
His eyes are cleaner than cold water,
Between his eyes the crucifix.

—John Heath-Stubbs

FROM its very beginning, Christianity adopted one important pagan idea about wild nature: namely, the belief that living in the wilderness in the company of wild beasts is a sign of sanctity. Tales of holy recluses dwelling alone in the desert are as old as Christianity itself.[1] The holiness of saintly hermits was not something they absorbed from the wilderness, which the early Christians (like their pagan and Jewish contemporaries) saw as a hostile territory associated with exile, alienation, and the wrath of God. Rather, it was the hermit's ability to tame the wilderness—to bring rebellious nature back under human dominion—that proved his sanctity. The wild birds and beasts that bring food to some hermit saint in many a Christian legend do so because the saint is good, not because the animals are good.

But it was not long before the wilderness and its animals began to take on the odor of sanctity as well. After all, if wild beasts reward saintliness with food and adoration while the human world rewards it with humiliation and martyrdom, it seems reasonable to think that the animals must be better than most people.[2]

In an apocryphal "Gospel of Matthew" written in Latin by some priestly forger around 800 A.D., the infant Jesus bluntly declares that the beasts, who recognize and worship him as the new Adam, are better than human beings, who do not:

> Suddenly a number of dragons came out of the cave . . . Jesus got down from his mother's lap and stood before the dragons, which worshipped him . . . Jesus walked before them and bade them hurt no one. Mary was alarmed for him, but he said, "Fear not, neither conceive that I am a child, for I always was and am a perfect man, and it is necessary that all the beasts of the forest should grow tame before me." In like manner lions and leopards adored him and accompanied them, showed them the way, and bowed their heads to Jesus . . . Jesus, eight years old, went from Jericho to Jordan. On the way there was a vault where there was a lioness with whelps. He went in and sat there, and the whelps played about him; the older lions stood at a distance and adored him, wagging their tails . . . His parents and the people looked on. Jesus said, "How much better than you are the beasts which know me and are tame, while men know me not."[3]

The reciprocal goodness of the saint and his animal friends is a familiar theme in folklore as well as in Christian mythology. In the Grimm fairy tales, kindly beasts help and comfort the good ("Cinderella") and punish the wicked ("The Bremen Town Musicians"). Kindness to animals is always rewarded appropriately ("The White Snake," "The Golden Bird," "The Queen Bee"), and cruelty to animals is punished ("The Dog and the Sparrow"). In folktales from all over Europe, just as in the medieval stories of the saints, friendship with the wild animals is proof of a pure heart.[4] This theme continues to be popular in our own time, especially in books and films intended for children.

The image of the saint attended by friendly animals is considerably older than Christianity, and it crops up in many other religions. When the Old Testament prophet Elijah fled into the wilderness at God's

The Celtic stag-god Cernunnos seated in state with animal attendants, as depicted on a ceremonial cauldron of the first century B.C. from Denmark. (National Museum, Copenhagen)

command, "the ravens brought him bread and flesh" (I Kings 17:2–6). Buddhist legends tell how the enlightened Gautama was worshipped and sheltered by adoring animals.[5] In Taoist myth, the perfect men of ancient times could grasp the tails of tigers and tread upon serpents without being harmed.[6] Still older animal-commanding gods and saints are hinted at by the divine figures flanked by animal attendants that appear on many of the seals recovered from sites of the ancient Cretan and Indus Valley civilizations. These prehistoric Greek and Indian cult figures are thought to be early versions of Artemis and Shiva, both of whom are divine hunters and lords of the wild beasts.[7] Students of comparative religion refer to such figures collectively as the Master of Animals, and some think that they originated as glorified depictions of stone-age shamans and their hunting magic.[8]

In the prehistoric religions of western Europe, the master of animals was represented by the antlered stag-god known to the Gauls as Cernunnos, whose image is preserved in sculptures and petroglyphs from the 4th century B.C. onward at Celtic sites from northern Italy to Scandinavia. On a votive cauldron recovered from a peat bog in Denmark and dated to the first century B.C., Cernunnos is shown sitting cross-legged, flanked by various animals including a majestic stag. This tableau looks much like the Indus Valley seals that show the pre-Shiva deity as a horned, cross-legged figure surrounded by animal attendants.[9] Although the representations of the horned god from ancient India are at least two thousand years older than those from western Europe, the two may have a common prehistoric source.

The memory of the Celtic stag-god appears to be preserved in British folklore of the Christian era—for instance, in certain enigmatic animal-guarding figures in Welsh and Irish mythology,[10] or in the stories told of Herne, the antlered bogeyman of Windsor Forest memorialized by Shakespeare:

> There is an old tale goes that Herne the Hunter,
> Sometime a keeper here in Windsor Forest,
> Doth all the wintertime, at still midnight,
> Walk round about an oak, with great ragg'd horns;
> And there he blasts the tree, and takes the cattle,
> And makes milchkine yield blood, and shakes a chain
> In a most hideous and dreadful manner.[11]

The image of the lord of the animals lingers on in Christian mythology as well as in British folklore. The conventional image of the devil as a man with horns and cloven hooves no doubt derives in part from the antlered and ram-horned gods that Celtic tribes throughout western Europe were worshipping at the time of their conversion to Christianity.[12] Conversely, it also seems likely that the powers over wild beasts attributed to Jesus and various saints in medieval legend owe something to the memory of the lord of the animals. The deer, which was the cult animal of Cernunnos and of the Greco-Roman mistress of the animals Artemis/Diana, is the symbol of more Christian saints than any other wild beast.[13] Most of the saints so symbolized were woodland recluses. Their legends show them visited in their forest sanctuaries by wild deer drawn to their aura of sanctity. Hinds give them milk (Giles, Goar) or bring them food (Egidius), stags light their way through the forest with miraculously flaming antlers (Ida), and hunted deer turn to the saints for salvation (Neot, Chad, Egidius, and Blaise). Giles, patron saint of beggars, is conventionally shown with his palm pierced by an arrow, which he intercepted when he threw himself in front of a hunted doe to protect her from the pursuing King Flavius of the Goths. The traditional Irish prayer known as the "Fáeth Fiada" (Deer's Cry), is said to have been composed by St. Patrick when he himself miraculously took on the semblance of a stag.[14]

In northern European tradition, the forest itself wears a faint aura of the supernatural. The forests of Germanic folktales are magical and uncanny places inhabited by strange characters, and those who enter them encounter enchantments, transformations, and luck. A different but related atmosphere hangs over the forest in medieval Celtic literatures: a sense that forests and other wild places are not spooky but *holy*. This feeling is particularly marked in early Irish poems, perhaps because many of them were written by monastic hermits:

> I wish, O Son of the living God,
> eternal ancient King,
> for a secret hut in the wilderness
> that it may be my dwelling.
>
> A very blue shallow well
> to be beside it,
> a clear pool for washing away sins
> through the grace of the Holy Ghost.
>
> A beautiful wood close by
> around it on every side
> for the nurture of many-voiced birds
> to shelter and hide it.[15]

The most powerful ancient Irish expression of the holiness of wild places is the *Buile Suibhne Geilt* (The Frenzy of Mad Sweeney). This work, half prose and half poetry, is a thirteenth-century reworking of older stories and verses about Sweeney, King of Dal Araidhe, and the madness that came over him after the battle of Magh Rath in 637 A.D.[16] Most of the *Buile Suibhne* consists of bursts of lyric madsong uttered by the crazed Sweeney, who believes he is a bird. (He also calls himself *fer benn,* man of antlers.[17]) As Sweeney runs naked and bleeding through the thickets and forests of Ireland, he sings in despair of his misery—but also in ecstatic praise of the clean sweetness of wild

A hunted doe flies to the embrace of St. Giles, whose right hand intercepts the arrow intended for her. (Anonymous, c. 1500; National Gallery, London)

nature, which he contrasts with the disorder and pollution of the human domain:

> From the cliff of Lough Diolar
> to Derry Colmcille
> I saw the great swans, heard their calls
> sweetly rebuking wars and battles.
>
> From lonely cliff-tops, the stag
> bells and makes the whole glen shake
> and re-echo. I am ravished.
> Unearthly sweetness shakes my breast.[18]

From some admixture of such Germanic and Celtic traditions with the conventional flowery May mornings that entered medieval literature through the troubadours' love songs,[19] there developed during the late Middle Ages the concept of the *greenwood,* the unsettled forest seen as a delightful seat of natural beauty and human pleasure. In the earliest English literature, the forest is still suffused with the ghostly gloom of Germanic folklore:

> . . . a mysterious land,
> wolf-haunted cliffs, windy headlands,
> fearful fen-paths; there the mountain torrent
> falls forever under the rocks' darkness,
> a flood under the earth. Not a mile hence
> lies the lake rimmed with rime-covered woods;
> the firm-rooted forest overshadows the water.
> There each night may be seen a terrible wonder,
> A fire on the flood. No man living
> is so wise that he knows that ground.
> Though the heath-stalker, the strong-horned stag
> hard-pressed by hounds, should seek the forest
> after a long chase, he would sooner yield up
> his life on the shore than plunge in there
> to hide his head.[20]

But the early Robin Hood ballads, which were in circulation by 1400 or so, paint a very different picture of the forest and its inhabitants:

> In summer, when the shawes be sheyne [copses are bright],
> And leaves be large and long,

58

It is full merry in fair forest
To hear the fowlès song:

To see the deer draw to the dale,
And leave the hillès hee,
And shadow them in the leavès green,
Under the green-wood tree.[21]

Throughout Old English poetry, "the aspects of nature described are stern or even gloomy";[22] but the prevalent vision of nature in Middle English poetry is sweet and welcoming. The transition from the ominous forests of Germanic sagas to the late medieval greenwood is reflected in the history of two English adjectives derived from Latin *silva* (woods). The older of the two is *savage,* which descends to English through French *sauvage* from Latin *silvaticus* (woodsy).[23] The newer word, borrowed from scholarly Latin into English in the late 1500s, is *sylvan.* The difference in meaning between *savage* and *sylvan* is precisely the difference between the images of the forest in the legends of Beowulf and Robin Hood.

THE savage forest was increasingly displaced by the sylvan forest in the medieval European imagination because the forest was becoming a different sort of place, with a new social significance. No longer feared as gloomy wildernesses infested with man-eating beasts and hobgoblins, the shrinking forests of northwestern Europe were transformed during the late Middle Ages into exclusive aristocratic playgrounds.

The transformation began with a population increase. New farming techniques, including three-field crop rotation and the use of horses in plowing, had led to a spurt in northern European population growth that began in the eighth century.[24] As northern Europe grew more and more populous, its forests grew fewer, smaller, and tamer. Interrupted briefly by the pandemic Black Death of 1348, these trends resumed in the mid-1400s and continued, with minor fluctuations, until the twentieth century. The balance shifted back and forth, and whenever pestilence or war diminished human numbers, fields reverted to woods and wild animals plagued the more isolated farms.[25] But in general human population grew and the forests and wild beasts retreated. By around 1200, both wolves and beaver had disappeared from southern Britain, and the surviving red deer and wild boar were largely restricted to royal forests and other game sanctuaries.[26]

As human settlements multiplied and the wild places dwindled, hunting increasingly became a privilege restricted to the nobility. Before the turn of the millennium, small landholders throughout northern and western Europe had been allowed to hunt more or less freely on their own land. But from the tenth century on, that right was increasingly taken over by the aristocracy. To quote David Dalby:

> From the Carlovingian period onwards . . . large areas were declared as royal "forests," within which the hunting or trapping of game was banned to the local population. The full effect of these new "hunting preserves" was not felt until later, however, when the right to set up and administer such areas began to pass from the King into the hands of local nobility, both spiritual and temporal. From the eleventh century onwards, these "hunting preserves" were being widely established in Germany, and the hunting rights of the free peasantry were progressively lost to their local overlords. This development marked the beginning not only of a new social period, but also of new hunting traditions: the stag-hunt and the sport of falconry, as practised by the nobility, became the most important forms of hunting, and the establishment of hunting retinues marked the growth of hunting as a regular profession.[27]

The Norman invaders who conquered England in 1066 lost no time in setting up hunting preserves there on the continental model. The Old English word for "game sanctuary," *deorfrith* (deerpeace), first appears around 1100, in a passage in the Anglo-Saxon Chronicles condemning William the Conqueror:

> *He set up many a deerfrith*
> *And laid down laws therewith,*

that whosoever slew hart or hind should be blinded. He protected the harts, likewise the boars as well. He loved the tall deer as dearly as if he had been their father.

> *He also ordered that the hare*
> *Should run freely everywhere.*

The rich protested and the poor grumbled,

> *But he was so set on his path*
> *That he would not heed their wrath,*

and they had to follow the king's orders if they wanted to keep their lives and lands.[28]

The ruling class's exclusive hunting privileges were tyrannically exercised and savagely enforced. Not only were peasants living near game preserves forbidden to hunt or even to own bows or nets; they were also forbidden to attack game animals that were devouring their crops. They were often required to raise and maintain hunting dogs for the use of their liege lords—and to mutilate their own dogs' feet to make them too lame to chase deer. In many parts of Europe, the peasantry were also compelled to serve without pay as beaters and bearers during hunts, and to build and maintain fences, lodges, and other structures for the use of noble huntsmen. Peasants suspected of taking game were punished with ruthless severity; accused poachers might be blinded, castrated, staked out to die in freezing water, or sewn into the fresh skin of a stag to be chased down and killed by deerhounds.[29]

The grossly unequal distribution of hunting privileges led people of different social classes to think about the hunt in different ways. For the peasant masses barred from the hunt, hunting became associated with freedom, feasting, and rebellion against the authorities. The English peasantry of the fourteenth century wove these motifs together in their songs and stories about Robin Hood, that free spirit clad in forest green who dwells in the woods with his band of proud outlaws, robbing the rich, giving to the poor, and merrily poaching the king's deer.[30] Similar though less celebrated legends were told about other deer-hunting fighters and fugitives in the greenwood: the eleventh-century Hereward the Wake, Fulk Fitzwarin, Gamelyn, Adam Bell of Carlisle, Johnie Cock, and so on.[31]

Hunting took on an opposite significance among the aristocracy. In those circles, hunting became associated with upper-class status, and hunting practices became encrusted with courtly ceremony that served to demonstrate the genteel manners (or expose the pretensions) of the participants in the chase. This formalization of the hunt appears to have started in thirteenth-century France. From there it spread first into England via its Norman-French aristocracy and subsequently into other countries.

The growth of ritual in the upper-class medieval hunt is documented in the how-to books produced for the education and training of aristocratic hunters. The oldest example extant, the *De Arte Bersandi* by the thirteenth-century German knight Guicennas, is a fairly straightforward practical treatise on the bowhunting of deer.[32] But its successors—especially those from France and England—became progressively more concerned with the forms of hunting etiquette and ceremony than with the practical task of bagging game.[33] The purpose of these books, as Anthony Dent puts it, is "not so much to teach the aspiring stag-hunter how to recognize signs of a stag having recently been in a covert as to ensure that he does not commit the social solecism of calling the stag's excreta by the wrong name."[34]

The importance of this particular topic is evident from George Turbervile's 1576 treatise *The Noble Arte of Venerie or Hunting*:

> If a young huntsman chance to light in company with elder masters, and that they ask him how he calleth the ordure of an hart, reindeer, goat, or fallow deer, he shall answer that they are to be called the fewmet or fewmishings, and that all beasts which live of browse, shall have the same term in that respect. But in beasts of raven or prey, as the boar, the bear, and such like, they shall be called the lesses. And of hares and coneys, they are called croteys. Of other vermin or stinking chases, as foxes, badgers and such like, they are called the feance, of the otter they are called the sprayntes.[35]

This catalogue is prefaced by a wood engraving of a huntsman on bended knee presenting a heap of deer turds to Queen Elizabeth I. Turbervile renders into heroic couplets a sample speech to be delivered on such occasions:

> Before the Queen, I come report to make
> Then husht and peace, for noble *Trystram's* sake,
> From out my horn, my fewmets first I draw,
> And them present, on leaves, by hunters' law:
> And thus I say: "My liege, behold and see
> An hart of ten, I hope he harbored be.
> For if you mark his fewmets every point,
> You shall them find, long, round, and well anoint,
> Knotty and great, withouten pricks or cares,
> The moistness shows, what venison he bears."[36]

A vast lexicon of technical terminology attended every aspect of the aristocratic hunt. The deer hunter who hoped to be regarded as a gentleman of breeding had to memorize lists of special terms for more

A huntsman presenting fewmets of the hunted stag to Queen Elizabeth I.
(Turbervile, 1576; Bodleian Library, Oxford)

than droppings. There were terms for every type and condition of hart and hind: for all the common configurations of antlers; for the hoofprints of deer and their variations; for the places where deer left signs of having lain or stood or walked or galloped: for all the other features of the landscape of possible interest to hunters; for the different sorts of hunting dogs and their anatomy, behavior, gear, and so forth. The would-be hunter also had to know all the appropriate signals, both cries and horn calls, to be given to his fellow hunters or to dogs at various turns and phases of the chase, together with hundreds of other details of terminology, etiquette, and ceremony.

"Breaking the stag"—the ceremonial gutting and butchering of the slain deer—was the most complicated part of aristocratic hunting ritual, and its details were minutely set forth in medieval literature. Gottfried von Strassburg's thirteenth-century poem *Tristan und Isolt,* the primary source for later versions of the Tristan legend, depicts Tristan as a particularly discriminating stag breaker,[37] which is why "noble Trystram" is invoked above in the fewmet bearer's rhymed speech. The huntsman who undertook to break the stag was watched and evaluated critically by all the participants in the hunt. He was expected to skin the animal using a certain number of cuts passing through certain points on the body, and to disjoint it and distribute specific pieces to traditional recipients. The ritual differed from century to century and from place to place. In sixteenth-century England, the tongue, testicles, rectum, and other highly relished tidbits went to the highest-ranking nobleman present; the right shoulder to the huntsman who found the stag; the brisket to the huntsman who drove the stag out of hiding; the neck to the master of the kennels; the back to the keeper of the bloodhounds; the occiput and brain to the hounds themselves; and the cartilaginous tip of the breastbone to the waiting ravens. In some forests, the ravens supposedly became so familiar with this ritual that they would fly down at the kill and pester the stag breaker until he gave them their handout.[38]

Most of these terms and rituals, like the terminology of feces, differed from one kind of quarry to another. The fantastic and amusing terms that Elizabethan huntsmen applied to groupings of different species—a *sloth* of bears, an *exaltation* of larks, a *trip* of goats, a *richesse* of martens[39]—are familiar today to lovers of quaint words. Every other aspect of the aristocratic hunt also afforded a different lexicon for each species of game. For example, a male fallow deer during its first six years of life was known successively as a *fawn, pricket, sorel, sore, buck of the first head,* and *buck,* while the corresponding terms for a red deer were *calf, brocket, spade, staggart, stag,* and *hart;* and some authorities held that the word *hart* should be reserved for a stag slain by a prince. To drive a red deer out of hiding was to *unharbor* it—but one was said to *rouse* a fallow deer, *find* a roebuck, *rear* a boar, *start* a hare, *bolt* a rabbit, *unkennel* a fox, *dig* a badger, *raise* a wolf, *bay* a marten, and *vent* an otter. Even the signals given to the dog pack were supposed to vary with the prey species. It was proper to say "To him, to him" when unleashing dogs to flush a red deer out of hiding; but if the quarry was a boar, the huntsman was expected to use the plural number ("To them")—a grammatical nicety presumably wasted on hunting dogs, even in Elizabethan England. The unhappy hunter who used the wrong pronoun to the dogs, called a brocket a pricket, or said "raise" when he meant "rouse" seldom escaped with mere derision. A public spanking with the flat of a hunting knife was the customary penalty for many such misuses of ritual language—for example, uttering the forbidden word "hedgehog" during a deer hunt.[40]

Obviously all these taboos and rituals and ceremonial usages were not needed for the practical business of killing deer; they served to advertise, or lay claim to, the social status of a gentleman. "Why you know," says a rustic social climber in the first scene of Ben Jonson's *Every Man in his Humour* (1598), "an a man have not skill in the hawking and hunting languages now-a-days, I'll give not a rush for him. They are more studied than the Greek, or the Latin. He is for no gallant's company without them."

The organization of the hunt also emphasized class boundaries, especially in France and England.[41] The importance of social class in English "sport" is made clear in the prefatory verses to Turbervile's book, in which the court poet George Gascoigne praises hunting as

> . . . a *Noble sport,*
> *To recreate the minds of Men, in good and godly sort.*
> *A sport for Noble peers, a sport for gentle bloods,*
> The pain I leave for servants such, as beat the bushy woods
> To make their masters sport. *Then let the Lords rejoice,*

> *Let gentlemen behold the glee, and take thereof the choice.*
> For my part (being one) I must needs say my mind,
> *That hunting was ordainèd first, for men of Noble kind.*
> And unto them therefore, I recommend the same,
> As exercise that best becomes, their worthy noble name.[42]

Hunting became an obsessive preoccupation of many aristocrats. Louis XV of France, who spent from three to five days a week in the saddle chasing deer, has been credited with killing some 10,000 red deer in the course of his fifty-year career in the royal game parks—an accomplishment possibly unique in the history of the human species.[43] The hunt attained bizarre levels of excess in elaboration as well as in quantity of killing in prerevolutionary France; Louis XIV is remembered in this context for the carriages, courtesans, and orchestras that followed the royal presence through his stag hunts at Versailles.

The elaborate ceremony that prevailed in the French royal game parks set a standard for aristocratic hunters throughout western Europe, and the French *parforce* hunt, in which no missile weapons were used and the quarry was essentially run to death, became the norm in Europe's princely courts. In England, French became as much the language of the hunt as it was of cuisine, diplomacy, and erotic intrigue. The principal hunting manuals of the late Middle Ages and Renaissance were written in French and translated into other European languages; Turbervile's manual, for example, is mostly a free translation of Jacques du Fouilloux's *La Venerie* of 1561.[44]

These ceremonious hunts found only rudimentary parallels in the lives and lore of the lower classes. By the end of the Middle Ages, the peasant masses of Europe had little opportunity to hunt openly. Peasants generally risked torture, mutilation, or death if they were caught taking game. Their hunting thus tended to be a rare, quick, and solitary affair, not a social occasion to be celebrated in song. A fair amount of hunting occurs in European folktales and ballads, but almost no details of technique are set forth. In Child's collection of traditional English and Scottish ballads, the only one that contains any description of hunting procedure is "Johnie Cock":

> Johnie shot, and the dun deer leapt,
> And she leapt wond'rous wide,
> Until they came to the wan water,
> And he stemmed her of her pride.

He has ta'en out the little pen-knife,
'Twas full three quarters long,
And he has ta'en out of that dun deer
The liver both and the tongue.

They ate of the flesh, and they drank of the blood,
And the blood it was so sweet,
Which caused Johnie and his bloody hounds
To fall in a deep sleep.[45]

Here the deer hunt is a solitary, bloody business of few words, simple apparatus, and no ceremony, as different as a hunt could possibly be from the courtly chases prescribed in the manuals of du Fouilloux and Turbervile.

YET despite all these differences between the aristocratic and folk traditions, legends and stories of the hunt from both high and low sources in medieval Europe share some important motifs that are not found in classical antiquity. These new themes have remained deeply imbedded in Western thought about hunting. They are summed up in a series of changes in the symbolic significance of deer.

The changing status of deer began to be reflected around 1000 A.D. in new meanings of words related to animals and hunting in several European languages. In English, German, French, and Irish during this period, words that had previously meant "animal" or "wild animal" (Old English *deor*, Old High German *wilt* and *tior*, Old Irish *fiad*, Latin *bestia*) narrowed in meaning to "deer" (modern English *deer*, German *Wild*, Irish *fiadh*) or "hind, doe" (Middle High German hunting jargon *tier*, French *biche*).[46] In short, for speakers of these languages, "animal" in general came to mean "deer" in particular, and deer became unqualified animals, paragons of the animal condition. Besides being animals par excellence, deer also came to be thought of throughout western Europe as the ideal objects of the hunt. This change is reflected in the usual modern Spanish word for deer, *venado,* which means "the hunted"; in the modern Irish verb *fiadhachaim* (to hunt), meaning literally "to deer-atize";[47] and in English *venison,* which originally meant "game, meat gotten by hunting" but now means the flesh of deer in particular.

In medieval German, the phrase *edel wilt* (noble wild animal), is an idiom meaning "stag."[48] Throughout western Europe, deer took on symbolic nobility during the Middle Ages. This was a new departure. In classical antiquity, deer had symbolized cowardice, as rabbits do today. In ancient Greek, "deerish" *(elapheios)* meant "cowardly." Achilles derides Agamemnon's cowardice in the *Iliad* by calling him "deer-hearted."[49] Characters likened to deer in classical literature are either cowards and losers (Turnus in the *Aeneid*, Penelope's suitors in the *Odyssey*) or innocent victims (Virgil's Dido). But in medieval literature, deer began for the first time to be invested with an aura of nobility and even of supernatural awe.

This symbolic elevation of deer to noble status must have resulted in part from the increasing restriction of deer-hunting privileges to the aristocracy. It may also in part be traceable to the ancient Celtic tradition of reverence for the stag; at any rate, the image of the stag as prince of the forest seems to be especially old in Celtic literatures. The earliest occurrence of this metaphor that I have come across is in the seventh-century Welsh poem, *Y Gododdin,* in which a heroic warrior is eulogized as a "noble stag."[50] Similar figures of the stag-hero persist in later Welsh poetry,[51] and they are echoed in Scots Gaelic folksong[52] and in medieval Irish literature:

> Those unharnessed runners
> from glen to glen!
> Nobody tames
> that royal blood,
>
> each one aloof
> on its rightful summit,
> antlered, watchful.
> Imagine them,
>
> the stag of high Slieve Felim,
> the stag of the steep Fews,
> the stag of Duhallow, the stag of Orrery,
> the fierce stag of Killarney.[53]

The ennobling of the stag made it possible to see the hunt as a tragedy. The deer hunt began to be used as a literary metaphor for the tragic fall of a noble victim at least as early as the thirteenth century, when the murdered Siegfried is likened to a slain stag in the epic *Nibelungenlied*. A more familiar sixteenth-century example is the lamentation of Shakespeare's Mark Antony over the corpse of the assassinated Caesar:

> . . . Here wast thou bay'd, brave hart;
> Here didst thou fall; and here thy hunters stand,
> Sign'd in thy spoil, and crimson'd in thy lethe.
> O world, thou wast the forest to this hart;
> And this indeed, O world, the heart of thee!
> How like a deer, strucken by many princes,
> Dost thou here lie![54]

Other hunting techniques furnished other metaphors.[55] But the stag was the hunter's ideal quarry, and so the ruling metaphors of the chase derived from the deer hunt. As hunting came to dominate the leisure and imagination of the medieval aristocracy, the deer hunt furnished their literati with metaphors for every sort of endeavor. The Christian pursuing God or fleeing Satan, the soldier pursuing or fleeing his foes on the field of battle, the courtly lover pursuing his beloved or struggling to escape the toils of desire—all became figurative deer, hounds, or huntsmen in medieval and Renaissance literature. The metaphor was applied to the most sacred subjects as well as the most profane. At the sacred extreme, the butchered stag becomes an emblem of the crucified Christ:

> He was todrawe [cut in pieces]
> So deer y-slawe [slain]
> In chase.[56]

At the opposite, profane extreme of the spectrum of hunting symbolism, the deer hunt becomes metaphoric coitus, the hunter's arrow a penis, and the stag's death an orgasm:

> For, O, love's bow
> Shoots buck and doe.
> The shaft confounds
> Not that it wounds,
> But tickles still the sore.
> These lovers cry Oh! ho! they die!
> Yet that which seems the wound to kill

> Doth turn oh! ho! to ha! ha! he!
> So, dying, love lives still.[57]

Ancient writers as far back as Plato had occasionally used the hunt as a metaphor for a lover's pursuit of the beloved.[58] But from the twelfth century to the sixteenth, stories and poems about the hunt of love became a full-blown literary genre. French and German poets in particular devised extraordinarily rich and elaborate allegories of the amorous chase, drawing all imaginable analogies between love and hunting.[59] In some of these erotic parables of the hunt, the hapless deer represents the male author—for instance, the sixteenth-century English poet Michael Drayton, portraying himself as a stag mortally wounded by rays from his lady's "darting eyes":

> Wallowing in his blood, some life yet left,
> His stone-cold lips doth kiss the blessed shaft.[60]

In others, the lady becomes the victim. She too may be represented as a hunted stag, as in the thirteenth-century French poem *Li dis dou cerf amoreus,* in which the beloved woman, "the stag of love," is harried and finally brought down by allegorical staghounds named "Wishes," "Longing," "Memory," "Pity," and "Love," who consummate their pursuit with a symbolic feast on the flesh of their fallen quarry.[61] More commonly, the lady is represented as a doe, and the chase has a less sanguinary conclusion. The fourteenth-century Welsh poet Dafydd ap Gwilym dreams of hunting dogs driving a symbolic white hind, "the color of waves of heat" *(hoen geirw tes),* into his arms:

> Tamed thus, she came
> (Threatening as I was) to my protection;
> Two naked nostrils: I awoke
> Ravenous, alone in my hut.[62]

As the late Middle Ages ripened toward the Renaissance, these allegorical hunts of love tended to become more delicately chivalrous, dwelling more on the ethereal beauty of the quarry and less on bloody flesh and naked nostrils. The narrator of one fifteenth-century German poem falls in love with a hind that he is too inept to pursue, and concludes his hunt instead by impressing the image of his beloved deer deeply into his heart.[63] In a more elaborate German allegory of

70

the fourteenth century, the hunter-poet is advised to abandon the amatory chase and turn to hunting Christ, the stag "whose hoof is stained / with blood, for He ransomed us at so great a price."[64] The hunter determines instead to spend his life in fruitless pursuit of the stag of love, embracing the unconsummated chase as an end in itself. The untouchable wildness of the woman-deer has here become an enchanting virtue, as in Thomas Wyatt's sonnet on the hunt of love two centuries later:

> Whoso list to hunt, I know where is an hind,
> But as for me, alas, I may no more:
> The vain travail hath wearied me so sore,
> I am of them that farthest cometh behind.
> Yet may I, by no means, my wearied mind
> Draw from the deer, but as she fleeth afore,
> Fainting I follow. I leave off therefore,
> Since in a net I seek to hold the wind.
> Who list her hunt, I put him out of doubt,
> As well as I, may spend his time in vain.
> And graven with diamonds in letters plain
> There is written her fair neck round about:
> "*Noli me tangere,* for Caesar's I am,
> And wild for to hold, though I seem tame."[65]

Allegories of the erotic hunt found expression in painting and sculpture as well as poetry and prose. A large number of decorative objects depicting the hunt of love—illuminated manuscripts, miniature paintings, carved and painted chests and coffers, ivories, musical instruments—have survived to bear witness to the popularity of the theme in upper-class circles during the Middle Ages and Renaissance.[66] A particularly elegant and witty sculptural expression of the metaphor is the *Diane d'Anet* from sixteenth-century France. The statue depicts a masterful Diana with unstrung bow, reclining amorously against a majestic but uneasy-looking stag. The statue was commissioned by another Diana, the king's mistress Diane de Poitiers, who displayed it in the courtyard of her country chateau.[67] Presumably this depiction of the bloodless conquest of a noble beast by a divine huntress was intended as a daring visual pun.

Another theme that separates medieval hunting symbolism from its classical antecedents is the motif of the uncanny or otherworldly quarry. In Greek myth, uncanny things sometimes happen *to* hunters: Actaeon is changed into a stag and killed by his hounds, Narcissus is changed into a flower, and the huntress Daphne becomes a laurel tree. But there is nothing uncanny about the deer and boar that these mythological hunters pursue.[68] Contrast with this a medieval myth of metamorphosis in the hunt. A young pagan named Placidas saw a peculiarly large and beautiful stag while hunting. After he pursued it into a lonely forest, the stag suddenly leapt up onto a rock and cried, "Ah, Placidas, why do you persecute me? It is even for your sake that I have come now, so that through this beast I might reveal myself to you. I am the Christ that you unknowingly worship . . . and I came so that I might reveal myself through this stag, and for him hunt and capture you with the nets of my mercy."[69] Converted by this miracle, Placidas was baptized into the church under the name of Eustace. Though he returned occasionally to the forest to meet and commune with the stag-Christ, he hunted no more. Wild beasts of prey henceforth left him unharmed, even when he was thrown to the lions in the arena. Eustace finally met a martyr's death at the hands of the emperor Hadrian—who was renowned as a huntsman. Despite all the antihunting symbolism associated with his legend, Eustace was adopted as the patron saint of hunters.

The legend of Eustace is only one of many popular medieval stories told about saints and heroes who encounter uncanny or supernatural stags or are transformed into stags themselves, like Patrick or the stag-Christ.[70] Tales of miraculous deer of divine beauty and supernatural portent are also common in Hindu mythology, and some historians think that this "stag motif" diffused into Europe in the fifth century from India.[71] But even if it had an Indian source, the stag motif must have struck a chord that harmonized with something in Western thinking, since it penetrated at once into European culture at all levels and has lingered ever since as a recurrent image in our art, our literature, and our folklore.

In medieval romances and in folktales and songs from all over northern Europe, otherworldly deer draw pursuing hunters on to love and glory or to tragic disaster. The uncanny quarry is often marked by its white color. A recurring theme in Irish mythology is the white

The *Diane d'Anet*. (Louvre, Paris)

stag that leads the hero to a royal crown.[72] In the rhymed stories called Breton Lays that were popular in medieval France and England, mysterious white deer often appear and draw hunters into chases that culminate in amorous adventure.[73] If the otherworldly white deer is female, it may prove to be the hunter's lover or sister transformed into a doe. In the horrid little Danish ballad *The Girl in Hind's Skin,* a hunter disregards his mother's warning and slays a mysterious "little white hind / That bears the gold under the shoulder." When he starts skinning the deer, he uncovers parts of his own sister's dead body.[74] Other ballads, from France, Brittany, and Great Britain, tell similar stories about shape-changing deer as lovers or sisters of hunters.[75] The uncanniest of all uncanny deer in balladry, the "fallow doe" of *The Three Ravens,* may originally have been another woman-deer lamenting the death of a human lover:

> Down in yonder green field
> There lies a knight slain under his shield.
>
> His hounds they lie down at his feet,
> So well they can their master keep.
>
> His hawks they fly so eagerly,
> There's no fowl dare come him nigh.
>
> Down there comes a fallow doe,
> As great with young as she might go.
>
> She lifted up his bloody head,
> And kissed his wounds that were so red . . .
>
> She buried him before the prime,
> She was dead herself ere evensong time.
>
> God send every gentleman
> Such hawks, such hounds, and such a leman.[76]

Stories of faery deer were carried by European settlers to the New World, where they persist in American folklore.[77] One widespread American tale tells of a reformed hunter endlessly following a doe that he loves and tries to protect from other hunters by tying a bell around her neck.[78] A North Carolina legend tells how the ghost of Virginia Dare, the first white child born in English North America, still haunts the forests of Roanoke Island in the form of a spectral white doe.[79] Folk wisdom in the Ozarks and the Cumberland Mountains holds that a white deer is a dire omen and that to shoot one is bad luck.[80]

In literary culture, the uncanny white deer has persisted for centuries as a symbol of the supernatural. In Thomas Malory's *Morte D'Arthur*, Sir Galahad is led by a white hart to a hermitage in the forest. There the holy hermit tells him that the hart is Jesus Christ and that "ofttimes ere this, our Lord showed him unto good men and good knights in likeness of an hart."[81] In John Dryden's long allegory *The Hind and the Panther*, a "milk-white hind" stands for the Roman Catholic Church, and the hind's hunted sons symbolize fallen martyrs. Later writers, from the English and German Romantics down to Yeats, Pound, and Eliot, have continued to use the white deer as an archaic symbol evoking feelings of otherworldliness, transcendence, and romance.[82]

At the beginning of the medieval period, hunting symbolism in Western art and literature had been rudimentary and peripheral. By the end of the Middle Ages, it was complicated and subtle, pervading many aspects of both the low and high cultural traditions of Europe. From the thirteenth century on, the hunt assumed antithetical connotations of license and aristocratic ritual. The gloomy forest converted itself into the gay and magical greenwood of medieval song and story, and the cowardly deer of Greek and Roman tradition came to be represented as noble and numinous figures, animal paragons charged with erotic and supernatural import. For the hunt to be perceived as a symbol of injustice and bloody tyranny, all that was needed was a smattering of systematic doubt about the divine origins of the dominion that men in general and gentlefolk in particular exercised over the world.

FIVE

The Sobbing Deer

1st Lord	Thus most invectively he pierceth through The body of the country, city, court, Yea, and of this our life, swearing that we Are mere usurpers, tyrants, and what's worse, To fright the animals and to kill them up In their assign'd and native dwelling place.
Duke Senior	And did you leave him in this contemplation?
2nd Lord	We did, my lord, weeping and commenting Upon the sobbing deer.

—Shakespeare, *As You Like It*

DOUBTS about the legitimacy of man's dominion began to surface in the sixteenth century, and with them came the first condemnations of hunting heard in Europe in fourteen centuries.[1] The attacks on hunting started at the very beginning of the northern Renaissance, in the writings of Erasmus and Thomas More.

In his *Praise of Folly* (1511), Erasmus ridiculed the elaborate rituals of the medieval hunt, dismissing hunting as mere butchery and hunters as empty-headed, snobbish aristocrats who

> renounce everything else in favor of hunting wild game, and protest they feel an ineffable pleasure in their souls whenever they hear the raucous blast of the horns and the yelping of the hounds. Even the dung of the dogs, I am sure, smells like cinnamon to them. And what is so sweet as a beast being butchered? Cutting up bulls and oxen is properly given over to the humble plebeian, but it is a crime for game to be slaughtered except by a gentleman! There, with his head bared, on

bended knees, with a knife designed just for this (for it is sacrilege to use any other), with certain ceremonial gestures he cuts just the proper members in the approved order . . . And if some bit of the animal is handed one of them to taste, he thinks he has gone up a step or so in the ranks of nobility. And thus with their butchering and eating of beasts they accomplish nothing at all unless it be to degenerate into beasts themselves, though they think, all the while, they are living the life of a king.[2]

Erasmus thought hunting simply a foolish waste of time, but his animal-loving friend Thomas More saw it as a sign of man's depraved nature.[3] In one of More's Latin epigrams, a trapped hare thrown alive to a pack of hounds for the hunters' entertainment cries out to condemn the human species: "O stony-hearted race, more savage than any wild beast, to find cruel amusement in bitter murder!"[4] More attacked sportive hunting at length in *Utopia,* published in 1516. His Utopians think of hunting as a species of butchery, not an aristocratic pastime. And just as they show contempt for ostentation by making their slaves' chains out of gold, they show contempt for killing and cruelty by making hunting a chore for slaves:

The Utopians think that this whole business of hunting is beneath the dignity of free men, and so they have made it a part of the butcher's trade—which, as I said before, they foist off on their slaves. They regard hunting as the lowest and vilest part of butchery, and the other parts of it as more useful and more honorable, since they kill animals only to meet human needs, whereas the hunter seeks nothing but pleasure from a poor little beast's slaughter and dismemberment . . . The Utopians think that this lust to witness violent death arises from a cruel disposition, or else eventually induces a cruel disposition through long indulgence in such a savage pleasure.[5]

More does not call hunting downright immoral, only low *(infimus)* and base *(indignus)*. But his distaste and outrage are evident. He repeatedly describes the hunters' quarry as "a poor little beast" and its killing as "murder," and he delivers a brief, angry sermon to his hunting readers:

Why should the sense of pleasure be any greater when a dog chases a hare than when a dog chases another dog? The same thing happens in both cases; there is racing in both, if you like to watch racing. But if what attracts you is the hope of slaughter and the expectation of seeing a beast killed, you ought rather to be moved by pity when you see a poor little hare torn to bits by a dog, the weak slain by the stronger, the fearful by the fierce, the innocent by the cruel and merciless.[6]

Montaigne expressed a similar distaste for the hunt in his 1580 essay, "Of Cruelty":

> Among other vices, I cruelly hate cruelty, both by nature and by judgment, as the extreme of all vices. But this is to such a point of softness that I do not see a chicken's neck wrung without distress, and I cannot bear to hear the scream of a hare in the teeth of my dogs, although the chase is a violent pleasure . . . For myself, I have not even been able without distress to see pursued and killed an innocent animal which is defenseless and which does us no harm. And as it commonly happens that the stag, feeling himself out of breath and strength, having no other remedy left, throws himself back and surrenders to ourselves who are pursuing him, asking for our mercy by his tears . . . that has always seemed to me a very unpleasant spectacle.

Like More, Montaigne felt that our joy in the hunt reflects some innate defect in the human spirit:

> Natures that are bloodthirsty toward animals give proof of a natural propensity toward cruelty . . . [and] Nature herself, I fear, attaches to man some instinct for inhumanity. No one takes his sport in seeing animals play with and caress one another, and no one fails to take it in seeing them tear apart and dismember one another.[7]

In the works of Montaigne's contemporary, Shakespeare, the hunt becomes a symbol of bloody oppression. Mark Antony eulogizes the assassinated Caesar as a "brave hart" struck down by "butchers." Innocent victims like Macduff's children are likened to "murdered deer," and hunted deer are depicted as injured innocents, like the "poor sequester'd stag / That from the hunter's aim had ta'en a hurt" in *As You Like It*:

> The wretched animal heav'd forth such groans
> That their discharge did stretch his leathern coat
> Almost to bursting, and the big round tears

Cours'd one another down his innocent nose
In piteous chase.[8]

Among Shakespeare's characters, a distaste for the hunt is a sign of common decency. "Come, shall we go and kill us venison?" cries the Duke in *As You Like It*—and then come the second thoughts:

. . . And yet it irks me the poor dappled fools,
Being native burghers of this desert city,
Should in their own confines with forkèd heads [hunting arrows]
Have their round haunches gored.

The Princess in *Love's Labor's Lost* has harsher things to say about her own deer hunt:

Then, forester, my friend, where is the bush
That we must stand and play the murderer in? . . .
But come, the bow. Now mercy goes to kill,
And shooting well is then accounted ill . . .
And out of question so it is sometimes,
Glory grows guilty of detested crimes,
When, for fame's sake, for praise, an outward part,
We bend to that the working of the heart;
As I for praise alone now seek to spill
The poor deer's blood, that my heart means no ill.[9]

When hunting is not a metaphor for murder in Shakespeare, it is frequently a metaphor for rape—for example, throughout *The Rape of Lucrece* or in *Titus Andronicus*, where the rape and mutilation of Titus' daughter Lavinia is treated as a metaphorical deer hunt. The metaphor begins with the villain's speech to his confederates:

My lords, a solemn hunting is in hand;
There will the lovely Roman ladies troop;
The forest walks are wide and spacious,
And many unfrequented plots there are,
Fitted by kind for rape and villany.
Single you thither then this dainty doe,
And strike her home by force, if not by words.[10]

"We hunt not," affirms one henchman, ". . . with horse nor hound, / But hope to pluck a dainty doe to ground."[11] They seize the girl in the hunting preserve by force, rape her, and then cut out her tongue and hew off her hands, so that she cannot accuse them in either speech or writing. Her uncle Marcus leads the mutilated girl to her father:

> *Marcus* O, thus I found her, straying in the park,
> Seeking to hide herself, as doth the deer
> That hath receiv'd some unrecuring wound.
> *Titus* It was my deer, and he that wounded her
> Hath hurt me more than had he killed me dead.[12]

The dislike that More and Montaigne expressed for the hunt, and Shakespeare's equation of hunting with rape, mutilation, and murder, were not yet common in the sixteenth century. Most English authors who wrote about hunting still saw it as a kind of bucolic romp, a jolly aristocratic frolic in the greenwood:

> The wild forest, the clothèd holts with green,
> With reins avaled, and swift y-breathèd horse,
> With cry of hounds and merry blasts between,
> Where we did chase the fearful hart a force.[13]

But though aversion to hunting was still something out of the ordinary, it does show up in important and influential sixteenth-century writers like More and Montaigne. We see it occasionally in the graphic arts too. Albrecht Dürer's 1504 drawing of a stag dying with a crossbow bolt in its skull testifies to the appearance of a new set of attitudes. This drawing could not have been turned out by a medieval artist; the technique is too subtle and complicated, and so are the feelings expressed. The respect with which Dürer has observed his subject reflects the new Renaissance practice of sketching from life instead of copying conventional models.[14] Getting away from medieval conventions of hunting art gave Dürer the freedom to express unconventional emotions in this work—powerful, complicated, ambivalent, and not easily put into words.[15]

As negative feelings began to be expressed toward the hunt, the theme of the erotic hunt gradually disappeared from Western art and literature. By the mid-seventeenth century, hunting had ceased to furnish a vital and popular metaphor for honorable love. When later writers compare love to hunting, they often either follow Shakespeare

Head of a Stag, by Albrecht Dürer (1504; Bibliothèque Nationale, Paris)

in making hunting a metaphor for rape,[16] or use the comparison satirically to ridicule hunters and their machismo.[17]

One of the most surprising places where antihunting sentiment crops up in the sixteenth century is in hunting manuals themselves. The standard treatise on hunting was the *La Vénerie* of Jacques du Fouilloux, first published in 1561.[18] The subsequent editions of *La Vénerie* contain a poem by Guillaume Bouchet, "Complainte du cerf" (Complaint of the Stag), in which the hunted deer bitterly reviles the senseless cruelty of mankind in general and du Fouilloux in particular. The "Complainte" begins with the same "unpleasant spectacle" of the stag at bay that Montaigne found so disturbing:

Since I in deepest dread do yield myself to Man,
And stand full still between his legs, which erst full wildly ran,
Since I to him appeal, when hounds pursue me sore,
As who should say *"Now save me Man, for else I may no more,"*
Why dost thou then, *O Man, O Hunter,* me pursue,
With cry of hounds, with blast of horn, with hallo, and with hue?
. . . Is it because thy mind doth seek thereby some gains?
Canst thou in death take such delight? breeds pleasure so in pains?[19]

81

After four pages of this, the stag ends by begging the gods to embroil
the human race in perpetual war as a substitute for hunting, and leave
the animals in peace:

> Lo, here I crave of mighty gods, which are both good and just,
> That *Mars* may reign with *Man;* that strife and cruel war
> May set Man's murdering mind on work, with many a bloody jar:
> That drums with deadly dub may countervail the blast
> Which they with horns have blown full loud, to make my mind
>   aghast;
> That shot as thick as hail may stand for crossbow shoots;
> That *cuisses, greaves,* and such may serve in stead of hunters' boots . . .
> That when their busy brains are exercisèd so,
> Harts may lie safe within their lair, and never fear their foe.

If there are any who will not turn from "killing harmless deer" to war,
prays the hart, let them share the fate of Actaeon:

> But if so chance there be some dastard dreadful mome,
> Whom trumpets cannot well entice, nor call him once from home:
> And yet will play the man in killing harmless deer,
> I crave of God that such a ghost, and such a fearful fear,
> May see *Diana nak'd:* and she (to venge her scorns)
> May soon transform his harmful head into my harmless horns:
> Until his hounds may tear that heart of his in twain,
> Which thus torments us harmless harts, and puts our hearts to pain.[20]

Turbervile, who translated Bouchet's "Complainte" in these words
into his 1576 hunting manual, added similar rhymed protests by other
game animals. The hare's condemnation of hunting and humanity is
particularly scathing:

> Are minds of men become so void of sense,
> That they can joy to hurt a harmless thing?
> A silly beast, which cannot make defense?
> A wretch? a worm that cannot bite, nor sting?
> If that be so, I thank my Maker than,
> For making me a Beast and not a Man.
>
> . . . So that thou show'st thy vaunts to be but vain,
> That brag'st of wit, above all other beasts,
> And yet by me, thou neither gettest gain

> Nor findest food to serve thy glutton's feasts:
> Some sport perhaps: yet *Grievous is the glee*
> *Which ends in Blood,* that lesson learn of me.[21]

This is strange stuff to find in a handbook for hunters. But perhaps it was not supposed to be taken too seriously. Turbervile might have added all the poetic weeping and cursing of the game animals to his book because he and his readers thought it was *funny*. Similar claims have been made about other literary characters of the period. Nietzsche and George Orwell argued that Cervantes' Don Quixote and Shakespeare's Falstaff, whom we tend to see as complex, half-tragic characters, were intended as simple comic buffoons, and that their sufferings seemed merely amusing to an audience that relished public executions and bear baiting.[22] The "sobbing deer" in sixteenth-century literature might likewise have been stuck in for laughs. If so, then what looks like an upwelling of antihunting sentiment in the 1500s might be only a figment of the modern imagination.

This interpretation, however, will not hold for More or Montaigne. Their distaste for the hunt seems sincere. And though Bouchet's "Complainte du Cerf" might have been intended humorously, there is not much to smile at in the hare's speech that Turbervile added to it. Shakespeare's description of the "poor sequestered stag" in *As You Like It* does have a comical ring to it; but if his audiences had found the suffering and death of hunted animals merely amusing, Shakespeare would not have used hunting metaphors for tragic effect in *Julius Caesar, Macbeth,* and *Titus Andronicus.*

Another sign that the morality of hunting really was being questioned in the sixteenth century is that Turbervile felt compelled to say he was *not* questioning it. In his section on deer hunting, he dutifully translates du Fouilloux's cautionary tale about a Byzantine emperor who was killed by a stag at bay. But Turbervile goes on beyond du Fouilloux to draw a moral, and the moral very nearly gets out of hand:

> Behold, gentle Reader, the unconstancy of variable Fortune. A Prince which had done so many deeds of prowess among men . . . was at the last in the pride of his pleasure . . . vanquished, slain, and gored with the horns of a brute Beast: yea (that more is) by a fearful beast . . . that fled from him, and a beast whom he constrained (in his own defense)

to do this detestable murder. This example may serve as a mirror to all Princes and Potestates, yea and generally to all estates, that they bridle their minds from proffering of undeserved injuries, and do not constrain the simple sakeless man to stand in his own defense, nor to do (like the worm) turn again when it is trodden on.

Having drawn this Orwellian analogy between mistreated animals and oppressed peasants, Turbervile hastens to take it back:

> I would not have my words wrested to this construction, that it were unlawful to kill a Deer or such beasts of venery: for so should I both speak against the purpose which I have taken in hand, and again I should seem to argue against God's ordinances, since it seemeth that such beasts have been created to the use of man and for his recreation: but as by all Fables some good morality may be gathered, so by all histories and examples, some good allegory and comparison may be made.[23]

Turbervile's protestations here show that he is alerted to the possibility of moral objections to hunting. If he had sought the same "good allegory and comparison" in, say, a story of a woodcutter killed by a falling oak, he would probably not have bothered to stop and insist that it is quite all right to chop down trees.

Sixteenth-century antipathy to hunting thus seems to be a real phenomenon, not just a literary convention. This antipathy was something new; there is nothing much like it in the art and literature of the Middle Ages. A medieval master of the hunt would have been astonished if somebody had come up to him and accused him of being a murderer. In the five centuries that have gone by since Thomas More started talking that way, this sort of rhetoric has grown commonplace, and hunters today have learned to expect it.

WHY, after sportive hunting had been admired and respected in Europe all through the Middle Ages, did it start to lose favor in the 1500s? The fabric of the medieval world order was coming unraveled everywhere by the end of the sixteenth century, and it is unrealistic to single out any one change as the sole result of any other; but we can point to a few changes that probably encouraged attacks on hunting. One was the erosion of the power and prestige of the old landed aristocracy. From the late fifteenth century on, the feudal barons of western Europe found themselves increasingly squeezed between the growing power of the centralized state and the restiveness of the lower classes. In England this began in earnest in 1485, when Henry VII came to the throne at the end of the Wars of the Roses and started to dismantle the barons' private armies and systems of justice. His Tudor successors continued the process, which was also going on elsewhere in Europe—in Spain under Ferdinand II, in Sweden under Gustav I, in France under Charles VIII and Louis XII. The old order was also undermined by the spread of Protestantism. By making salvation a matter between each individual and God, Protestant belief not only undercut the power of priests and prelates but also prompted subversive thoughts about individual sovereignty in other sectors of society.

As a legal monopoly of the upper class and an aristocratic status symbol, hunting became a focus for class conflict during the 1500s. Actual class warfare broke out over aristocratic hunting in the Peasants' War of 1524. Encouraged by Lutheran doctrines and egged on by radical Protestant leaders, the peasants of northern Germany rose up against their feudal lords, sacking castles and monasteries and demanding an end to oppressive practices—especially the ruling-class monopolization of hunting.[24]

The rebellious German peasants were only demanding a fair share of the venison, not objecting to hunting as such. Opposition to hunting was a middle-class phenomenon, which expressed a bourgeois rejection of aristocratic values. Not all middle-class folk, of course, rejected those values; and some who longed to hobnob with the gentry bought hunting manuals and eagerly boned up on the lore of morts, prickets, and fewmets. But others, who resented the privileges and pretensions of the aristocracy, were disposed to denounce hunting as cruel or foolish. Erasmus (who was the bastard son of a priest) shows this sort of resentment in the passage from *Praise of Folly* quoted earlier. Similar bourgeois ridicule of the hunting gentry crops up in Richard Pace's humanist manifesto of 1517, *On the Fruits of Learning:*

> One of those whom we call gentlemen, who always carry a horn slung at their backs as though they were going to hunt during dinner, overheard us talking about literature, and he suddenly burst out in a rage, "What rubbish! Devil take all your stupid book learning! . . . I swear by God's Body I would rather that my son should hang than study

literature. It behooves the sons of gentlemen to blow horn calls correctly, to hunt skilfully, to train a hawk well and carry it elegantly. But the study of literature should be left to the sons of peasants."[25]

This middle-class caricature of the gentleman hunter is turned upside-down in book 2 of *Don Quixote,* where Cervantes mocks anti-hunting feelings as the base sentiments of a peasant. When Sancho Panza climbs a tree to escape from a hunted boar and is fetched down in disgrace, he declares that the pleasure of hunting "should not be one at all, for it consists in killing an animal that has done no harm to anyone." His host the Duke replies that it is a question of one's social class:

"for hunting is the most suitable and necessary exercise of all for kings and princes. The chase is the image of war: it has its stratagems, wiles, ambushes by which one can overcome the enemy in safety . . . and indeed it is an exercise which can be taken without harming anyone and with benefit to many. And the best point about it is that it is not for everybody, as other kinds of sport are, except hawking, which also is only for kings and great lords. So, Sancho, change your opinion, and when you are governor, go in for hunting, and you will soon find that it will do you a world of good."

"By no means," replied Sancho: "a good governor should have a broken leg and keep at home. Wouldn't it be a fine thing if people came to see him on business, foot-weary, and he's away in the woods enjoying himself? . . . By my faith, sir, hunting and amusements are more for lazybones than governors. Now my bit of amusement will be a game of cards at Easter, and bowls on Sundays and holidays. Them huntings and such-like don't suit my temper or my conscience."[26]

But not all the tension surrounding hunting in sixteenth-century writing can be attributed to class conflict. Shakespeare and More evince little hostility to the aristocracy. Montaigne was himself a nobleman of sorts. Hunting manuals like Turbervile's were written for an audience of real and would-be gentlefolk. These writers' uneasy feelings about the hunt must have had some source beyond baseborn resentment of bluebloods.

One likely source was the literature of pagan antiquity. The sixteenth-century writers who deplored hunting were steeped in Renaissance humanism and the revival of classical learning that went with it, and some of their opinions probably derive from Greek and Roman models. More's Utopians sound like Sallust when they dismiss hunting as a chore for slaves. Sancho's opinions in *Don Quixote* are reminiscent of Varro's. In his diatribes against hunting and cruelty to animals, Montaigne was clearly influenced by Ovid and Plutarch.

Still, none of this explains why these particular antique notions abruptly began to attract attention in the 1500s. Even in the Renaissance, old ideas were not adopted just because they were old. Class conflict and classical scholarship no doubt had something to do with the birth of antihunting sentiment in the sixteenth century, but they do not add up to a satisfactory explanation of it. Opposition to hunting incorporated something else as well, something that can be described as a new skepticism about the place of human beings in the world.

That skepticism is clearly evident in the work of Montaigne, whose doubts about hunting were rooted in doubts about man's special status. Montaigne refused to acknowledge any important differences between people and other animals. All of man's supposedly unique spiritual qualities can be seen at work, he declared, in the behavior of beasts. Birds show judgment and craft in the construction of their nests. Dogs use logic in tracking prey, and they show altruism and consideration in guiding blind masters. Horses and mules use slyness and trickery to get out of work. Forethought and imagination are evident in many animal actions. Even religion has its counterpart among beasts; ants reverently bring home the bodies of their dead, and elephants salute the rising sun.[27] Admitting that no beast has learned to speak a human language, Montaigne countered that the sounds and gestures through which animals communicate are not well understood by people. "This defect that hinders communication between them and us, why is it not just as much ours as theirs?" he asked. "We have some mediocre understanding of their meaning; so do they of ours, in about the same degree. They flatter us, threaten us, and implore us, and we them."[28]

Montaigne thought our supposed physical distinctions to be as imaginary as our spiritual ones. Since the time of Socrates, various pagan and Christian writers had argued that human beings were made bipedal and upright so that they can look upward toward God, instead of gazing down at the earth like soulless quadrupeds.[29] Montaigne recognized this as nonsense:

> And that prerogative that the poets make much of, our erect stature, looking toward heaven, its origin, "While other animals face down to earth . . ." (Ovid), is truly poetic, for there are many little creatures whose sight is wholly overturned to the sky; and I find that camels and ostriches have their necks set even higher and more erect than ours. What animals do not have their face up high and in front, and do not look straight forward like ourselves, and do not discover, in their proper posture, as much of heaven and earth as man? And what qualities of our corporeal constitution, in Plato and Cicero, cannot apply to a thousand kinds of beasts? Those that resemble us most are the ugliest and most abject of the whole band: for in external appearance and shape of the face, it is the apes . . . for the insides and vital parts, it is the hog.

Even the human weaknesses that we find so distinctive—our nakedness, our feeble strength, our lack of natural weapons—are nothing special. Many creatures are even feebler, less hardy, and more defenseless than we are. Neither our virtues nor our defects distinguish us from our fellow beasts. "It is apparent," Montaigne concluded, "that it is not by a true judgment, but by foolish pride and stubbornness, that we set ourselves before the other animals and sequester ourselves from their condition and society."[30]

Montaigne's skepticism reflects the growing intellectual insecurity of his age. Although most sixteenth-century writers continued to see the world as a marvelous stage set for the drama of human salvation, nearly every detail of that vision came to be corroded by doubt by the end of the century. The medieval world picture had centered on human concerns and destinies, and fallen man occupied the literal center of things; but by the late sixteenth century, it was no longer clear that the world had any center at all. The uncentering of the Renaissance world was well under way by 1440, when Nicholas of Cusa declared that "the world machine has its center everywhere and its circumference nowhere."[31] It reached a sixteenth-century climax in the fiercely debated ideas of Copernicus, who saw the earth as just another planet circling the sun, and of Bruno, who saw the sun as just another star in an infinity of worlds.[32]

The discoveries made by European voyages of exploration and conquest also contradicted the traditional world picture in a hundred baffling and disturbing ways. As Thomas Browne put it,

> There is another secret, not contained in the Scripture, which is more hard to comprehend . . . and that is, not only how the distinct pieces of the world and divided islands should be first planted by men, but inhabited by tigers, panthers, and bears. How America abounded with beasts of prey and noxious animals, yet contained not in it that necessary creature, a horse: by what passage those, not only birds, but dangerous and unwelcome beasts came over: how there be creatures there, which are not found in this triple continent; all which must needs be strange to us, that hold but one Ark, and that the creatures began their progress from the mountains of Ararat.[33]

Pervasive doubts were not restricted to the intelligentsia. Fundamental religious doctrines and social precepts were being called into question at every level of society by the multiplication of Protestant sects and creeds in northern Europe. Against the background of all these uncertainties, the Renaissance humanism that celebrated the human spirit as "the knot and bond of the universe"[34] looks less serenely confident and more defiantly argumentative.

Even in the Florentine inner sanctum of Renaissance humanism, we occasionally find some uncertainties about human status peeking through the facade. In the 1549 dialogue *Circe,* by the Florentine academician Giovanni Battista Gelli, Ulysses begs the witch Circe to restore human form to the Greeks she has changed into animals. She agrees to do so, if Ulysses can gain the animals' consent. But no matter how Ulysses pleads and argues with the animals, they all refuse, declaring themselves saner, freer, and happier as beasts than they were as human beings. Finally a former philosopher, whom Circe had transformed into an elephant, accepts Ulysses' offer. Made human again, he exclaims joyfully, "What a marvellous sensation it is to be a man!" and sings a hymn of praise to God for having bestowed upon man alone the power to know and love the world's creator.

Yet though humanism triumphs in the end in *Circe,* Ulysses' final score still stands at ten failures to one success. And after each failure, Ulysses consoles himself by reflecting that those who rejected his offer had been human beings of such inferior sorts—a fisherman, a farmer, a woman, and so on—that the life of a beast understandably looks good to them by comparison. He does not draw the obvious conclusion that most people would be better off as animals, but it is hard for the reader to escape that implication. Worse yet, some of the animals in *Circe* put up arguments that seem more persuasive than Ulysses' humanistic sophistries. This is especially true of the doe, who speaks for the women of sixteenth-century Florence. Every word that Ulysses addresses to her is a gross, chauvinistic insult, to all of which she replies with good humor and logical objections. She will not become human again, she insists, because

> you men make mere slaves and servants out of us, whereas we were originally designed for your assistants and associates, and that's what we should be; and your degrading us is so impious, and so much against the rule of nature, that no animal but man ever attempts it. Among animals, any animals you want to name, the female partakes equally with the male in his pleasures and diversions, as well as in the care and labor; but man assumes to himself a tyrannical power and prerogative, styling himself lord and master of the whole species . . . At least as a deer, I have as much privilege and authority as any male in the herd.[35]

Even in 1549 Ulysses' contemptuous reply—that women have to be ruled by their husbands because human females are all foolish, feather-brained, pig-headed chatterboxes—could hardly have seemed like a telling rejoinder to Gelli's coolly dialectical doe. *Circe* leaves the modern reader feeling that Ulysses has won his case by rhetorical tricks, and that human superiority over the beasts is something of a fraud. This is not just a twentieth-century perception; Gelli's seventh dialogue, between Ulysses and a horse, is thought to have inspired the bitter misanthropy of the fourth book of *Gulliver's Travels*.[36] It seems reasonable to suppose that the ambiguities in these dialogues reflect Gelli's own ambivalent feelings about human society and man's status in the world.

The sobbing deer in sixteenth-century art and literature are subversive creatures, whose plaints are intended to cast doubt on the legitimacy of established hierarchies. Some of them, like Gelli's doe or Turbervile's regicidal hart, express questions about social justice in a more or less symbolic way. But others, like the weeping deer of Dürer and Shakespeare, express more literal questions about the relationship between people and animals. In Montaigne's influential essays, such

90

questions reflect a profound skepticism about human superiority to the beasts. That sort of fundamental skepticism was not congenial, and it was not tolerated for long. The great systematic thinkers of the succeeding century made it their business to transform that skepticism into science and harness it to the service of man's dominion over nature.

SIX

The Noise of Breaking Machinery

Lamb, what makes you tick?
You got a wind-up, a Battery-Powered,
A flywheel, a plug-in, or what?
You made out of real Reelfur?
You fall out the window you bust?
You shrink? Turn into a No-no?
Zip open and have pups?

I bet you better than that.
I bet you put out by some other outfit.
I bet you don't do nothin.
I bet you somethin to eat.

—George Starbuck

FOR a century or more after his essays were published, Montaigne was widely condemned as an enemy of morality and religion. His critics feared that people who learned from him to think of themselves as beasts would feel free to do beastly things.[1] Reading Montaigne, concluded Pascal, "is absolutely pernicious to those who have any inclination toward impiety or vice."[2] But others rejected Montaigne for almost the opposite reason—not because he granted too much animal license to libertines, but because he conceded too much human autonomy to the animals. Montaigne's generous estimate of the beasts' mental abilities was at odds with the new way of looking at things. In the mechanistic philosophies that came into fashion among Eu-

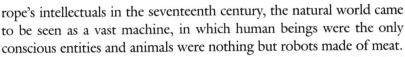

rope's intellectuals in the seventeenth century, the natural world came to be seen as a vast machine, in which human beings were the only conscious entities and animals were nothing but robots made of meat.

These ideas were not altogether new. European theologians had long debated the notion that God might be a sort of divine clockmaker who had built the universe to run all by itself without any subsequent adjustments or tinkering.[3] And philosophers all the way back to the Greeks had argued that the other animals lack free will. Beasts, said Aristotle, do not act by choice, for they cannot deliberate their actions.[4] Nature and circumstances—or, as we say nowadays, heredity and environment—were commonly thought to dictate everything that the lower creatures do. Some said that the actions of beasts are controlled by the stars.[5] Among all the animals, proclaimed St. Bernard of Clairvaux, man alone is free.[6]

What was novel about the new philosophy of the 1600s was not that it saw things as predetermined but that it saw them as *predictable*. The new science sought to make out the whole natural world as a mechanism governed by fixed equations that could be discovered by human inquiry. Powerful new mathematical techniques—symbolic algebra, logarithms, analytic geometry, calculus—allowed Europe's natural philosophers to reason clearly for the first time about such tricky subjects as vectors and acceleration, and to essay mathematical predictions about basic physical phenomena.

Their efforts met with swift and stunning success. The revolution in mechanics began in 1637 with Galileo's demonstration that a projectile traces a parabola; it culminated a mere fifty years later in Newton's epochal proclamation of the law of universal gravitation. Similar revolutionary transformations took place in hydrostatics, pneumatics, optics, and other realms of physical science in the latter half of the seventeenth century. In a few decades, essentially medieval theories of the world's fundamental workings had been swept away and replaced by essentially modern ones, capable in principle of explaining and predicting the movement of all the inanimate matter in the universe.

Since these theories worked best on inanimate matter, the new world picture had more inanimate matter and less mind in it than the old one. To the new philosophers, the only really satisfactory explanations for natural phenomena were mechanical ones. "The whole burden of philosophy," wrote Newton in the preface to his *Principia,* "seems to consist in this—from the phenomena of motions to investigate the forces of Nature, and then from these forces to demonstrate the other phenomena . . . I wish we could derive the rest of the phenomena of Nature by the same kind of reasoning from mechanical principles."[8]

The same sort of program was widely adopted in all the branches of natural philosophy. The planetary intelligences—spirits or angels that had been thought to move the heavenly spheres as the body is moved by the soul—were tossed out by seventeenth-century astronomers and replaced with celestial clockwork.[9] Other seventeenth-century scientists went looking for mechanism in the bodies of beasts. Eager vivisectors laid open the bodies of writhing dogs and cats to determine what effects ensued if this nerve was cut or that vessel was tied off. Harvey announced in 1628 that the heart is just a blood pump, and the veins and arteries are only its intake and outflow hoses. Other scientists all over Europe—Bartholin in Denmark, Rudbeck in Sweden, Willis in England, Borelli in Italy, Swammerdam and Boerhaave in Holland—carried out similar experiments and offered similarly mechanical or hydraulic interpretations of the workings of muscles, lymphatics, and nerves.[10] Thomas Hobbes drew the obvious conclusion at the beginning of his *Leviathan* in 1651:

> For seeing life is but a motion of Limbs . . . why may we not say, that all *Automata* (Engines that move themselves by springs and wheels as doth a Watch) have an artificial life? For what is the *Heart,* but a *Spring;* and the *Nerves,* but so many *Strings;* and the *Joints,* but so many *Wheels,* giving motion to the whole Body, such as was intended by the Artificer.

The brusque and irreligious Hobbes saw the human spirit itself as merely a gaseous component of the bodily mechanism. In the subtler, more reverential mechanistic philosophy preached by René Descartes, man's immortal soul was carefully kept out of the workings of the world machine.

Descartes' insistence on the special status of the soul stemmed from his fundamental doubts about everything else. My thoughts, argued Descartes, are the only thing of which I have reliable first-hand knowledge. Everything I perceive in the world, including my own body, might be a hallucination; but I cannot be mistaken in thinking that I am thinking. The one solid fact about the universe is my awareness of my own mental activity. From this lone fact, Descartes reasoned God and the universe into existence. Since I think (he argued), I must exist; therefore I am a thinking substance, whose essence it is to think; therefore I am indivisible and cannot be destroyed. It follows that I must be immortal.[11] But I know that I am not perfect; therefore I must have picked up the idea of perfection from something that is perfect. Thus there must be a perfect being—whom we call God. Since such a being would not suffer me to be tricked by my senses, the material world must exist after all.[12]

For Descartes, mind-stuff and body-stuff were equally real but utterly different substances. Human beings he recognized as strangely composite entities, part mind and part matter; but he regarded all other things as either pure matter (like a rock) or pure mind (like an angel). The beasts, he insisted, are entirely made of body-stuff—and so they have no feelings or sensations. If beasts had minds, they would be immortal like us, which is absurd.[13] Besides, we know that animals have no thoughts, because they cannot speak:

> All human beings no matter how dull or stupid, even madmen, can arrange various words together and fashion them into a discourse through which they make their thoughts understood. Contrariwise, no animal however perfect or well-bred can do anything of the sort. This is not simply because they lack the right organs, because magpies and parrots can learn to utter words as well as we can . . . and people born deaf and mute—who are at least as handicapped as the beasts are—have the custom of inventing their own signs, with which they communicate . . . [All of which] proves not that the beasts have less reason than people, but that they have none at all.[14]

"It seems incredible," concluded Descartes, "that the very best and brightest of monkeys or parrots could not learn to speak at least as well as the stupidest child—or at any rate a child with a disturbed brain—unless their souls were of an entirely different nature from our own."[15]

Furnished with such arguments as these, the followers of Descartes undertook physiological experiments on animals without compassion or compunction. "They kicked about their dogs and dissected their cats without mercy, laughing at any compassion for them and calling their screams the noise of breaking machinery."[16] "It was said that [beasts] were clocks; that the cries they made when beaten were nothing but the sound of a little spring that had been actuated; but that all of this was without sentience or feeling."[17]

This is a vicious doctrine, and the whole Cartesian world picture—a world of deathless, introspective spirit-agents riding through a mechanical landscape inside dying body-machines—affords an ugly and depressing prospect. Today's scientific world view, which retains Descartes' contempt for the fleshly machines but eliminates their ghostly occupants, presents an even bleaker picture. Why have these grim visions of a mechanical world dominated the imaginations of so many great minds for the past three centuries?

Part of the answer lies in the promise of power that is inherent in the idea of universal mechanism. If we can predict what comes after from what has gone before, then we can reliably control the future by altering the present. The whole point of Descartes' natural philosophy was to replace "that speculative philosophy taught in the Schools" with a more practical science, through which we could make ourselves "masters and possessors of nature."[18] Descartes' contemporary Francis Bacon similarly denounced the old "sophistical and inactive" philosophies of scholasticism and laid out a program for a new kind of experimental inquiry that would bring about "the amplification of the power and kingdom of mankind over the world" and "a restitution of man to the sovereignty of nature."[19] The objective of the new philosophy, he said, would not be the fruitless logic chopping that had preoccupied the medieval academics, but rather "the enlarging of the bounds of human empire to the effecting of all things possible."[20]

The subsequent growth of natural science has in the main fulfilled Bacon's promise. What was not foreseen was that science would abandon that distinction between matter and spirit that had given the human race its special status in the philosophies of Bacon and Descartes, as a sovereign of nature rather than just a part of it. But the loss of human distinctiveness was implicit in the scientific program from the beginning. Because science seeks explanatory generality, it tries to find a single system of explanation that will cover everything. And because science is grounded in experimental practice, it justifies its inquiries in practical terms, by pointing to the resulting amplification of the power and kingdom of mankind. Science therefore inevitably tends toward a description of the universe as composed of lumps of uniform, neutral matter, the value of which lies in their utility as means to human ends. The bargain that science offers us is Faustian: in exchange for getting control over these lumps, we must ourselves consent to become lumps of the same uniform stuff.

From the late 1600s on, successive schools of Western thought about the natural order have been looking for loopholes in the compact we have made with science. Most of them have done this by trying to put spirit back into the operations of the world machine—starting with the bodies of animals.

THE Cartesian philosophy faced one intractable difficulty: it was hard to see how anything as ethereal as the human soul could move something as gross as the human body. Descartes suggested that a peculiar little nubbin in the brain, the so-called pineal gland, is the seat of the soul, and that by pulling and pushing on it the soul makes the fingers wiggle or the legs dance.[21] This is not a very convincing suggestion, since there is no reason to think that the soul would find a pineal gland any easier to push around than a finger or a leg. Besides, animals also have pineal glands.

By the 1670s, Descartes' disciple Malebranche had given up on the pineal gland and worked out a mad, ingenious theory that identified God as the immediate cause of all events, whether fleshly or spiritual. According to Malebranche, my fingers wiggle when I will it only because God makes the willing and the wiggling happen simultaneously. The willing does not *cause* the wiggling, because mind can have no effect on matter. Conversely, matter cannot affect mind. So when I seem to see a horse, it is only because God chooses to thrust a horse-shaped image into my mind at the very same moment when he chooses to bring a horse around.[22] This theory, which demands an act of God to account for every twitch of a finger or glimpse of an object, reduces the elegant mechanism of the Cartesian universe to a whimsical puppet show. It was too much to swallow, even to keep the human soul out of the machinery.

One way out of this impasse was to deny the reality of mind-stuff and to accept thinking as something that the body does. Some Christians rejected this possibility as an ungodly absurdity, but others argued that an omnipotent God can make a piece of meat think if he wants to. God, wrote John Locke in 1690, "can, if he pleases, bestow on any parcel of matter, ordered as he thinks fit, a faculty of perception and thinking."[23]

Locke's ideas gradually gained ground on those of Descartes during the 1700s. As the barrier between mind and matter was lowered, the barrier between people and animals fell with it. Even those who felt that it takes a soul to think increasingly tended to reject the Cartesian view of animals as soulless machines. Brutes, concluded John Wesley, "perform a thousand actions which can never be explained by mere mechanism . . . so that we are constrained to own there is in them also some superior principle" of a spiritual kind, resembling the human soul.[24] Other animals, insisted Wesley, resemble man in having understanding, will, passions, reason, and liberty. The only real difference between us and them is that we can know God and they cannot.[25]

A surprising range of eighteenth-century thinkers, from the pious Wesley at one extreme to the atheistic physician Julien de la Mettrie at the other, agreed in seeing human thought as a souped-up version of capacities widely shared among the beasts.[26] Alexander Pope, upholding the traditional view that the two differ in kind, still put most of his stress on the thinness of the dividing line:

> Far as Creation's ample range extends,
> The scale of sensual, mental pow'rs ascends:
> Mark how it mounts, to Man's imperial race,
> From the green myriads in the peopled grass . . .
> How Instinct varies in the grov'ling swine,
> Compar'd, half-reas'ning elephant, with thine:
> 'Twixt that, and Reason, what a nice barrier;
> For ever sep'rate, yet for ever near!
> Rememb'rance and Reflection how ally'd;
> What thin partitions Sense from Thought divide![27]

In trying to bridge the gulf between man and beast, Pope and other eighteenth-century writers invoked the ancient notion of the great chain of being. This notion goes back to Plato, who had wondered why a perfect creator would bother to make less perfect creatures. Plato concluded that the universe as a whole would not be perfect unless it were *complete* and that it could not be complete unless it comprised a spectrum of all possible kinds of beings: a chain or ladder descending from the immortal gods on high down through people, beasts, and plants to mere stones and dust at the bottom.[28] Later philosophers and theologians invoked the image of this great chain of being in many contexts—especially to explain why God had made so many useless or noxious creatures or why one social class should be subordinate to another.

Medieval schoolmen and Renaissance humanists alike had argued that man holds a uniquely important place in the chain of being, as the "great and true *Amphibium*" that unites the worlds of matter and spirit. But many eighteenth-century writers used the image of the great chain to the opposite effect, to debunk human pretensions to special status in the world. The poems of von Haller and Pope derided our partly bestial, partly spiritual nature and called man a sorry hodge-podge, a "wretched composite of angel and cow."[29] *Homo sapiens* was commonly described as merely another link in the chain, nearer the bottom than the top, and of no more intrinsic importance than the beasts below us or the angels above us on the ladder of nature. "The life of a man," wrote Hume with characteristic bluntness, "is of no greater importance to the universe than that of an oyster."[30] Pope put it more elegantly:

> Nothing is foreign: Parts relate to whole;
> One all-extending all-preserving Soul
> Connects each being, greatest with the least;
> Made Beast in aid of Man, and Man of Beast;
> All serv'd, all serving! nothing stands alone;
> The chain holds on, and where it ends, unknown.[31]

Though few denied that people are superior to the other animals, many increasingly doubted that the beasts were put on earth solely for our convenience. If the animals were made to benefit man, Pope insisted, man was likewise made for the benefit of the animals.

> Has God, thou fool! work'd solely for thy good,
> Thy joy, thy pastime, thy attire, thy food? . . .
> While Man exclaims, "See all things for my use!"
> "See man for mine!" replies a pamper'd goose;
> And just as short of Reason he must fall,
> Who thinks all made for one, not one for all.[32]

Almost all earlier Western thought about ethics had left animals out of the picture. The few moral philosophers who had bothered to mention animals at all had argued that human beings have no duties of any kind to beasts and are not even obliged to treat them humanely.[33] But the widespread eighteenth-century acknowledgment of our psychological likeness to other animals encouraged people to try to find some place for beasts in their theories of moral rights and duties. The Enlightenment habit of deprecating man's special status in the universe also contributed to the rethinking of the moral standing of beasts. So did the growing egalitarianism that culminated in the American and French revolutions. Maupertuis and Rousseau began talking about animal rights in the 1750s.[34] By 1780 Jeremy Bentham was demanding rights for beasts and human slaves in almost the same breath and for the same theoretical reasons:

> The day *may* come, when the rest of the animal creation may acquire those rights which never could have been withholden from them but by the hand of tyranny. The French have already discovered that the blackness of the skin is no reason why a human being should be abandoned without redress to the caprice of a tormentor. It may come one day to be recognized, that the number of the legs, the villosity of the skin, or the termination of the *os sacrum*, are reasons equally insufficient for abandoning a sensitive being to the same fate. What else is it that should trace the insuperable line? Is it the faculty of reason, or, perhaps, the faculty of discourse? But a full-grown horse or dog, is beyond comparison a more rational, as well as a more conversible animal, than an infant of a day or a week, or even a month, old. But suppose the case were otherwise, what would it avail? the question is not, Can they *reason*? nor Can they *talk*? but, Can they *suffer*?[35]

That question had not come up much in previous European thinking about ethics. Before the eighteenth century, the suffering of animals had not been generally perceived as a matter of moral consequence. In the new climate of opinion, animal suffering came to be seen for the first time as an important evil. This perception raised some unwelcome questions about the supposed goodness of God.

EVER since the scientific revolution of the 1600s, God's hand has become progressively harder to discern in everyday life. Christian thinkers of the Middle Ages and the Renaissance felt God's immediate presence in all sorts of events, from the weather to plagues and earthquakes. Today these phenomena are regarded as acts of God only by fundamentalists and insurance companies. We blame pestilences on germs, earthquakes on plate tectonics, and droughts on the greenhouse effect. If scientists concede a role in these things to God, it is usually only as the remote celestial planner behind the Big Bang, who created matter and set up the rules at the beginning.

This attitude goes back to the natural philosophers of the Newtonian age. The pioneering chemist Robert Boyle summed it up in 1665: "the universe being once framed by God, and the laws of motion settled, and all upheld by his incessant concourse and general providence, the phenomena of the world are physically produced by the mechanical operation of the parts of matter, and . . . they operate upon one another according to mechanical laws."[36] This vision of God as the divine but remote designer of the world machine—a vision embraced in one form or another by most of the architects of the Enlightenment—can be seen as a sort of cosmic projection of the theories of government and political economy that emerged in Britain after the Cromwellian revolution. The removal of the British king's hands from the reins of power is mirrored in the removal of God's hands from the day-to-day management of the world; the beneficent equilibrium of the ideal marketplace, untroubled by governmental meddling, is mirrored in the eternally balanced operation of the world machine without any miraculous intervention.[37] In this model, the universe (like the nation) is governed by impartial, universal laws, not by the ruler's personal whims. God never has any second thoughts about the implications of those laws, and so he has no need to intervene in history.

> How most exact is nature's frame!
> How wise th' eternal mind!
> His counsels never change the scheme
> That his first thoughts design'd.[38]

If God is a benevolent and perfect Designer who has set up the world machine to operate by itself, then the machine must be perfectly designed and the results it produces must be the best possible results.

As Leibniz pointed out in 1710, it follows that this must be the best of all possible worlds.[39] What appear to be evils in its constitution are really blessings, or God would not have conferred them upon us. In Pope's often-quoted words,

> All Nature is but Art, unknown to thee,
> All Chance, Direction which thou canst not see;
> All Discord, Harmony not understood;
> All partial Evil, universal Good;
> And, spite of Pride, in erring Reason's spite,
> One truth is clear: 'Whatever IS, is RIGHT.'[40]

This sort of cosmic optimism has acquired a bad odor from the ridicule Voltaire heaped on it in *Candide*, in which the deluded Dr. Pangloss staggers from one catastrophe to another mindlessly insisting that all's for the best in this best of all possible worlds. But Christian optimists can fairly easily reconcile their faith with Voltaire's catalogue of human misery. Human suffering, after all, is not simply and invariably evil. We learn from pain, and it helps keep us out of trouble. Painful experiences sometimes make us stronger, braver, or more sensitive. Punishment that we earn for misbehavior today may keep us out of dangerous mischief tomorrow, like a child who has been spanked for playing with matches. Christian theologians have always pointed to such examples in trying to explain why God allows us to suffer. They can reasonably argue that it is at least *possible* that all our suffering serves some greater good, either as punishment that we have earned for our wicked behavior or as pricks and blows warning us against nature's perils and directing us along the narrow path to Heaven. The punishments demonstrate God's justice; the pricks and blows manifest His grace.

The suffering of animals, however, is harder to reconcile with the goodness of God. Christian tradition holds that beasts cannot sin and have no immortal souls. Their suffering therefore manifests neither retributive justice nor redemptive grace. No doubt animals (like people) need to feel pain when they injure themselves, so that they learn not to do it again. But most of the pain that beasts suffer is caused not by bumping into things, but by starvation, disease, and predation. If this sort of animal suffering is the unredeemed and unrecompensed evil that it seems to be, then it is unjust; and if such a large aspect of the world is unjust, it is hard to see how God can be both almighty and good.

Descartes avoided this problem simply by denying that animals suffer. His eighteenth-century follower Louis Racine stood the problem on its head and argued that we can infer animal unconsciousness from our knowledge of God's goodness. If the poor creatures could feel pain, Racine reasoned, then God would be unjust. But since we know that God is just, we can safely conclude that the beasts feel nothing—and so we can slaughter, hunt, and vivisect them with a clear conscience.[41] The Enlightenment thinkers who regarded animal consciousness as a fact and God's goodness as the matter in question could not accept this shortcut. Earlier philosophers had not troubled their minds much about animal suffering, but it came to be perceived as a major problem by eighteenth-century theologians. Animal suffering, lamented John Wesley, furnishes "a plausible objection against the justice of God, in suffering numberless creatures that had never sinned to be so severely punished."[42] The French prelate Jean Meslier lost his faith through such reflections and became an atheist.[43] Wesley, on the other hand, concluded that a just God would recompense animals in the next life for their suffering in this one; and he hoped that the beasts would be restored to life with human intelligence so that they could participate in the joys of the new Jerusalem after the second coming of Christ.[44] Other Christian thinkers, less receptive to the idea of billions of resurrected livestock and poultry erupting from the earth at the Last Trumpet, insisted that the animals' pain is recompensed (on the whole and in the long run) by their pleasure in this life, and that their suffering "is but as the dust of the balance in comparison of the happiness that is communicated."[45]

However they chose to exonerate God of the charge of cruelty to brutes, the eighteenth-century thinkers who agonized over the problem of animal pain agreed that much of the animals' suffering could be blamed on man, not God, and that we are obliged to spare the beasts whatever suffering we can—especially if they have no hope of an afterlife. "The more entirely the inferior creation is submitted to our power," wrote Pope, "the more answerable we should seem for our mismanagement of it; and the rather, as the very condition of nature renders these creatures incapable of receiving any recompence in another life for their ill treatment in this."[46]

THERE was a lot of mismanagement to be answered for. Brutal and sadistic treatment of beasts, much of it perpetrated for the sake of amusement, was commonplace throughout eighteenth-century Europe.[47] At the courts of royalty, lords and ladies enjoyed watching assorted large animals—lions, bears, horses, wolves, bison—goaded into fighting and killing each other in Roman-style arenas. In the establishments of princelings too poor to slaughter lions and bison for entertainment, courtiers gathered in rings to toss small animals in nets until they died from accumulated fractures, concussions, and shock. At one fete held at the Dresden court in 1747, 414 foxes, 281 hares, 32 badgers, and 6 wild cats were tossed to death for the delectation of the noble assembly.[48] Commoners amused themselves with bull baiting and bear baiting, bull, dog, and cock fights, throwing at cocks (hurling sticks to maim and kill tethered cocks), and riding for geese (riding at a gallop to pull the head off a greased goose hanging in a tree). Meat animals were tortured to death in various ways to make their flesh more tender and savory.[49] Cats were routinely set on fire, hung up in bags and smashed like piñatas, or killed in dozens of other ingeniously painful ways for recreation. The quickening tempo of life and the growing importance of clocks and timetables prompted teamsters, post riders, and coachmen to drive draft animals to death in ever-increasing numbers in their efforts to keep to schedules.[50]

Attacks on all these practices began in the late 1600s and grew louder and more frequent throughout the eighteenth century.[51] In a few German states, whose autocratic rulers could legislate by decree and did not have to contend with bull-baiting rural parliamentarians, cruelty to animals began to be punished by executive order during the late 1700s.[52] In England, persuasion was the reformers' chief recourse. Britons at all levels of society were exhorted to be kind to animals, not only in literary writing but also through more popular media, such as cheap engravings, sermons, and nursery rhymes.[53] Children's books, which became a commercial genre in the mid-1700s, conformed from the start to Locke's dictum that children should "be bred up in an abhorrence of killing and tormenting any living creature."[54] Throughout the rest of the eighteenth century, a steadily increasing flood of books for children urged their readers to love all sorts of beasts from horses to houseflies, treat them kindly, and rescue them

FIRST STAGE OF CRUELTY.

The Progress of Cruelty, Stage 1, by William Hogarth (1751). The poem below the picture ends: "Learn from this fair example—You / Whom savage *Sports* delight, / How *Cruelty* disgusts the view / While *Pity* charms the sight."

SECOND STAGE OF CRUELTY.

The generous Steed in hoary Age
Subdu'd by Labour lies,
And mourns a cruel Master's rage,
While Nature Strength denies.
Designed by W. Hogarth
Published according to act of Parliament Feb 1 1751.

The tender Lamb o'er drove and faint,
Amidst expiring Throws:
Bleats forth its innocent complaint
And dies beneath the Blows.

Inhuman Wretch! say whence proceeds
This coward Cruelty?
What Intrest springs from barbrous deeds?
What Joy from Misery?

Hogarth's *Progress of Cruelty*, Stage 2. An overloaded donkey and a baited bull appear in the background. The first verses below the picture contrast animal innocence with human depravity: "The generous Steed in hoary Age / Subdu'd by Labour lies; / And mourns a cruel Master's rage, / While Nature Strength denies. // The tender Lamb o'er drove and faint, / Amidst expiring Throws; / Bleats forth its innocent complaint / And dies beneath the Blows."

from the clutches of bad children who torment them.[55] These books also condemned adult misuses of animals, including inhumane slaughter, vivisection—and hunting.[56]

In this intellectual climate, hunting came increasingly under attack as another cruel entertainment, similar to fox tossing or bear baiting.[57] The Abbé Fleury called the hunt "a relic of ancient barbarism" and an "unmanly and destructive exercise . . . as disgraceful to humanity as it is to common sense."[58] "It is very strange, and very melancholy," said Samuel Johnson, "that the paucity of human pleasures should persuade us ever to call hunting one of them."[59]

The *parforce* hunt of the nobility continued to inspire particular distaste. In an anonymous German pamphlet that appeared around 1780, *Letter from a Parforce-Hunted Stag to the Prince Who Hunted Him,* the wretched deer addresses this pathetic petition to his royal persecutor:

I had the honor today of being hunted *parforce* by your Noble and Serene Highness, but I humbly beseech your Worship to spare me this honor in the future. If Your Noble and Serene Highness could only once experience being coursed *parforce* yourself, you would think this a modest enough request. I lie here now unable to lift my head, while blood streams from my mouth and nostrils. How can Your Highness have the heart to run to death a poor innocent animal that lives on grass and herbs? Next time, please shoot me dead and get it over and done with.[60]

Although Alexander Pope had grown up hunting in Windsor Forest, he nevertheless denounced the *parforce* chase as a sort of lynching on horseback, and he assailed another custom of the royal stag hunt as

barbarous enough to be derived from the Goths, or even the Scythians; I mean that savage compliment our huntsmen pass upon ladies of quality who are present at the death of a stag, when they put the knife in their hands to cut the throat of a helpless, trembling, and weeping creature,

—*Questuque cruentus,*
Atque imploranti similis.[61]

Uneasy feelings about the slaughter of birds and beasts for food considerably antedate the eighteenth century. Words like *butcher, slaughterhouse,* and *shambles* have been terms of ill repute at least since the Renaissance, and butchers have long been stereotyped as bloody and merciless men.[62] Butchers were supposed to be excluded from English juries trying capital crimes, because it was felt that their trade inured them to killing the innocent.[63]

But the morality of eating the butcher's goods was rarely questioned by Europeans before the Age of Reason. Ethical vegetarianism—abstention from meat on the theory that it is wrong to kill animals for food—was only the eccentric habit of a few cranks like Leonardo da Vinci until the late 1600s, when ethical vegetarianism began to be widely discussed, and books promoting it began to appear.[64] One influential book on the subject, Thomas Tryon's *The Way to Health, Long Life and Happiness, or A Discourse of Temperance,* convinced young Benjamin Franklin to give up meat when he read it in 1722. After a year of strict vegetarianism, Franklin found himself aboard a ship where the sailors were frying up a mess of freshly caught codfish:

> I consider'd with my Master Tryon, the taking every Fish as a kind of unprovok'd Murder, since none of them had or ever could do us any Injury that might justify the Slaughter . . . But I had formerly been a great Lover of Fish, and when this came hot out of the Frying Pan, it smelt admirably well. I balanc'd some time between Principle and Inclination: till I recollected, that when the Fish were opened, I saw smaller Fish taken out of their Stomachs: Then thought I, if you eat one another, I don't see why we mayn't eat you. So I din'd upon Cod very heartily and continu'd to eat with other People, returning only now and then occasionally to a vegetable Diet. So convenient a thing it is to be a reasonable Creature, since it enables one to find or make a Reason for every thing one has a mind to do.[65]

Other savants of the Enlightenment proved equally adept at rationalizing the fish fry and the barbecue. Voltaire and Rousseau criticized meat eating but did not give it up, and Pope and Bentham concluded that the slaughter of animals for food was justifiable if it was done painlessly. But all these moralists, and many others of the period, saw meat eating as a questionable habit that needed to be given some sort of moral justification.[66]

These doubts and questions about human carnivory raised further questions concerning human nature. Eighteenth-century European writers often pointed to the Indians of North America as a model of natural man. Since hunting was commonly described as the Indians' chief activity and the main prop of their existence,[67] it was a commonplace of eighteenth-century thought that "in the rudest state of mankind . . . hunting is the principal occupation, and the only mode of acquiring food."[68] If hunting is both the primordial human enterprise and morally objectionable, then something like the hunting hypothesis must be true. These beliefs about hunting, coupled with the prevailing interest in savages—noble and otherwise—combined in the eighteenth century to yield the earliest foreshadowings of the killer ape in Western literature.

Alexander Pope more or less explicitly attributed the fall of man to the adoption of meat eating. He wrote in the "Essay on Man":

> Pride then was not, nor arts, that Pride to aid;
> Man walk'd with beast, joint tenant of the shade;
> The same his table, and the same his bed;
> No murder cloathed him, and no murder fed . . .
> Ah! how unlike the man of times to come!
> Of half that live the butcher and the tomb;
> Who, foe to Nature, hears the gen'ral groan,
> Murders their species, and betrays his own.
> But just disease to luxury succeeds,
> And ev'ry death its own avenger breeds;
> The Fury-passions from that blood began,
> And turn'd on Man a fiercer savage, Man.[69]

This poetic interpretation of Adam's fall differs significantly from the biblical myth. In Pope's version, the fall results not from disobeying God's orders but from transgression against the state of nature and animal innocence, and war and murder are seen as the wages of carnivory.

In his 1774 version of the hunting hypothesis, Lord Monboddo postulated that man in his natural state "is a wild animal, without language or arts of any kind." The few anatomical descriptions and travelers' tales available to Monboddo convinced him that the great apes of Africa and Indonesia are persistently primitive human beings—sociable and cooperative animals, "as the beavers are, living together in cabins and huts, and carrying on of concert some common work," but communicating only with inarticulate cries and body language, like the other beasts. Thousands of years ago, Monboddo conjectured, our apelike ancestors became "so multiplied that the natural fruits of the earth could not maintain them," and so they were forced to start hunting other animals. Lacking natural armaments and hunting instincts, the hungry proto-humans were driven to invent weapons and language to carry on the hunt. As people took more and more to eating meat, they "grew fierce and bold, delighting in blood and slaughter" and became "the most dangerous and mischievous of all the creatures that God has made"—save for a few primitive troops of "Orang Outangs" and "Chimpenzas" still living peacefully on fruit in the tropical jungles.[70]

The high-water mark of this misanthropic speculation about man's animal nature is the concluding book of *Gulliver's Travels,* in which Gulliver is cast ashore in a land where horses can reason and human beings cannot. Here he finds that the horses (Houyhnhnms) are godlike paragons of sweet reason, natural beauty, and virtue, while the human beings (Yahoos) are the most odious and disgusting brutes imaginable:

> Their Heads and Breasts were covered with a thick Hair, some frizzled and others lank; they had Beards like Goats, and a Long Ridge of Hair down their Backs, and the fore Parts of their Legs and Feet; but the rest of their Bodies were bare, so that I might see their Skins, which were of a brown Buff Colour. They had no Tails, nor any Hair at all on their Buttocks, except around the *Anus;* which, I presume Nature had placed there to defend them as they sat on the Ground; for this Posture they used, as well as lying down, and often stood on their hind Feet. They climbed high Trees, as nimbly as a Squirrel . . . [and] would often spring, and bound, and leap with prodigious Agility . . . Upon the whole, I never beheld in all my Travels so disagreeable an Animal, or one against which I naturally conceived so strong an Antipathy . . . My Horror and Astonishment are not to be described, when I observed, in this abominable Animal, a perfect human Figure.[71]

From Orrery down to Orwell, Swift's critics have denounced the last part of *Gulliver* as lunatic misanthropy.[72] Thackeray advised people to stop reading Swift's book at the end of Book 3 to keep from being sucked into the "horrible, shameful, unmanly, blasphemous" conclud-

A yahoo-like portrayal of *Australopithecus* from Dart and Craig (1959). In this depiction, the killer apes are female.

ing chapters, which he thought "filthy in word, filthy in thought, furious, raging, obscene."[73] In painting Yahoos, sniffed Orrery, Swift "becomes one himself."[74] And yet, as Sheridan pointed out long ago,[75] Swift's depiction of the Yahoos is a logical consequence of three highly orthodox beliefs: that reason distinguishes people from brutes, that reason is a godlike faculty that ennobles our animal nature, and that people are nevertheless more wicked than the beasts. If all this is true, then our purely animal nature must be uniquely debased—or else adding reason to it would leave us better, not worse, than the other animals. And if our animal nature is uniquely debased, then Swift's degrading portrait of the Yahoos follows as a corollary. The Yahoo is what is left of man when reason is subtracted. It is no coincidence that Swift's picture of our animal nature is strikingly reminiscent of Dart's picture of *Australopithecus*. It is also no coincidence that the Yahoos feed chiefly on the flesh of asses, dogs, and cows, while the Houyhnhnms live chastely on hay, oats, and milk.[76]

SEVEN

The Sorrows of Eohippus

> "What is the meaning of it, Watson?" said Holmes solemnly as he laid down the paper. "What object is served by this circle of misery and violence and fear? It must tend to some end, or else our universe is ruled by chance, which is unthinkable."
>
> —Arthur Conan Doyle

BY THE latter part of the eighteenth century, many European intellectuals were getting tired of hearing that they were only animals, and not very nice animals at that. "It really seems," fumed Johann Gottfried von Herder in 1774, "as though all the great geniuses of our century—Helvetius, Rousseau, Voltaire, Buffon, Maupertuis—have been trying each in his own way to vilify the human race."[1] From the mid-1700s on, young French and German intellectuals began increasingly to rebel against the materialism and empiricism of the Enlightenment. Their protests marked the onset of the Romantic movement.

The Romantic rebellion took different forms in different countries, and it was always more of a style than a real philosophy; but there were some distinctive ideas that many Romantics shared. They added up to a sort of inversion of the Enlightenment. The Enlightenment prized clarity; the Romantics craved mystery and mists and shadows. The Enlightenment extolled reason; the Romantics praised feelings, and the stronger the better. ("The tygers of wrath are wiser than the horses of instruction," proclaimed William Blake. "The lust of the goat is the bounty of God. The wrath of the lion is the wisdom of God."[2]) Romantics also tended to be philosophical idealists, who saw the world as somehow constructed by the mind. The leading lights of the Enlightenment had been materialists who regarded the mind as an activity of the body; the Romantics, taking their cue from Kant, saw matter itself as a largely mental phenomenon. "The world is mind precipitated," insisted Ralph Waldo Emerson. The Romantic accordingly "takes his departure from his consciousness, and reckons the world an appearance . . . His thought,—that is the Universe."[3]

Another thing that many Romantics shared was a reverence for nature. This was not new or unique to Romanticism. The *philosophes* of the French Enlightenment had also felt a reverence for nature—as they defined it—and they had looked forward to the dawn of a bright new day when natural science and natural religion would supplant base clerical superstition and inaugurate a reign of reason and happiness. "Man," declared the Baron d'Holbach in 1770, "is unhappy because he is ignorant of nature."[4] But whereas d'Holbach and other Enlightenment thinkers thought nature and reason almost synonymous, many Romantics saw reason as the very thing that alienates us from nature:

> Sweet is the lore that nature brings:
> Our meddling intellect
> Mis-shapes the beauteous forms of things;
> —We murder to dissect.[5]

Early portents of the Romantic taste for undissected nature can be made out as far back as the late 1600s, when a new, "natural" look began to appear in European gardening styles. Before then, Europeans had generally admired geometrical regularity, culture, and artifice in landscape,[6] and the formal gardens of the upper classes had been laid out with Euclidean precision. But toward the end of the century, as merchants and travelers returning from the east spread reports of the exquisitely contrived wildness of Chinese and Japanese gardens, tastes in landscape began to change, and Europeans too began to strive for a more natural appearance in their gardens. In an essay of 1712, Addison compared Europe's ornamental gardens unfavorably to those of the Orient:

There is generally in nature something more grand and august than what we meet with in the curiosities of art. When, therefore, we see this

113

imitated in any measure, it gives us a nobler and more exalted kind of pleasure than what we receive from the nicer and more accurate productions of art . . . Writers who have given us an account of China tell us the inhabitants of that country laugh at the plantations of our Europeans, which are laid out by the rule and line, because, they say, anyone may place trees in equal rows and uniform figures . . . For my own part, I would rather look upon a tree in all its luxuriancy and diffusion of boughs and branches, than when it is thus cut and trimmed into a mathematical figure.[7]

Ornamental gardens in seventeenth-century Europe had typically been enclosures bounded by walls and hedges, within which unruly nature was pruned into shape, subdued, rationalized, and restored to the docility of Eden.[8] Pope mocked this older style in his *Moral Essays* in 1731:

> His gardens next your admiration call,
> On ev'ry side you look, behold the wall!
> No pleasing intricacies intervene,
> No artful wildness to perplex the scene;
> Grove nods at grove, each Alley has a brother,
> And half the platform just reflects the other.[9]

In the early eighteenth century, the British aristocracy began to share the preference of Pope and Addison for artful wildness. On one estate after another, the garden walls came tumbling down, and the garden expanded to encompass the natural landscape. England's tastemakers spared no effort or expense to have their grounds landscaped in accordance with the doctrines of the landscape architect William Kent, who saw all nature as a garden and declared that the gardener's function was only to "brush nature's robe."[10]

These new theories were promoted by Jean-Jacques Rousseau in his 1761 novel *La Nouvelle Héloïse,* an enormously popular book that helped to start a fashion for "English" gardens on the continent.[11] Rousseau, the great eighteenth-century proponent of natural goodness, primitive virtue, and the noble savage, has often been called the first Romantic. He was thoroughly Romantic in his love of wild and rugged nature: "You know by now what I mean by 'beautiful' country. A flat stretch of land, though ever so beautiful to some, never seems so in my eyes. I must have torrents, rocks, firs, dark woods, mountains,

114

The Romantic ego confronting nature in Caspar David Friedrich's painting *The Wanderer above the Mists*. (1818; Kunsthalle, Hamburg)

steep paths hard to climb or descend, with precipices on every side to make me afraid."[12]

Before the eighteenth century, European poets and painters had generally found mountains ominous and had preferred to celebrate pastoral and agricultural scenes: lush meadows, gently rolling woodlands dotted with sheep, and amber waves of grain. But in the later 1700s, Europeans began to enjoy feeling scared and insignificant in the presence of the forces of untamed nature, and to find beauty in them. "The passion caused by the great and sublime in nature," wrote Edmund Burke in 1756, "is astonishment; and astonishment is that state of the soul, in which all its motions are suspended, with some degree of horror . . . Terror [is] the common stock of everything that is sublime."[13] From the time of Burke and Rousseau on, towering peaks, cataracts, and giddy abysses came to be viewed as sublime; and painters and poets increasingly fixed their attention on such picturesque vistas.

The loneliness as well as the sublimity of wild landscapes lent them charm. Nature, it was felt, is somehow spoiled by the human presence. "Nature seems to want to conceal from human eyes its real attractions, of which men are all too little aware and which they disfigure when they are within reach," wrote Rousseau. "Nature flies from frequented places. It is on the summits of mountains, in the depths of forests, on deserted islands that she reveals her most affecting charms."[14]

Wild and lonely landscapes were attractive to the Romantics because they could perceive them as an extension of themselves. Romantic sensitivities were attuned to subjective, inward experience, and Romanticism was systematically egotistical to an extent unprecedented in earlier philosophies. The Romantic love of nature was grounded in that egotism. It arose from what Keats called the "egotistical sublime" and Freud called the "oceanic feeling"[15]—the feeling that the boundary between self and nature has dissolved and that the Romantic's emotions are one with the whole universe. "I rustle with the wind," gushed Herder, "and become alive—give life—inspire—I inhale fragrance, and exhale it with the flowers; I dissolve in water; I float in the blue sky; *I* feel all these feelings."[16] Shelley's "Ode to the West Wind" is typically Romantic in straining to tear down the boundary between the poet's emotions and the forces of nature:

Make me thy lyre, even as the forest is:
What if my leaves are falling like its own!
The tumult of thy mighty harmonies

Will take from both a deep, autumnal tone,
Sweet though in sadness. Be thou, Spirit fierce,
My spirit! Be thou me, impetuous one!

Drive my dead thoughts over the universe
Like withered leaves to quicken a new birth!

Emerson's description of the oceanic feeling is famous: "Standing on the bare ground—my head bathed by the blithe air and uplifted into infinite space—all mean egotism vanishes. I become a transparent eyeball; I am nothing; I see all; the currents of the universal Being circulate through me; I am part or parcel of God."[17] It takes a more or less "natural" setting to evoke this kind of feeling. One cannot become a transparent eyeball on a subway platform. In a city, human company and human artifice conspire to make the Romantic unpleasantly aware that the world contains other selves and that he is not the central focus of Universal Being. "Nature" is important to the Romantic partly because it offers a refuge from that unpleasant awareness of other people.

In the Romantic imagination, nature accordingly ceased to be a normative system of laws and tendencies and became a *place:* a realm to which one might travel to get away from people, a nonhuman domain removed from (and symbolically opposed to) civilization and its works. Lord Byron's poetry bears witness to the importance of nature as a sanctuary for the Romantic ego:

I live not in myself, but I become
Portion of that around me; and to me
High mountains are a feeling, but the hum
Of human cities torture: I can see
Nothing to loathe in nature, save to be
A link reluctant in a fleshly chain,
Class'd among creatures, when the soul can flee,
And with the sky, the peak, the heaving plain
Of ocean, or the stars, mingle, and not in vain.[18]

Eugene Delacroix, *Tiger Attacking a Wild Horse.* (c. 1825; Louvre, Paris)

The Romantics delighted not only in wilderness, but in *wildness,* in things inhuman and violent and imbalanced, in what Shelley called "the tempestuous loveliness of terror."[19] These Romantic enthusiasms signaled and helped to precipitate a lasting change in western tastes in scenery. Before the late 1700s, European travelers rarely went out of their way to look at torrents, rocks, and abysses. From the end of the eighteenth century on, Europeans and Americans of all classes began to do so, and eventually to set aside particularly sublime or scary stretches of landscape as preserves and parks. The pleasure we take in wildness has probably been the most enduring legacy of Romanticism.

The big fierce animals that figure in the art of Romantic artists like Eugene Delacroix express the same delight in wildness. But Romantic attitudes toward animals were ambivalent. Because most Romantics were idealists who believed that nature is a construct of the human mind, they thought of themselves as spiritual beings superior to the beasts. "He is blessed who is assured that the animal is dying out in

118

him day by day, and the divine being established," declared Thoreau.[20] Many Romantics were just as reluctant as Byron to see themselves classed among creatures in a fleshly chain of living things. On the other hand, they wanted to touch something transcendent in communing with nature. Animals—the wild ones, at any rate—thus had to be perceived as low brutes in some contexts and as signposts toward God in others.

This difficulty was managed by thinking of all creatures as participants in a great upward striving toward a misty pantheistic spirituality—Goethe's Weltgeist, Hölderlin's Father Aether, Emerson's Oversoul. This World Spirit creates the great chain of being, declared Shelley, as it

> sweeps through the dull dense world, compelling there,
> All new successions to the forms they wear;
> Torturing th' unwilling dross that checks its flight
> To its own likeness, as each mass may bear;
> And bursting in its beauty and its might
> From trees and beasts and men into the Heaven's light.[21]

In communing with nature, the Romantic poet perceives and reaches out to the spiritual reality behind nature's transient forms:

> The torrent shooting from the clear blue sky,
> The rocks that muttered close upon our ears . . .
> Tumult and peace, the darkness and the light—
> Were all like workings of one mind, the features
> Of the same face, blossoms upon one tree;
> Characters of the great Apocalypse,
> The types and symbols of Eternity,
> Of first, and last, and midst, and without end.[22]

In typical Romantic thought, the universe becomes a vast organism animated by something like a human spirit. ("A general organism," wrote Friedrich Schelling,[23] "is the prerequisite for everything mechanical.") We are higher and better creatures than the beasts because we are aware of this underlying spiritual reality and they are not. On the other hand, because the beasts are less conscious of themselves than we are, they *participate* in the world spirit with an immediacy that we can approach only now and then during fleeting illuminations of transparent eyeballhood. "Dark is the world to thee," lamented Tennyson. "Thyself art the reason why: / For is not He all but that which has power to feel 'I am I'?"[24] Shelley's skylark is filled with a profound, unconscious joy that self-conscious creatures like ourselves can never feel:

> Waking or asleep,
> Thou of death must deem
> Things more true and deep
> Than we mortals dream,
> Or how could thy notes flow in such a crystal stream?
>
> . . . Teach me half the gladness
> That thy brain must know,
> Such harmonious madness
> From my lips would flow
> The world should listen then—as I am listening now.

The Romantic ambivalence toward beasts was associated with mixed feelings about hunting. Some Romantics, especially in Germany, celebrated the hunter as a noble half-savage, a sort of Romantic poet with a gun who roams the forest communing with nature and brimming over with bittersweet longings.[25] Overtones of the erotic hunt persist in German Romantic poetry:

> The sweetest joys on earth are found
> In forests green and deep,
> Where thrushes sing and hawks cry out
> And stags and roebucks leap.
>
> O let my love sing like a thrush
> In the greenwood's blossoming crown
> And leap away like a fleeing roe
> So that I can hunt it down.[26]

The American version of the Romantic huntsman is Natty Bumppo, the hero of James Fenimore Cooper's Leatherstocking novels. In his love of the wild and his spiritual communion with nature, Natty is a rustic Wordsworth or Thoreau:

a man of strong, native, poetical feeling. He loved the woods for their freshness, their sublime solitudes, their vastness, and the impress that

120

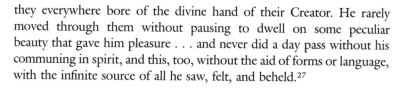

they everywhere bore of the divine hand of their Creator. He rarely moved through them without pausing to dwell on some peculiar beauty that gave him pleasure . . . and never did a day pass without his communing in spirit, and this, too, without the aid of forms or language, with the infinite source of all he saw, felt, and beheld.[27]

Natty dreads and detests the relentless advance of English civilization into God's wilderness. "If I were King of England," he declares, "the man that felled one of these trees without good occasion for the timber should be banished to a desarted and forlorn region in which no four-footed animal ever trod."[28] Evidently he thinks it punishment enough to be deprived of the company of quadrupeds. Although he is a deerslayer clad in buckskins, he kills only reluctantly and from need, never for sport. Although he is a white man, he lives on intimate and friendly terms with the natives and admires many of their customs. His chief objection to the Indians' religion is their idea of heaven as a happy hunting ground—which he regards as unreasonable and immoral:

> I can't fall into all these notions, seeing that they appear to be ag'in reason. Spirits can't eat, nor have they any use for clothes, and deer can only rightfully be chased to be slain . . . for the venison or the hides. Now I find it hard to suppose that blessed spirits can be put to chasing game without an object, tormenting the dumb animals just for the pleasure and agreeableness of their own amusements. I never yet pulled a trigger on buck or doe, Judith, unless when food or clothes was wanting.[29]

Cooper's hero entered American folklore as the archetype of the frontier hunter: the man in the buckskin suit who lives by himself in the wilderness, avoiding human entanglements, despising modern civilization, and cherishing the animals he hunts. This image of the hunter as a sort of male maenad recurs in the subsequent legends of all our nature-loving frontiersmen, from Daniel Boone to Grizzly Adams.

But not all Romantics regarded the hunter as a fellow nature-lover. Some saw him as a vicious fool who enjoys destroying his fellow creatures because he cannot empathize with them or grasp their spiritual significance. "Whenever anything moves," lamented Goethe and Schiller, "the hunter shoots it. He thinks that every living creature, no matter how vital and alive, was made just for him to pop in his game bag."[30] "Each outcry of the hunted Hare," groaned Blake, "A fibre from the Brain does tear."[31] Romantic indignation about hunting culminated in Coleridge's *Rime of the Ancient Mariner*. In this well-known poem, which is probably the most widely read attack on sport hunting ever written, the sailor hero shoots an albatross for fun and is punished by being plunged into a living hell—from which he is released only when he forswears hunting and learns to love "both man and bird and beast."

The American Romantics who called themselves Transcendentalists also disliked hunting. "Hast thou named all the birds without a gun," demands one of Emerson's poems, "Loved the wood-rose, and left it on its stalk?"[32] Thoreau saw the hunt as a matter of arrested development, a reversion to the primitive impulses of children or savages:

> There is a period in the history of the individual, as of the race, when the hunters are the "best men," as the Algonquins called them . . . Even in civilized communities, the embryo man passes through the hunter stage of development . . . [But] no humane being, past the thoughtless age of boyhood, will wantonly murder any creature which holds its life by the same tenure that he does. The hare in its extremity cries like a child. I warn you, mothers, that my sympathies do not always make the usual phil-*anthropic* distinctions.[33]

"Is it not a reproach that man is a carnivorous animal?" Thoreau went on. "I have no doubt that it is a part of the destiny of the human race, in its gradual improvement, to leave off eating animals, as surely as the savage tribes have left off eating each other when they came in contact with the more civilized."[34]

Other Romantics also thought flesh-eating repulsive and barbaric. "It is only by softening and disguising dead flesh by culinary preparation," wrote Shelley, "that it is rendered susceptible of mastication or digestion; and that the sight of its bloody juices and raw horror does not excite intolerable loathing and disgust."[35] Louisa May Alcott's vegetarian father Bronson Alcott, a friend of Emerson's, recorded similar feelings on one of his last shopping trips to the butcher's:

> What have I to do with butchers? . . . Death yawns at me as I walk up and down in this abode of skulls. Murder and blood are written on its

stalls. Cruelty stares at me from the butcher's face. I tread amidst carcasses. I am in the presence of the slain. The death-set eyes of beasts peer at me and accuse me of belonging to the race of murderers. Quartered, disembowelled creatures suspended on hooks plead with me . . . I am a replenisher of graveyards.[36]

The Romantic writers who condemned human exploitation of animals had less to say about the animal suffering inherent in the course of nature itself. They wanted to see nature as a veil over the face of the world spirit, but they were confounded and dismayed by all the predators and parasites they found crawling on that veil. Blake was more honest than most in facing up to the facts of God's "murderous Providence,"[37] but even Blake tried to escape from this distasteful spectacle into a platonic fantasy, persuading himself that the death and suffering we see in nature are only distorted shadows of a better reality on some higher plane of being:

> How are the Beasts & Birds & Fishes & Plants & Minerals
> Here fix'd into a frozen bulk subject to decay & death?
> Those Visions of Human Life & Shadows of Wisdom & Knowledge
> Are here frozen to unexpansive deadly destroying terrors,
> And War & Hunting, the Two Fountains of the River of Life,
> Are become Fountains of bitter Death & of corroding Hell.[38]

"Whoever believes in Nature," said Blake to his friend Crabb Robinson, "disbelieves in God. For Nature is the work of the Devil."[39] Blake's best-known poem, "The Tyger," expresses his rejection of nature in words of such ambivalent grandeur that they are commonly mistaken for admiration:

> When the stars threw down their spears
> And water'd heaven with their tears,
> Did he smile his work to see?
> Did he who made the Lamb make thee?
>
> Tyger! Tyger! burning bright
> In the forests of the night,
> What immortal hand or eye,
> Dare frame thy fearful symmetry?

Later, more typically Romantic writers were unwilling to reject nature as evil, and so they could offer no real answers to Blake's questions. Shelley hinted that when the goddess Liberty ushers in the new age of freedom, animal predation will somehow cease, but the details were left to the reader's imagination.[40] Those unable to comfort themselves with mystical nonsense could only lament with Tennyson that "Nature is one with rapine, a harm no preacher can heal."[41] British theologians of Tennyson's day, for whom it was practically an article of faith that God's goodness is revealed in nature,[42] agonized over these same questions to little better effect. It was increasingly hard to accept the old line that the fall of man had brought carnage into a vegetarian paradise. The supposed connection between Eve's disobedience and the lion's diet had never made much sense anyway; and as more and more was learned about physiology and comparative anatomy, it became difficult to believe that an animal built like a lion could ever have eaten straw like the ox in the first place. Those who hoped to discern God's goodness in the natural order were hard pressed to understand why so many of his creatures should be predators and parasites, cunningly designed for inflicting misery, terror, and death on innocent victims.

Different scholars came up with different excuses. Some shared Wesley's faith that the "mysterious anguish" of the beasts would be compensated in the world to come.[43] In an 1835 treatise on the manifestation of divine providence in the instincts and anatomy of animals, William Kirby suggested that predators were created as natural symbols of demons. God, he said, has put them here to warn us that just as in nature there are both peaceful deer and savage wolves, so "in the invisible world there are two classes of spirits—one benevolent and beneficent, and the other malevolent and mischievous."[44] But probably the most influential and widely read Christian justification of the cruelties of nature was the one that the Anglican archbishop William Paley laid out in his 1802 classic, *Natural Theology*. Paley offered two excuses for predation. His first was the strange and distinctly Victorian argument that without predation and disease there would be no room in the world for reproduction—and therefore, "as things are constituted, no animal happiness." His second argument was that predation is a necessary providence of God to permit what he called *superfecundity*—the capacity of a species to reproduce beyond the capacity of its environment to sustain it. This superfecundity, wrote Paley, is a good and useful thing, which justifies the predation needed to maintain it:

> The advantages of such a constitution are two: first, that it tends to keep the world always full; while, secondly, it allows the proportion between the several species of animals to be differently modified, as different purposes require, or as different situations may afford for them room and food . . . But then this *superfecundity,* though of great occasional use and importance, exceeds the ordinary capacity of nature to receive or support its progeny. All superabundance supposes destruction, or must destroy itself . . . It is necessary, therefore, that the effects of such prolific faculties be curtailed.[45]

No doubt Paley was right in thinking that the blessings of superfecundity could not be maintained without predation and its attendant suffering. But it is hard to believe that he felt strongly persuaded that the two balanced each other out, and that the benefits of superfecundity were worth all the agony inflicted on the world by sharks and tigers, spiders and vipers, hookworms and liver flukes. It seemed like a high price to pay for the privilege of unlimited copulation.

The suffering and death of individual animals was not the worst of it. By the beginning of the nineteenth century, the accumulating fossil record had made it painfully clear that species too are mortal and that most of the animal kinds that used to exist are now extinct. In the light of all these unpleasant facts, many began to worry about God's evident lack of care for his creatures, including our own species. Tennyson's famous lines about nature red in tooth and claw express these worries:

> Are God and Nature then at strife,
> That Nature lends such evil dreams?
> So careful of the type she seems,
> So careless of the single life . . .
>
> 'So careful of the type'? but no.
> From scarpèd cliff and quarried stone
> She cries, 'A thousand types are gone:
> I care for nothing, all shall go.'
>
> . . . And he, shall he,
> Man, her last work, who seem'd so fair . . .

> Who trusted God was love indeed
> And love Creation's final law—
> Tho' Nature, red in tooth and claw
> With ravine, shriek'd against his creed—
>
> Who loved, who suffer'd countless ills,
> Who battled for the True, the Just,
> Be blown about the desert dust,
> Or seal'd within the iron hills?[46]

A better justification of nature and its cruelties was needed to link all that struggle, death, and extinction to some nobler objective. Darwin's work would fill that need, by identifying suffering and superfecundity as the twin engines of universal historical progress.

FAITH in progress is relatively new. Until the seventeenth century, Western thinkers who considered the big historical picture tended to assume that the golden age was in the past and that people, manners, and institutions have been going downhill ever since. Most classical writers shared this assumption, and its biblical formulation—the story in Genesis about Eden and the Fall—was a cornerstone of Jewish sacred history and Christian doctrine.

But in the wake of the scientific revolution, the old Christian belief in the decadence of natural man began to be replaced by a widespread confidence that things will naturally get better as time goes by. The savants of the Enlightenment felt sure that human freedom and happiness were bound to increase as more and more people saw the light and threw off the chains of ancient tyranny, superstition, and ignorance.[47] That faith, which is implicit in the word "enlightenment" itself, helped to fuel the great revolutions that swept America and France in the late 1700s.

Eighteenth-century faith in progress also affected thinking about the larger order of nature and our place in it. The natural order, like the social order, began to be seen not as a static hierarchy but as a historical process perpetually tending toward better things. As the biologists and visionaries of eighteenth-century Europe began to think about how a whole species might over time change into something higher and nobler, the old fixed Ladder of Being was—as Loren Eiseley put it—gradually converted into an escalator.[48] By 1750, the

German poet Christoph Martin Wieland was prophesying that all creatures are destined in the distant future to become reasoning animals like human beings, while man rises above them to unimaginable spiritual heights. All animals, he said, are sentient creatures like ourselves, and all of us are climbing the same ladder of being toward God. People of course have a few rungs' head start on the others:

> They are not now our peers; and though in coming days
> Fate may the beasts to human station raise,
> We shall by then have climbed on far above their heads
> Along the rising stair that every spirit treads . . .
> God ordered all things thus, that all might rise toward
> The fount of being and adore their Lord.
> All things strive upward toward one lofty end:
> Whatever feels, feels God; and all ascend
> Infinite ladders through eternity,
> Approaching God in ever-rising ecstasy.[49]

In the distant future, speculated the visionary French biologist Charles Bonnet, man will pass on to higher realms of being and be replaced on this earth by upgraded beasts:

> Man—who will by then have been transported to another dwelling-place, more suitable to the superiority of his faculties—will leave to the monkey or the elephant that primacy which he, at present, holds among the animals of our planet. In this universal restoration of animals, there may be found a Leibniz or a Newton among the monkeys or the elephants, a Perrault or a Vauban among the beavers.[50]

These mystical notions were at bottom just another way of expressing Wesley's vision of the animals coming back to life with human faculties at the resurrection. But such fantasies furnished the seedbed for the idea of biological evolution. Erasmus Darwin, Lamarck, and other speculative biologists of the late eighteenth and early nineteenth centuries took up the notions of universal progress articulated by Wieland and Bonnet and others, and translated them into groping, quasi-scientific talk about "progress toward perfection of organization" and "improving excellence . . . increasing by the activity of inherent principles" in the development of modern plants and animals from lowlier ancestors.[51]

These evolutionary speculations found support in geology. The accumulating fossil record showed that the strange, primitive plants and animals of earth's remote past had been progressively replaced by more and more modern-looking organisms as time went on. Orthodox geologists held that this succession was the record of successive divine creations; but the "development hypothesis," the idea that the older species had somehow changed into the modern ones, was becoming increasingly popular on the fringes of science in the early nineteenth century. In Disraeli's 1847 novel *Tancred,* one gushy lady sums up her readings in this pre-Darwinian evolutionary literature:

> But what is most interesting, is the way in which man has been developed. You know, all is development. The principle is perpetually going on. First, there was nothing, then there was something; then, I forget the next, I think there were shells, then fishes; then we came, let me see, did we come next? Never mind that; we came at last. And the next change will be something very superior to us, something with wings. Ah! that's it; we were fishes, and I believe we shall be crows.[52]

Disraeli's caricature reflects the dim view that the leaders of British science and society took of all this talk about evolution. Their aversion to the notion was partly a matter of politics. Evolutionary ideas were associated with radicalism and materialism, and establishment intellectuals generally saw them as a threat to religious orthodoxy, social stability, and ruling-class privilege.[53] If evolution is a fact, sputtered the English geologist Adam Sedgwick, then "the labours of sober induction are in vain; religion is a lie; human law is a mass of folly, and a base injustice; morality is moonshine; our labours for the black people of Africa were works of madmen; and man and woman are only better beasts!"[54]

But many scientists balked at the idea of evolution for more strictly scientific reasons. Materialists who had no problem swallowing its religious or political implications were repelled by all the misty Romantic assumptions that the development hypothesis trailed behind it. To Thomas Henry Huxley and others, that hypothesis seemed scientifically dubious for the same reason that speculation about telepathy is today: nobody had any direct evidence for it or knew of a mechanism that might make it work.[55] The theory of evolution did not attract a corps of fierce scientific partisans until after 1858, when

Charles Darwin and Alfred Russel Wallace came forth with the pleasingly mechanical hypothesis of evolution by natural selection.

That hypothesis was a simple one. Not all members of a species survive to reproduce, and survival is not wholly a matter of luck. Some individuals do better than others because they have inherited superior features: longer legs, deeper roots, bigger brains, or whatever else makes for survival in that species' way of life. On the whole and in the long run, these superior individuals will leave more offspring than others. Therefore their hereditary advantages will tend to spread throughout the population. In time, all the members of that species will have longer legs (or deeper roots or bigger brains). The species will then have changed from what it was. As long as new and useful variations keep appearing, the species can go on changing forever, getting more and more perfectly adapted to a succession of changing environments. Over hundreds of millions of years, Darwin concluded, this process of natural selection could have evolved all the world's organisms from a few ancestral forms, with no need for divine planning or intervention.

Darwin's ideas were assailed by those who could not bear to see design in nature replaced by blind mechanism. Many of these people were religious reactionaries, but they also included great scientists like William Herschel, who dismissed natural selection as the "law of higgeldy-piggeldy,"[56] and radical humanists like George Bernard Shaw, who denounced the whole theory as

> a ghastly and damnable reduction of beauty and intelligence, of strength and purpose, of honor and aspiration, to such casually picturesque changes as an avalanche may make in landscape, or a railway accident in a human figure . . . If it be no blasphemy, but a truth of science, then the stars of heaven, the showers and dew, the winter and summer, the fire and the heat, the mountains and the hills, may no longer be called to exalt the Lord with us by praise: their work is to modify all things by blindly starving and murdering everything that is not lucky enough to survive in the universal struggle for hogwash.[57]

But other Victorians found the mechanical character of the Darwinian theory attractive. Skeptical scientists, and even some liberal theologians,[58] were pleased to see the diverse adaptations of living things attributed to homely natural causes instead of a vast cascade of prehistoric miracles. Others were drawn to Darwinism because it seemed to put the prevailing faith in progress on a hard scientific footing. The great spiritual upward striving that the Romantics had discerned throughout nature was reinterpreted in Darwin's work as a no-nonsense, thoroughly material struggle for existence—which nevertheless "inevitably leads to the gradual advancement of the organisation of the greater number of living beings throughout the world."[59] Since "natural selection works solely by and for the good of each being," Darwin assured his readers, "all corporeal and mental endowments will tend to progress towards perfection."[60] The universal progress that the Romantics had proclaimed and the universal suffering that they had bewailed thus turned out to be two aspects of the same benign mechanism.

Analogies between Darwinism and laissez-faire Victorian theories of political economy were obvious, and the two influenced each other from the start. At first, social theory had a greater impact on Darwin than Darwin had on social theory. Both he and Wallace had hit on the idea of natural selection by reading Malthus' treatise on population, which explained at length why society would collapse unless the children of the poor were allowed to starve. Ten years before Darwin and Wallace put their own theories into print, the philosopher Herbert Spencer was already preaching the gospel of social progress through what he called the "survival of the fittest." Spencer likened the misery imposed upon the poor and ignorant under laissez-faire capitalism to "the stern discipline of Nature" in weeding out the weak and sickly members of a species. "It is impossible in any degree to suspend this discipline," he wrote in 1850, "without suspending progress."[61]

Darwin incorporated these ideas into his own work. "Man," he insisted,

> has no doubt advanced to his present high position through a struggle for existence consequent on his rapid multiplication; and if he is to advance still higher, it is to be feared that he must remain subject to a severe struggle. Otherwise he would sink into indolence, and the more gifted men would not be more successful in the battle of life than the less gifted. Hence our natural rate of increase, though leading to many and obvious evils, must not be greatly diminished by any means. There should be open competition for all men; and the most able should not

be prevented by laws or customs from succeeding best and rearing the largest number of offspring.[62]

As some of Darwin's critics noted, "the place vacated by Paley's theological and metaphysical explanation [had] simply been occupied by that suggested to Darwin and Wallace by Malthus in terms of the prevalent severity of industrial competition."[63]

But as Darwin's fame and reputation soared, the influences started to run in the other direction, and the Darwinian vision of the struggle for existence began to be invoked as a model for human society. Apologists for late nineteenth-century capitalism often pointed to Darwinian analogies in arguing for unchecked competition between human nations, classes, and individuals. Like Darwin himself, many insisted that such competition is a good thing because it results in progress through the survival of the fittest, who prosper most under free-market conditions.[64] William Graham Sumner assured his readers that the millionaire captains of industry "are a product of natural selection . . . [They] hold the world of trade, industry, finance, transportation, law, and politics in their hands; and they hold it, not because they inherited it or because they belong to any privileged class, but [because] they have obtained control of it by natural selection."[65] Sumner had no real idea of what "natural selection" meant, but he was sure that it must account for the power of the millionaires because both things were part of the order of nature. The social Darwinism preached by people like Spencer and Sumner was warmly embraced by the ideologues and boosters of nineteenth-century capitalism, and such beliefs are still important themes in conservative political philosophy and entrepreneurial folklore.

Another appealing thing about Darwinism, as Shaw observed,[66] was that it eliminated the philosophical problem of animal suffering. If nature was not a contrivance of God, then there was no need to find some sort of divine purpose in nature's cruelties. Instead of struggling to justify those cruelties as the deliberate choice of an almighty deity, Darwinians could forgive nature's harshness as unintentional—and even applaud it as the motive force behind evolutionary progress.[67] The majestic closing sentences of the *Origin* sum up the Darwinian justification for natural evil and animal misery:

Thus, from the war of nature, from famine and death, the most exalted object which we are capable of conceiving, namely, the production of the higher animals, directly follows. There is grandeur in this view of life, with its several powers, having been originally breathed by the Creator into a few forms or into one; and that, whilst this planet has gone cycling on according to the fixed law of gravity, from so simple a beginning endless forms most beautiful and most wonderful have been, and are being evolved.

Yet the suffering of the components in the machinery of progress continued to be seen by some Victorians as an objection to the supposed goodness of the present order of things, whether natural or social. "The order of nature, in so far as unmodified by man," wrote J. S. Mill in his vitriolic posthumous essay *Nature,*

> is such as no Being whose attributes are justice and benevolence would have made with the intention that his rational creatures should follow it as an example. If made wholly by such a Being, and not partly by beings of very different qualities, it could only be as a designedly imperfect work which man, in his limited sphere, is to exercise justice and benevolence in amending . . . In sober truth, nearly all the things which men are hanged or imprisoned for doing to one another are nature's everyday performances.[68]

A grim pessimism concerning the cruelty of nature was in fact an important part of the Darwinian world view, since the "murderous creation" of which Blake had complained made more sense in Darwinian terms than it did in the context of creationist belief. As Darwin put it: "I cannot persuade myself that a benevolent and omnipotent God would have designedly created the Ichneumonidae with the express intention of their feeding within the living bodies of Caterpillars, or that a cat should play with a mouse. Not believing this, I see no necessity in the belief that the eye was expressly designed."[69] But some Darwinians (including Darwin) sometimes went beyond this skeptical conclusion and talked as though the promise of future progress somehow *justified* present suffering. This maneuver was not much of an improvement on the natural theodicy of Paley or the animal heaven postulated by Wesley and Wilberforce. Huxley's 1888 essay on "The Struggle for Existence in Human Society" addressed Christian and Darwinian meliorism alike with impartial contempt:

From the theological side, we are told that this is a state of probation, and that the seeming injustices and immoralities of nature will be compensated by and by. But how this compensation is to be effected, in the case of the great majority of sentient things, is not clear. I apprehend that no one is seriously prepared to maintain that the ghosts of all the myriads of generations of herbivorous animals which lived during the millions of years of the earth's duration . . . and which have all that time been tormented and devoured by carnivores, are to be compensated by a perennial existence in clover; while the ghosts of carnivores are to go to some kennel where there is neither a pan of water nor a bone with any meat on it . . . On the evolutionist side, on the other hand, we are told to take comfort from the reflection that the terrible struggle for existence tends to final good, and that the suffering of the ancestor is paid for by the increased perfection of the progeny . . . [but] it is not clear what compensation the *Eohippus* gets for his sorrows in the fact that, some millions of years afterward, one of his descendants wins the Derby.[70]

EIGHT

The Sick Animal

For certainly man is sicker, less secure, less stable, less firmly anchored than any other animal; he is the *sick* animal . . . How could such a brave and resourceful animal but be the most precarious, the most profoundly sick of all the sick beasts of the earth?

—Friedrich Nietzsche

ALTHOUGH Darwinism had some Romantic elements in it, Darwinian ideas about nature and animals were basically at odds with those of the Romantics. The Romantics looked at nature and saw an underlying spiritual unity everywhere; Darwinians looked at nature and saw competition and hierarchy.

The Darwinian vision had a special appeal for the rich and powerful. Such people often prefer hierarchical conceptions of nature, which tell them that their high station is part of the natural order of things. In the late nineteenth century, the literature of Social Darwinism assured the people at the top of the heap that natural selection among competing individuals had given them rightful power over the poor. The power that Europeans exercised over the rest of the human race was also justified in Darwinian terms, by analogy with man's dominion over the lower animals.

By the end of the nineteenth century, fully two-thirds of the habitable surface of the planet was either administered from Europe or occupied by European colonists who had driven the native peoples from their land. Most of the world's peoples and cultures that were not derived from Europe or under direct European control were reeling under the impact of European political and military pressure, technology, religion, political ideas, intoxicants, and money. In the context of European empire, the subtitle of the *Origin of Species,* "The Preservation of Favoured Races in the Struggle for Existence," had obvious political overtones. It seemed clear to many Europeans that the white race had proved itself superior to the lower races of man by bringing them under its sway, just as the human species as a whole had proved itself superior to the other animals by dominating and subduing them. Darwin himself predicted that "the civilised races of man will almost certainly exterminate, and replace, the savage races throughout the world." The great apes, he added, are also bound to become extinct before long, and when white men have finally exterminated all the Negroes and gorillas and chimpanzees, the gulf between people and animals will be even wider than it is now:

> for it will intervene between man in a more civilised state, as we may hope, even than the Caucasian, and some ape as low as a baboon, instead of as now between the negro or Australian and the gorilla.[1]

The analogy between man's dominion over the beasts and Europe's supremacy over the "savage races" was reflected in the symbolism of big-game hunting in the tropics. The chase had long been regarded as a token of human dominion over the animals, and European aristocrats had always thought of it as a sort of war game in which a gentleman could hone his military skills by pursuing and killing unfriendly beasts. Naturally the gentlemen who went off to run Europe's colonies took up hunting there, as a familiar recreation appropriate to their high station—and just as naturally their hunting came to be seen as a symbol of the whole imperial enterprise.[2] There were obvious parallels between organizing a hunting party to kill wild animals and leading a military expedition against hostile aborigines. Colonial hunting rituals celebrated those parallels through symbols of European dominion over the land, its animals, and its people.

In East Africa, the white hunter traveling into the bush in search of game went on safari, employing a train of forty to a hundred black natives as bearers and servants. The differences between the local folk and their foreign conquerors were emphasized in every aspect of the proceedings. On safari in British East Africa, the white hunter sported a distinctive outfit topped off by a pith helmet, to call attention to his supposed need for protection from the tropical sun. He slept in an elaborate tent and was addressed as *bwana, baas,* or *master;* his bearers slept in the open and were addressed as *boy.* Even the bearers' food, consisting chiefly of cornmeal mush, was called by a special name *(potio),* like animal fodder. The natives marched along day after day balancing sixty-pound packs on their heads; the hunter carried nothing, not even his own gun. His weapons were carried for him by a gunboy, who handed them to the hunter on demand, like a caddy passing clubs to a golfer.[3]

In India, where there was a native civilization of considerable wealth and splendor, some Englishmen adopted the gorgeous hunting customs of the native aristocracy, donning formal dress to shoot at game from the back of an elephant. On one such luxurious elephant-back hunt in 1876, the Prince of Wales and his entourage flushed a tiger by pelting it with the empty mineral-water bottles that had accumulated in their howdah. Truly serious white hunters in India, who regarded such practices as un-British, preferred to fare forth in the African manner in front of a procession of native attendants; nevertheless, they were punctilious about bringing along the proper wines to drink with their meals and the proper evening clothes to wear to dinner every night.[4]

All this ritual was part of the imperial show, intended in part to "keep up the side," impress the natives, and make it clear who was *baas.* "The object of this hunt," the great tiger hunter Ralph Stanley-Robinson reminded his companions at the beginning of one hunt, "is imperial. We are the rulers here."[5] And the natives were not the only ones who were impressed. The imperial hunt also made for good public relations back in the homeland, where it appealed to a wide audience as a token of the white man's dominion over the jungle creatures. For over a century, from the early 1800s down through the 1930s, the presses of Europe and America poured out a torrent of popular books and articles by colonial hunters, with such titles as *Field Sports in India, African Game Trails,* and *The Land of the Lion,* illustrated by pictures of intrepid sportsmen firing away at charging buffaloes, lions, and elephants or posing with a foot planted negligently on the vanquished quarry.

Gustave Courbet, *The End of the Chase*. (orig. *Hallali du cerf*, 1867; Musée des Beaux-Arts et d'Archéologie, Besançon)

From all these books and images, there emerged a new mythic stereotype: the Great White Hunter. This contrasted sharply with the older, Romantic vision of the huntsman as a friend of nature. The Romantic ideal of the hunter-colonist is Cooper's Leatherstocking: a white man dressed in buckskins, who lives simply in the wilderness on intimate and friendly terms with the natives, dislikes white civilization, and hunts only to satisfy his basic needs for food and clothing. The Great White Hunter is exactly the opposite: an upper-class white man wearing a conspicuously "civilized" costume, who leads an army of servile natives on a foray into the bush to kill for thrills, glory, and trophies. For the Romantic hunter, the Man in the Buckskin Suit, the hunt is an act of loving communion with nature. For the imperial and Darwinian hunter, the Man in the Pith Helmet, it is an assertion of his competitive superiority over the natives and other local fauna.

Both conceptions of European man's relationship to nature found many expressions in the popular culture of the late nineteenth and early twentieth centuries. In English-speaking countries, the stern Darwinian vision of a world ruled by the law of the jungle and lorded over by the white man was celebrated in the paintings of Winslow Homer and set forth in the bestselling books of Rudyard Kipling and Jack London. Great White Hunters like Jim Corbett and Teddy Roosevelt were idolized by the young boys who devoured their tales of wilderness adventure.[6] But the tender-minded Romantic view of animals and nature seized the public's fancy as well, and probably had an even bigger impact on the popular imagination. It pervades so many works of nineteenth-century art and literature that hard-nosed critics have complained ever since about "the sentimentality and anthropomorphism of Victorian animal lovers."[7] There was nothing new or distinctive about anthropomorphism as such. Dressed-up talking animals had for millennia been used to caricature people or satirize institutions, and eighteenth-century children's authors had written talking-animal stories to discourage cruelty to animals. But before the nineteenth century, realistic animals had rarely been featured as viewpoint characters in serious art and writing.

This tendency began to be visible in art galleries in the early 1800s. Animal genre painting of the seventeenth and eighteenth centuries had generally celebrated animals as possessions, memorializing the expensive livestock and the hunting exploits of the rural gentry who bought the artists' works.[8] But in the nineteenth century, animal painting began to celebrate the animals themselves as subjects, in a psychological as well as an artistic sense, and famous animal painters like Courbet, Bonheur, and Landseer vied with each other to capture the souls of beasts in their canvases.

It was generally acknowledged that Sir Edwin Landseer, Queen Victoria's favorite artist, painted animals more expressively than anyone else. "He penetrates the secret of these dark brains, he knows what makes these unconscious little hearts beat, and reads in these dreamy eyes the faint astonishment produced there by the spectacle of things," exclaimed Théophile Gautier. "He is on intimate terms with beasts: the dog, giving him a shake of the paw like a comrade, tells him the news of the kennel [and] the stag, which like a woman has the gift of tears, comes to weep on his breast over the cruelty of man."[9] The critic John Canaday summed up Landseer's oeuvre less charitably by calling him "the Sarah Bernhardt of taxidermy."[10] Landseer's death in 1873 evoked this eulogy in *Punch:*

> Mourn, all dumb things, for whom his skill found voice,
> Knitting 'twixt them and us undreamed-of ties,
> Till men could in their voiceless joy rejoice,
> And read the sorrow in their silent eyes.[11]

Like many other salon painters of the nineteenth century, Landseer painted his pictures with an eye on a mass audience. New printing techniques allowed middle-class Victorians to hang chromolithographs and steel engravings of famous paintings in the parlor as household icons; and some artists, including Landseer, derived most of their income from copyright fees on these reproductions. His pictures had a widespread influence on the way people thought about animals. Clarence Day's memoirs of a New York childhood in the 1870s attest to the impact of Landseer's images:

> On one wall was an engraving of Rosa Bonheur's rearing horses . . .
> On the opposite wall was an engraving of Landseer's "Stag at Bay." We
> stood and stared at him in awe. Our other heroes, Crusoe and Christian,
> and still more of course Gulliver, in spite of all the adventures they had,
> were somehow at heart pretty humdrum. That stag was quite different.
> He was tragic and male and magnificent.[12]

Earlier hunting art had mainly provided artists with a pretext for painting still life of dead game or portraits of rich patrons on horseback. But in the hunting scenes painted by Landseer and other nineteenth-century animal painters, the focus shifted to the suffering of the quarry: writhing otters impaled on spears, exhausted foxes screaming in terror at the advancing hunt, and red deer by the metric ton, tragic and male and magnificent, confronting death with their pointed faces frozen in masks of noble agony.[13] Although Courbet, Bonheur, and Landseer were themselves enthusiastic hunters, at least some of these paintings were clearly intended to stir feelings of pity and indignation at the things hunters do. In a letter written to Lord Ellesmere in 1837, Landseer expressed his own mixed feelings about deer hunting in Scotland:

Sir Edwin Landseer, *A Random Shot*. (c. 1848; Bury Museum, Bury, England)

There is something in the toil and trouble, the wild weather and savage scenery that makes butchers of us all. Who does not glory in the death of a fine stag? on the spot—when in truth he ought to be ashamed of the assassination . . . Still, with all my respect for the animal's inoffensive character—my love of him *as a subject for the pencil* gets the better of such tenderness.[14]

The concern for animal suffering that Landseer and other animal genre artists poured into their paintings and engravings was mirrored in many aspects of Victorian culture. Its bestselling literary expression was Anna Sewell's 1877 novel *Black Beauty,* which animal-welfare societies bought by the carload and gave away to cabbies and stablehands to encourage them to be kind to horses. Its political wing was the SPCA movement, of which both Landseer and Bonheur were dedicated members.

ORGANIZED political agitation for the humane treatment of animals began in Britain during the first two decades of the nineteenth century, when bills criminalizing the mistreatment of animals started to be introduced in Parliament. The first such bill to win passage, the Cruelty to Animals Act of 1822, made it a crime to mistreat horses, asses, and cattle but provided no means of enforcement.[15] That omission was met in 1824 by the formation of the Society for the Prevention of Cruelty to Animals. The SPCA started out as a little band of much-derided zealots who went around bravely dragging horse-floggers into court and pressing charges against them. It soon evolved into a private constabulary that worked hand in hand with the official police. The young Princess Victoria joined the society in 1835, catapulting it into the loftiest spheres of English respectablity. When she became queen, Victoria commanded that her pet charity be renamed the Royal SPCA. More stringent anticruelty laws were soon pushed through Parliament by the RSPCA and its influential friends. During the latter half of the nineteenth century, similar animal-protection societies sprung up throughout Europe and North America, lobbying for similar legislation and sometimes getting it.[16]

These humane societies were disproportionately made up of rich people, and they directed most of their energy against such lower-class abuses of animals as dog fighting, bull baiting, and driving horses to death. Some historians have accordingly viewed the humane movement as a largely symbolic expression of the fear and guilt that the people at the top of Victorian society felt toward those at the bottom.[17] This picture has a great deal of truth in it, but it leaves out some important facts. No matter what we think about the symbolic dimensions of the humane movement, we must recognize that its members really were concerned about cruelty to animals, which was a genuine problem and a legitimate object of moral concern. And some of them looked beyond bull baiting and dog fights to condemn two distinctly upper-class ways of hurting animals: vivisection and hunting.

Cutting up living animals to figure out how their bodies work, a practice that goes back at least to Galen, became a commonplace laboratory procedure during the scientific revolution of the seventeenth century. It was a hellish affair redolent of the torture chamber, in which the animal suffered the agonies of being dissected alive and the only anesthetic employed was the Cartesian philosophy that dulled the sensibilities of the experimenter. Protests against vivisection began to be heard in the early 1700s and grew during the nineteenth century into a substantial political movement that enlisted several of the early SPCA luminaries, including Queen Victoria herself.[18] One of the first shelters for homeless animals in France was founded by the estranged wife and daughters of the French physiologist and fanatical vivisector Claude Bernard, as an act of penance to atone for the sufferings and deaths of all the stray dogs that Bernard had brought home over the years and vivisected in the cellar.[19] A campaign against vivisection that the British RSPCA launched in 1857 culminated in the passage of the Cruelty to Animals Act of 1876—the world's first law restricting the use of animals in scientific research.

The introduction of ether anesthesia in 1849 made most vivisection a relatively painless affair, but the change had little effect on antivivi-sectionist rhetoric. For many opponents of vivisection, what made scientific experimentation on animals objectionable was not so much the suffering of the animal as the detachment and arrogance of the vivisector. Victorian antivivisectionists "saw scientific experimentation on animals as . . . a symbol of what was wrong with a world in which people had assigned the highest priority to themselves, their reasoning power, and the gratification of their desires."[20] Many working-class Britons came to see vivisection in even more bluntly political terms, as a symbol of the power that doctors and other men of wealth and influence exerted over the poor. This aspect of the antivivisectionist movement was made clear in the Brown Dog riots of 1907, in which trade unionists fought medical students in the streets of Battersea to preserve a statue erected in memory of a vivisected terrier.[21]

Hunting had similar sorts of symbolic meaning, and it stirred similar emotions and political responses. In England, where hunting was still a marker of upper-class status, aristocrats chasing a fox or a stag occasionally found their quarry protected from them by a hostile lower-class mob.[22] And just as the hunter's dominion over the beasts furnished a model for European dominion over the rest of humanity, so denunciations of hunting sometimes embodied doubts about the legitimacy of empire. The antihunting sentiments voiced by Coleridge, Thoreau, and other early nineteenth-century writers were rooted in a Romantic love of animals and unspoiled nature; but in later Victorian literature, such sentiments were often commingled with corrosive doubts about the value of progress, the superiority of European cul-ture, and the goodness of man.

One of the first writers to tie these various doubts together was the American essayist and novelist Charles Dudley Warner. In his short story "A-Hunting of the Deer," which appeared in the *Atlantic Monthly* in 1878, Warner attempted to express "the pleasurable excitement of a deer-hunt . . . from the deer's point of view." Warner's tale is an ironic and savagely sarcastic tearjerker, the story of a hunted doe who gets her throat cut in the antepenultimate paragraph. Warner invokes the suffering of the doe and her starving fawn to castigate mankind in general, so-called Christian civilization in particular, and hunting in all its forms, drawing explicit parallels between deer hunting and Western imperialism:

> The hunters, in winter, find [the deer] congregated in "yards," where they can be surrounded and shot as easily as our troops shoot Comanche women and children in their winter villages.

> . . . In a panic, frightened animals will always flee to humankind from the danger of more savage foes. They always make a mistake in doing so. Perhaps the trait is the survival of an era of peace on earth; perhaps it is a prophecy of the golden age of the future. The business of this age is murder—the slaughter of animals, the slaughter of fellow-men, by the wholesale.[23]

These sentiments were echoed by Warner's friend and collaborator Mark Twain, whose views of his culture and his species grew increasingly bleak as he got older. In his early travel books, Twain was scornful of the backward foreigners and savages he encountered and was always ready to assign them amusingly low ranks on the scale of existence. *The Innocents Abroad* describes European peasants as half-animal types, "little better . . . than the donkeys they eat and sleep with"; and in *Roughing It* Twain dismisses the "degraded" South African Bushmen and the "inferior" natives of the Great Basin as "manifestly descended from the same gorilla, or kangaroo, or Norway rat, whichever animal-Adam the Darwinians trace them to."[24]

But even in these early books, Twain often poked satirical fun at the supposed superiority of white people and their culture; and as his life and the nineteenth century drew to a close, he grew less and less inhibited about attacking the hierarchical Darwinian vision of nature and the prevailing assumptions about white supremacy. Returning from an 1895 lecture tour that took him through much of the British

Empire, Twain proclaimed himself an "anti-imperialist."[25] In his memoirs of that tour, he lacerated the semislavery inflicted upon Polynesians by white "labor recruiters,"[26] praised the stone-age culture and skills of the Australian aborigines, and sardonically commended a white Australian farmer for the mass murder of a group of aboriginals to whom he had fed arsenic-laced Christmas pudding. That farmer, wrote Twain, had acted in the time-honored traditions of Christian civilization:

> The white man's spirit . . . was the spirit which the civilized white has always exhibited toward the savage, but the use of poison was a departure from custom . . . and therefore a mistake, in my opinion. It was better, kinder, swifter, and much more humane than a number of the methods which have been sanctified by custom, but . . . its unusual nature makes it stand out and attract an amount of attention which it is not entitled to . . . In many countries we have chained the savage and starved him to death; and this we do not care for, because custom has inured us to it; yet a quick death by poison is lovingkindness to it. In many countries we have burned the savage at the stake; and this we do not care for, because custom has inured us to it; yet a quick death is lovingkindness to it. In more than one country we have hunted the savage and his little children and their mother with dogs and guns through the woods and swamps for an afternoon's sport, and filled the region with happy laughter over their sprawling and stumbling flight, and their wild supplications for mercy; but this method we do not mind, because custom has inured us to it; yet a quick death by poison is lovingkindness to it . . .
>
> There are many humorous things in the world, among them the white man's notion that he is less savage than the other savages.[27]

Twain saw little difference between the hunting of people and the hunting of animals. Recounting horror stories he had heard in India about Thuggee, the ritual murder of unsuspecting travelers by devotees of the goddess Kali, Twain concluded that there was only a "microscopic" moral difference between the Thug and the hunter:

> The joy of killing! the joy of seeing killing done—these are traits of the human race at large. We white people are merely modified Thugs . . . who long ago enjoyed the slaughter of the Roman arena, and . . . who now, with the Thugs of Spain and Nimes, flock to enjoy the blood

and misery of the bull-ring . . . We are gentle Thugs in the hunting season, and love to chase a tame rabbit and kill it . . . There are many indications that the Thug often hunted men for the mere sport of it; that the fright and pain of the quarry were no more to him than the fright and pain of the rabbit or the stag to us; and that he was no more ashamed of beguiling his game with deceits and abusing its trust than are we when we have imitated a wild animal's call and shot it when it honored us with its confidence and came to see what we wanted.[28]

Although Twain never wrote a story like Warner's depicting hunting from the perspective of the quarry, he published similar stories attacking bullfighting and vivisection, and he joined Warner in condemning hunting as a barbarous amusement that demonstrates the innate depravity of man.[29] His last works are saturated with a profoundly misanthropic conviction that *Homo sapiens* is "the lowest animal," supreme in intellect but defective in all other respects, who differs from higher creatures chiefly in his cruelty, avarice, spite, and pathological joy in doing evil.[30] "If you pick up a starving dog and make him prosperous," Twain wrote, "he will not bite you. This is the principal difference between a dog and a man."[31] This aphorism is often taken as a wisecrack, but Twain's later writing makes it clear that he believed every word of it.

Other Victorian intellectuals were thinking similar dark thoughts toward the end of the nineteenth century. Twain's loss of faith in human and European superiority finds a particularly close parallel in the poetry of Alfred, Lord Tennyson. His poem "Locksley Hall," published in 1842, is an elegant poetic expression of early-Victorian confidence in the white male's position at the top of the hierarchy of nature. "Woman is the lesser man," Tennyson assured his readers, and European civilization is the best civilization: "Better fifty years of Europe than a cycle of Cathay." And as man is superior to the lower animals, so civilized white people are superior to dark-skinned savages "with narrow foreheads, vacant of our glorious gains, / Like a beast with lower pleasures, like a beast with lower pains!"[32] In this early poem, Tennyson foresaw only perpetual progress and the dawning of universal peace. But when he sat down in 1885 to write the sequel, "Locksley Hall Sixty Years After," all these happy expectations had evaporated. Progress, European superiority, and human authority over the beasts seemed illusory. The future he now prophesied for humanity was one of extinction through overpopulation and ceaseless war, "till this outworn earth be dead as yon dead world the moon." Civilized man's chief difference from "the kindlier brutes" and "the primal clan," as he saw it, lay in a refinement of cruelty:

> Have we grown at last beyond the passions of the primal clan?
> 'Kill your enemy, for you hate him,' still, 'your enemy' was a man.
>
> Have we sunk below them? peasants maim the helpless horse, and drive
> Innocent cattle under thatch, and burn the kindlier brutes alive.
>
> Brutes, the brutes are not your wrongers—burnt at midnight, found at morn,
> Twisted hard in mortal agony with their offspring, born-unborn,
>
> Clinging to the silent mother! Are we devils? are we men?
> Sweet St. Francis of Assisi, would that he were here again,
>
> He that in his Catholic wholeness used to call the very flowers
> Sisters, brothers—and the beasts—whose pains are hardly less than ours![33]

The great nineteenth-century exponent of this sort of tender-hearted despair was the German philosopher Arthur Schopenhauer. Schopenhauer is not read much today, but disaffected young intellectuals a hundred years ago adored him. Deeply influenced by Buddhist philosophy, Schopenhauer was a melancholy pessimist who regarded nature as a living hell and human life as a bottomless cup of anguish. Like Darwin and Huxley, he thought that the world's flaws refuted the hypothesis of design:

> There are two things which make it impossible to believe that this world is the successful work of an all-wise, all-good, and at the same time all-powerful being: firstly, the misery which abounds in it everywhere; and secondly, the obvious imperfection of its highest product, man, who is a burlesque of what he should be.[34]

"If you accustom yourself to this view of life," Schopenhauer went on, ". . . you will find that everything is as it should be, in a world where each of us pays the penalty of existence in his own peculiar way

. . . In fact, the conviction that the world and man is something that had better not have been is of a kind to fill us with indulgence toward one another."[35] For Schopenhauer, the great mystery was why the *lower* creatures had to suffer:

> By taking a very high standpoint it is possible to justify the sufferings of mankind. But this justification cannot apply to animals, whose sufferings, while in large measure brought about by people, are often considerable even apart from human agency. And so we are forced to ask, "Why and for what purpose does all this torment and agony exist?"[36]

Even an irreligious pessimist like Schopenhauer still wanted to believe that somehow, somewhere there must be a *justification* for animal suffering. But the only ray of sunshine that Schopenhauer could find in the dark abyss of animal misery was his conviction that the beasts are at any rate better off than people—mainly because they are too stupid to realize how miserable they are. ("In proportion as knowledge attains to distinctness, as consciousness ascends," lamented Schopenhauer, "pain also increases, and therefore reaches its highest degree in man . . . [and] the man who is gifted with genius suffers most of all."[37]) The will to go on living is thus inversely correlated with intelligence. Because the lower animals are unimaginative creatures of the present moment, they are spared all the agonies that we suffer from our embittered recollections of the past and anxieties about the future.[38] The beasts might be relatively happy in their enjoyment of their eternal present, were it not for human cruelty:

> But man, that selfish and heartless creature, misuses this quality of the brute to be more content than we are with mere existence, and often works it to such an extent that he allows the brute absolutely nothing more than mere, bare life. The bird which was made so that it might rove over half the world, he shuts up into the space of a cubic foot, there to die a slow death . . . And when I see how man misuses the dog, his best friend; how he ties up this intelligent animal with a chain, I feel the deepest sympathy with the brute and burning indignation against its master.[39]

Schopenhauer's influential writings helped to nourish spreading doubts about the hierarchies underlying the prevailing notions of progress. Those doubts reflected a growing insecurity about the legitimacy of human and Western authority over the rest of the world. The excellence of the human condition and Western civilization were not so obvious to European and American intellectuals at the end of the nineteenth century as they had been at its beginning. The injustice and oppression inherent in European imperialism were becoming painfully evident to many thoughtful people—especially after the Boer War, in which the African natives suppressed by Britain's armies aroused particular sympathy because they had white skins and spoke Dutch.

Man's dominion over the lower orders of nature also seemed increasingly questionable (in part because of its metaphorical connections with European empire), and many Victorians sought to limit that dominion through political means. Two important nineteenth-century political movements shared this goal. The humane movement that began in England strove to limit our dominion over the animals by prohibiting certain human behaviors. The conservation movement, which blossomed in the United States after the Civil War, sought to limit human exploitation of nature in a different way, by taking large chunks of it out of the hands of man forever.

The first stirrings of the conservation movement began in the United States in 1833, at a time when there was still more wilderness than anything else in North America. In that year, the frontier artist George Catlin proposed that some of the immense forests that still flourished on the banks of the Missouri River "might in future be seen (by some great protecting policy of government) preserved in their pristine beauty and wildness, in a magnificent park, where the world could see for ages to come, the native Indian in his classic attire, galloping his wild horse . . . amid the fleeting herds of elks and buffaloes."[40] The idea of a national park was also urged by Emerson, Thoreau, and the painter Thomas Cole, all of whom shared Catlin's Romantic reverence for the sublimities of unspoiled nature. Like Catlin, Thoreau wanted to see the Indians preserved with the rest of the fauna, as part of the natural American landscape, "in which the bear and panther, and some even of the hunter race, may still exist, and not be 'civilized off the face of the earth'—our forests, not to hold the king's game merely, but to hold and preserve the king himself also, the lord of creation—

not for idle sport or food, but for inspiration and our own true recreation."[41]

During the 1850s, as the railroads crept west and the gold rush brought California its first feverish land boom, a new genre of newspaper stories, panoramic paintings, photographs, and books about the glory and majesty of the western wilderness emerged in the eastern media. This river of publicity for the western territories was encouraged by entrepreneurs and speculators, who sought to promote migration from the east by advertising the scenic beauties of western nature. In 1852, a couple of California go-getters stripped 7,000 square feet of bark from a sequoia and sent it on a publicity tour of the east coast and London, where onlookers were sold a pamphlet urging them to visit California and see the Big Trees for themselves.[42] This publicity gimmick evoked indignant outbursts from James Russell Lowell, Oliver Wendell Holmes, and other influential writers, who protested the exploitation of the redwoods and demanded that they be protected from unscrupulous moneymakers.

That demand began to be realized in 1864, when President Lincoln signed a bill deeding the Yosemite Valley and the Mariposa sequoias to the state of California on the condition that they be held in public trust forever. The first national park was formed in 1872 to protect Yellowstone in its natural condition, and new parks and monuments established under federal control were added to it at an average rate of one per year for the next thirty-six years.[43] In the succeeding years of this century, a third of the area of the United States has become sequestered public land of some sort, temporarily or permanently placed off limits to human development, and the American experience has provided a model for similar conservation efforts throughout the rest of the world.

From the very beginning, the American conservation movement has encompassed two rather different sorts of nature lovers: tender-minded Romantics who want to preserve nature because it is holy, and tough-minded Darwinian types, who want to preserve it because it is healthy. For the Romantics, nature is an open-air chapel in which one can commune with the Infinite and make friends with the forest creatures; for the Darwinians, nature is a kind of vast exercise salon, in which one can get rid of bodily flabbiness and spiritual malaise, work up a glorious appetite, and polish off a couple of those forest creatures for supper. These views are not mutually exclusive, and most nature lovers hold both to varying degrees; but there is a tension between the two attitudes, which sometimes breaks out into fights over such matters as hunting.

The most notorious of these fights was the celebrated controversy over "nature fakery" that erupted in the United States at the turn of the century. At that time perhaps the best-known and most beloved American naturalists were two grave, white-bearded sages in their mid-sixties: John Muir, whose outlook on nature was essentially Romantic, and John Burroughs, who was an emphatic Darwinian. The two were on friendly terms, but they were fundamentally different in temperament and did not like each other very much.

Burroughs, whom one reviewer once described as "a sort of reduced Thoreau,"[44] was a quiet, bookish, precise man who had been writing charming, popular books about natural history for thirty years. Although he had been a disciple of Emerson's, Burroughs had little patience with mystical notions about animals or nature. Nature study, he thought, ought to cure people of that sort of thing, not encourage it. "Intercourse with nature," he wrote, "tends to beget a habit of mind the farthest possible removed from the myth-making, the vision-seeing, the voice-hearing habit and temper. In all matters relating to the visible, concrete universe it substitutes broad daylight for twilight; it supplants fear with curiosity; . . . it blights credulity with the frost of skepticism." He saw nature in a hard, cold, Darwinian light:

> Nature is not benevolent; Nature . . . makes no exceptions, never tempers her decrees with mercy, or winks at any infringement of her law. And in the end is not this best? Could the universe be run as a charity or a benevolent institution, or as a poorhouse of the most approved pattern? . . . It is a hard gospel; but rocks are hard too, yet they form the foundations of the hills.[45]

Muir, the founder of the Sierra Club, was a bounding, arm-waving, ceaselessly preaching mystic, who saw the western wilderness as holy ground "where everything is wild and beautiful and busy and steeped with God."[46] He consecrated his life to the protection of wilderness and wildlife from the depredations and overweening presumption of

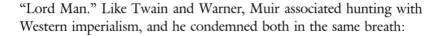

"Lord Man." Like Twain and Warner, Muir associated hunting with Western imperialism, and he condemned both in the same breath:

> Let a Christian hunter go to the Lord's woods, and kill his well-kept beasts, or wild Indians, and it is well; but let an enterprising specimen of these proper, predestined victims go to houses and fields and kill the most worthless person of the vertical godlike killers,—oh! that is horribly unorthodox, and on the part of the Indians atrocious murder! Well, I have precious little sympathy for the selfish propriety of civilized man, and if a war of races should occur between the wild beasts and Lord Man, I would be tempted to sympathize with the bears.[47]

By the turn of the century, Burroughs was starting to feel threatened by this sort of attitude—not just ideologically but economically. During the 1880s, American educators had introduced what was called "nature study" into the public school curriculum, in the belief that boning up on birds, bugs, and woodcraft would not only teach American schoolchildren some natural science but instil in them an appreciation of nature's beauties, a respect for her creatures, and a reverence for her Author. Since raw nature often failed to yield these moral lessons without some prompting, schoolbooks were needed to tell children what they were supposed to see in nature and how they were supposed to feel about it. Nature-study textbooks were big business; successful ones might sell hundreds of thousands of copies. And no writer of such books was more successful or more highly esteemed than John Burroughs, whose sales were considerably boosted by the network of John Burroughs societies that his publishers promoted in schools across the country.[48]

But by 1900 Burroughs was getting some strong competition from a younger generation of nature writers, whose books sported breezier prose and prettier illustrations, and whose animal characters did more clever things. The two most popular writers of this younger generation were a pair of Canadians, Ernest Thompson Seton and William J. Long, whose attitudes toward nature were considerably more sentimental and Romantic than Burroughs'. Seton, an accomplished artist whose first published book was an elegant atlas of animal anatomy, was also a reformed hunter who had once made a living out of killing wolves for government bounty money. The experience had turned him against hunting. His first two nature books, *Wild Animals I Have Known* and *Lives of the Hunted,* are powerful antihunting propaganda, presenting the lives and tragic deaths of hunted animals with an affecting sentimentality and an attention to realistic-seeming detail that suggests a prose version of Landseer's paintings. Long's books were cheerier but generally similar collections of animal stories, full of equally stylish illustrations and containing similar preachments against hunting.

Burroughs studied the works of Seton and Long and brooded over them, and then launched a thunderbolt at his upstart competitors' heads. In the February 1903 issue of the *Atlantic,* he denounced them as mercenary fabulists, willing to make up any sort of story "to float into public favor and into pecuniary profit." Seton's bestselling *Wild Animals I Have Known,* snarled Burroughs, should be retitled "Wild Animals I *Alone* Have Known." And Long was even worse. His little Nature Readers for schoolchildren were nothing but collections of tall tales—about a porcupine that curled into a ball and rolled downhill for fun; about ospreys that trained their young to fish by maiming minnows for them to practice on; about a trapped fox that deliberately played possum to escape the trapper; about another fox that caught roosting chickens for supper by running in circles until the giddy fowl swooned from their perches; and so on and on, from one preposterous whopper to another. Burroughs hinted that Long had acquired all this woodsy lore at home in an armchair, by reading the fish stories in rod-and-gun magazines.

What chiefly irked Burroughs was not so much the inaccuracy of these would-be naturalists as their anthropomorphism. He found Long's book *School of the Woods* especially annoying. "There is a school of the woods," he fumed, "just as much as there is a church of the woods, or a parliament of the woods, or a society of united charities of the woods, and no more; there is nothing in the dealings of animals with their young that in the remotest way suggests human instruction . . . The young of all the wild creatures do instinctively what their parents do and did. They do not have to be taught; they are taught by nature from the start."[49] Animals, Burroughs insisted, are machines made of meat, "almost as much under the dominion of absolute nature, or what we call instinct, innate tendency, as are the plants and trees."[50]

In a rejoinder published that May, Long retorted that animals are individuals, with their own peculiar quirks and idiosyncracies. In "the world of facts and law, with which alone Science concerns itself," Long argued, "the individual, whether animal or man, must struggle against fact and law to develop or keep his own individuality." Anecdotes and stories, not laws and statistics, are what it takes to document that individuality. Because Burroughs perceived living things only as stereotyped representatives of their species, he was a bad naturalist, who would never fully understand the creatures he pretended to study.[51]

A storm of controversy promptly broke around the two men, as America's leading natural historians, birdwatchers, and editorialists came down on one side or the other—and American cartoonists gleefully caricatured the delicious spectacle of so many rich society people fighting about whether birds reason and porcupines roll downhill. The nation's foremost amateur naturalist, President Theodore Roosevelt, paced back and forth impatiently on the sidelines, writing letter after indignant letter criticizing Long to various magazine editors. Finally, in early 1907, Roosevelt went public. In an interview for a Chicago paper, he denounced Long and other nature writers as charlatans and humbugs. "I don't believe for a minute," he protested, "that some of these men who are writing nature stories and putting the word 'truth' prominently in their prefaces know the heart of the wild things." The president took particular exception to a story Long had written, about a wolf killing a bull caribou by piercing its heart with a sudden snap of the teeth. Calling this feat "a mathematical impossibility," Roosevelt compared it to trying to open a grapefruit buried in a barrel of flour by biting through the barrel.[52]

In picking on this particular mistake of Long's, Roosevelt exposed a vulnerable spot in his own public image. He was a devout conservationist, but his view of man's relationship to nature was thoroughly hierarchical and Darwinian. An enthusiastic imperialist and a staunch believer in the superiority of the Anglo-Saxon race, he was also a renowned Great White Hunter who devoted much of his life to killing large animals throughout the world and writing books recounting his adventures. He favored the preservation of America's wildlands because he thought that wilderness adventures inculcated "fighting, masterful virtues" and "that vigorous manliness for the lack of which in a nation, as in an individual, the possession of no other qualities can possibly atone." His exploits as a hunter thrilled schoolboys, but many conservationists and nature lovers of a more Romantic bent regarded him as something of a butcher. When Roosevelt traveled west for the first time to meet John Muir and go camping with him, Muir promptly asked, "Mr. President, when are you going to get beyond the boyishness of killing things?"[53]

Long's counterattack focused squarely on the tension between Roosevelt's image as a lover of nature and his exploits as a Great White Hunter:

> Who is he to write, "I don't believe for a minute that some of these nature writers know the heart of a wild thing." As to that, I find after carefully reading two of his big books that every time Mr. Roosevelt gets near the heart of a wild thing he invariably puts a bullet through it. From his own records I have reckoned a full thousand hearts which he has thus known intimately. In one chapter alone I find that he violently gained knowledge of 11 noble elk hearts in a few days.[54]

The debate rumbled on through the newspapers and magazines until September, when Roosevelt brought it to a swift end in the time-honored American way, by inventing what we now call a sound bite. Long and his ilk, wrote Roosevelt, were nothing but a bunch of "nature fakers." The catchy tag stuck. By the end of the year, Long and Seton and their friends were generally referred to as the nature fakers, and they have been remembered that way ever since. They soon retired from the public debate and turned their attention elsewhere. Most historians of the subject conclude that they were humiliated by Roosevelt and Burroughs and their works and ideas discredited, and that the whole affair was a grand triumph of science over sentimentality.

But seen in its larger cultural and historical context, the nature-faker affair seems less clear-cut. It looks more like a temporary triumph of one political ideology over another. Long wanted to see nature as benevolent and the life of wild animals as essentially happy, whereas Roosevelt and Burroughs viewed nature as a harsh disciplinarian with no mercy for the soft and weak. Since nature is actually neither be-

"Instinct!"

The President and Mr. Burroughs observing carefully the antics of tomtits and snipe. Theodore and John together: "Instinct, sheer instinct!"

A caricature of the "scientific" side in the nature-fakers controversy: Teddy Roosevelt and John Burroughs, sporting halos labeled "Homocentric" and chanting "Instinct, sheer instinct!" in unison. (*Collier's Weekly,* September 5, 1908) nevolent nor harsh, it is a mistake to regard one of these views as realistic and the other as fanciful. At bottom, both are little more than projections of different political attitudes. Long's Mother Nature was a liberal Democrat; Burroughs' was a conservative Republican and Social Darwinist. Long and his friends thought that animals (or at any rate mammals and birds) were little persons with the rudiments of reasoning ability and self-awareness, whereas Burroughs saw them as automatons driven by instinct. This issue too was left unsettled by Roosevelt's victory, and it is still being debated today in the controversy over animal rights.

In sum, the Darwinian view of the world order espoused by Burroughs and Roosevelt has not supplanted the more Romantic view of nature favored by Long, Seton, and Muir. Both views have persisted throughout the twentieth century and have helped to inspire ongoing political movements. The tender-minded, romantic vision of nature as a harmony threatened by human incursion has encouraged the growth of such political phenomena as animal-rights activism, Greenpeace, tree spiking, ecofeminism, and the Green parties of Western Europe. The tough-minded, Rooseveltian view of nature as a competitive hierarchy was intimately connected with nineteenth-century European imperialism and doctrines of white supremacy, and it continues to make an important contribution to conservative political thinking. As manifested in the works of philosophers like Haeckel and Friedrich Nietzsche, the hierarchical view of nature became one of the main intellectual currents feeding into the ideology of Nazi Germany.[55]

THE philosophy of Nietzsche is in essence that of Schopenhauer turned upside down. Nietzsche agreed with Schopenhauer that life does indeed entail perpetual suffering. But to be healthy, Nietzsche insisted, is to affirm life, and so suffering must be embraced. A sane and healthy person neither struggles to avoid suffering nor hesitates to inflict it on others. In fact, to cause others to suffer is a sign of vitality. Man, having invented mercy and empathy, has become the sick animal and will not regain his health until he has once again become cruel, villainous, and splendid:

Man, with his need for self-torture, his sublimated cruelty resulting from the cooping up of his animal nature within a polity, invented bad conscience in order to hurt himself, after the blocking of the more natural outlet of his cruelty . . . What a mad, unhappy animal is man! What strange notions occur to him; what perversities, what paroxysms of nonsense, what bestialities of ideas burst from him, the moment he is prevented ever so little from being a beast of action![56]

Nietzsche's description of the mentally healthy is notorious:

They revert to the innocence of wild animals: we can imagine them returning from an orgy of murder, arson, rape, and torture, jubilant and at peace with themselves as though they had committed a fraternity prank . . . Deep within all these noble races there lurks the beast of prey, bent on spoil and conquest. This hidden urge has to be satisfied from time to time, the beast let loose in the wilderness.[57]

It is hard to read this passage sympathetically because we know what happened when one self-proclaimed noble race adopted a national policy of letting the beast loose in the wilderness. But Nietzsche's fundamental notion here, that civilization is a sickness that we can be cured of by giving occasional free rein to our animal instincts and participating in the natural order, is still a widely accepted idea. It underlies all the naturist and Strenuous Life movements, from scouting to nudism, that blossomed in Europe and North America around the turn of the century. The proposition that mental well-being entails occasionally getting out into the woods and killing something is one that nearly all thoughtful and literate hunters endorse. And the idea that mental illness results from the suppression of man's animal nature is one that we no longer recognize as Nietzsche's, since we are so used to thinking of it as Sigmund Freud's.[58]

Like Nietzsche, Freud assumed that man's psychic health lies in the satisfaction of animal instincts and that civilization has demanded the repression of those instincts.[59] But unlike Nietzsche, Freud prized civilization and had no fondness for rapine and pillage. He was correspondingly unable to prescribe a return to animal simplicity as a cure for the human condition. Instead, Freud fretted repeatedly over the impending extinction of mankind. At first he thought this might happen because human beings were becoming too civilized and re-pressed to reproduce.[60] But after living through the vast idiotic carnage of World War I, Freud decided that the real threat to human survival lay in what he called the death instinct: an innate human desire for self-destruction that when frustrated (or redirected into sadism) ex-presses itself in aggression against others.[61] The terrible weaponry that science had now put at the service of this "human instinct for aggres-sion and self-destruction," Freud concluded, made it impossible to feel any confidence in the future of the human race.[62] Starting from premises resembling Nietzsche's, Freud found himself driven back toward Schopenhauer's notion that intelligence is in some sense in-nately bent on self-destruction.

Freud's enormously influential writings have lent authority ever since to the view of man as a sick animal whose frustrated instincts give him the power and inclination to destroy the world. "Freud in combination with Darwin suffice to give us our philosophical vision," wrote T. H. Huxley's grandson Julian. "Man is the only organism normally and inevitably subject to psychological conflict."[63] During the years between the two world wars, Western intellectuals generally accepted the grim Freudian view of things as an unsettling fact revealed by modern science, like the red shift in astronomy or the Lorentz-Fitzgerald contraction in physics. Even Marxists like the young W. H. Auden followed Freud in contrasting man's sickness and internal con-flict with animal health and wholeness:

> Beneath the hot incurious sun,
>   Past stronger beasts and fairer
> He picks his way, a living gun,
>   With gun and lens and bible . . .
>
> And ruled by dead men never met,
>   By pious guess deluded,
> Upon the stool of madness set
>   Or stool of desolation,
> Sits murderous and clear-headed . . .[64]

The Freudian vision of the human condition has affected both Darwinian and Romantic views of the relationship between man and nature, and has become incorporated on both sides into twentieth-century debates about hunting. Hunters themselves have tended to adopt a Nietzschean view of the hunt as therapy for the human sickness, a cleansing participation in the healthy violence of the natural order. Others, including the theorists of the hunting hypothesis, have preferred to see the hunt in a more Romantic light, as a pathological symptom of the sickness of man, an assault by mad human disorder on natural order and animal innocence. This negative view of the hunt has probably been more popular. Even some hunters see their sport as a token of human depravity. "Deer are the most beautiful animals of the woods," writes the author of a 1925 treatise on bowhunting. "Why men should kill deer is a moot question, but it is a habit of the brute. For so many hundreds of years have we been at it, that we can hardly be expected to reform immediately. Undoubtedly, it is a sign of undeveloped ethnic consciousness. We are depraved animals."[65]

One factor that nudges us toward this unfavorable view of hunting is the complex of conventional meanings that we attach to the hunter's quarry. Deer and rabbits, the traditionally favored objects of the hunt,[66] symbolize harmlessness, vitality, and innocent sexuality, and they are respective icons of the Christmas and Easter festivals of birth and resurrection.[67] Anybody who wants to kill an animal that stands for love, beauty, innocence, and Christmas has a serious public-relations handicap to overcome.

The symbolic values attached to deer have long exerted a powerful influence on Western attitudes toward hunting and hunters. Literary, artistic, and folk conventions built up through centuries of Western cultural history have established deer as stereotypically perfect, magical animals: innocent ("doe-eyed"), swift, graceful, beautiful, delicately feminine as does and powerfully masculine as stags, emblematic of nature and the wilderness, numinous and otherworldly,[68] tragic figures and innocent victims.[69] It is easy to think that there must be something wrong with people whose idea of sport is shooting such creatures dead. In his 1835 treatise on natural theology, the Reverend William Kirby argued that deer were intended by God to be "amongst the peculiar favorites of [the world's] king and master man," and that our fondness for killing these "elegant and airy" creatures is a sign of fallen man's innate depravity.[70] The modern American poet Kenneth Rexroth summed it all up in six lines:

Deer are gentle and graceful
And they have beautiful eyes.
They hurt no one but themselves,
The males, and only for love.
Men have invented several
Thousand ways of killing them.[71]

Feelings of reverence toward deer are widely shared today and widely expressed by all sorts of people, including Hispanic biologists, Native American novelists, black prizefighters, and American presidents.[72] A similar reverence is obvious in the writings of many deer hunters. It reaches a unique pitch of intensity in the writing of James Dickey, whose bowhunting experiences form the basis for his novel *Deliverance* and several of his poems. In one of these, the poet is thrown into such religious transports by the appearance of a buck silhouetted against the sunrise that he throws off his clothes to dance naked with his quarry:

I put an unbearable light
Into breath skinned alive of its garments:
I think, beginning with laurel,
Like a beast loving
With the whole god bone of his horns:
The green of excess is upon me
Like deer in fir thickets in winter
Stamping and dreaming of men
Who will kneel with them naked to break
The ice from streams with their faces
And drink from the lifespring of beasts.[73]

For Dickey and a great many other devoted hunters, deer hunting obviously connotes something larger and more mysterious than a harvest of high-quality protein. The symbolic significance of deer and its bearing on the meaning of hunting were made even clearer in an offhand remark by the animal-rights activist Cleveland Amory, when he arrived at the Everglades in 1982 to protest a hunt ordered to control the whitetail population. "When some of these Fish and Wildlife people get to heaven—*if* they ever do, which I doubt," declared Amory, "they're going to be awfully surprised if they find out that God is a deer."[74]

NINE

The Bambi Syndrome

We know by now, or ought to know, that what gets us off
as entertainment is rarely simple and never innocent.

—Fred Pfeil

IT IS easy enough to describe how various symbols and images associated with the hunt have changed throughout Western history. It is
harder to say how much those changes really meant to most people
in the past. There are ordinarily no grounds for thinking that such
changes affected anyone much beyond the fringes of the ruling class.
We cannot assume, for example, that the signs of distaste for hunting
that began to appear in sixteenth-century English and French literature
expressed much more than the feelings of a small set of bookish
urbanites.

The mass media have changed all that. The manufacturers of mass
culture are generally members of the literate elite, and they can and
do mine the high cultural tradition for ideas they can use in concocting
works for mass consumption. This insures a wider audience for those
ideas. For every person who has read Shaw's *Pygmalion,* a hundred
have seen *My Fair Lady.* Almost nobody has heard of Edmond Ro-
stand, but millions know the story about the big-nosed guy who
spouts poetry to help a friend woo the woman they both love—and
those who do not remember him as Jose Ferrer in *Cyrano de Bergerac*
can catch him as Gérard Depardieu, or as Steve Martin in *Roxanne.* I
and many other middle-aged Americans learned the principal Greek
deities from poring over Captain Marvel and Wonder Woman comic
books in the 1940s. The mass media have taken a vast number of high-

culture themes and ideas that were once the private concerns of the intelligentsia and marketed them as entertainment to a mass audience. By so doing, they have enhanced the social relevance of intellectual history.

In the matter of hunting and man's relationship to nature, we can actually document the impact of high culture on mass attitudes. Although few Americans have read Thoreau or Freud or Schopenhauer, there is reason to think that these writers have influenced popular American attitudes toward nature and wildlife, because material and ideas from their works went into the making of one of our most familiar mythic images of the natural order: the image of a cartoon fawn gazing enraptured at a butterfly perched on his upraised tail.

For all its saccharine sweetness and childish whimsy, Disney's *Bambi* has had a deep influence on modern attitudes toward the hunt, wildlife, and the wilderness. The movie derives its mythic force from the skill with which it combines a wide variety of elements from both high and low cultural traditions—including all the rich symbolism associated with deer as innocent, doe-eyed victims and numinous monarchs of the wilderness. Hunters regard *Bambi* as the most powerful piece of antihunting propaganda ever produced, and they are probably right.

THE Bambi myth has its literary roots in Freud's Vienna. Bambi's creator was a young, blazingly ambitious Hungarian named Siegmund Salzmann, who was born into a Magyar-speaking Jewish family in Budapest in 1869. Salzmann learned German as an adolescent and came to Vienna in the mid-1880s in search of literary fame and fortune. Changing his inauspiciously Jewish-sounding name to Felix Salten, he soon fell in with the crowd of bohemians and aesthetes that frequented the Café Griensteidl on the Michaelerplatz. He began to write and publish prolifically—plays, novels, essays, short stories, theater criticism—and to develop lasting friendships with better writers than himself, such as Hugo von Hofmannsthal and Arthur Schnitzler. By the turn of the century, Salten had become a major force in Viennese theatrical and literary circles.[1]

Salten's life—like those of many other middle-class citizens of imperial Vienna—seethed with public and private contradictions. On the surface, Salten was a pillar of establishment propriety: the drama critic for Vienna's leading pro-government newspaper, the president of the Austrian PEN club, and a flag-waving supporter of the Austro-Hungarian war effort in World War I. But he was also the secret author of *The Memoirs of Josephine Mutzenbacher,* a notorious classic of Viennese pornography that he published anonymously in 1906. He was an aristocratically contemptuous critic of American society and culture, who described "the great majority of Americans" as Babbits;[2] but he was also a Rotarian and the German translator of *Abie's Irish Rose.* He liked to go hunting with Habsburg aristocrats and eventually acquired a private hunting preserve of his own just ten miles outside of Vienna.[3] But he was also an ardent animal-lover, and his hunting experiences led him to produce a masterpiece of antihunting sentiment.

Salten's novel *Bambi: A Forest Life* appeared in 1924. Written in the decaying capital of a defeated and dismembered empire, in an intellectual atmosphere dominated by Freudian gloom and the increasingly hysterical voices of artistic and political extremists, the book radiates a cold aura of Schopenhauerian pessimism. "Death is the central theme of *Bambi,*" writes sportsman and conservationist George Reiger. "Something fears dying, or does die in terrible agony, in almost every chapter."[4] The forest world, which Salten describes in sometimes exquisitely poetic prose, only provides a backdrop of intense color and beauty in front of which his animal characters suffer and bleed and limp and die awful, uncomprehending deaths.

A tally of the carnage conveys much of the flavor of Salten's book. Walking through the forest behind his mother, the newborn roebuck Bambi watches a ferret killing a mouse; the spectacle terrifies him, but his mother will not discuss it. Crows attack a sick baby hare and kill him "in a cruel way. He could be heard moaning pitifully for a long while." A squirrel who escapes from a ferret goes running about in the snow "with a great wound in his neck where the ferret had caught him . . . From time to time he stopped, sat down, raised his forepaws desperately and clutched his head in terror and agony while the red blood oozed on his white chest." (After an hour or so of this, the squirrel drops dead and is eaten by magpies.) A wounded fox develops an infection and lingers for days "suffering terribly . . . biting the snow and the ground." But the evils of nature are trivial compared to the terrors inflicted on the forest creatures by the satanic two-legged demigod they call Him with a capital H. Bambi barely manages to survive his first encounter with the human presence:

> On the edge of the clearing, by a tall hazel bush, a creature was standing. Bambi had never seen such a creature before. At the same time the air brought him a scent such as he had never smelled in his life. It was a strange smell, heavy and acrid. It excited him to the point of madness.
>
> Bambi stared at the creature. It stood remarkably erect. It was extremely thin and had a pale face, entirely bare around the nose and the eyes. A kind of dread emanated from that face, a cold terror. That face had a tremendous power over him. It was unbearably painful to look at that face and yet Bambi stood staring fixedly at it.
>
> For a long time the creature stood without moving. Then it stretched out a leg from high up near its face. Bambi had not even noticed that there was one there. But as that terrible leg was reaching out into the air Bambi was swept away by the mere gesture. In a flash he was back into the thicket he came from, and was running away.[5]

The bullet does not go home on that occasion. A few pages later, as Bambi is getting up his nerve to speak directly to an adult roebuck for the first time, the buck is suddenly shot dead by a concealed hunter and tumbles into the shrubbery in a bloody heap. Another buck, Ronno, has a leg smashed by a hunter's bullet and limps through the rest of the book. Bambi himself is shot and recovers slowly and painfully from a shoulder wound. His mother and a host of other animals are assassinated in an autumn game drive as man stalks through the forest shooting anything that moves. Besides being indiscriminately bloodthirsty, man is also perversely treacherous, as the full-grown Bambi learns when he finds a human hunter imitating the love call of his mate Faline.

But what gives Salten's *Bambi* its peculiar misanthropic force is that it depicts the human presence as not only dangerous but corrupting. Getting maimed or killed by man proves to be less dreadful than being befriended by Him. Wounded in the game drive, Faline's brother Gobo is taken away by the hunters and made into a pet. Months later, the recovered Gobo is dumped back into the forest with a collar around his neck, and begins preaching the good news of human kindness and mercy to the astonished deer. When man reappears in the forest, Gobo bounds joyously out to commune with his master— and is felled by a gut shot, to die screaming in a mess of blood and viscera. Even poor Gobo is better off in some ways than the dogs and other truly domesticated animals, who pass their lives in a psycho-pathic tumult of worshipful adoration, hatred, and fear of man and detestation of themselves.

Though the tame animals revere man as a jealous god and the wild animals abominate him as a mad demon, they agree on the fact of his dominion over nature. "No one can escape Him," says one forest creature after another throughout Salten's book. "He kills what He wants . . . He can do anything." "I worship Him, I serve Him," yelps a dog to a maimed fox. "Do you think you can oppose Him, poor creatures like you? He's all-powerful. He's above all of you. Everything we have comes from Him. Everything that lives or grows comes from Him."

This delusion is dispelled for Bambi at the end of the book. White-haired and half blind with age, Bambi's dying father takes his son to view the corpse of a murdered poacher, to learn thereby the great secret: man is only another dying animal, and the governance of the world lies elsewhere.

> "Do you see, Bambi," the old stag went on, "do you see how He's lying there dead, like one of us? Listen, Bambi. He isn't all-powerful as they say. Everything that lives and grows doesn't come from Him. He isn't above us. He's just the same as we are. He has the same fears, the same needs, and suffers in the same way. He can be killed like us, and then He lies helpless on the ground like all the rest of us, as you see Him now."
>
> There was a silence.
> "Do you understand me, Bambi?" said the old stag.
> "I think so," Bambi said in a whisper.
> "Then speak," the old stag commanded.
> Bambi was inspired, and said trembling, "There is Another who is over us all, over us and over Him."
> "Now I can go," said the old stag.[6]

The English translation of *Bambi* appeared in 1928. The translator was the young Whittaker Chambers, who had joined the Communist

Party not long before and was later to become famous as Richard Nixon's star witness in the Alger Hiss case. The English novelist and Nobelist John Galsworthy, a virulent opponent of hunting,[7] contributed a foreword to Salten's book, calling it "clear, illuminating . . . moving . . . a little masterpiece." "I particularly recommend it to sportsmen," he concluded acidly. Reviewers were ecstatic. "The author," wrote John Chamberlain in the *New York Times,* "has, while writing wholly of animals, somehow transcended his subject. He has given us the life story of a forest deer, and Felix Salten's comprehension of the entire universe as well . . . Throw away your Spinozan tomes on pantheism and read *Bambi*."[8]

Salten's books would probably be as little read today as Spinoza's were it not for another event of 1928. That September in a New York recording studio, a young film maker named Walt Disney managed to get a sound recording of "Turkey in the Straw" synchronized with the movements of a cartoon mouse. As a result of this cinematic breakthrough, Bambi's name would become virtually synonymous with "deer," though neither Disney nor Salten suspected it yet.

WALT Disney was born in Chicago in 1901. His father Elias was a perpetually unsuccessful, blue-nosed, Bible-thumping socialist who abominated liquor, tobacco, foul language, and hanky-panky. Disney's biographers generally agree that it was no coincidence that Elias' youngest son Walt grew up into a chain-smoking, hard-drinking, hard-cursing, hard-driven champion of free enterprise.

In 1906, Disney's father decided to try his hand at farming. He moved the family to a farm about 80 miles northeast of Kansas City. Disney always remembered his four years on that Missouri farm as the happiest part of his childhood, and the idyllic farmyard and the animal friends he made there turn up again and again in his films. Significantly, one of his few unpleasant memories of the place involved hunting. As Disney told the story in later life, the farm was overrun with rabbits when his family arrived, and he and his older brother Roy crept into the fields to watch them in their springtime mating rituals. Charmed and excited by all the March-hare antics, Walt spent the next few days memorializing them in his very first cartoons: childish sketches of cottontails playing peekaboo in the grass. But when Roy next returned to the fields, he brought along his air rifle and shot the biggest buck bunny he saw. Walt dissolved in tears when Roy broke the thrashing rabbit's neck, and he refused to touch the rabbit stew their mother served up that evening.[9] The contrast that this incident embodied between innocent animal desire and malign human contrivance was to recur in several Disney films. He would impress that love-and-death opposition on the world with particular force in *Bambi*.

Disney began his film career in 1920 making animated ads to be shown in movie theaters. The silent cartoons that he and his coworkers put together during the early 1920s, first in Kansas City and later in Hollywood, were nothing special and attracted no particular attention. But from 1928 on, Disney began to press toward heights of animation that no one had dreamed of reaching. Before Disney, the animated cartoon was only a species of trick film. Its whole purpose was to get a laugh, usually by depicting comic impossibilities. What Disney envisioned and drove his staff to create for him was *artistic* animation, rich and subtle and realistic enough to hold the attention of an audience over longer periods and engage its emotions more fully. Starting from the crude drawing, barnyard humor, and body-distortion gags of the first Mickey Mouse cartoons in 1928, Disney and his artists took less than a decade to learn how to inspire pity and terror as well as laughter with a twelve-per-second flow of talking-animal caricatures.

The world went wild over Disney in the 1930s. His productions were favorites not only with the general public but in intellectual circles as well. Drawings from *Snow White* and *The Three Little Pigs* were exhibited by the Metropolitan Museum and the Art Institute of Chicago.[10] Disney received a shelfful of honors, including honorary degrees from Harvard and Yale. "Taken as a whole," wrote Gilbert Seldes, "the work of Walt Disney is by far the most satisfying creation of the moving picture with sound . . . a great many people consider Disney as the great satirist of the machine age."[11] George Orwell thought it not incongruous to praise Henry Miller as a peer of Walt Disney.[12] In the collectivist intellectual climate of the 1930s, the communal character of animation production had a particular charm for many of the intelligentsia; Disney films were widely viewed as a kind of high-tech folktale turned out by an artistic collective, and the Disney studio was described as "the most successful art cooperative of all time." Disney encouraged this attitude. "We can't have individualists around here," he told interviewers, "not even me . . . Do you know how long it would have taken one man to make [*Snow White*]? I figured it out—just 250 years."[13] As one writer put it: "All of [Disney's] people are working, not for the expression of their own souls; they are working calmly and objectively toward an expression of the popular soul, the divination of which is not the result of one man's intuition but the outgrowth of years of organized, purposeful collective experience."[14]

Work on *Bambi* began in 1937. Although it was the second feature that Disney put into production, after *Snow White,* it was the fifth to be released, because of the unique difficulties it presented. Those difficulties were of two sorts: animation problems and story problems.

In an animated film, all attributes of the depicted universe are controlled by the animator. The animator's godlike jurisdiction over natural law has always been exploited to produce comic impossibilities for sight gags; but emotionally expressive changes in the properties of animated matter were a Disney specialty. In the mature Disney productions of the late 1930s and early 1940s, when the studio was at its artistic zenith, animated objects rise and fall, stretch on acceleration and squash on impact, in obedience to laws of physics that have been artistically distorted to enhance the emotions that the movement is intended to express or evoke. Golden-age Disney animation universalizes the pathetic fallacy; all things in the depicted world respond to the joy, grief, and rage of the viewpoint characters.

At first those characters were typically creatures of rounded outlines, rubbery consistency, and quasi-human form. Their rounded outlines made it easier to visualize and draw their movements in three dimensions (a sphere looks the same from all angles). Their rubbery appearance was a corollary of all the exaggerated squashing and stretching that gave their movements the conviction of overstatement. All the Disney talking-animal characters—Mickey Mouse, Donald Duck, the Three Little Pigs—were drawn as anthropomorphic bipeds with human hands, so that the animators could rely on the use of familiar gestures to express the characters' emotions.

But all of these painfully acquired skills and habits had to be discarded in approaching *Bambi.* Disney knew from the start that what Salten had to say about life, death, suffering, and God could not be put in the mouth of a cartoon deer that looked like Clarabelle Cow with antlers. To have the potential for tragedy, the animated deer had to move with authority and grace—which meant that an unprecedentedly realistic set of drawing conventions had to be developed. The *Bambi* project was put on hold while the animators spent month after month sketching deer, studying films of deer, and holding their noses and gagging as they watched artist-anatomist Rico Lebrun dissecting the rotting carcass of a newborn fawn.[15]

Learning to draw deer was one thing; making them move expressively was another. The animators were permitted to use whatever human facial expressions could be imposed on the stiff, elongated face of a deer, but no human body language was allowed. Vainly they pleaded to be allowed to introduce a few vertical postures: could Bambi rear up on his hind legs for one little gesture? Couldn't he at least put his front legs up on a stump? No, answered Disney and the film's directors;[16] human-looking postures and movements were forbidden. The animators gritted their teeth and began imagining themselves into the bodies of deer, learning to express human feelings with shifts in weight support and gait patterns, with head and neck posture, with flicks of the ears and tail.

The rubbery, squash-and-stretch animation techniques that the Disney studio had pioneered in the 1930s could not be used in *Bambi* either. A deer's body is all rigid segments and thin unyielding members, and it cannot undergo much distortion from one frame to the next if it is going to look like a deer. Unusual precision thus had to be exercised in tracing and interpolating animation drawings in *Bambi*. Maintaining this precision was the job of the lower echelons of the animators' hierarchy. Disney's master animators usually only sketched every eighth or tenth frame of a film, and their widely separated rough sketches were supplemented, tidied up, and painted onto transparent plastic cels by a long train of subordinates: assistant animators, inbetweeners, cleanup men, inkers and painters. As you descended through the ranks of this hierarchy at Disney, from supervising animators down to inkers and painters, the artists' pay, status, and screen credits dropped accordingly—and the percentage of women employees rose, from zero at the top to 100 percent at the bottom.[17]

To everyone's dismay, the first rushes of the *Bambi* animation showed the limbs of the deer jiggling and vibrating as if seized by some nervous tremor whenever the characters moved slowly. Tiny errors in the copying and tracing were destroying the precision needed to maintain the illusion of constant slow movement in those long, thin, rigid legs. The only way to get rid of the tracing errors was to bypass the middlemen and hand the animators' sketches directly to the ink and paint department. To finish the sequences involving slow movement, the lowly inkers would have to learn to combine the better-paid jobs of the inbetweeners and cleanup artists in a single operation, inking the inbetween drawings directly onto the cels.[18]

This procedure was followed in *Bambi*. It had never been used before and will probably never be used again in commercial animation.[19] Even at the ink and paint department's depression-era wages, it was ruinously expensive,[20] and its subversion of the studio's artistic hierarchy must have contributed to the severe labor unrest that racked the Disney organization in the early 1940s. But the precise control over slow movement that it permitted lends a unique beauty to the finished movie. Smooth, slow animated movement requires painstaking labor, and most animators tend to avoid it by moving their characters in quick bursts from one static pose to another, producing a staccato rhythm of incident that is characteristic of much animation (and is exploited to elegant comic effect in Chuck Jones's Roadrunner cartoons). By contrast, the rhythms of *Bambi* are *largo* and *maestoso*. A dreamy languor pervades the film. The animated deer move through the forest with deliberate and sentient delicacy; autumn leaves fall with stately precision through shifting patterns of light to nestle weightlessly into the forest floor. The timeless, floating quality that results from all this minutely controlled slow movement makes a statement about the natural order that is more powerful than anything in the film's written continuity.

The evolution of that continuity began with the first story treatments in 1937. The early sketches preserved in the Disney Archives generally follow Salten, but they focus more closely on the survival lessons that Bambi gets from the other forest creatures. This gives them a robust Darwinian flavor reminiscent of Kipling's Jungle Books, as though Bambi were a sort of four-legged Mowgli. Most of the writers' ingenuity seems to have gone into thinking up cornball dialogue and Silly Symphony sight gags.

But between late 1937 and early 1939, a fierce earnestness crept over the writers working on *Bambi*. Long passages from Thoreau were mimeographed and circulated. What looks like a sketch for a song lyric is written in agonized, solemnly awful heroic couplets ("Perplexed before the catastrophes of earth / That stalk you from the moment of your birth, / Your span shall know no respite from the pain / Of racking hunger, stinging sleet and rain"). Script drafts began to center on human cruelty and what the animals have to say about it. One sketch of the animals' debate on man's place in nature quotes verbatim from some of the most sardonically misanthropic passages of Don Marquis' *archy and mehitabel*. By September 1, 1939, the film's story editor Perce Pearce was telling Disney that all predators other than *Homo sapiens* had to be excised from the script. "There's nobody swooping down and eating someone else and their one common enemy is Man. That's the conflict there—and keep it simple."[21]

What explains this shift in tone? September 1, 1939, was also the day when German armor struck across the border into Poland and plunged Europe into the first phase of World War II. There are reasons for thinking that the increasingly tense and despairing script materials produced by the Disney writers during 1938 and 1939 reflect the gathering storm in Europe and the Pacific. The team working on the *Bambi* continuity were well aware of their story's relevance to the war. "Psychologically, that forest fire—this destruction—and then you see you can't stop life from going on," said story editor Larry Morey to Disney in March 1940, "has a terrific impact today with the trouble in the world today."[22]

Other reasons for thinking that the grim tone of the early *Bambi* scripts has something to do with the outbreak of World War II are furnished by an oddly parallel short cartoon produced over at the MGM studios during the same dark closing months of 1939. The cartoon, *Peace on Earth,* opens with two baby squirrels asking their grandfather what "men" were. He explains that they were "uniformed monsters" who were continually at war with one another. After he tells his grandchildren the story of how men fought each other to

171

The happy forest animals celebrating the end of the human race in Hugh Harman's 1939 cartoon *Peace on Earth*. (Turner Entertainment Co.)

extinction, the cartoon ends with the cute forest animals frolicking through a landscape of rusting weapons and bullet-riddled helmets, singing Christmas carols that proclaim peace on earth, good will toward men. *Peace on Earth* received a great deal of praise and numerous awards, including a 1939 Academy Award nomination.[23]

The first reasonably complete sketch of the *Bambi* continuity that survives appears on internal evidence to have been written during the three months after the Nazi invasion of Poland.[24] It is saturated with bitter detestation of human beings and their weaponry. The fawns Bambi and Faline are shot at (but missed) as they play in a sunny meadow. "Whenever man comes into the forest, there's nothing but fear!" cry the forest animals. "He kills without mercy! He's killed many of my family!" The deer gather for a colloquium on human depravity. "Will He never stop hunting us?" wails one buck. The following dialogue ensues between Bambi's mother and the young stag Ronno:

> M: They say that some day He'll come and live with us. He'll be gentle then, and play with us. And we'll be friends with Him—and there will be love in the forest.
>
> R: (angrily) Let Him stay where He is and leave us alone! He's vile and loathsome and I hate Him!
>
> M: (quietly) You shouldn't talk like that, Ronno.
>
> R: (fiercely) And why not! Hasn't He murdered us ever since we can remember? Every one of us—our sisters—our mothers—our brothers—ever since we came into this world, He's given us no peace—but has killed us wherever we've shown our heads. And now we're going to be friends with Him and love Him—what nonsense!
>
> M: (quietly) Love is no nonsense—it has to come.[25]

Shortly after Bambi's mother declares her faith in the possibility of human love, she and Bambi are stalked by a hunter. They flee, but a shot rings out; we see her jerk in mid-leap and fall dead. As Bambi wanders the forest crying for his lost mother, he hears what he thinks is her voice and runs toward it joyously—to discover a hunter with a deer call, who shoots him. He runs over a hill and collapses. Driven back onto his feet by the frantic urging of his father and the other forest animals, Bambi staggers along, bleeding and gasping with pain, back to the thicket where he was born. He begins calling for his mother again and falls down, apparently dead. His anxious father watches him until at last the unconscious fawn begins to breathe once more.

Man reenters the forest after Bambi has grown into an antlered buck. Hunting dogs run in man's vanguard, praising His omnipotence and tearing cornered animals to bits. Pheasants and quail are shot down as they flee in terrified hysteria. Friend Hare, the prototype of Thumper, intercepts a bullet and dies at Bambi's feet, murmuring, "I don't understand—What have I ever done to Them?" After a fire set by the intruders devastates the forest, Bambi's father leads him through the smouldering stumps and ashes to a charred human cadaver, over which they exchange Salten's dialogue. The film ends in a scene of rebirth, with the forest sprouting anew and Bambi glimpsing Faline with two newborn fawns.

In succeeding drafts, all this was toned down and the script grew simpler and sweeter as the screenwriters gave up their attempts to interpret the human condition within their story framework. All the animals' assessments of humanity—Gobo's tragic delusions, the dialogue of the deer on human depravity, the dogs' hymn to human power—were cut out for one reason or another, until no dialogue remained to establish the animals' superstitious awe of man. The climactic scene with the cooked cadaver was accordingly no longer a resolution of anything. It was reluctantly dropped from the film in the last stages of production, and with it went the last vestiges of Salten's attempted reconciliation of man with nature. The only remaining discussion of the human presence is Bambi's question, "What happened, Mother? Why did we all run?" and Mother's slow, portentous response: "Man [long pause] was in the forest."[26]

The thorny uncertainties of Salten's story are replaced in the film by the crystalline simplicities of myth. Deer biology is distorted to mythological effect by making the deaths and births of the deer correspond with winter and spring respectively and shifting their mating season to the springtime; Bambi, like John Barleycorn and Osiris, is born and sows his seed in the spring and is cut down in the fall. Some of the mythic elements in *Bambi* are specifically Christian, particularly the introductory nativity scene. After the adoring animals finish hailing the birth of the young prince and leave the thicket, the camera pulls back to show mother and child nestled in a circlet of thorns, while a remote and godlike father looks down from a heavenly crag. This borrowing of Christian symbolism was not wholly unconscious; Pearce referred to the tableau as "that madonna-like picture."[27]

The madonna image in *Bambi* may have leaked across from the setting of Schubert's "Ave Maria" at the end of *Fantasia,* which originally centered on an icon of the madonna and child.[28] *Fantasia* was also influential for its elimination of sound effects and dialogue, which Disney and his directors tried to emulate in *Bambi.*[29] The final script contains less than a thousand spoken words, and all the hero's lines put together account for less than two hundred of them. Almost the only sound effects in *Bambi* are a few gunshots, rabbit thumps, and bird songs. *Bambi* is an essentially silent movie: a wordless, rhythmical ballet performed to an orchestral accompaniment. The alienation of man from the natural order is symbolized by barring the human presence completely from the universal dance. Man is represented only by ominous, lurching music that—unlike the rest of the score—is unaccompanied by onscreen choreography.

As the motif of the reconciliation of man with nature evaporated from the film, a new narrative structure came into being. The succession of events in *Bambi* forms a huge palindrome pivoting on the death of Bambi's mother. This sort of A-B-A structure was a favorite device of Disney's. Many of his best and most characteristic short films—*Skeleton Dance, Flowers and Trees, The Band Concert, Through the Mirror, The Old Mill,* the "Sorcerer's Apprentice" and "Night on Bald Mountain" sequences from *Fantasia*—move from an initial harmony through dark chaos back to a restoration of the initial harmony. This pattern is particularly noticeable and elaborate in *The Old Mill,* which was undertaken as a trial run for the feature films. The palindrome in *Bambi* becomes evident when all the sequences centered on the minor characters are left out of the picture (see the accompanying table). How much of this structure was consciously imposed is hard to say, but it is certain that the minutely detailed repetition of incident in the A and C blocks was deliberate and that much of it was inserted into the film by Walt Disney himself.[30]

It is still less clear how much of the elaborate psychological apparatus in *Bambi* was consciously intended by the filmmakers. The first English translation of Carl Jung's *Archetypes of the Collective Unconscious* appeared in 1939. Around the end of that year, the Disney conception of Faline abruptly changed from a shy fawn to a teasing, seductive minx who repeatedly shows up as a double of Bambi's reflection in the water. The new, 1939-model Faline bears a suspiciously close resemblance to Jung's description of the Anima archetype.[31] Moreover, the Two Winds sequence, in which Bambi and Faline are picked up and whirled away by the night winds in a transport of passion, is strikingly reminiscent of the images Jung uses to describe the archetype of the Shadow.[32] Much of this imagery was added by Walt Disney.[33] Although it may be hard to believe that Disney had been reading Jung's new book, it is harder still to believe that all the Jungian figures in *Bambi* are either coincidences or spontaneous archetypal eruptions from the studio's collective unconscious. Perhaps a couple of coincidentally Jungian images put forward by Disney suggested others to screenwriters who had been following the Californian tradition of keeping up with new trends in psychotherapy.

The Freudian devices in the film are equally numerous. Salten, as one might expect of a Jewish intellectual in the Vienna of the 1920s, put a generous amount of oedipal tension into his book, including primal scenes both observed and fantasized and an attempted parricide.[34] These incidents are dropped in the film, but the book's monumentally remote, Kafkesque father figure is retained. The Disney version resolves some of the oedipal conflict by remaking Bambi's mate in his mother's image. The equation of the two begins with the

---

Disney's *Bambi*: Motifs and Structure

A1. Birth, adoration, stag on crag. (Theme: "Love Is a Song.")

B1. Falling, getting up: Mother supervising. Frightening forces of nature (thunderstorm): Mother protects. [*Dance with mother in meadow. Theme: "I Bring You a Song."*]* Passes through water to meet Faline.

C1. Drink, see Faline's reflection, retreat and fall, kiss, chase. Fighting stags. Crows flying: Great Prince warns of danger. ("Man's Theme" on soundtrack.) Mother and Bambi in peril: flight, separation ("Mother? Mother!"). Parents rescue Bambi. Near-death: shot not fatal.

D1. Explanation and warning: death ("Man was in the forest.")

E1. Seasonal-change production number (autumn).

F1. Snow: hunger. (Wordless chorus on soundtrack.)

MOTHER'S DEATH: PIVOT

F2. Snow: abandonment. (Same wordless chorus on soundtrack.)

E2. Seasonal-change production number (spring).

D2. Explanation and warning: love ("Twitterpated").

C2. Drink, see Faline's reflection, retreat and fall, kiss, chase. Fighting stags. [*Dance with Faline in meadow. Theme: "I Bring You a Song."*]* Crows flying; Great Prince warns of danger. ("Man's Theme" on soundtrack.) Faline and Bambi in peril: flight, separation ("Faline? Faline!"). Bambi rescues Faline. Near-death: shot not fatal.

B2. Falling, getting up: Father supervising. Frightening forces of nature (fire): Father protects. Passes through water to meet Faline.

A2. Rebirth, adoration, stag on crag. (Theme: "Love Is a Song.")

---

*The dance sequence indicated in italics is a repeated motif but does not conform to the overall A-B-A pattern.

Two Winds sequence, which has the same locale and the same musical accompaniment as Bambi's earlier romp on the meadow with his mother. His dance with Faline culminates in a symbolic orgasm—a sustained wordless cry from the tenors, a cascade of flower petals into the dark water, and so forth—whereupon the scene fades out, to be replaced by a shot of the two lovers sleeping together in dead leaves beneath a cold autumnal dawn. When Faline opens her eyes, they have changed from a virginal blue to a warm russet, leaving her indistinguishable from Bambi's late mother.

Freud or no Freud, such a morning-after shot would not have passed the film industry's censors in 1942 if it had involved human characters,[35] and a few warning flags went up over the sexual symbolism in *Bambi* after the studio staff got to see the preliminary version in 1940.[36] It may seem surprising, in view of Disney's reputation for producing nothing but doggedly clean-minded children's entertainment, that he would deliberately put out anything with obvious sexual content. But early Disney films are not so studiedly innocent as the later ones became;[37] and although Disney was known to walk out of private showings of films he found suggestive, and once denounced typical Hollywood movies as "putrid, pornographic shit" at the top of his voice at an Academy Award dinner,[38] he seemed to find animal sexuality a different matter—fascinating, innocent, and beautiful. He kept in his office a reel of pasted-together film clips of wild animals copulating, which he liked to show to selected visitors.[39] His Oscar-winning 1954 documentary *The Vanishing Prairie* shows a buffalo giving birth, a sequence that Disney found unobjectionable but that caused the film to be banned as indecent in New York.

The contrast between human pollution and animal innocence that is implicit in these attitudes of Disney finds a classic and powerful expression in *Bambi*. The film portrays the natural world as a realm of beauty, saturated with innocent love in all its varieties—hot erotic love, warm maternal love, strong paternal love. The amorous warmth of this sylvan pastorale is subtly intensified by the animals' permanently dilated pupils, like those of a Renaissance courtesan on belladonna.[40] The one important source of discord in the magic forest is the human presence, which manifests itself as a wave of mad slaughter and ecological catastrophe. The Freudian opposition between the instincts of life and death, between Eros and Thanatos, is forcefully equated throughout the film with the symbolic opposition of man to nature; and no resolution of the conflict is offered or even hinted at, as it had been in Salten's novel.

All these psychological and symbolic devices chugging away in Disney's *Bambi*—its erotic and oedipal symbolism, its archetypal characters, its invocation of Christian and pagan mythology, its perfectly choreographed universal dances of all things not human, its A-B-A architecture silently preaching the Eternal Recurrence, its superbly executed and controlled animation, its occasionally breathtaking visual beauty, and its despairing subliminal consciousness of the implacable onrush of World War II—give the movie the force of a sledgehammer for many viewers, despite its pervasive and repellent cuteness. "I came out of *Bambi* on my hands and knees," recalled director Richard Williams in a 1989 interview.[41] The film has been pushing all the buttons of film critics and reducing them to incoherence for fifty years. Its 1982 rerelease prompted Pauline Kael first to denounce it as "gooey," "uncannily awful," and "berserk" and then to turn around two weeks later and praise its "primal power."[42] Reviewing *Bambi* during its 1988 theatrical release, Roger Ebert described it as "a parable of sexism, nihilism, and despair, portraying absentee fathers and passive mothers in a world of death and violence," and called it unsuitable for young and impressionable children.[43] When *Bambi* first came out it was greeted by the London *Times* as the single great masterpiece produced thus far by the cinema.[44] At the other extreme, Manny Farber attacked it in the *New Republic* as "entirely unpleasant . . . . an affectation of reality, like a Maxfield Parrish painting."[45] Similar denunciations of *Bambi* as mere photographic realism became nearly universal among critics when fashions in animated graphics styles changed abruptly in the 1950s.[46]

HUNTERS have criticized *Bambi* even more severely. The first attack on the film by America's outdoorsmen came in the summer of 1942 from the editor of *Outdoor Life,* Raymond J. Brown. Denouncing the movie as "the worst insult ever offered in any form to American sportsmen," Brown complained that *Bambi* showed hunters engaging in low, unsportsmanlike practices—killing a doe, shooting deer in the spring, hunting deer with dogs, and setting the autumn woods ablaze to drive game. He called on Disney to correct this slur by adding a disclaimer to the film, to tell audiences that this sort of foul play was of course not typical of America's 15 million law-abiding hunters, who help to preserve our wild heritage through their selfless good citizenship, and so on and so forth.[47]

Disney's response to this demand was simple, clever, and decisive. American sportsmen, he replied, had not been slurred because Salten's story was about *German* hunters. In 1942, the first year of America's war against Nazi Germany, there was not much left to be said after that. Although Brown protested that Disney's Bambi was no Black Forest roebuck, but a Virginia whitetail whose forest friends included such distinctively American animals as opossums, skunks, raccoons, gray squirrels, chipmunks, and bobwhite quail,[48] Disney regarded the matter as closed. No apology or disclaimer was ever offered.

A more straightforward defense of *Bambi* was put forward in the July 1942 issue of *Audubon Magazine* by Donald Culross Peattie, a leading member of America's growing community of birdwatchers and conservationists. Peattie hotly denied that the movie had misrepresented anything; American hunters were just as rotten as Disney had painted them. Every fall, he insisted, the Forest Service finds the woods full of maimed and dying does and fawns. "Either the hunters who shot them cannot tell does and fawns from bucks," Peattie concluded, "or they don't give a damn." As for the use of fire, Peattie found it suspicious that forest fires in California's mountains had for many years always begun on the first day of deer season. Peattie admitted that "spring hunting is not practiced much," but he thought it made little difference to the deer or to Disney's audience whether deer were shot down "against a background of spring greenery or autumn splendor."

The Audubon Society was not opposed to hunting as such. Still, Peattie noted, it had been working since the turn of the century "to foster in children . . . . a sympathetic understanding of wild life" through its junior auxiliaries; and the aim and effect of Disney's *Bambi* was exactly the same. "Speaking only for myself," he went on,

I would hazard the guess that the National Audubon Society, both among its officers and by referendum to its constituency and membership, would endorse *Bambi* . . . However, our endorsement is not needed. The message of *Bambi* is sweeping the country; it is appealing above all to the men and women of tomorrow who are now our children. To a child, in his simplicity, the life of an innocent, harmless, and beautiful animal is just as precious as that of a human being, so many of whom do not appear altogether innocent and harmless and beautiful.[49]

In the half-century that has gone by since the film came out, hunters' attacks on *Bambi* have become even more strident and insistent; but they no longer criticize Disney's film as a slur on the honor of sportsmen. The line commonly encountered nowadays is that the movie is nature-fakery, a fantastically misleading distortion of the scientific facts about the behavior of wild beasts, and that children who see it are thereby gulled into a foolish sentimentalism about wildlife and an unjustifiable hatred of hunters. Many hunting writers seem to think that if *Bambi* and other Disney products could somehow be suppressed, opposition to hunting would evaporate. The prevailing view in the hunting community today was expressed in a 1973 speech by Warren Page, formerly Shooting Editor of *Field and Stream:*

The serious hunter of the U.S. [is] under strong and conspirated and deliberate and planned attack and the causes of our ridicule are brutally simple. Every one of them, unfortunately, emotional. It's very difficult to answer by a rational approach. For one thing, in this country we have undergone an entire generation of brainwashing. Not only our kids but our wives, our brothers, our mothers, our cousins, our brothers-in-law have for 25 years been subjected to constant film and TV presentations of the Disney myth. In the Wonderful World of Disney animals are cuter than people. Wolves spend their time playing like kittens. The lion and the lamb love one another and only man is the bastard in the black hat . . . whose chief aim is the spilling of Bambi's blood. Now this is the Bambi Syndrome. The Disney films may not have started out that way, but once it became clear that sentimentality and outright anthropomorphism would make money, that's the way the films went . . . They deliberately misinform viewers of basic biological facts.[50]

Bambi-baiting pervades the defensive rhetoric of today's outdoorsmen. "Too many anti-hunters," writes the rod-and-gun columnist Jim

Wilson, "believe in the Bambi quality of animals . . . The animals that so concern those people are not real, but are idealized versions. Those animals don't procreate or eliminate wastes or eat one another, they gaily romp and play their lives away . . . these people never knew or don't want to know that death is as quotidian in the wild as sucking air in and blowing it out."[51] "In other countries," laments another hunter, "hunters are admired. The difference is that Americans live in a world of fantasy where all animals are supposed to be Bambi."[52] Antitrapping protestors, snorts a furriers' representative, are "under the impression that if these animals aren't trapped, they live happily ever after, like Bambi or something."[53]

Nobody wants to be stigmatized as either a Bambi-lover or a Bambi-killer, and so both proponents and opponents of hunting tend to get edgy when the name of Bambi comes up. A recent article in *Field and Stream* urges hunters to start protesting against the "Bambi-killer jokes" they are subjected to when they check their guns in at airports.[54] Following the 1982 Everglades deer hunt at which Cleveland Amory suggested that God is a deer, a successful hunter displayed his kill to a reporter. "Not bad for a low-down Bambi-killer, hey?" he quipped.[55] Amory himself, on the other hand, resents being thought of as a "namby-pamby Bambi-lover."[56] The philosopher Tom Regan likewise insists that he and other animal-rights activists are not "crazy, emotional, and uneducated" people who "all have Bambi complexes."[57]

American hunters tend to cluster toward the right of the political spectrum, and it is not surprising that they have picked up the scent of Marxism and atheism in *Bambi*. In an attack on *Bambi* in the March 1980 issue of *Field and Stream,* George Reiger suggests that the whole Bambi syndrome is somehow connected with leftist ideology. "Liberals," writes Reiger, "argue that if they are permitted to take away guns, man will give up hunting and war."[58] Conservatives know better. Felix Salten, who it seems had been driven into the liberal delusion by "the senseless slaughter of World War I," dreamed that "if man could first be made to amend his attitudes toward nature, then in time he could also amend his view of himself." The novel he wrote accordingly sentimentalized nature and vilified man. Reiger imagines that that combination must have appealed to an idealistic young Communist like Whittaker Chambers, who was like Salten "unable to accept the impersonal realities of nature." Reiger concludes his article by hinting darkly that the identity of Bambi's translator is being intentionally suppressed by liberal Washington bureaucrats—a cover-up evidenced by the disappearance of Chambers' name from the novel's catalogue cards in the Library of Congress.

But what Disney himself "and his staff of little helpers" are guilty of in Reiger's eyes is not Marxism but "blasphemy"—specifically, mockery of Christ. "In Disney's version," Reiger complains, "Bambi is not just another deer born into the woods, he is the 'young Prince,' a Christ-like figure to whom all other creatures turn for guidance . . . Naturally, once Bambi is raised in status from mere deer to Jesus Whitetail Superstar, man's hunting of deer becomes a crime comparable to the persecution of Christ."

How much truth is there in what Reiger and other hunting journalists say about the Bambi syndrome? Clearly, none of the things that hunters object to in the film originated with Disney. The "fawn" chorus from the *Bacchae* of Euripides is virtually a synopsis of *Bambi*. The vision of the wilderness as an Eden and of man as a destructive intruder into the harmony of nature has ancient roots, extending back into classical and medieval thinking. Wounded deer have been symbols of injured innocence for centuries; the specific identification of the hunted stag with Christ dates to the Middle Ages. Moral indignation over hunting flared up now and then even in classical antiquity and has become steadily more commonplace in Western culture since the Renaissance. The notion that all this is somehow Walt Disney's fault is wishful thinking on the part of many outdoorsmen.

Yet if Disney did not invent the symbolism that portrays hunted deer as ravished maidens and martyred princes of peace, he gave it a mass audience, an irresistible graphic expression, and a mythical embodiment it would not otherwise have had. The mythical stature of the figure of Bambi is evident from its symbolic use in common speech and literary and political rhetoric.

Bambi is emblematic of deer in general. The simplest way to experience this is to stand for an hour or two in front of a deer pen at a zoo; some child or its mother is sure to point to a deer and exclaim, "Look! Bambi!" (I have heard the name applied to sika, axis, white-tailed, and mule deer, as well as to various more or less gracile antelopes, up to and including the big cowlike nilgai of India.) The use of the

Bambi's mother meets George Bush in a 1989 editorial cartoon by Mike Lane. (*Baltimore Evening Sun*)

name to mean "deer" is widespread in the news media, and has international currency.[59] Scientists are as prone to this usage as anyone: Jane Goodall describes newborn Thompson's gazelles as "miniature Bambis,"[60] and I once heard a biologist who was unable to think of the word "fawn" substitute "Bambi" for it. Even some jocular hunters like to call their quarry "Bambis."[61] Bambi seems to be on his way to becoming a lower-case generic noun, as his predecessor Reynard the Fox did in the French language.

As the stereotypic deer, Bambi symbolizes all those things that deer in general symbolize—in particular, harmless, dewy-eyed innocence. Denouncing President Reagan's drug policies in a speech to the 1988 Democratic convention, Senator John Glenn protested that "you can't talk like Rambo and act like Bambi."[62] The huge, vaguely sexy eyes of the Disney deer are proverbial.[63] Associated as it is with bedroom eyes, naiveté, and innocence, the name "Bambi" (like "Fawn") is sometimes given to girls but never to boys, even though the fictional Bambi is male.[64] Bambi also symbolizes wilderness and the natural order. This was seen clearly when James Watt became U.S. Secretary of the Interior: editorial cartoons showed the forest animals shouting, "Run, Bambi, Run!" and comedian Mark Russell announced that Bambi was leaving for Canada.[65] During the national furor in 1989 over the importation and sale of semiautomatic rifles, an editorial cartoon in the *Baltimore Sun* showed Bambi whispering "Mother?" to a smoking mound of hamburger, bones, and eyeballs, while President Bush lurked behind a tree with an AK-47.

In short, hunters are probably right to think that *Bambi* has had a pervasive effect on western attitudes toward hunting, wildlife, and the natural order. Children who see the film often appear to be deeply disturbed by the killing of Bambi's mother, and people sometimes confess in private that seeing *Bambi* on one of its periodic rereleases turned them against hunting or made vegetarians or conservationists out of them. Popular reluctance to control the spread of Lyme disease by wiping out whitetailed deer has been blamed on the Bambi syndrome.[66] Some historians of forestry think that the forest-fire sequence in *Bambi* was what drove the Forest Service to launch a no-burn policy two years later.[67] Once in a fancy Arizona restaurant, I saw a woman at an adjoining table hurl her napkin to the floor and cry, "It's like eating *Bambi*!" when a waiter announced roast pronghorn as the evening's special entrée. An ex-hunter interviewed by John Mitchell for his book on hunting said that his attitude was changed by his two daughters, who "got the idea every deer is named Bambi. And I began to wonder what is sport and what isn't." In the last paragraphs of the book, Mitchell has his own first buck held in his rifle's sights. Suddenly he stops, ejects his cartridge, and collapses shaking uncontrollably after staring into "the eyes—the huge glistening eyes that had torn my own away from the cross hairs on the shoulder."[68] Elsewhere, he frankly attributes his hesitation to the Bambi syndrome:

> I am torn by ambivalence when it comes to the white-tailed deer. Walt Disney got to me early. I wept for Bambi when the huntsmen slew its mama; yet today I count deerslayers among my closest friends, and understand what drives them to it and bear no grudge and, in fact, occasionally join them afield, bearing arms. But I have never shot a deer, or at one. Perhaps someday I will. Perhaps I won't.[69]

Bambi has also exerted an important indirect influence as the prototype from which the modern nature film evolved. The first such films to reach a mass audience were Disney's True-Life Adventures of the 1950s, which took much of their theme and format from *Bambi.* The True-Life Adventures were so novel and successful that they defined the nature-movie genre and established its subsequent conventions. Two central conventions of the Disney wildlife films and their successors derive from *Bambi:* the exclusion of the human presence from the picture (and, by implication, from the natural order), and the Eternal Recurrence in which a final return to the starting place marks one round of an ancient and unchanging cycle. ("Again an ending is but a beginning. With the advent of Spring, Nature's miracles have come full circle . . . In the turning cycles of time and tide and eternal change, Nature will forever create and re-create—and in her timeless pattern, replenish the earth again and again with her Secrets of Life."[70])

The antihunter bias that outdoorsmen complain of in Disney films is pervasive in animated cartoons from other studios as well. It is implicit, at least in part, in the technique of animation itself, which is why most of the best animated cartoons are about talking mice, ducks, and rabbits. Because animated drawings must be kept extremely simple, they cannot reproduce the complexities and subtleties of photographed human expression and movement. Instead, animation drawings tend to rely on exaggeration for their effectiveness. When human characters are animated with too little exaggeration, they come across as stiff and wooden (Snow White). If animated with a lot of exaggeration, they can come to life—but only as comic grotesques (the Seven Dwarfs) or menacing villains (the Wicked Witch). Animated people are therefore almost always defective in one way or another, whereas animated animals, with their humanlike speech and intelligence, are better than the real thing. In animation, people accordingly seem less interesting and attractive than animals.

The expense of drawing a movie frame by frame also tends to restrict the use of animation to stories that cannot be made convincing by photographic means—which usually means stories with talking-animal protagonists. The enormous artistic and rhetorical energy of animation is thus intrinsically linked to animalitarian sentiments. The most appealing and memorable animated characters, from Gertie the Dinosaur in 1914 to Roger Rabbit in 1988, have all been anthropomorphized beasts; and the plot lines of many animated films, from *Dumbo* and *Bambi* down to *The Secret of NIMH, Watership Down,* and *The Plague Dogs,* have revolved around the persecution or killing of animal protagonists by the human race in general.

The popularity of the animal characters produced by Disney and other animated-filmmakers accounts in part for the fact that books, movies, and toys made for young children today are dominated by dressed-up, anthropomorphic talking animals. This domination predates Disney, but it is relatively recent and may not long antedate the first animated cartoons.

Children's literature in the English language started to emerge as a separate genre around the end of the seventeenth century. The first books written specifically for children were grim Puritan religious tracts, intended to instill a fear of God and hellfire in unregenerate youth.[71] These were soon joined by a variety of secular but equally didactic works, including Aesop and other moral fables about talking animals.[72] A second type of talking-animal story, the animal biography, made its appearance in the late 18th century. The heroes or narrators of such stories, from Dorothy Kilner's *The Life and History of a Mouse* in 1783 down through *Black Beauty* to *Bambi* and *Watership Down,* are realistically depicted beasts who go naked and walk on all fours but think human thoughts. Like other early children's books, the eighteenth-century animal biographies were written with a didactic purpose—in this case, to persuade children to treat animals with kindness and sympathy. Most subsequent animal biographies have had the same moral intent. A third variety of talking-animal story, the animal burlesque, stands the animals on their hind legs and furnishes them with human clothes, technology, society, and manners as well as speech. This subgenre has antecedents in such folktales as "Puss in Boots," and it goes back in western literature at least to the ancient Greek mock epic "The Froggo-Mousian War" *(Batrachomyomachia)*. But its first appearance in children's literature was from 1807 to 1809 in a number of English picture books—*The Butterfly's Ball, The Peacock at Home, The Lion's Masquerade, The Lion's Parliament,* and so on—which showed dressed-up animals imitating human customs and foibles.[73]

During the first half of the nineteenth century, talking animals,

186

fairies, and other such fanciful elements fell into disfavor in books intended for children, as the rising tides of evangelism and early-Victorian moral earnestness moved children's literature back again toward the preachy didacticism of the early 1700s. Wrote one American schoolbook author in 1823,

> Beasts, reptiles and insects are not represented in this volume, as the equals of rational beings; because such a supposition is repugnant to nature, science, and correct moral sentiment. Most of the fables so long employed in schools, are particularly improper for small children, who should be taught by literal examples, before they can comprehend figures of rhetoric . . . The fancy of converting inferior animals into "teachers of children" has been carried to ridiculous extravagance.[74]

"Dialogue between wolves and sheep, cats and mice," sniffed the American reformer Lyman Cobb in 1832, "is as destructive of truth and morality as it is contrary to the principles of nature and philosophy."[75]

But beast fables and animal burlesques again became standard fare in later Victorian children's books and have generally gained ground over moral homilies and fairy tales during the twentieth century. Today, talking-animal stories actually comprise a majority of the books aimed at young American children.[76]

Young children's toys have also become animal-oriented within this century. Stuffed animals, such as the Gingham Dog and Calico Cat of Eugene Field's 1889 verse "The Duel," were occasionally made for children in the nineteenth century,[77] but they were not common. When the teddy-bear craze struck the U.S. in 1906, there was a serious debate over the effect that stuffed animals would have on children; some feared that small girls who played with plush bears instead of baby dolls would be inadequately prepared for motherhood.[78] Although teddy bears did not cut into the U.S. birth rate, they did precipitate a permanent change in the furnishings of the nursery. We now regard stuffed animals as archetypal toys for children of both sexes. As archetypes, they have tended to replace the work- and human-oriented toys—dolls, drums, trumpets, popguns, rocking horses—that the nineteenth century associated with childhood (and that are still conventionally shown protruding from Santa's sack).

It is not clear why this animalization of children's culture has taken place, and the change has attracted surprisingly little comment. One of the few people to comment on it at length was J. R. R. Tolkien, who deplored animalitarian sentiments from a Christian standpoint and suggested that adults force talking-animal stories and stuffed animals on children because such things are somehow seen as up-to-date and scientific.[79] This seems implausible. An alternative explanation, based on Jungian rather than Christian premises, is offered by D. D. Pitts, who thinks that we subconsciously hate animals as symbols of "our instinctual or (pejoratively) bestial nature," but feel guilty about hating them and about repressing that instinctual nature in ourselves and our children.[80] We therefore, says Pitts, try to expiate our guilt by making the children listen to talking-animal stories. This explanation seems just as far-fetched as Tolkien's.

In recent years, the spread of talking animals in productions intended for children has undoubtedly been furthered by the fact that anthropomorphic beasts are racially and ethnically neutral (and therefore universally acceptable) in a way that human figures cannot be.[81] But the animalization of children's culture is not simply a product of our post-1960s desire to avoid stepping on anybody's ethnic sensitivities. The change was well underway before World War I, at a time when insulting jokes about minorities were still a staple of American humor. Moreover, some classic children's books (for example, the Dr. Doolittle and Oz books) contain sympathetically presented talking animals side by side with offensive racial stereotypes.

However we choose to account for it, the preponderance of animal fables, biographies, and burlesques in the entertainment and educational media we produce for young children is a real phenomenon. It embodies an unspoken belief—and a message to children—that animals are good and innocent, whereas human beings are darker and more dubious creatures. In teaching our children about the world they are to inherit, we prefer to leave human society out of the picture, or at least to approach it through talking-animal allegories, until childhood and innocence have started drawing to a close.

TEN

A Fatal Disease of Nature

The other anthropoid apes were safe
In the great southern rain-forest and hardly changed
In a million years: but the race of man was made
By shock and agony . . . Blood-snuffing rats:
But never blame them: a wound was made in the brain
When life became too hard, and has never healed.
It is there that they learned trembling religion and
    blood-sacrifice,
It is there that they learned to butcher beasts and to
    slaughter men,
And hate the world.

—Robinson Jeffers

DARWIN had tiptoed around the touchy question of human evolution in the *Origin of Species,* saying only that "light will be thrown on the origin of man and his history" by his hypothesis. His critics immediately focused on that evasion as a weak link in the Darwinian theory. Natural selection, they argued, could never account for the evolution of man. Our natural weapons seemed too feeble, our moral impulses too disinterested, and our intellects too vast to have arisen through mere survival of the fittest among apes and savages.[1] These peculiar human traits therefore required some special cause—or special Providence—to explain them.

Darwin published his own story about human origins in 1871. It was only nominally Darwinian, since it did not represent human traits as adaptations *to* anything. Rather, Darwin thought that man's domination of nature made human origins self-explanatory. Our distinctive traits, he argued, are advantageous because they help to make us the lords of the jungle. Man, even in "the rudest state in which he now exists," wrote Darwin, "is the most dominant animal that has ever appeared on this earth. He has spread more widely than any other highly organised form; and all others have yielded before him. He manifestly owes this immense superiority to his intellectual faculties, to his social habits . . . and to his corporeal structure. The supreme importance of these characters has been proved by the final arbitrament of the battle for life."[2] If these characters have made man king of the beasts, they must confer some sort of universal advantage. Therefore, reasoned Darwin, any rudimentary humanlike traits that happened to crop up in our apelike ancestors would have been favored by natural selection. Of bipedalism, for example, Darwin wrote:

> If it be an advantage to man to stand firmly on his feet and to have his hands and arms free, *of which, from his pre-eminent success in the battle of life, there can be no doubt,* then I can see no reason why it should not have been advantageous to the progenitors of man to become more and more erect or bipedal . . . The best built individuals would in the long run have succeeded best, and have survived in larger numbers.[3]

In short, no special theory is needed to account for the traits that give us dominion over nature.[4] Such traits would naturally be expected to evolve in apelike primates. In this context, what seemed mysterious was not the origin of humanity but the *failure* of the other apes to become human. If apes naturally tend to evolve into people, why are there still apes?

Darwin had nothing to say about this problem, but later Darwinians tried to deal with it. The consensus that emerged in the early 1900s held that the other apes had never gotten anywhere because they had gone in for swinging through the trees by their arms. As a result, they had evolved long arms and long, hooklike fingers—which had left them too top-heavy and clumsy-handed to evolve into tool-using bipeds like ourselves.[5]

Many scientists thought that the apes had failed to advance for another reason: their tropical environments were too cozy. Instead of moving into the bracing northern climes that had made men of our ancestors, the apes' ancestors had merely lingered on in the jungle munching bananas—"living in a land of plenty, which encouraged indolence in habit and stagnation of effort and growth."[6] Such explanations sound silly today, but they must have seemed more plausible back in the heyday of European colonialism. They express the deep-seated colonialist belief that the natives of the tropics are shiftless, simian oafs who need to be whipped into shape by smarter, more energetic Nordic types. "In tropical and semi-tropical regions where natural food fruits abound, human effort—individual and racial— immediately ceases," proclaimed H. F. Osborn, dean of American paleontologists, in 1926. "In forested lands evolution of man is exceedingly slow, in fact there is retrogression, as plentifully evidenced in forest-living races of today."[7]

During the 1920s and 1930s, the notion that human peculiarities are self-explanatory blossomed into a full-blown theory of human and primate evolution. The man who did the most to formulate and promote that theory was the English anatomist W. E. Le Gros Clark, whose ideas about primate evolution dominated the anthropology textbooks of the English-speaking world from the 1930s through the 1960s. Le Gros Clark thought that all primates naturally tend to evolve big brains, upright posture, nimble hands, and other humanlike traits. These "predetermined trends of development"[8] culminate in the appearance of man. The other living primates failed to become human because their ancestors wandered off into evolutionary blind alleys, taking up specialized habits like arm-swinging. Their "divergent specialization . . . has led them away from the main line of evolution culminating in the human species."[9]

Thus, from Darwin's time down through the first half of the twentieth century, it was generally agreed among anthropologists that human beings are what evolution produces when it is left to its own devices and not perverted by "divergent specialization." The idea that human traits themselves might have started out as specializations for a particular way of making a living was not seriously discussed.

The hunting hypothesis was the first truly Darwinian explanation of human origins to be proposed. Between 1880 and 1920, three authors put forward early versions of the killer-ape story, which anticipated most of the ideas and arguments that Dart came up with in the 1950s. Some of these accounts were thoughtfully worked out in great detail. They appeared in long articles in major scientific journals and in books put out in multiple editions by reputable publishers. In spite of all this, they attracted no notice and were ignored by the leading experts on human evolution. Anthropologists were not ready to hear about the killer ape until after the end of World War II.

THE first version of the hunting hypothesis to enter the scientific literature was proposed by the American editor and science writer Charles Morris. In two papers written in the 1880s, Morris suggested that man's ancestor was a fruit-eating ape that had taken up hunting, which increased "the strain upon his faculties and the consequent activity of his mind."[10] In his 1900 book *Man and His Ancestor,* Morris tried to reconstruct the transition from ape to man in more detail. Our simian forebears, he argued, must have become upright bipeds even while they were still living in the trees. If they had moved through the trees with long arms like those of a chimpanzee, then they would have gone on all fours like a chimpanzee when they came down from the trees and would never have started walking upright.

But apes find their long arms useful in swinging and hanging from tree branches. Why, then, would our tree-dwelling ancestors have developed short arms and long legs? Morris suggested that they had evolved these body proportions for predatory purposes. An ape that was trying to capture prey with its hands would be more successful if it could get up and run on its hind feet alone. To do that, it would need more powerful legs and less massive arms. These changes "would act as a predisposing agency in inducing the animal to desert the tree for the ground, and to employ weapons in the chase." Brain enlargement occurred later, when people began to live in cold climates and to wage war. "It is, undoubtedly, to war between man and man, and the conflict with the adverse conditions of nature in the colder regions of the earth," wrote Morris, "that man's development from his lowest to his highest intellectual state has been largely due."[11]

The hunting hypothesis next surfaced in a series of articles that the British surgeon Harry Campbell published from 1904 to 1921 in the medical journal *Lancet*. He suggested that the transition from ape to man began when our apelike "homo-simian" ancestors began coming to the ground in search of food—"above all animal food, which was probably the main attraction towards a terrestrial life." At first, these homo-simians were "able to secure little more than vermin." But even vermin were more elusive than bananas, and catching prey therefore encouraged the evolution of brains and the invention of tools. "Lacking alike the instinct and natural weapons of the carnivora, [the homo-simian] was obliged to rely upon his superior intelligence in hunting his prey [and] intelligence began to count in the struggle for existence as it had never counted before . . . With the advent of the hunting period mental evolution received a great impetus."[12]

This "great impetus," in Campbell's view, was "all in favour of the male," since the males did all the hunting. Female homo-simians, it seems, confined themselves to gathering vegetables—an activity that "did not involve any high degree of intelligence."[13] Warfare, which was another exclusively male pursuit, also helped make the males smarter. All this, Campbell thought, explains why men today have more "nervous activity, love of adventure, courage, bellicosity, ingenuity, and intellectuality generally" than women have.[14] Male superiority over women became still more pronounced after polygamy was introduced. "The custom of polygamy renders it more difficult for some members of the tribe to get offspring than others, the most brainy on the whole getting the largest number," wrote Campbell. "The most intelligent men secured the most wives and left the most children." Since intelligence was more valuable to men than to women, it tended to be inherited as a secondary sexual characteristic peculiar to the male, like big muscles and beards. "The superiority of the man's mental endowment over the woman's," Campbell concluded happily, is "traceable in some degree to his polygamous past."[15]

In his 1904 and 1913 essays, Campbell sounds like the perfect Edwardian member of the Royal College of Physicians: fearful and disdainful of the poor, condescending toward women and nonwhites, and fatuously confident of the evolutionary benefits of war. These early articles seem to prove everything that leftist, pacifist, and feminist critics have had to say against the hunting hypothesis.

But Campbell's next article, written in 1917, presents things in a different light. Although Campbell still depicts hunting and warfare as the engines of human progress, he is no longer sure about the value of that progress or of the rightness of the English social order. His whole hypothesis now expresses a different set of attitudes. In 1913, it had seemed self-evident to Campbell that the English class system constituted "not merely a social but a mental hierarchy—one, namely, in which innate mental endowment increases from below upwards"— and that "The members of each social class are, on the average, more richly endowed in . . . brains and grit . . . than those of the class immediately below."[16] But in 1917, we find Campbell angrily denouncing "the moneyed fool" and "the employer who sweats his workers" and equating investment bankers with burglars. "Has not the informed and skilful speculator something in common with the house-breaker?" demands this new Campbell. "Each uses his skill in annexing the property of others by taking advantage of their ignorance." Campbell ends his 1917 essay by calling for a "moderate, sane Socialism," universal democracy, and the formation of a United States of Europe.[17]

Somewhere between his 1913 and 1917 articles, Campbell had stopped talking like Herbert Spencer's parrot and begun to sound like a member of the Fabian Society. Yet during those four years, his opinion of humanity had plummeted to something recalling Mark Twain's or Raymond Dart's. Man, wrote Campbell in 1917,

> is the arch-slaughterer—*facile princeps*. Since the time the pre-human ape took to hunting he and his human descendants have wrought ruthless havoc among the lower animals, and at the present day man not only hunts them, but breeds them for the express purpose of destroying them, chiefly for food, partly for amusement . . . The animal which attacks another and in so doing causes pain merely responds to a blind unthinking instinct; but man, proud man, who looks before and after, is able to realise and take pleasure in the pain he deliberately . . . sets out to cause. It is clearly absurd to speak of his conduct as "brutal." Rather we should call it devilish, the Devil usually being credited with a goodly share of intelligence.[18]

The last of the early proponents of the hunting hypothesis was Carveth Read, a psychology professor at University College London. Read published a brief sketch of his theories in 1914 and followed it up with a book six years later. Like Morris and Campbell, Read thought that human bipedalism and brains had gotten their start when our ancestors came to the ground in pursuit of prey and began to need predatory cunning and artificial weapons. But Read worked out the whole hypothesis in far more detail. He was particularly interested in the effects of hunting on human society and psychology. Human beings, he argued, are the most cooperative of primates because they are predators. The apes have no need to cooperate to get what they want; but when man first took to hunting game,

> especially big game (not being by ancient adaptation, in instinct and structure, a carnivore), he may have been, and probably was, incapable of killing his prey single-handed; and, if so, he would profit by being both social and co-operative in hunting, like the wolves and dogs, a sort of wolf-ape. The pack was a means of increasing the supply of food; and gregariousness increased by selection. Hence in character man is more like the dog than he is like any other animal.[19]

In his 1920 book *The Origin of Man,* Read dubbed his imaginary hunting primate *Lycopithecus* (Greek for "wolf-ape"), and went on to speculate about its social life. Darwin and Freud had contended that the primitive human group was a harem lorded over by a single jealous patriarch.[20] Read called this idea a baseless speculation, noting that all people known to history have always lived in multimale, multifamily groups. The smallest and simplest of such groups today are "tribes or bands of about fifty." Read took this to be the primitive form of human society, and he interpreted it as a hunting adaptation—"a society entirely different from that of any of the Primates, or of cattle, and most like that of the dogs and wolves—a hunting-pack." To Read, many things about human society seemed strikingly doglike, including monogamous pairings within the larger confines of a pack, territoriality, peck order, coordinated hunting, and cooperation of both sexes in feeding offspring. The human mind, he concluded, "is a sort of chimpanzee mind adapted to the wolfish conditions of the hunting-pack."[21]

The misanthropy that colors other versions of the hunting hypothesis shows up in Read's book as well. He attributed human "greed, cruelty, pride and every sort of aggressiveness" to the predatory heritage of the wolf-ape and quoted approvingly from the German anatomist Robert Hartmann: "Both savage and civilized people are capable of showing unspeakable and, as it is erroneously called, inhuman cruelty towards each other. These acts of cruelty, murder and rapine are . . . truly human, since nothing like them can be traced in the animal world . . . In this respect the anthropoid ape stands upon a higher plane than many men."[22] Read adds an ironic postscript to Hartmann:

> We ought not, I think, to attribute unnecessary cruelty or destructiveness to Lycopithecus, except so far as the novelty of his life may have led him into excesses compared with the economical life of true, adapted carnivores. He too was a narrow-minded beast. All these atrocities cited by Hartmann (and the list might be expanded into a volume) have resulted from the expansion of imagination . . . Aggressive cruelty, no doubt, was born in the hunting-pack, but it did not attain the "truly human" dimensions until it was enlisted in the service of ideas.[23]

Here and elsewhere, Read anticipated Konrad Lorenz's view of man as a crazy, weapon-wielding killer ape who lacks the inbred decency of true, biologically adapted carnivores. "True carnivores are not generally cannibals," wrote Read, because of "their more ancient and perfect adaptation to a predatory life. For them persistent cannibalism would have been too destructive."[24]

Pacifist critics have argued that the hunting hypothesis was cooked up to furnish a pretext for condoning war as an inevitable evil grounded in man's aggressive nature. The writings of Morris, Campbell, and Read suggest otherwise. For Morris, hunting and war had little to do with each other. To prewar Campbell, both hunting and war seemed like beneficial forces promoting evolutionary progress; but for later Campbell, war was an evolutionary vestige to be put behind us. These differences evidently express the disgust that Campbell felt toward the carnage of World War I. There are similar differences between Read's prewar and postwar writings. These comparisons strongly suggest that in 1917, as in the 1940s, the misanthropy associated with the hunting hypothesis appeared as a reaction against the preceding world war—not as an excuse for having another one. The writings of Campbell also show that the hunting hypothesis is equally compatible with politics of the left and of the right.

THE ideas proposed by Morris, Campbell, and Read quickly sank into oblivion. Morris' book was snubbed altogether by scientists.[25] A synopsis of one of Campbell's *Lancet* articles appeared in 1918 in the *American Journal of Physical Anthropology,* but it did not even mention the hunting hypothesis.[26] Read's 1920 book was reviewed in a few scientific journals. Twenty-eight years later, the British anthropologist Arthur Keith mentioned Campbell and Read offhandedly as forgotten precursors of Raymond Dart.[27] William Etkin, in his influential 1954 paper on hunting and early hominid social organization, traced some of his ideas back to Read. And until recently, that seems to have been the sum total of scientific attention paid to these men—at least in print.[28]

One or two facts suggest that Campbell's writings may have influenced Raymond Dart. When Dart described *Australopithecus* in 1924, he consigned it to a new family of primates, the "Homo-simiadae." This strange name, which breaks several of the rules of zoological nomenclature,[29] sounds suspiciously like an echo of Campbell's imaginary "homo-simians." Dart could have picked up that name—and the germ of the hunting hypothesis with it—by stumbling across one of Campbell's articles in *Lancet,* most of which appeared while Dart was still a medical student.[30] But even if he did read Campbell during those years, the experience left no great impression. He never cited either Campbell or Read. Asked outright about the matter sixty years later, Dart denied any acquaintance with Campbell's writings.[31] Dart's early articles point to changes in climate, not diet, as the cause of human origins, and they do not portray the man-apes as mighty hunters. As late as 1940, Dart was still describing *Australopithecus* as a hard-pressed scavenger scrounging scraps to stay alive in a hostile environment.[32]

In short, scientists and popular science writers paid little or no attention to the hunting hypothesis during the first half of the twentieth century. If anthropologists had taken Read's 1920 book seriously, the discovery at Taung four years later would have been hailed as the fulfillment of Read's predictions, and Dart's "bird-nest-rifling and bone-cracking ape" probably would have been named *Lycopithecus* instead of *Australopithecus.* But Read's book was shrugged away, and no one made the connection.[33]

Scientists in the 1920s and 1930s of course recognized that our ancestors had been (among other things) hunters; and the prehistoric caveman who went around bashing prey and mates alike with his stone ax was already a familiar stereotype in the mass media.[34] But none of the experts on human prehistory saw hunting as the big breakthrough that had brought all the other human peculiarities into existence. Some authors doubted that hunting had played any important role in man's emergence at all. "It is in the highest degree improbable that the human savage ever hunted animals much larger than the hare, the rabbit, and the rat," declared H. G. Wells in his classic *Outline of History*. "Man was probably the hunted rather than the hunter."[35] As recently as 1946, W. W. Howells concluded that hunting "may not be of any great significance" in human evolution.[36]

Why was the hunting hypothesis brushed aside in 1920 and embraced everywhere in 1960? Preposterous as it sounds today, one reason why nobody took Read's theories seriously in 1920 is that they were perceived as Darwinian and therefore quaint. When Read's book came out, the fortunes of Darwinism had reached their lowest ebb, and the whole theory of natural selection was widely dismissed as a Victorian superstition.[37] Some biologists, influenced by the new science of experimental genetics, sought to portray evolution as a more or less random process driven by chance mutations. Others claimed that mysterious internal forces, unrelated to the environment, had directed the course of evolution. The Romantic evolutionary theories of Henri Bergson were popular in literary circles. As Ernst Mayr put it, "Up to the 1920s and 1930s, virtually all the major books on evolution . . . were more or less strongly anti-Darwinian. Among nonbiologists Darwinism was even less popular."[38] This bias against Darwinism is clear in the reviews of Read's book. "The time when such hypotheses had any scientific interest or were capable of arousing any enthusiasm is gone for good," wrote one reviewer.[39] "Suffice to say," sniffed another,

> that the Theory of Natural Selection plays a prominent part [in Mr. Read's argument]. For some years past this theory has, however, been losing its hold on biological inquirers into origins, and there can be little doubt that Natural Selection has been a far less important factor in evolution than was thought in the last century.[40]

The anti-Darwinism of the 1920s was swept away in the 1930s by a triumphant Darwinian counterrevolution, which put natural selection

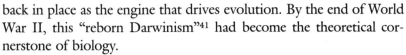

back in place as the engine that drives evolution. By the end of World War II, this "reborn Darwinism"[41] had become the theoretical cornerstone of biology.

The triumph of neo-Darwinism had important implications for the study of human evolution. The anthropologists of the 1950s no longer felt comfortable explaining man as the inevitable result of the general evolutionary process. The origins of human peculiarities, like those of any other group of animals, now had to be traced to an *adaptive shift*— that is, to some change in way of life that had imposed new demands on our apelike ancestors and started them evolving in a new direction. Dart's hypothesis filled the bill perfectly, and it came along at just the right time, when physical anthropology was being made over along neo-Darwinian lines by Sherwood Washburn and the other champions of the postwar "new physical anthropology."[42] This cozy fit between Dart's ideas and the demands of neo-Darwinism helped to make the hunting hypothesis more acceptable to anthropologists in the 1950s than it had been in 1920. But anthropologists were also happy to hear about the adaptive shift for other reasons—reasons that had more to do with the Holocaust than with evolutionary theory.

FROM Darwin's time down to the beginning of World War II, most scientists who studied human evolution were shocking racists by today's standards. Most of them firmly believed that some living human races are closer to the apes than others. Darwin's psychological disciple George Romanes described today's "savages" as living fossils, who help to bridge "the psychological distance which separates the gorilla from the gentleman."[43] The leading German Darwinian, Ernst Haeckel, classified living human beings into twelve different species and concluded that the most primitive of them are psychologically closer to dogs and baboons than they are to white people.[44] Haeckel's ideas had a profound influence on Nazi ideology, and German anthropologists trained in the Haeckelian tradition collaborated eagerly with the SS program of "race hygiene" in the 1930s.[45] Physical anthropology in the English-speaking countries, though not so actively genocidal, was almost equally racist prior to World War II.[46] As late as 1946, Earnest Hooton, one of the seminal figures in American physical anthropology, could write without blushing:

> The native Australian is almost as incapable of absorbing civilization as the chimpanzee of adopting the method of life and tribal customs of the aboriginal Australian . . . We are fairly safe in assuming that the Australian is far less intelligent than is the Englishman, and that the chimpanzee is much farther removed in his mental capacity from the native Australian. The Australian has had as much time to develop a culture as has the Englishman; so has the chimpanzee . . . I can see no reason why the gorilla should not have become man, no reason why the pygmy should not have acquired a culture, except inherent lack of mental capacity—which in terms of gross anatomy means an inferior brain.[47]

Such assertions did not abruptly cease after World War II, but in the shadow of Auschwitz they were no longer intellectually respectable. The collapse of Germany and the unveiling of the systematic mass murders committed by the German government thoroughly discredited the ideology of the Nazi state. Doctrines of white supremacy were also undercut by the recession and swift collapse of the European empires in Africa and Asia during the 1950s. The whole notion of racial hierarchy, the idea that some human populations are more human than others, could no longer be tolerated in postwar anthropological thought. It had become an abomination, and it had to be extirpated.

Unfortunately, extirpating that racist notion went against one important aspect of the Darwinian tradition. Darwinists had always sought to minimize the gulf between man and ape. Most of the leading experts on human evolution, from Thomas Henry Huxley on,[48] had tried to fill in some of the missing links by using "inferior races" and "lower savages" to bridge the gap between gentlemen and gorillas. If anthropologists wanted to affirm human unity and equality, they would have to accept a sharper discontinuity between people and animals.[49]

Postwar anthropologists not only accepted that discontinuity, they embraced it. Leslie White's influential writings declared that there are no intermediate stages between human and animal behavior. "Because human behavior is symbol behavior," wrote White, "and since the behavior of infra-human species is non-symbolic, it follows that we can learn nothing about human behavior from observations upon or experiments with the lower animals."[50] Noam Chomsky, whose theories ushered in a revolution in linguistics in the late 1950s, likewise drew an absolute distinction between human and animal communication. Language, he concluded, could not have evolved from animal antecedents; it must have sprung into being instantaneously, by some mysterious genetic mutation.[51] Similar views of human culture, language, and history as phenomena without animal parallels or precedents are strongly held by many anthropologists and linguists today.[52]

Physical anthropologists were committed to Darwin, and so they could not proclaim an absolute difference between people and animals. But during the 1950s and early 1960s, they did what they could to contribute to the new postwar perception of the unity, equality, and distinctness of the family of man. Racial hierarchies disappeared from physical-anthropology textbooks, and the whole concept of race came to seem quaint and disreputable. Our primitive fossil relatives were granted more fully human taxonomic status: Java Man *(Pithecanthropus)* and Peking Man *(Sinanthropus)* were admitted to the genus *Homo,* and Neanderthal Man was welcomed into our own species, *Homo sapiens.* At anthropology meetings during the 1960s, scientists who questioned the mental capacities or human status of the Neanderthals were sometimes accused of bigotry, as if they had cast a slur on some ethnic group.

The australopithecines also won a taxonomic promotion in the postwar decade. Before that, most of the experts had agreed that these South African creatures were cousins, not ancestors, of ours, and that they lay on a side-branch of ape evolution that had ultimately gone extinct. "Because they lacked brains," wrote Hooton, "they remained apes, in spite of their humanoid teeth."[53] Many scientists thought that the australopithecines and our ancestors had evolved their humanlike traits separately, and that the South African fossils just proved how easy and natural it is for apes to evolve in a human direction. As W. W. Howells put it in 1946, "Development toward men is a ready and natural channel for evolving apes, and might take place in several different groups."[54] Howells granted, however, that the man-apes would probably have to be recognized as our close relatives if it turned out that they were upright bipeds. The very next year, in 1947, a fossil pelvis of *Australopithecus* came to light in one of the Transvaal caves. It proved to be short and wide like a human pelvis, not tall and narrow like a chimpanzee's. The logical conclusion from its anatomy was that *Australopithecus* had walked upright on its hind feet alone.[55]

In the light of this find, even previously skeptical anthropologists were driven to rethink their ideas about the essence of humanity. The new fossils proved that "differences in the brain between apes and man . . . were attained *after* full human status had been achieved in the limbs and trunk."[56] For Hooton, the index of humanity had been the brain; but the new generation of anthropologists saw the man-apes' upright posture and small front teeth as the crucial human innovations. Both traits were thought to be connected with the use of weapons. Throwing rocks or swinging a club, it was argued, encourages bipedal postures and makes canine fangs superfluous. The human condition thus came to be seen as the product of weapon technology.

Conversely, dependence on tools and weapons was taken as the hallmark of human status. An "essential humanity" was therefore attributed to all hominids, even the australopithecines.[57] "All species now identified as hominids," wrote Alan Mann in 1972, "shared with modern man a dependence on human cultural behavior, and . . . for this reason, they should all be referred to as 'human.'"[58] One group of scientists identified "culture" (technology) as the hominid ecological niche. Since a single niche can support only one species at a time, they concluded that there could never have been more than one hominid species. This conclusion was known as the "single-species hypothesis."[59] It portrayed the human family as a unitary entity by its very nature, bound together by bonds of universal equality and brotherhood from the moment the ancestral australopithecine first stood upright and started hitting things with a stick.

Thus the story that human origins had involved an adaptive shift to hunting was welcomed for reasons of politics as well as science. The hunting hypothesis posited a big adaptive difference between early hominids and apes, which satisfied the demands of neo-Darwinian theory on the one hand and racial egalitarianism on the other. The pessimism and misanthropy inherent in Dart's killer-ape story were popular for a different set of reasons: they reflected the decay of the scientific intelligentsia's faith in progress.

THE nineteenth century had bequeathed to the twentieth a widely shared belief in the inevitability of progress. Victorian thinkers as diverse as Hegel and Darwin, Karl Marx and Andrew Carnegie, had agreed that the forces of history tend inexorably toward the perfection of the world. Though bruised by World War I, that mechanical optimism nevertheless persisted among lesser Babbits and Bolsheviks through the 1920s and 1930s. The American public's faith in progress probably reached some sort of zenith in the 1950s, when every line of consumer goods was packaged to look like a spaceship and advertised as the latest technological breakthrough into the exciting world of tomorrow.[60] Even today, many ideologues continue to insist that the workings of the class struggle or the free marketplace can be relied upon to lead mankind automatically into a rosy future.

But thoughtful people who surveyed what World War II left behind at Dachau and Hiroshima found it hard to keep smiling. The systematic extermination of Europe's Jews by the German government demonstrated that nations of the highest scientific and technological attainments can turn frothing mad almost overnight; and the invention of nuclear weapons ensured that insane nations of the future would command the means to destroy life on earth. It was difficult, in the face of those facts, to sustain the sunny conviction that all would be well once we had universal literacy, One Big Union, and sanitary drains.

As the implications of death camps and nuclear weapons sank in, a bleak pessimism became increasingly common among intellectuals of all political and religious persuasions.[61] "Man has proved to be so insane, so corrupt, that the more power you give him the more he will destroy himself," wrote the popular preacher Harry Emerson Fosdick. "We are Frankensteins, who have created a technological civilization that in the hands of sin can literally exterminate us."[62] "No thoughtful person whom I know," declared George Orwell in 1946, "has any hopeful picture of the future. The notion that a war between Russia and America is inevitable within the next few decades, and that [we are] bound to be blown to pieces by atomic bombs, is accepted with a sort of vague resignation."[63] H. G. Wells, a perennial optimist who had devoted much of his life to prophesying the wonders of the coming age of science, concluded in 1945 that "the end of everything we call life is close at hand and cannot be evaded."[64] Marston Bates observed this epidemic despair with an ecologist's eye:

> Why are we so pessimistic? Chiefly, I suspect, because we have come more and more to doubt our ability to act rationally . . . The great immediate threat, of course, is the misuse of nuclear power, the danger of catastrophic war. The long-term threat is the cancerous multiplication of the numbers of men . . . It looks as though, as a part of nature, we have become a disease of nature—perhaps a fatal disease. And when the host dies, so does the pathogen.[65]

The metaphors of postwar despair have become so familar that we scarcely notice them. Humanity is a fatal disease of nature.[66] The human brain is a maladaptive overgrowth that has doomed us to extinction, like the tusks of the extinct saber-toothed cats.[67] Human beings are insane evolutionary mistakes mindlessly destroying the natural order—"like vultures flapping / Belching, gurgling, / near a dying Doe."[68]

"There is no darkness of nature so dark as the darkness of men," wrote Richard Rhodes in 1969, after watching a coyote hunt and a cockfight in rural Kansas:

> We observe with a cold arrangement of brain cells that do not reproduce and feel no pain. We stare, unblinking eyes, at dying beasts and see only casual transformations. Corn grows, and we pluck it; wheat grows, and we cut it; coyotes run, and we tear them; cocks crow, and we murder them; men die, and we send others after them. We are nature's full circle, the end product of her millennial butchery of forms, form feeding on form unto the ends of the earth. We nest as animals: we hunt as men. We huddle as animals: we murder as men.[69]

This fear and detestation of ourselves and our capacity for destruction found a wide variety of postwar expressions, from Robinson Jeffers' poetry to Hollywood movies about bomb-spawned mutant monsters.[70] In the realm of science, the fear was expressed in the hunting hypothesis of human origins.

It seems clear in retrospect that the origin and spread of the hunting hypothesis in the 1950s had more to do with with postwar anxiety about man's future than with Dart's new discoveries. Golding and

Jeffers started depicting hunting as man's original sin before they could have heard about the Transvaal fossils. Other writers had begun to come up with bits and pieces of the killer-ape picture even before that, while the war was still going on. In 1922 H. G. Wells thought hunting irrelevant to human origins; but in his last book, published in 1945, he described man's remote ancestors as apes that had been forced to take up killing as a way of life when their forests disappeared.[71] The conclusion of T. H. White's tetralogy *The Once and Future King*, written in wartorn England in 1941, is one long misanthropic rumination on warfare's roots in human biology—especially in man's hunting habits. "Man," says White, is "a slayer by instinct . . . that rarity in nature, an animal which will kill for pleasure! . . . If nature ever troubled to look at man, the little atrocity, she would be shocked out of her wits." White's mouthpiece Merlyn concludes that "war is an inestimable boon to creation as a whole, because it does offer some faint hope of exterminating the human race."[72]

During the war, my father Cleve Cartmill published a science-fiction story, "The Link," about Lok, a funny-looking hairless mutant born into a tribe of prehistoric apes.[73] Weak of jaw but strong of brain, Lok is driven to invent the club, with which he kills first a lion and then a dozen members of his own tribe. Struggling to explain his exploits to an adoring female, Lok boasts in the story's last line that he has killed a lion, and—he searches for a word—"and other animals." In that punchline, as in the killer-ape stories told by scientists twenty years later, the human-animal boundary springs into being abruptly with the invention of the first weapon. "The Link" was reprinted in a popular postwar anthology,[74] and it is tempting to speculate that it might have influenced William Golding—whose 1955 novel *The Inheritors* also features an apeman hero named Lok.

The science-fiction genre started out in the early 1900s in gadgeteers' magazines like *Popular Mechanics,* and most of its early productions celebrated the marvels of future technology. The gee-whiz attitude of the early writers and fans is captured in the names of the old pulp magazines: *Amazing Stories, Thrilling Wonder Stories, Astounding Science Fiction.* But after World War II, fear of technology and resentment of human domination of nature became common themes in science fiction.[75] These themes are especially conspicuous among some of the science-fiction writers—Ray Bradbury, Ursula Le Guin, Stanislaw Lem—who have been taken the most seriously by the mainstream literary establishment.

Kurt Vonnegut Jr., probably the most important writer to emerge from the science-fiction ghetto, has devoted his career from the mid-fifties on to attacking "sin," defined as "anything human that seriously threatens the planet and the life thereon."[76] As a war prisoner in Germany Vonnegut lived through the Allied firebombing of Dresden, and after the war he began writing bitter, satirical fiction decrying technology and human nature. Throughout his work, animals appear as symbols of sanity, decency, and innocence that contrast with man's devilish ingenuity and twisted compulsions.[77] "This was a very innocent planet, except for those great big brains," says the narrator of Vonnegut's 1985 novel of evolutionary theory, *Galápagos*. "There was no end to the vile schemes that a thought machine that oversized couldn't imagine and execute."[78] *Galápagos* ends happily when a plague wipes out the human race. A few survivors remain stranded on the Galápagos Islands; but fortunately their descendants evolve into stupid, seal-like animals with flippers instead of hands, and the world is saved at last from the threat of technology.

Recent science-fiction movies, for all the high-tech glitter of their special effects, have picked up the antitechnology message of postwar science fiction and repackaged it for a mass audience. The good guys in these films—Obi-wan Kenobi, Luke Skywalker, Yoda, E.T., Star-man—live simply in harmony with their environment and rely on occult spiritual powers to defeat the elaborate killing machines of their wicked adversaries. Kubrick's *2001*, the progenitor of this whole special-effects genre, puts the killer ape himself on screen and dramatizes the same connections that Dart drew between early technology, hunting, and murder.[79]

POSTWAR fears of weapon technology helped to bring the hunting hypothesis into being, and they promoted its swift acceptance in the late 1950s and early 1960s. During the same years, fear of technology also fueled the rapid growth of the ecology movement.

Before World War II, ecology was just another scientific subject, like aerodynamics or biochemistry. The word began to take on its present political, philosophical, and religious overtones in the postwar writings of the wildlife biologist Aldo Leopold. Leopold grew up on a farm in Iowa at the turn of the century. His parents, both devoted hunters and fishers, instilled a love of nature and wildlife in their son. Leopold went to Yale Forestry School and then into the U.S. Forest Service. Posted to the New Mexico Territory in 1909, he helped to promote and carry out the federal government's campaign to exterminate the wolf in the southwest.[80] The experience revolted him as it had revolted Ernest Thompson Seton. But instead of turning against hunting as Seton did, Leopold entered on a more fundamentally subversive line of thought: he began to turn against the treatment of the earth as a resource to be managed or "improved" for human ends.

Leopold summed up his revolutionary ideas in his posthumous 1949 book *A Sand County Almanac,* in which he criticized existing conservation programs as "based wholly on economic motives" and called for the creation of a "land ethic." By this he meant nothing less than a new system of morality, in which nonhuman organisms and the ecosystem as a whole would be granted rights and respected as ends in themselves:

> All ethics so far evolved rest upon a single premise: that the individual is a member of a community of interdependent parts . . . The land ethic simply enlarges the boundaries of the community to include soils, waters, plants, and animals . . . A land ethic changes the role of *Homo sapiens* from conqueror of the land-community to plain member and citizen of it. It implies respect for his fellow-members, and also respect for the community as such.[81]

Leopold had mixed feelings about the hunt. His own hunting thrilled him with a sense of ecological participation, and he could find poetic metaphors of the food chain in a plate of venison chops and bear-grease gravy over biscuits.[82] But he had a veiled contempt for hunters who kill when they are not hungry, or who kill for trophies, or who drive cars instead of hiking to their hunting grounds, or who use newfangled gadgets in the field.[83] That adds up to just about all the hunters there are in modern America.

Leopold's feelings about science were also mixed. He approved of science as a means to understanding, but he disliked the mushrooming technology, the cold detachment, and the fragmentation of knowledge that science brings with it. The balance of nature, he wrote, is like a great song, and a scientist is someone who "selects one instrument and spends his life taking it apart" without listening for the music or understanding how the parts go together. The ultimate outcome of science is the destruction, through technology, of the natural order that science purports to study:

> Professors serve science and science serves progress. It serves progress so well that many of the more intricate instruments are stepped upon and broken in the rush to spread progress to all backward lands. One by one the parts are thus stricken from the song of songs. If the professor is able to classify each instrument before it is broken, he is well content . . . Science [insists] that every river needs more people, and all people need more inventions, and hence more science; the good life depends on the indefinite extension of this chain of logic. That the good life on any river may likewise depend on the perception of its music, and the preservation of some music to perceive, is a form of doubt not yet entertained by science.[84]

The most decisive postwar attack against technological "progress" was mounted in 1962 by the marine biologist Rachel Carson in *Silent Spring,* which awakened the world to the environmental effects of the flood of pesticides being dumped into our air and water. Carson's book begins with a grimly pessimistic quote from Albert Schweitzer: "Man has lost the capacity to foresee and to forestall. He will end by destroying the earth." It ends with an image of science itself as a killer ape-man:

> The "control of nature" is a phrase conceived in arrogance, born of the Neanderthal age of biology and philosophy, when it was supposed that nature exists for the convenience of man . . . It is our alarming misfortune that so primitive a science has armed itself with the most modern and terrible weapons, and that in turning them against the insects it has also turned them against the earth.[85]

Silent Spring led to the banning of DDT and other pesticides in the late 1960s, and was a major force behind the creation of the U.S. Environmental Protection Agency in 1969. Leopold's writings began to be translated into law during the same period. The sponsors of the

1964 Wilderness Act, which put two percent of American soil off limits to human construction forever, cited Leopold as their chief inspiration.[86] During the 1960s, the ideas of Leopold and Carson developed mass political support. Every passing year since then has seen more square miles set aside as nature preserves, more pollutants banned, more species protected, and more environmental issues confronted by the world's parliaments. Despite some reverses during the conservative reaction of the 1980s, all these trends are back in the headlines today and seem likely to continue beyond the end of the twentieth century.

Although the environmental movement probably derives most of its mass support from such pragmatic and widely shared goals as reducing air pollution, its theoreticians have always kept an eye on a deeper moral agenda.[87] In recent years, Leopold's vague talk about the innate value of beasts, plants, and landscapes has begun to give way to more carefully reasoned systems of environmental ethics. As might be expected, there is no agreement on the moral status of hunting. Advocates of "deep ecology" praise hunting as a ceremonious and sacramental participation in the food chain, whereas some "eco-feminists" condemn it as symbolic rape, and animal-rights advocates see it as (in effect) murder of the mentally retarded for a thrill.[88] But all these schools of thought agree on Leopold's fundamental points: that other species have a right to exist that transcends the claims of human wishes and convenience, and that the Baconian program for the control and domination of nature through science is shortsighted, foolish, and immoral.

This ecological vision of things has affinities with Dart's, which traces man's worst flaws to the onset of technology. Since the early 1960s, these affinities have been reflected in the ideas and rhetoric of both anthropologists and environmentalists. Lamentations about man's killer-ape heritage turn up occasionally in the environmentalist literature, and dire ecological prophecies now often come in as moral taglines to accounts of human evolution.[89] One exponent of the killer-ape picture who has been a particularly important influence on the environmental movement is Robinson Jeffers, whose poetry has begun to take on an almost scriptural aura in some environmentalist circles.[90] Although the scientific proponents of the hunting hypothesis never gained that sort of prophetic status, the upsurge of ecological consciousness in the 1960s helped to make their ideas generally acceptable. Dart's postwar hunting hypothesis succeeded where earlier versions had failed, because it harmonized with the needs of neo-Darwinist theory, the demands of racial egalitarianism, and the pervasive fear of nuclear Armageddon—and also because it furnished the rising ecology movement with a suitable origin myth.

ELEVEN

The Spirit of the Beast

I said in mine heart concerning the estate of the sons of men, that God might manifest them, and that they might see that they themselves are beasts. For that which befalleth the sons of men befalleth beasts . . . as the one dieth, so dieth the other; yea, they have all one breath; so that a man hath no preeminence above a beast . . . Who knoweth the spirit of man that goeth upward, and the spirit of the beast that goeth downward to the earth?

—Ecclesiastes, 3:18–21

JOSEPH Wood Krutch's 1929 book *The Modern Temper* is an eloquent statement of the lost-generation funk that afflicted many intellectuals in the 1920s. It ends with a declaration on behalf of the human race: "Ours is a lost cause and there is no place for us in the natural universe, but we are not, for all that, sorry to be human. We should rather die as men than live as animals."[1]

These words sound noble, but they are hard to interpret. What does Krutch mean by saying that we should prefer to die as men than live as animals? After all, we *are* animals. (What else could we be?) "Animals" here must mean only the nonhuman beasts, but somehow spelling that out does not clear things up much. "Better to die a man," Krutch appears to be saying, "than live as any other sort of organism." It is hard to believe he meant that literally. Surely it would be interesting to be something as strange and beautiful as a dolphin or a kudu for a while—more interesting, at any rate, than being a human cadaver. Krutch would probably have said so himself, judging from his later work as a nature writer.[2]

We can guess at the sort of thing Krutch had in mind in rejecting the life of an animal. Nonhuman animals, he might have said, are not persons but *objects,* chattels that we can buy and sell and use as we see fit. They do not aspire to better their lot, for they do not judge their own circumstances, actions, and accomplishments. They are thoughtless, or at any rate unreflective. Because people can perceive and reflect on their lives as a whole, they have a kind of mastery over their lives and destinies that other animals apparently lack. Human beings are accordingly alive and conscious in a way that beasts are not. For a human being, becoming a beast would be something like a halfway station to death. It is not clear whether all these claims are true, but some such beliefs probably underlie Krutch's words. By refusing to accept the life and status of an animal, he is declaring that he would rather die as a subject than live as an object.

But this is almost as peculiar a declaration as the original version was. Why did Krutch need to voice such a preference? Nobody was threatening to change him into a kudu. This refusal to become an animal has to be read as expressing a different sort of anxiety. What he was really worried about was science, which filled him with foreboding and despair. Our nineteenth-century forebears, wrote Krutch, were optimistic enthusiasts for science because they assumed "that truths . . . were necessarily useful, and that the human spirit flowered best in the midst of realities clearly perceived." But that assumption has proved to be a sad mistake:

> We have learned how certain truths—intimate revelations concerning the origin and mechanism of our deepest impulses—can stagger our souls, and how a clear perception of our lonely isolation in the midst of a universe which knows nothing of us and our aspirations paralyzes our will . . . We have come to realize that the more we learn of the laws of that universe—in which we constitute a strange incongruity—the less we shall feel at home in it.[3]

Science, in other words, has revealed that our desires are mechanical, our values arbitrary, and our lives as vain and futile as those of the beasts. The best response we can make to these sorry disclosures is to ignore them. When Krutch insisted that he would rather die as a man than live as an animal, what he really meant was that he preferred not to think about certain topics.

In one form or another, this sort of resentment, dread, and willful ignorance of scientific knowledge has been current among intellectuals for two hundred years. It began with the earliest Romantics, and it persisted through a long succession of literary and artistic movements all the way down to the postmodernists of today. Some of this allergy to science springs from religious reaction; yet many of the writers that have had it the worst have not been traditional Christians. Some of it arises from fear of new technology, and some from envy of scientists' power and money. But there must be deeper reasons for it, because it goes back long before the era of big grants, recombinant DNA, and H bombs—all the way back to the days when scientists wore knee britches and "new technology" meant Leyden jars.

C. S. Lewis, who had the allergy worse than most, tried to justify it by pointing to internal contradictions in the whole scientific enterprise. Science, he argued, has always had two fundamental aims: to understand all things as parts of nature and to control nature. Both sound like reasonable aims; but it would be a disaster to attain both at once because it would entail treating people as part of nature—that is, as objects to be controlled.

"From this point of view," Lewis wrote, "the conquest of Nature appears in a new light. We reduce things to mere Nature in order that we may 'conquer' them. We are always conquering Nature, because 'Nature' is the name for what we have, to some extent, conquered." And conquest is what motivates scientists. Despite all their pious declarations about the disinterested quest for objective truth, they have gone after power from the very beginning:

> If we compare the chief trumpeter of the new era (Bacon) with Marlowe's Faustus, the similarity is striking. You will read in some critics that Faustus has a thirst for knowledge. In reality, he hardly mentions it. It is not truth he wants from his devils, but gold and guns and girls . . . In the same spirit Bacon condemns those who value knowledge as an end in itself: this, for him, is to use as a mistress for pleasure what ought to be a spouse for fruit. The true object is to extend Man's power to the performance of all things possible.

But the scientist's insatiable Baconian thirst for power is self-defeating, for human power ceases to be power when it is extended over man himself. "As soon as we take the final step of reducing our own species to the level of mere Nature," concluded Lewis, "the whole process is stultified, for this time the being who stood to gain and the being who has been sacrificed are one and the same."[4]

Whether or not Lewis was right about all this, he spoke for a lot of people. His doggedly premodern writings against science foreshadow the postmodernist view that science is at bottom a kind of political discourse, chiefly concerned with extending and legitimizing the power of the ruling class. Like Carol Merchant and other feminist writers today, Lewis argued that the scientific revolution of the seventeenth century was led astray from the beginning by its obsession with power and control. Lewis also anticipated the feminists' call for a more humane sort of science that will admit spiritual values into its world picture.[5] Although Lewis would probably have found radical feminist thinking almost as hateful as scientific materialism, he would certainly have endorsed Merchant's complaint that "mechanistic assumptions about nature push us increasingly in the direction of artificial environments, mechanized control over more and more aspects of human life, and a loss of the quality of life itself."[6] And similar complaints about the scientific world view and the devaluation of human life that it brings with it have been voiced by a vast chorus of other modern writers, representing every kind of politics and ideology: reactionaries like Lewis, fascists like Roy Campbell, mystics like Aldous Huxley, old-line socialists like Orwell, and new-age radicals like Theodore Roszak.

Until the end of World War II, there was a counterbalancing Baconian literature, whose authors saw themselves as an enlightened scientific vanguard promoting the expansion of human power over nature. One such writer of the 1920s was W. H. Auden, who actually welcomed the "impoverishment in feeling" brought about by increasing mechanization and hailed it as a sign of man's maturity.[7] Another was Bertrand Russell, who argued in 1925 that "to respect physical nature is foolish" and that we will attain true freedom only when we have attained the same technical control over the human mind that we already have over physical nature.[8] Some Marxist thinkers of the 1930s urged that it was time to put an end to nature and that animals and plants that serve no human purpose ought to be exterminated.[9]

We read these "enlightened" propositions nowadays with dismay.

Almost no one talks like that any more, and the few who do are not taken seriously. The Baconian tradition no longer has any literary champions. There is a growing consensus—outside the scientific research community, at any rate—that limits must be placed on human power over nature.

World War II was something of a turning point in this change. Most of the old confidence in science evaporated with the flash of the atomic bomb over Hiroshima. Even before that, the rise of Nazi Germany had led many thoughtful people to deny the supposed connection between science and progress. As George Orwell put it in 1941:

> Unfortunately the equation of science with common sense does not really hold good. The aeroplane, which was looked forward to as a civilising influence but in practice has hardly been used except for dropping bombs, is the symbol of that fact. Modern Germany is far more scientific than England, and far more barbarous . . . The order, the planning, the State encouragement of science, the steel, the concrete, the aeroplanes, are all there, but all in the service of ideas appropriate to the Stone Age.[10]

Similar thoughts drove Russell and Auden to take an increasingly skeptical and politicized view of the power that science wields over the natural order. Technological progress in the twentieth century, warned Russell in 1945, has led to an expanded belief in power: "first, the power of man in his conflicts with nature, and then the power of rulers as against the human beings whose beliefs and aspirations they seek to control . . . Nature is raw material; so is that part of the human race which does not effectively participate in government."[11] In Auden's poetry of the 1940s, science is personified as a totalitarian Big Brother whose technological dominion spreads beyond the realm of inanimate matter to encompass the minds of the masses:

> Great is Caesar: He has conquered Seven Kingdoms.
> The Seventh was the Kingdom of Popular Soul:
> Last night it was Order-Order, tonight it is Hear-Hear;
> When he says, You are happy, we laugh;
> When he says, You are wretched, we cry;
> When he says, It is true, everyone believes it;

> When he says, It is false, no one believes it . . .
> Great is Caesar: God must be with Him.[12]

These lines express a distinctively modern emotion, the fear of being an organic puppet controlled by a technocrat. That sort of fear underlies Krutch's otherwise baffling declarations in *The Modern Temper*, and it is responsible for much of the aversion that Lewis and other humanist intellectuals feel toward science.

Fear of science is not something peculiar to intellectuals. It permeates popular culture. Scientists in movies, comic books, and television shows are stereotypically malign figures. They are usually portrayed as ivory-tower incompetents blind to the dire implications of their research, or as malevolent warlocks bent on blowing things up and enslaving mankind. The popular aversion to science and scientists is expressed in a thousand variants of the Frankenstein story, in which the scientist is providentially destroyed by the unholy powers he has unleashed in his laboratory. Another recurring myth is the story of the Revolt of the Lab Animals, which tells how the vivisected creatures rise up against the evil powers of science and overthrow them.[13] These stories are at bottom political allegories. We enjoy hearing them because we know what it is like to be regarded as an experimental object by doctors, social scientists, industrial and military researchers, government experts, and other wizards empowered to mess with our lives. The sufferings of laboratory animals arouse indignation and political action, because we ourselves are afraid of scientists; the (probably greater) sufferings that factory farmers inflict on their livestock inspire far less protest, because we are not afraid of farmers.

If all this is true, then C. S. Lewis was basically right about the grounds of the intelligentsia's hostility to science. But Lewis' religious biases led him to omit something important from his picture. Although he was a learned historian of words and their changes in meaning, Lewis was willfully blind to the radical transformation in the meaning of the word "nature" that went on during his lifetime. Nature, wrote Lewis,

> is a word of varying meanings, which can best be understood if we consider its various opposites. The Natural is the opposite of the Artificial, the Civil, the Human, the Spiritual, and the Supernatural. The

Artificial does not now concern us. If we take the rest of the list of opposites, however, I think we can get a rough idea of what men have meant by Nature . . . She seems to be the world of quantity, as against the world of quality: of objects as against consciousness: of the bound, as against the wholly or partly autonomous: of that which knows no values as against that which both has and perceives value.[14]

Lewis saw nature as the land of the dead, a sterile, value-free domain of numbers and inanimate objects. For him, the important antonyms of *natural* were *civil, human, spiritual,* and *supernatural;* and *nature* was "the name for what we have, to some extent, conquered." But this whole idea of nature is a semantic antique. Some such concept prevailed in the seventeenth and eighteenth centuries, when the usual antonym to *natural* was still *supernatural,*[15] and it had some currency even in the early twentieth century. When Krutch wrote that there is no place for people "in the natural universe," he meant that human values find no objective counterpart in the godless waste land revealed by science. But this image of nature and the natural is no longer current. If you poll a dozen acquaintances at random and ask them what the opposite of *natural* is, most of them will tell you it is *artificial,* the one word Lewis did not want to talk about. A few of them may hit on *unnatural, abnormal, perverse,* or some other vaguely pathological term—a class of antonyms that Lewis did not even mention. Nobody will come up with *supernatural.*

Lewis retained the essentially medieval view of nature as a low, gross dominion, placed by God under the heel of man and symbolically opposed to the sacred realm of the supernatural. The modern conception of nature is just the opposite: nature is the land of the living, a sacred domain in symbolic opposition to the dominion of human technique. "Nature," as we use the word today, is that part of the world that we have kept our dirty fingers off of. It is precisely the name for what we have *not* conquered. When something comes under human control, it ceases to be nature for us and enters the realm of artifice, with all the connotations of perversion, pollution, and insincerity that attach to the unnatural. In short, nature for us means the nonhuman, and the nonhuman has become holy.

The hallowing of wildness began to become commonplace among European intelligentsia in the late eighteenth century, during the rise

217

of the Romantic movement. In England, the same decades also witnessed the onset of the Industrial Revolution and the first mass propaganda for humane treatment of animals. Many historians have sought connections between these phenomena. One of the first to do so was the young Karl Marx, who thought that the modern image of man as a sick animal estranged from nature is merely a superficial symptom of the real disease—namely, the oppression of the working class under capitalism. In capitalist economic systems, the products of labor are taken from the worker and appropriated by the capitalist. Under such conditions, argued Marx, the worker "only feels himself freely active in his animal functions—eating, drinking, and procreating, or at the most in his dwelling and dressing up, etc.: and in his human functions he no longer feels himself to be anything but an animal."[16]

In this alienated state, the distinctive human activity of labor assumes the mechanical pointlessness of a hamster running in a wheel, and our images of man become increasingly mechanical or bestial.[17] As the human self-image becomes debased, our images of the nonhuman—animals, nature, wilderness—become correspondingly humanized and idealized. "Nature acquires the meaning of what has grown organically, what was not created by man, in contrast to the artificial strictures of human society." It is accordingly credited with "a value opposed to the social institutions which strip man of his essence and imprison him." "Since the products that workers make in this type of industrial society are expropriated . . . there evolves the sense of alienation whereby the product (of labor), and indeed the whole of science and technology, appear as something alien, an independent threatening force that enslaves man and destroys the quality of his life."[18]

If such perceptions are only a pathological side effect of capitalism, then we would expect the citizens of communist countries not to venerate nature. For a long time they did not—but mainly because they were forbidden to do so. Under Stalinism, official art and propaganda painted wild nature as an enemy of the working class, calling on all Soviet citizens to help tame the wilderness and make it serve the needs of the proletariat. Novels, paintings, and posters showed heroic Soviet workers damming rivers, draining marshes, felling forests, and dotting the tundra with factories. Every good Marxist was expected to support the struggle of "collectively organized reason against the elemental forces of nature." "Praise of nature," declared Maxim Gorky, "is praise of a despot."[19]

This sort of orthodox Stalinist line can no longer be taken seriously. Ironically, the recent collapse of Soviet-bloc Marxism was probably hastened by the disastrous environmental effects of "collectively organized reason," which killed off the forests and poisoned the air and groundwater across large areas of eastern Europe.[20] During the Soviet Union's final decade, as the underpinnings of official Marxism sagged and disintegrated, Soviet attitudes toward nature and the environment converged on Western ones. The antitechnological misanthropy of postwar science fiction in the West found a popular eastern European counterpart in Stanislaw Lem's works;[21] the Bambi syndrome became conspicuous in Russian children's culture;[22] and the animal-rights movement began to develop a Soviet consituency.[23] By 1984, the old Bolshevik view of wild nature as the enemy of human progress—a view that used to be attributed to Gorky or Lysenko or Stalin and praised—was being attributed to Eric Hoffer and denounced.[24] The end was clearly in sight in 1988, when the Kremlin's chief ideologist announced that saving the environment takes precedence over the class struggle.[25]

All this casts doubt on the Marxian notion that reverence for nature is a capitalist aberration. Besides, some of the chief icons of that reverence—the hermit saint, the greenwood, the magic forest, the uncanny quarry, the sobbing deer—cannot be products of capitalism or industrialism, since they predate industrial civilization. The whole Romantic attitude toward nature had crystallized in Rousseau's thinking by the early 1750s, ten years before the invention of the spinning jenny, when the typical relationship of capital to labor was still typically that of a master to his apprentices and the most advanced industrial machines were Newcomen's steam pumps. In its inception, the Romantic attitude was more a response to the mechanistic rationalism of the age of Descartes, Hobbes, Locke, and Newton than a reaction against an industrial revolution that had not yet happened. Insofar as it was a reaction against anything, it was a reaction against scientific thinking.

SCIENCE threatens people. This is not something we can fix by trying to institute a gentler, more spiritual science of the sort urged by Lewis

and Merchant. Science is threatening by its very nature, for it undercuts the special status we accord to human beings. Because science
seeks universal laws that apply to all things, it encourages us to see all
things, including ourselves, as lumps of one universal stuff, subject in
theory to the same sort of prediction and control. Most of us find this
self-image demeaning and threatening. We can relieve the threat in
only two ways: by restricting technology's power over nature or by
taking ourselves out of nature.

Sanctifying the wilderness encourages us to restrict our power over
nature. Our reverence for wild nature lies at the heart of a system of
legal and ideological checks and balances that we have set up to try
to prevent the forces of science and technology from getting out of
hand. Many of the other beliefs and attitudes and myths examined in
this book are parts of the same system. The animalization of children's
culture inculcates a kind of nursery Romanticism that portrays the
world of animals as more innocent and friendlier than the world of
humanity. The Frankenstein story admonishes us that limits must be
placed on the scope of science and the growth of technology. The
postmodernist view of science reassures humanistic intellectuals that
the control scientists have over the world is only a matter of politics
and is therefore negotiable. Some of these ideological devices are saner
and more sensible than others, but they all work to restrict the claims
of science and technology to dominion over our minds and lives.

The hunting hypothesis of human origins was a similar ideological
device. In it, technology figures as something that sprang up out of
predatory bloodlust and divorced humanity from nature; that divorce
is depicted as a Fall, with explicit reference to the Genesis story. Some
of Dart's critics have tried to make out the hunting hypothesis as an
ideological prop for capitalist imperialism; but that seems unlikely,
since some Marxist anthropologists of the time also pointed to hunting
as the crucial development that had launched the human career.[26] In
its context in the writings of Dart, Ardrey, Lorenz, Golding, and
Jeffers during the postwar decade, the hunting hypothesis carried
much the same message as the writings of Aldo Leopold and Rachel
Carson: it sounded a warning against the dangers inherent in technology.

The hunting hypothesis also drew a sharper boundary between man
and beast than previous evolutionary accounts of human origins had

done. Dart's account of the hominid story began with an adaptive shift, from the life of a lazy fruit-eating simian to that of a cruel but clever predator. Although anthropologists have abandoned the hunting hypothesis itself, they have gone on looking for some other abrupt adaptive change to mark the onset of the human career. We are anxious to identify a discontinuity between nature and history, in order to exclude humanity from the compulsions of nature and to support our perceptions of human uniqueness. We want such human traits as big brains, bipedalism, language, and technology to be uniquely and uniformly human, because they have mythic importance for us as markers of human status. Seen as *uniquely* human traits, they explain and justify our dominion over the beasts; seen as *uniformly* human traits, they forbid us to explain or justify the dominion of one human group over another in similar terms.

Animals with human traits—big-brained dolphins, tool-making chimpanzees, talking parrots, signing gorillas—make us correspondingly uneasy. Even scientists, who are in general comfortable thinking of people as nothing but smart animals, are rarely comfortable seeing other animals as stupid people (which is the same equation put the other way round). Science is supposed to make the "higher" intelligible by reducing it to the "lower." Describing people in animal terms is therefore regarded as explanation and a triumph for science, whereas describing beasts in human terms is condemned as unscientific anthropomorphism.

This presupposition helps to explain why so many biologists and social scientists get huffy whenever humanlike feelings, thoughts, or abilities are attributed to animals. Jane Goodall's suggestion that chimpanzees' termiting sticks should count as tools, for example, recently evoked this riposte from Lord Zuckerman:

> During the first five years of my career as a scientist . . . I got to "know" many captive chimpanzees. A mature female with whom I often played was in the habit of picking up a piece of straw in order to "manicure"— I can think of no better word—my nails. It never occurred to me to regard her as a tool user, any more than I felt an "empathy" with her when I offered her my head so that she could "groom" my hair.[27]

Zuckerman offers this statement to prove himself a better scientist than Goodall, but it can equally well be read as a confession of prejudice. Like many scientists, Zuckerman cannot bring himself to apply even simple psychological and motivational terms ("know" or "groom") to any beast, no matter how intelligent and humanlike, without wrapping those words in snigger quotes.

In policing the animal-human boundary, scientists have shown considerable ingenuity in redefining supposedly unique human traits to keep them from being claimed for other animals. Consider our supposedly big brains. Human beings are supposed to be smarter than other animals, and therefore we ought to have larger brains. But in fact, elephants, whales, and dolphins have bigger brains than ours; and small rodents and monkeys have relatively bigger brains (their brains make up a larger percentage of body weight than ours do). Scientists who study these things have accordingly labored to redefine brain size, dividing brain weight by basal metabolic rate or some other exponential function of body weight to furnish a standard by which these animals' brains can be deemed smaller than ours.[28] The unique bigness of the human brain thus turns out to be a matter of definition.

The uniqueness of human language is also partly a matter of definition. Apes and parrots can learn to understand our signed or spoken questions, and to respond to them with semantically appropriate answers.[29] However, these animals cannot handle syntax (the grammatical rules underlying word order). Seizing on this inability, scientists have found reasons for claiming that syntax, not semantics, is the hallmark of true language and indispensable for humanlike thought processes—or even for consciousness itself.[30]

Early Darwinians, most of whom were by our standards racists and imperialists, felt comfortable seeing the boundary between man and ape as a difference in degree, bridged to some extent by the savages of Africa and Australia. Anthropologists today struggle to see it as a difference in kind, because that seems essential to our faith in universal human rights. A sharp animal-human boundary is the cornerstone of democracy. Unfortunately, this way of seeing things is hard to reconcile with Darwin. As Bertrand Russell put it: "If men developed by such slow stages that there were creatures which we should not know whether to classify as human or not, the question arises: at what stage in evolution did men, or their semi-human ancestors, begin to be all equal? . . . An adherent of evolution may maintain that not only the doctrine of the equality of all men, but also that of the rights of man, must be condemned as unbiological, since it makes too emphatic a distinction between men and other animals."[31]

Our culture offers to justify that distinction by viewing human beings as separate from nature and innately superior to it. At the same time, however, we view the natural order as sacred and establish elaborate machineries to protect it from human intervention. Though different subcultures place different stress on these two views, probably most of us would assent in some degree to both. But it is obvious that they do not fit very well together. Our vision of nature as man's holy slave is both incoherent and dishonest, like the patriarchal Victorian vision of Woman as a sort of angelic chattel.

The incoherence and dishonesty inherent in that Victorian ideology were eventually corrected by recognizing that the similarities between master and chattel had greater moral and political importance than the differences. Since there proved to be no morally interesting differences between women and men, the only way men could preserve their self-respect and integrity was to extend citizenship to women. The same was true of masters and slaves and of whites and blacks. In each of these cases, a heavily marked status boundary ultimately had to be given up because it was intellectually indefensible. And if the cognitive boundary between man and beast, between the world of history and the world of nature, is equally indefensible, we cannot defend human dignity without extending some sort of citizenship to the rest of nature—which means ceasing to treat the nonhuman world as a series of means to human ends.

Regan, Rachels, and other philosophers of the animal-rights movement have urged us to do exactly that for just that reason. At bottom, their philosophy is concerned less with the rights of animals than with furnishing a rational and defensible justification for the universal rights of humanity. Recognizing that people are animals and that, as Darwin put it, "there is no fundamental difference between man and the higher mammals in their mental faculties," the animal-rights philosophers seek to protect people from becoming mere things by stretching a corner of the mantle of human dignity around our dumb relatives.[32] The same anxieties that made Krutch insist he would not be an animal lead them to conclude that animals must in some sense be people.

For the reasons sketched by Russell, it may in the final analysis not be possible to harmonize democratic political theory with science without accepting some such conclusion. To reconcile our hard-won understanding of the continuity between man and animal with our equally hard-won insistence on the universal rights and dignity of human beings, we must find foundations in animal existence for the recognition of those rights and that dignity. Unfortunately, it is hard to see how this can be done consistently without giving up such exploitative conveniences as animal experimentation, furs, and meat eating. And despite all the forces that have promoted the growth of animalitarianism in the past three centuries, most of us—like Bentham, Franklin, and Pope—still prize consistency less highly than sausage.

TWELVE

A View to a Death in the Morning

So far from hunting's being a reasoned pursuit, reason can be described more appropriately as the greatest threat to the existence of hunting.

—Ortega y Gasset

THE hunting hypothesis originated as a myth, concocted out of antique preconceptions and wishful thinking. But that does not prove it false. Sometimes people guess at the truth for no good reason. Lucretius rightly surmised that prehistoric people had used stones as weapons. Anaximander guessed that men had developed from fish. Swift accurately described the moons of Mars before any astronomer had seen them.[1] The hunting hypothesis might be another one of those lucky guesses. Even if it was advanced for the wrong reasons, we still need to ask whether it embodies some sort of truth about human origins or human nature.

Was hunting really an important factor in human origins? Some anthropologists have recently been trying to reopen this question,[2] but I am inclined to think that it is a question that science cannot hope to answer—at least, not as it is usually posed.

It is a safe bet that our australopithecine ancestors were hunters in a broad sense: that is, they sometimes killed and ate other animals, just as chimpanzees and people do today. And since people today are more predatory than chimpanzees, it is another safe bet that hunting took on an increased importance during the course of our evolution from a chimpanzee-like ancestor.

But none of this implies that hunting was what "made us human." To draw that conclusion, we need good reasons for thinking that our ancestors' predatory habits somehow *caused* some of the distinctive human traits we want to explain. Such reasons are hard to find. It is never easy to demonstrate causality in evolution—and it becomes logically impossible when the effect we want to explain is human uniqueness.

Science cannot furnish us with grounds for thinking that hunting, or anything else, made human beings uniquely different from other animals. This is not a deficiency we can cure by launching more expeditions to look for fossils in Africa; it is a matter of the logic of causal explanation. To explain something is to show that it is an instance of some general rule, familiar to us from other instances. As David Hume pointed out long ago, science can have nothing to say about the causes of unique phenomena that do not fit into any sort of larger pattern. It follows that the only evolutionary changes we can hope to explain are what are called *parallelisms:* recurrent modifications that show up over and over again in different lineages for the same structural or adaptive reasons, such as the sleek body lines of fast-swimming animals like porpoises or the long, slender legs of swift runners like deer. If there really are human peculiarities that find no parallels in other creatures, then they are inexplicable. As long as we insist on hearing stories that "explain" human uniqueness, we will have to forgo genuine explanations and content ourselves with narrative fables, in which all the causal links are supplied by the imagination.

The hunting hypothesis was such a fable. Its abrupt acceptance by science in the years after World War II had more to do with new conceptions of the animal-human boundary than it did with the facts about *Australopithecus africanus*. We should recognize it as an origin myth, dreamt up to justify the dubious distinction we draw between the human domain and the wild kingdom of nature.

This does not, however, imply that we can afford to smile at the hunting hypothesis as a quaint mistake and sweep it into the dustbin of history. Good myths embody big truths; and this one is likely to

226

be a good myth, because it has for centuries been lovingly embroidered by great storytellers. Even if hunting does not have the causal importance that anthropologists once attributed to it, it may still be linked to some essential human taint, some fundamental disorder or sickness that makes the human condition peculiarly tragic or dangerous. If so, we ought not to disregard the myth of the killer ape.

THESE questions took on personal meaning for me on a bright, cold September morning in 1991, when I got up at dawn and drove to the small farm in Hillsborough, North Carolina, where my wife Kaye and I keep a couple of horses. Driving down the country road that goes by our farm, I saw a beat-up sedan with a peeling vinyl top parked in the weeds alongside the road. A stranger was bent over beside the car, messing with what looked like a discarded crib mattress. He straightened up when he saw my car coming. He was a white man in his thirties, with the kind of bony, desperate-looking face you see on Confederate cannon fodder in old Civil War photos. He looked wary and guilty and dangerous, and so did his buddy sitting behind the wheel. I stopped and looked back after I had gone a hundred feet. The two men sat motionless, watching me and waiting for me to drive on; so I did.

Two whitetail deer, a doe and a half-grown fawn, bounded across the road as I came to our farm. I knew those deer. The doe had been crossing the road at this spot every morning for a month with a pair of twin fawns—one male, one female. Kaye had christened them—what else?—Bambi and Faline. I waited for the second fawn to show up and follow the doe, but no fawn came. After a few minutes, I drove on and did the stable chores.

The two men had left by the time I started back home, so I stopped to look at the mattress, which turned out to be something wrapped up in a bloodstained pink sheet. I threw back the sheet and discovered the decapitated, skinned, and gutted body of a small deer. One hind leg had been wrenched off and taken away. The empty hip socket looked up at me like a blind pink eye. I decided not to poke through the sticky, oozing mess in search of reproductive organs to find out whether this was the remnants of Bambi or Faline.

I have thought a lot about those two hunters and their motives since then, driving back and forth past the decaying cadaver and watching the birds and insects reduce it to a skeleton. Why do people do such things? Why would two grown men stay up all night, risking all sorts of penalties for killing prohibited quarry on posted property (which my neighbor has been known to defend with a shotgun), just to convert a graceful and beautiful wild animal into that stinking ruin? Why had they bothered to clean and dress the carcass and then kept only a few handfuls of meat, leaving the rest to rot by the roadside? And why on earth had they carefully wrapped the discarded body in a little pink sheet before they took off?

The motives of hunters are vague and visceral, and nonhunters find them hard to understand. To most of us, ceremoniously going into the woods once a year to kill deer with a rifle sounds about as attractive as marching into the dairy barn once a year to bash cows with a sledgehammer. Because hunters have trouble articulating and defending their motives, nonhunters often conclude that they are simply crazy. From the Renaissance to the present day, writers who have seen hunting as a sign of man's depravity have assumed that the hunter takes a psychopathic pleasure in inflicting pain and death. As Joseph Wood Krutch put it:

> Killing "for sport" is the perfect type of that pure evil for which metaphysicians have sometimes sought. Most wicked deeds are done because the doer proposes some good to himself . . . [but] the killer for sport has no such comprehensible motive. He prefers death to life, darkness to light. He gets nothing except the satisfaction of saying, "Something which wanted to live is dead. There is that much less vitality, consciousness, and, perhaps, joy in the universe. I am the Spirit that Denies."[3]

Many others see hunters in this same light, as inscrutable, bloodthirsty lunatics. Hunters, writes Joy Williams, "are persecutors of nature who should be prosecuted":

> They're overequipped . . . insatiable, malevolent, and vain. They maim and mutilate and despoil. And for the most part, they're inept. Grossly inept. Camouflaged toilet paper is a must for the modern hunter, along with his Bronco and his beer. Too many hunters taking a dump in the woods with their roll of Charmin beside them were mistaken for white-tailed deer and shot. Hunters get excited. They'll shoot anything—the

pallid ass of another sportsman or even themselves. A Long Island man died last year when his shotgun went off as he clubbed a wounded deer with the butt. Hunters get mad. They get restless and want to fire! They want to use those assault rifles and see foamy blood on the ferns.[4]

Williams thinks sport hunting should be prohibited by law. That proposal is supported by a large number of pro-animal organizations, from hardcore animal-rights groups like PETA and Friends of Animals all the way over to mainstream humane societies like the Massachusetts SPCA.[5] One recent poll indicates that almost a third of all Americans agree with them. And pro-animal activists are not the only ones who see hunters as crazy killers. Even some U.S. Fish and Wildlife agents, who presumably ought to support sport hunting if anyone does, complain about "four-wheel-drive, assault-rifle, gun-and-run, shoot-anything yahoos who think they're Rambo."[6]

This stereotype of the hunter—as a violent, psychopathic male compulsive eager to shoot anything that moves—is a staple of popular culture, recurring in innumerable films, TV shows, and comic strips.[7] It has been set to music, in Tom Lehrer's *Hunting Song:*

> I always will remember,
> 'Twas a year ago November,
> I went out to hunt some deer
> On a morning bright and clear.
> I went and shot the maximum the game laws would allow:
> Two game wardens, seven hunters, and a cow.[8]

Even some hunters concede that the main motive for hunting is a simple, weasel-like joy in killing things and seeing foamy blood on the ferns. "We *like* to kill animals," admits the hunting journalist Humberto Fontova. "Hunters are simply guys who get a thrill out of killing animals." Fontova thinks that evolution has implanted an instinctive love of killing in his breast. "I recognize the urge as a predatory instinct to kill. Man is a predator—has been for tens of thousands of years. It's going to take a while to breed that out of us, and thank God I won't be around by then."[9]

Fontova is not the only hunting writer who offers the hunting hypothesis as a rationale for hunting. A lot of them insist that their urge to kill is something they were born with, an instinctive blood lust inherited from our killer-ape ancestors. Those who do not thrill to the chase seem rootless and degenerate to them. "For some unfortunates," wrote Robert Ruark,

> prisoned by city sidewalks and sentenced to a cement jungle more horrifying than anything to be found in Tanganyika, the horn of the hunter never winds at all. But deep in the guts of most men is buried the involuntary response to the hunter's horn, a prickle of the nape hairs, an acceleration of the pulse, an atavistic memory of his fathers, who killed first with stone, and then with club, and then with spear, and then with bow, and then with gun, and finally with formulae. How meek the man is of no importance; somewhere in the pigeon chest of the clerk is still the vestigial remnant of the hunter's heart; somewhere in his nostrils the half-forgotten smell of blood.[10]

The hunting writer Tom McIntyre thinks that a distaste for the hunt is a perversion of our instincts, like celibacy or anorexia:

> Being hunters is what made humans what they are . . . from millions of years of a hunting past that shaped everything from our bodies to our brains to our social relationships. Ten thousand years of grubbing in the dirt is hardly an adequate period for the impulse to hunt to be extinguished in our lives. And so the real aberration is not that some humans still hunt and kill, but that some do not.[11]

But if the desire to hunt and kill is a human instinct, it is a curiously restricted one. Only about 12 percent of Americans hunt, and their numbers grow smaller every year.[12] Though most of us still think it all right to hunt for meat, polls show that large majorities are opposed to hunting simply for trophies or for recreation.[13] If killing animals were an intrinsically pleasurable activity like eating, drinking, and making love, then the majorities would presumably lean the other way—and, as the hunting naturalist Valerius Geist points out, a lot more of us would be eager to land a job cutting steers' throats in a slaughterhouse.[14]

In short, there is no reason to think that human beings have any innate fondness for bloodshed. No doubt some people hunt because they enjoy killing animals. But those people are kidding themselves when they claim that their love of killing is something all of us are born with—or even something they have in common with all hunters.

Other hunters, in fact, argue the reverse: that "buck fever," the nervous trembling and paralysis of the trigger finger that afflicts novice hunters, stems from an ingrained *reluctance* to kill that the beginner must learn to overcome.[15] And at the other end of their hunting careers, many experienced outdoorsmen finally hang up their weapons because they have simply grown sick of killing. In an interview with the great bowhunter Fred Bear, John Mitchell asked him why he had given up hunting. Bear thought it over before he answered:

> "Oh, I suppose it was all those years, and trips," he said. "Every damn time I went hunting, I had to *kill* something." He stopped then and turned his face toward the rain, and in a voice so soft and low I could barely hear it, said at last, "I figure you know damn well what I mean."[16]

If hunters themselves often start out and end up with a distaste for killing, then why do they hunt? The writings of hunters and the studies that have been undertaken of their motives show that different people hunt for different reasons. Some of these reasons are easy for the nonhunter to understand. Others are not.

Simple economic need furnishes the best and most easily understood reason for hunting. But it is not a real motive for most modern hunters, many of whom spend large sums of money every year in the hope of fetching home a few wildfowl or a few dozen pounds of venison. The hunters who sink $20,000 or $30,000 into building specialized all-terrain vehicles to chase deer through the swamps of southern Florida are not trying to economize on their grocery bills.[17] In the past, many people hunted because the bodies of wild animals provided them with food and clothing and other materials that they could not so easily obtain in any other way. This still holds true for a few rural Americans today. For the vast majority of hunters in modern America, however, hunting is a net drain on assets and has no real economic value.[18] One sign of this fact is the carrion that accumulates during hunting season alongside many rural American roads where hunters have killed deer or wildfowl, hacked off a few choice cuts of meat, and left the rest of the carcass for the crows.[19]

Some hunters condemn this sort of careless slaughter as "unethical," and make a point of trying to eat, wear, or utilize in some other way every possible scrap of their quarry's body. "I don't waste anything," proclaims one hunter held up as a model in a 1985 National Rifle Association ad. "I process the meat, tan the buckskin, make thread and lacings from the sinew, even scrimshaw the bones."[20] The underlying notion here, that a truly ethical hunter is one who wastes no part of the animals he kills, is a fairly new idea. There are hints of this clean-plate ethic in the nineteenth century—for example, in the pronouncements of Cooper's Deerslayer or in Oscar Wilde's famous characterization of English fox hunting as "the unspeakable in pursuit of the uneatable."[21] But before World War II, the plebeian "pot hunter" or meat hunter was commonly looked down on as the social and moral inferior of the classier sport hunter, who killed for amusement rather than from vulgar need.[22] The clean-plate ethic seems to be mainly a postwar phenomenon, probably connected with the general rise in ecological consciousness during the second half of this century.

Another ecology-related rationale sometimes offered for hunting is the need to keep population numbers down so that the prey animals will not die a lingering death from starvation in lean seasons. A great deal of ink has been expended in articulating and attacking this rationale,[23] but all that needs to be said here is that population control has never been a *motive* for hunting. Hunters do not trudge reluctantly off into the woods out of a sense of humanitarian duty, to locate starving animals and put them out of their misery. In fact, hunters are usually the first to protest when wolves, coyotes, cougars, feral dogs, or other nonhuman predators move into an area and start taking over the job of controlling game populations.[24] Perhaps the most interesting fact about this whole controversy is that it is always focused exclusively on those archetypal martyrs of the wildwood, the deer. No one has much to say one way or the other about the hunter's obligation to keep opossums, foxes, or ravens from starving to death in the snows of winter.

Many hunters hunt for social reasons that have nothing to do with hunting as such. Whenever hunting has been a marker of the ruling class, social climbers have joined the chase in order to gain status and cozy up to the gentry. Conversely, hunting is a seasonal ritual of working-class solidarity for many rural American men. When they go hunting, they feel that they are renewing their bonds with friends and kinfolk and reaffirming their ties to the land and way of life they have inherited from their ancestors.[25] Still other men like to go hunting precisely because it gets them away from their kinfolk and into the exclusively male company of old buddies, with whom they can relax, "drink beer, shoot at inoffensive animals, and talk about pussy."[26] For such men, hunting addresses a different kind of social need—a need for what is sometimes called "male bonding."

The connection of hunting with masculinity runs deep, and both hunters and their critics often comment on it. Hunting has been a stereotypically male activity throughout most of Western history. In America today, the vast majority of hunters are male; some 21 percent of men but only about 2 percent of women hunt.[27] Women who hunt generally do so with male companions, and their participation in a hunt is often resented by male hunters. Many male hunters believe that hunting affirms their identity as men, and feel that taking a boy hunting cements his bonds to other males and helps make a man of him.[28]

Some hunters think that their sport affirms their virility as well as their masculine identity. "The sentiment of self-importance makes the enjoyment of women all the more pleasant after hunting," wrote the sixteenth-century Indian king Rudradeva of Kumaon.[29] Though few modern hunters would put it that candidly, some of them obviously believe that hunting makes them sexier. You can see it in the double-entendres on their bumper stickers. BOWHUNTERS HAVE LONGER SHAFTS, asserts one such sticker. I HUNT WHITE TAIL YEAR ROUND, proclaims another (which is decorated with drawings of a deer's scut and a woman's buttocks to make sure nobody misses the pun). And some women do seem to be attracted to the aura of deadly force and competence that surrounds an accomplished hunter. That aura pre-sumably explains why some clothing manufacturers peddle hunting togs to nonhunters as intriguingly sexy getups.[30]

Since hunters often think of hunting as a marker of manhood, each side in the debate over hunting tends to suspect that there is something shaky about the other side's sexual identity. Opponents of hunting are not above intimating that hunters go out and kill things because they are neurotically anxious to prove their virility.[31] For their part, hunters have been known to suggest that their critics are either limp-wristed sissies with too little testosterone or bull-necked viragos with too much. Antihunting activists, scoffs one hunting writer,

> are mostly aging hippies still asking what's called their women if 1968 was their best year . . . What's called men in that group wear turtlenecks and Earth Shoes, and have granny glasses hanging around their skinny necks. The men would rather be eating a bowl of granola than chasing pipefitters from Pittsburgh but their larger women and matriarchal mores won't let them.[32]

Going back and forth over this muddied ground is not likely to yield any clear answers. No doubt some men are attracted to hunting because it makes them feel manly. But there are many devoted hunters who show no evident need to prove themselves in this way, and who hunt for reasons that apparently have nothing to do with their gender identification.

Many articulate hunters, the ones who are most apt to write books on the joys of the hunt, say that they hunt in order to feel that they are part of nature. Hunting is for them mostly a pretext for being outdoors, an "excuse to get out into the hills, away from the crowds, to live, if only for a few days, beyond the wall."[33] Such hunters relish the pursuit of the quarry because it disciplines and focuses what might otherwise become a careless stroll through the woods.[34] John Mitchell recalls that he and his other boyhood friends who took up hunting were set apart from their fellows by their "land sense," their love of and sensitivity to the natural order: "a way of looking at the land, and noting where the acorns fell, and which side of a tree the moss grew on, and how the prickly buckeye fruits split open in October, and why the stirred-up leaves and wisp of rabbit fur probably meant there was an owl nearby, dozing on a full stomach."[35] Hunting, writes the sports columnist Craig Holt, is a way of "keeping a promise with the land," which prevents him from becoming "isolated from the natural world."[36] Valerius Geist, struggling to define his reasons for hunting, describes it as an "intercourse with nature":

> It's a welcome weight on one's shoulders when one hikes home with game in the bag and a set of antlers or horns protruding from the pack.

During a rest break, the hand touches the gleaming points (or the horn tips), caresses the antler beams (or the burr), and plays with the soft hair on the head. Hunting is a passion better men than I have tried to describe . . . and attempted to explain. Some have called it sport. I disagree. Some have called it cruel and unjust—an uncultured act, done for the sake of killing. I disagree. It is no more "sport" than is gardening; it is no more done for the sake of killing than gardening is done for the sake of killing vegetables. If it is sporting, with whom is one competing? The animals? I should blush at such a comparison, given the weapons we possess and the skills in hunting we are capable of . . . Were someone to call it an intercourse with nature, I should shake my head at the choice of words, but I shall know what that person gets out of hunting. When stalking, one's guts must tell one that one is doing something right, that one is reliving the very drama that caused man's ancestors to rise from the apes to become men.[37]

Nature-loving hunters can be found working either side of the animal-human boundary. For some of them, like Geist, part of the charm of hunting is that it gives them a sense of what that boundary means. Others like to hunt because it dissolves that boundary for them and lets them know that they themselves are beasts. One such hunter is James Dickey, with his fantasies of stripping naked to dance with deer and breaking the creek ice with his face to "drink from the lifespring of beasts." The syndicated outdoorsman Bob Simpson is another. "I know that I can eat better and cheaper on beef that was raised in confinement," Simpson admits, "but I must know that I can survive without an intercessor, that I am part of, and have common bond with, the wilderness, a common citizen of this planet along with the other animals."[38] "I go hunting," insists one lyrical hunter, "to have shadowy, sometimes violent encounters with my brother animals."[39] The essence of sportive hunting, claimed the philosopher Ortega y Gasset, is "a conscious and almost religious humbling of man which limits his superiority and lowers him toward the animal."[40]

This whole system of motives, and the world view they entail, are akin to those of the animal-rights activist. The activist and the devout hunter worship at different chapels in the same church. Both long to break through the animal-human boundary, and both tend to see the wilderness as a realm of order and harmony from which the human species is alienated. For the theorists of the hunting hypothesis, hunting was the cause of man's alienation from nature; for many nature-loving sportsmen, it represents the cure for that alienation. "The human being," wrote Ortega, "tries to rest from the enormous discomfort and all-embracing disquiet of history by 'returning' transitorily, artificially, to Nature in the sport of hunting," which "alone permits us the greatest luxury of all, the ability to enjoy a vacation from the human condition."[41]

One important difference that separates nature-loving hunters from their opponents is that the antihunting activist worries about the lives and welfare of individual members of an animal species, whereas the hunter-ecologist regards the species as the enduring entity and sees the hunted animal chiefly as an ephemeral sample of it. This was one of the issues that divided Burroughs and Roosevelt from Long and the other "nature fakers," and hunters today often bring it up in reply to their critics. "The problem with animal-rights advocates," complains one sports columnist, "is that they have a fundamental ignorance of animals. They tend to view animals as individuals, not species."[42] Though the hunters' population-centered attitude is condemned as "environmental fascism" by animal-rights people,[43] it is widely shared by environmentalists and biologists.

Many hunters say that killing their own food gives them a feeling of cutting through the trivia and hypocrisy of civilization and getting in touch with life's elemental realities. "Part of what makes hunting such an emotional experience," writes one deer hunter, "is the physical responsibility you take for the death of your food . . . Hunting takes us out of the world of telephones, fluorescent lights, and bus exhaust into a primal world where, yes, the drama of the kill, the smell of the prey, and the feel of warm blood help restore our sense of belonging to nature."[44] (The underlying assumption here is that warm deer blood is real in a way that hot bus exhaust is not.) Hunters who share this perspective often deride antihunters as Disney-deluded dreamers unable to face the grim realities of life on earth. "Killing animals is not wrong. It is certainly part of the real world. God does it," replied rock singer Ted Nugent when the animal-rights activist Teresa Gibbs wrote imploring him to give up hunting. "Come on, Teresa, get your fat ass out of the office and let me take you along with my children and friends to the beautiful world of truth and experience."[45]

For hunters like Nugent, part of the attraction of hunting is that it keeps them in touch with "the beautiful world of truth and experience." The hunt reassures them that life is harsh and therefore earnest and meaningful. The conflict between such hunters and their critics reflects differing visions of what the world is really like. The hunter sees nature as cruel, whereas the antihunter sees nature as kindly and thinks of cruelty as a uniquely human trait.[46] The notion that we should all try to get along in peace and harmony with our woodland friends disgusts many hunters, in the same way that someone who breeds and trains attack dogs might be disgusted by a wriggling Pekinese. Such hunters enjoy hunting because it confronts them with cold, beautiful truths—what George Orwell called "the simple, intelligible disasters that give you the feeling of being up against the bedrock facts of life."[47]

In this respect, hunting has an appeal like that of dramatic tragedy. We like tragedy, argued Francis Gummere, because it gratifies our craving for truth:

> Only the tragic can be finally true . . . Day in, day out, it is pleasanter to keep the screen of comedy before us, and to take the curtain for the play; but to every man come times when he desires to see the thing as it is, and then what he sees is tragedy . . . Tragedy plays the game, without complaint, and with no thought beyond the limits of the scene . . . [Tragic poets] know by instinct . . . that only the anguish of some inevitable conflict is worth while.[48]

Similar things are sometimes said in defense of hunting and other blood sports. "Life," wrote Ortega y Gassett, "is a terrible conflict, a grandiose and atrocious confluence. Hunting submerges man deliberately in that formidable mystery and therefore contains something of religious rite and emotion in which homage is paid to what is divine, transcendent, in the laws of Nature."[49]

ALL these considerations help to make the attraction of the hunt clearer to the nonhunter. But we need to recognize that hunters have other,

237

less comprehensible motives, which are not so easy to sympathize with. Much of the art and literature of sport hunting expresses a strangely conflicted set of emotions that strike the nonhunter as unsane—not just harmlessly dotty, but twisted and sick. Consider, for example, this poetic description of deer hunting by William Thompson, one of the founding fathers of the sport of bowhunting in America:

> To see the soft and devious approach of the wary thing; to see the lifted light head turned sharply back toward the evil that roused it from its bed of ferns; to feel the strong bow tightening in my hand as the thin, hard string comes back; to feel the leap of the loosened cord, the jar of the bow, and see the long streak of the going shaft, and hear the almost sickening "chuck" of the stabbing arrow. No one can know how I have loved the woods, the streams, the trails of the wild, the ways of the things of slender limbs, of fine nose, of great eager ears, of mild wary eyes, and of vague and half-revealed forms and colors. I have been their friend and mortal enemy. I have so loved them that I longed to kill them.[50]

That last sentence would seem pathological in any other context, and it seems reasonable to regard it as pathological here. Yet the emotion Thompson describes, the lyrical love that expresses itself as a wish to slay, is commonplace among serious hunters. One thinks of James Dickey dancing naked with his quarry, or Valerius Geist caressing the severed heads of his victims. "Love," wrote the German hunter Heinrich Laube in 1841, "is the passion-mystery between one person and another, and hunting is the passion-mystery between people and all non-human things."[51] "You see the animal and it becomes a love object," one intellectual hunter told John Mitchell. "There is tremendous sexuality in this . . . in the sense of wanting something deeply, in the sense of *eros*. All quests, all desires are ultimately the same."[52] This motif crops up again and again throughout the literature of hunting: many hunters deeply and sincerely love the animals they kill, and they identify that love as one of their reasons for wanting to kill them.

There is no reason to think that this murderous amorousness characterizes all hunters, or that it has any historical or adaptive connection with the predatory habits of our prehuman ancestors. But it does show that hunting is often entangled with something dark, violent, and irrational in the human psyche, whatever the source of that darkness may ultimately prove to be.

This is also implied by the feelings of guilt that pervade the art and literature of hunting. Those feelings are clear in the writings of Montaigne and in the antihunting propaganda produced by reformed hunters like Seton and Galsworthy.[53] The hunter's guilt is more guarded, but still unmistakable, in Renaissance hunting manuals and in the works of animal-loving hunters like Oudry, Courbet, Landseer, Bonheur, and Salten. It attains a bizarre intensity in the fiction of T. H. White—who spent the fall of 1938 alternately shooting geese and working on a novel, *Grief for the Grey Geese,* about a reformed hunter who loves wild geese and tries to save them from being shot.[54] This sort of inner conflict is usually a sign that something wrong is going on.

In fact, that wrongness may itself be part of the attraction of hunting. Some men, like William Thompson, seem to enjoy feeling evil; and some hunters—say, those who kill wild animals for no discernible reason and dump them beside country roads—may enjoy their sport precisely because it makes them feel wild and wicked and crazy. This sort of hunting is Dionysian. It is the modern equivalent of the *diasparagmos,* or the rural equivalent of running through Central Park at night, raping and murdering random New Yorkers.

Hunters sometimes put forward the same excuse for hunting that many rapists offer for rape: they insist they are not to blame because the victim was asking for it.[55] Ortega y Gasset recounts the experience of a Spanish hunting party en route to a hunting preserve, who skidded their car to a stop and got tangled up in an insane scramble to find their weapons when they passed a couple of wolves by the side of the road. Ortega blames the hunters' frenzy on the *wolves*:

> It is a question of reflex and not of deliberation, not even for an instant. It is not man who gives to those wolves the role of possible prey. It is the animal—in this case the wolves themselves—which demands that he be considered in this way, so that not to react with a predatory impulse would be anti-natural . . . [Hunting] is a relationship that certain animals

239

impose on man, to the point where not trying to hunt them demands the intervention of our deliberate will . . . Before any particular hunter pursues them they feel themselves to be possible prey, and they model their whole existence in terms of this condition. Thus they automatically convert any normal man who comes upon them into a hunter. *The only adequate response to a being that lives obsessed with avoiding capture is to try to catch it.*[56]

By the same token, presumably, the only adequate response to a woman who is obsessed with avoiding rape is to rape her—at least, if one is a "normal man."

Some of the feelings that many hunters express—the murderous love and other incoherent emotions, the Hemingwayesque anxiety about sexual identity, the relish for doing delicious evil, the false and contemptuous affection for the victim, the refusal to think of the victim as an individual—are also common feelings among rapists.[57] The same sort of psychology is evident in the pornographic allure of cheap rod-and-gun magazines, with their snapshot galleries of grinning hunters holding up the heads of big, beautiful deer corpses. It is implicit in the stories that many deer hunters tell about how majestic bucks are lured to their death by their fatal weakness for the seductive doe.[58] All these things support the contention of some feminist writers that sportive hunting is sometimes a symbolic attack on women.[59] Perhaps the real social pathology linked to hunting is not war, as the hunting hypothesis would have it, but rape.

FINALLY, we need to ask whether hunting is wrong. There may be no clear-cut answer to this question. But we can at least decide whether the answer we give is in principle compatible with other things we believe.

There is a consensus today, at any rate in the industrialized West, that the suffering of sentient animals is something that is intrinsically undesirable: that, other things being equal, the deliberate infliction of such suffering is something that must be *justified,* by showing that it serves a higher or more urgent goal. If we accept any sort of laws against cruelty to animals, we must accept this proposition. And if we do, it is hard to see how we can justify sportive hunting, since it inflicts grave suffering for the sake of mere amusement. If killing animals is wrong as a spectator sport, it ought to be equally wrong as a participatory sport.

Hunters generally dismiss this issue as irrelevant. After all, everything dies sooner or later. Something must kill these animals eventually, they say, and it might as well be us.[60] The trouble with this argument is that it provides an equally good (or bad) rationale for sportive homicide. One hunting writer argues that the suffering of the quarry is not the sort of thing that grownups can afford to worry about: "We must, by the time we finish growing, have learned that you can never stop and think or it will break your heart."[61] But this is exactly backwards. Children, not grownups, are the people who are unconcerned about the results of their behavior. Growing up involves learning to recognize the consequences of our actions and taking responsibility for them; and one consequence of hunting is the infliction of pain and death for no very urgent reason.

Probably most critics of hunting conspire in the killing of beasts in other ways for various purposes of their own. Philosophical sportsmen often accuse such critics of hypocrisy. If hunting is objectionable because it inflicts pain and death for the sake of amusement, these sportsmen argue, then other killing of animals for aesthetic purposes ought to be equally objectionable—and in an age of soy protein and plastics, eating steak and wearing leather are just as purely a matter of aesthetics as trophy hunting and bullfighting are.[62] Yet even granting the justice of this argument, the antihunter can still legitimately retort that enjoying the fruits of the kill is not the same thing as taking pleasure in killing itself. Even the most enthusiastic lover of fried chicken may suspect that there is something wrong with a man who finds recreation in wringing the necks of pullets.

As a last recourse, the hunter can always fall back on Nietzsche and insist that we cannot affirm life unless we affirm killing and its attendant suffering. Most thoughtful hunters today would probably agree with Nietzsche that "life itself is violent, rapacious, exploitative, and destructive and cannot be conceived otherwise."[63] Although probably not many would wholeheartedly endorse Nietzsche's corollary that "to speak of right and wrong *per se* makes no sense at all," milder assertions to the same effect are common in hunting literature:

> There is almost no way for one form of life to exist *except* at the expense
> of another . . . Those who wish to make a moral issue out of hunting [do
> not understand that the hunt] . . . is absolutely beyond accepted, formal
> morality in the way, at essence, that other fundamental human activity,
> sex, is . . . by itself it is neither good nor evil; it only is.[64]

This amounts to saying that questions of morality may be brushed
aside in talking about hunting because hunting is natural and real,
whereas morality is cultural and arbitrary. Both of these judgments
seem mistaken.

There is no reason to think that hunting is natural in the sense of
being instinctive for human beings. (Probably most of the people who
have ever lived have never hunted.) Our tendency to think of it as
"natural" in a looser sense, as a woodsy, primitive sort of activity
unconstrained by social niceties, is a Romantic conceit that has distant
roots in the myths of Dionysus and Robin Hood and more recent
ones in eighteenth-century delusions about noble savages. Prior to the
rise of Romanticism, the chase was not regarded as something primitive or undisciplined. Throughout most of European history, from
ancient Greece down to the colonial empires of the early twentieth
century, hunting was a highly formalized pursuit dominated by the
military aristocracy, and its governing myths and symbols centered on
images of reason, dominion, and control.

In America today, hunting has ceased to be a marker of high social
status, and hunting writers tend to describe their sport as a return to
nature rather than as a punitive expedition against the wilderness.
Many of them invoke the hunting hypothesis to support this view.
Hunting, they assure their readers, is the primordial human enterprise.
It brings us back to the edge of nature where everything human began,
where "the drama of the kill, the smell of the prey, and the feel of
warm blood help restore our sense of belonging to nature." Perhaps
the quickest way to disabuse oneself of this sort of primitivist fantasy
is to study all the elaborate ceremonial usages surrounding the killing
and dismemberment of quarry in a Renaissance hunting manual.
Hunting in modern America is a relatively rustic and informal business
because we have chosen to make it so. That choice is itself a matter
of social convention.

Hunting, then, is not a "natural" activity in any meaningful sense, and moral issues have as much bearing on the hunt as they have on any other human undertaking. It is a mistake to dismiss such issues as artificial and arbitrary. Although moral values are artificial, they are not arbitrary. Like the monetary values we put on commodities, moral values are constrained by the facts of nature and the prices that people are willing to pay.

Several large facts of nature bear on the morality of the hunt. It is a fact of nature that human beings are animals. Science has taught us to regard ourselves as the descendants and cousins of beasts, and to acknowledge that most or all of our capacities are expressed to some degree among our close animal relatives. As materialists and Darwinians, scientists are compelled to recognize those relatives as being in effect deformed human beings, differing from us only in certain genetic rearrangements that make them grow up funny-looking and stupid.

Since (as Bentham noted) nothing distinguishes all humans from all beasts, we have no grounds for valuing human life per se above all other sorts of life. We cannot sustain our belief in the intrinsic value of human life unless we can identify something about animal life itself that we value and are prepared to balance in the scales of decision making against other, conflicting goods and values. We have so far avoided doing that, because such a move would carry a high price. It would mean abandoning the moral boundary we draw between people and beasts, the line separating responsible agents with rights and duties from more or less neutral stuff that can be made into soap and lampshades. And abandoning that boundary and expanding the moral community to include nonhuman things would mean giving up the parallel boundary we have erected between the human domain and the wild kingdom of nature.

The erosion of the animal-human boundary threatens the moral foundations of hunting, as it does of any activity that assumes a qualitative moral difference between people and beasts. But anything that tends to dissolve the boundary between man and nature poses a still more fundamental threat to hunting, by undercutting its conceptual foundations. Throughout Western history, the hunt has been defined as a confrontation between the human world and the wild. Giving up the distinction between those two worlds means discarding the whole system of symbolic meanings that have distinguished hunting from mere butchery and given it a special importance in the history of Western thought. If the edge of nature is a hallucination, then hunting is only animal-killing, and we are compelled to see it in the same harsh light in which it appeared to More's Utopians.

Even if the boundary between the human order and the natural order ceases to be recognized, no doubt people will go on killing friendly and unfriendly animals for various reasons. But no matter what sort of animals they kill or how they do it, they will have ceased to hunt.

244

. . . .

Sometimes, as one can see
Carved at Amboise in a high relief, on the lintel stone
Of the castle chapel, hunters have strangely come
To a mild close of the chase, bending the knee
Instead of the bow, struck sweetly dumb
To see from the brow bone

Of the hounded stag a cross
Grown, and the eyes clear with grace. Perfectly still
Are the cruising dogs as well, their paws aground
In a white hush of lichen. Beds of moss
Spread, and the clearing wreathes around
The dear suspense of will.

But looking higher now
To the chapel steeple, see among points
   and spines of the updrawn
Vanishing godbound stone, ringing its sped
Thrust as a target tatters, a round row
Of real antlers taken from dead
Deer. The hunt goes on.

—Richard Wilbur

Notes

1. The Killer Ape

EPIGRAPH: S. A. Barnett, 1980.

1. R. A. Dart and D. Craig, 1959, pp. 30–31; A. Paton, 1964, pp. 77, 80–82, 94.
2. A. Paton, 1964, pp. 96 ff.
3. P. V. Tobias, 1984, p. 9.
4. R. A. Dart and D. Craig, 1959, p. 32.
5. R. A. Dart and D. Craig, 1959, p. 7.
6. P. V. Tobias, 1984, p. 33.
7. R. A. Dart, 1926.
8. R. A. Dart, 1925a.
9. R. A. Dart, 1926.
10. R. A. Dart, 1940.
11. Dart (1940) quotes this last phrase approvingly from W. K. Gregory and M. Hellman, 1939.
12. R. A. Dart, 1940, 1948, 1949.
13. R. A. Dart, 1957a; 1957b, p. 30.
14. R. A. Dart and D. Craig, 1959, p. 195.
15. B. G. Campbell, 1972.
16. W. Etkin, 1954.
17. W. La Barre, 1954, p. 107.
18. S. L. Washburn, 1960, pp. 73–74.
19. C. F. Hockett and R. Ascher, 1964.
20. S. L. Washburn, 1960, p. 74.
21. S. L. Washburn and C. S. Lancaster, 1968.
22. W. Laughlin, 1968.
23. R. A. Dart, 1949, 1953, 1955, 1957a, 1957b; R. A. Dart and D. Craig, 1959; K. P. Oakley, 1951, 1954, 1959, 1961; G. A. Bartholomew and J. B. Birdsell, 1953; W. Etkin, 1954; W. La Barre, 1954, pp. 347–348, 1964; S. L. Washburn and V. Avis, 1958; S. L. Washburn, 1960; S. L. Washburn and I. DeVore, 1961; S. L. Washburn and C. S. Lancaster, 1968; A. Brues, 1960; J. T. Robinson,

1961, 1962, 1963; F. B. Livingstone, 1962; F. C. Howell, 1963, 1964, 1967; I. DeVore, 1964; G. Clark and S. Piggott, 1965, p. 40; W. E. Le Gros Clark, 1967, pp. 116–124; D. Morris, 1967, 1978; W. Laughlin, 1968; R. L. Holloway, 1968; M. R. A. Chance and C. J. Jolly, 1970, p. 207; D. L. Wolberg, 1970; L. Tiger and R. Fox, 1971, pp. 100, 121 ff; J. Pfeiffer, 1969, pp. 105–149, 1971; G. B. Schaller, 1972a, 1972b, pp. 379, 386–387; D. Pilbeam, 1972, pp. 4, 84, 190; D. Cohen, 1975, pp. 35 ff; R. E. Leakey and R. Lewin, 1977, ch. 7.

24. R. Ardrey, 1976, pp. 10–11.
25. R. A. Dart, 1955, p. 325.
26. R. A. Dart and D. Craig, 1959, p. 201.
27. R. A. Dart and D. Craig, 1959, p. 201; R. A. Dart, 1953.
28. S. L. Washburn and V. Avis, 1958. Cf. S. L. Washburn, 1959, p. 26.
29. S. L. Washburn and C. S. Lancaster, 1968. Cf. S. L. Washburn and R. S. O. Harding, 1975, p. 10.
30. K. Lorenz, 1963, pp. 241–242.
31. S. L. Washburn and C. S. Lancaster, 1968.
32. R. Ardrey, 1961, p. 316.
33. Ibid., p. 325.
34. For example, E. Leach, 1966; R. L. Holloway, 1967; C. L. Brace, 1971, 1977; A. Walker, 1976.
35. For example, C. Coon, 1962, pp. 76–80, 237–239, 287–289; T. Dobzhansky, 1962, pp. 198–199; B. G. Campbell, 1966, pp. 200–204; R. J. Harrison and W. Montagna, 1969, p. 364; D. Pilbeam, 1972, p. 84; J. Buettner-Janusch, 1973, pp. 324–325; F. E. Poirier, 1973, pp. 104–111; J. B. Birdsell, 1975, pp. 270–273; J. E. Pfeiffer, 1978, pp. 95–100.
36. C. L. Brace and J. Metress, 1973, p. 57.
37. The South African anthropologist Phillip Tobias, a junior colleague, biographer, and longtime friend of Dart's, is said to have been the technical adviser on this part of Kubrick's film (J. Reader, 1988, p. 127).

2. The Rich Smell of Meat and Wickedness

EPIGRAPH: Michael Flanders and Donald Swann, "The Reluctant Cannibal," *At the Drop of a Hat,* Angel LP 35797, 1968.

1. Some anthropologists, including R. Linton (1956, p. 76), C. J. Jolly (1970), and F. C. Howell (1973, pp. 59, 69), put a certain amount of stock in Dart's "osteodontokeratic" (bone-tooth-and-horn) tools, but most authorities, including Dart's staunch defender Robert Broom (1949), remained persistently skeptical (D. L. Wolberg, 1970).
2. C. K. Brain, 1970; 1981, pp. 15–17, 54, 64, 72, 85, 141.
3. R. A. Dart and D. Craig, 1959, p. 113; R. Ardrey, 1961, p. 300; C. K. Brain, 1970; 1981, pp. 266–270.
4. C. K. Brain, 1981, pp. 136, 210–211, 260–261; A. Walker, 1976, p. 81.
5. I. Tattersall, 1970, p. 48; D. Pilbeam, 1972, p. 144; F. C. Howell, 1973, pp. 74–75; J. D. Speth and D. D. Davis, 1976.

6. P. V. Tobias, 1965; J. A. Wallace, 1975; A. Walker and R. E. F. Leakey, 1978; G. Ll. Isaac, 1976, 1978. The Ethiopian deposits that contain the earliest known stone and bone tools have not yet yielded remains of *Homo* (J. Chavaillon, 1976; D. C. Johanson and M. A. Edey, 1981, p. 231).

7. E. Vrba, 1975, 1976, 1980.

8. C. K. Brain, 1981, pp. 213–218; P. Shipman, 1986.

9. C. O. Lovejoy, 1981. Cf. M. H. Nitecki and D. V. Nitecki, 1987.

10. G. Teleki, 1973, 1981; N. M. Tanner, 1981, p. 81; J. Goodall, 1986, pp. 267–312; C. Boesch and H. Boesch, 1989.

11. R. B. Lee, 1968.

12. M. F. A. Montagu, 1968b, p. 10. Cf. M. F. A. Montagu, 1978, p. 100.

13. N. Eldredge and I. Tattersall, 1982, pp. 23, 92.

14. P. Bowler, 1986, p. 248.

15. N. Tanner and A. Zihlman, 1976. Cf. S. Linton, 1971; N. M. Tanner, 1981, ch. 1; D. Haraway, 1988, pp. 232–234.

16. T. Perper and C. Schrire, 1977.

17. G. Boas, 1933; A. O. Lovejoy and G. Boas, 1935, Chapt. 13.

18. K. E. Bock, 1980, p. 34.

19. R. Ardrey, 1961, chs. 1 and 6; 1976, p. 6 ff.

20. R. Jeffers, 1948, p. 146. W. H. Nolte (1978, p. 14) describes this passage as "misanthropy . . . so nearly pure as to cancel even the tribute that loathing pays to its subject."

21. W. Golding, 1954, pp. 140–141, 172.

22. W. Golding, 1966, p. 86.

23. W. Golding, 1955, p. 54.

24. Ibid., pp. 173–177.

25. W. Everson, 1977.

26. W. Golding, 1966, p. 85.

27. R. A. Dart, 1953, p. 207. Cf. R. A. Dart and D. Craig, 1959, p. 202.

28. Ardrey himself later decided that what he and Dart had written in the late 1950s had been warped by a "weapon fixation." "These were Cold War years," he wrote, "dominated by our fears concerning the ultimate weapon. Like Dart, I was preoccupied by the implications of the hypothesis in terms of our ancient dependence on the weapon" (1976, pp. 13–14).

29. J. Burnett, 1774, pp. 396–397.

30. Ibid., pp. 397, 415.

31. Ibid., pp. 415–416. Monboddo distances himself from this outburst by putting it into the mouth of Momus, the Greek god of invective.

32. Plato, *Laws,* 7; Xenophon, *Cynegeticus,* 12; T. Roosevelt, 1893, pp. 448–464.

33. This claim accords with all the religious language—"African Genesis," "mark of Cain," "Eden's outcasts," "Paradise lost," "original sin"—that Dart, Ardrey, Jeffers, and Golding use in talking about our predatory ancestors. But Genesis language is a rhetorical commonplace among paleoanthropologists, most of whom recognize at some level that their stories about human origins are in competition with biblical mythology.

3. Virgin Huntresses and Bleeding Feasts

EPIGRAPH: Euripides, *Hippolytus,* lines 215–224 (D. Grene, 1942, p. 178). The words "and you a lady" are not explicit in the original Greek.

1. In 1982, 13 million American deer hunters spent an estimated $2.5 billion to kill 2 million whitetailed deer yielding an average of 60 pounds of meat per carcass, for an average expenditure of $20.93 per pound (J. G. Mitchell, 1982). I have seen similar estimates of the cost of venison for specific areas: $19.98 per pound for Michigan's lower peninsula (J. G. Mitchell, 1980, p. 8), and $16.67 per pound for Montana (B. Simpson, 1986). These figures represent cash outlay only, not the cost of the labor involved. In an experiment in which nine whitetail bucks were stalked in a fenced enclosure under ideal hunting conditions (fair midwinter weather with a light tracking snow on the ground), Michigan wildlife officials found that a team of six experienced hunters took 51 hours spread over four days—a total of 306 man-hours—to kill one deer (E. Bauer, 1983, p. 25). These figures indicate that the average total cost of a pound of venison in the early 1980s was approximately $20 cash and at least 5 man-hours of labor.

2. A. D. Haight, 1939, pp. 207–208.

3. The verb "to hunt" also means "to search after, seek." This seems to be a metaphorical extension of its original meaning, "to pursue and kill wild animals" *(Oxford English Dictionary)*. Similar extensions are commonplace in other languages: see Plato's dialogues *Sophist* and *Laws* (E. Hamilton and H. Cairns, 1961, pp. 961–965, 1393).

4. The hunting writer J. B. Whisker (1981, pp. 5–8), who agrees that "hunting requires that the pursued be a wild animal," misconstrues the issue as one of nobility rather than docility. "One finds no pleasure in slaughtering a cow," writes Whisker, "because the cow cannot possibly be a worthy foe." But it is clear from Whisker's examples that what defines a worthy foe for him is that it runs away from people. Dodo birds, giant tortoises, and cows are not "worthy subjects of a hunt" because they can be killed easily without being chased.

   Feral cows have in fact been hunted; they were a favorite quarry of sport hunters in nineteenth-century Georgia (C. Hallock, 1860; C. Gohdes, 1967, pp. 78–79). Conversely, the bison of Yellowstone National Park are no longer wild enough to be entirely fair game. In 1985 the Montana state government authorized local hunters to kill any bison that wandered out of Yellowstone. Hunters who bought a bison license for $200 each were accompanied into the field by state game wardens, who herded the animals into killing areas and lined them up for convenient dispatch (G.E. Sabbag, 1986). Most of the park's northern herd was slaughtered in this way in 1989, when they left the burned-over park in search of food. This "harvest" was widely denounced in newspaper editorials as a travesty of the hunt, a "sick parody of sport [that] panders to perverted blood lust" (Raleigh, N.C., *News and Observer,* February 23, 1989, p. 10A). Even news stories described the buffalo shooters as "hunters"

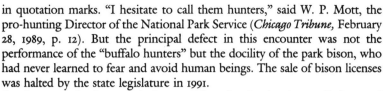

in quotation marks. "I hesitate to call them hunters," said W. P. Mott, the pro-hunting Director of the National Park Service (*Chicago Tribune,* February 28, 1989, p. 12). But the principal defect in this encounter was not the performance of the "buffalo hunters" but the docility of the park bison, who had never learned to fear and avoid human beings. The sale of bison licenses was halted by the state legislature in 1991.

5. Surplus zoo animals are sometimes purchased to be shot in so-called canned hunts, but this is generally not regarded as real hunting. "True hunters," declared a recent *Time* article, "should be delighted to join in bringing an end to [this] perverted bloodlust" (June 10, 1991, p. 61).

6. This may explain why fowling is not mentioned in medieval books on hunting. Birdcatching with trained hawks was an aspect of falconry (which had its own highly specialized language and literature), and other sorts of birdcatching did not count as hunting until nets and limed twigs were supplanted by the more violent fowling pieces.

7. S. Lonsdale, 1981, p. 59. Cf. M. Detienne (1979, p. 24): "As a fundamentally masculine activity in which confrontation with wild animals leads to the spilling of blood at the same time as it provides meat as food, hunting contrasts with farming but is closely linked to war."

8. *Iliad,* 5.133 ff; 8.338 ff; 10.360 ff; 1241 ff; 13.102, 198, 470 ff.

9. The deer hunt in the *Odyssey* begins with Agamemnon's outburst in book 4 (R. Fitzgerald, 1961, p. 63):

> Intolerable—that soft men, as those are,
> should think to lie in that great captain's bed.
> Fawns in a lion's lair! As if a doe
> put down her litter of sucklings there, while she
> quested a glen or cropped some grassy hollow.
> Ha! Then the lord returns to his own bed
> and deals out wretched doom on both alike.
> So will Odysseus deal out doom on these.

These lines are repeated verbatim by Telemachus in book 17, just before Odysseus returns home. The poem climaxes in a shower of hunting images. The disguised Odysseus is recognized first by his old hunting dog; then his former nursemaid recognizes him from an old hunting scar. His wife challenges any suitor that would win her hand to string her vanished husband's mighty hunting bow. Odysseus alone can do it; and when he has the bow strung, he starts killing the suitors and their confederates. Those who escape his hunting arrows are killed by spear, sword, or noose, and their deaths furnish yet other metaphors of predation (*Odyssey,* 22.302 ff, 383 ff, 399 ff, 468 ff).

10. Xenophon, *Cynegeticus,* 12 (E. C. Marchant, 1968, pp. 443–444, 453–454).

11. Aristotle, *Politics,* 1.8 (E. Walford, 1910, pp. 19–20).

12. Cicero, *De natura deorum,* 2.64 (H. Rackham, 1933, pp. 276–279); Julius Pollux, *Onomasticon,* 5 (D. B. Hull, 1964, p. 144); Vegetius, *De re militari,*

1.7 (F. Wille, 1986, pp. 35–36). Cf. K. V. Thomas, 1983, p. 183. Similar analogies occur in Sanskrit literature (M. Chand, 1982, p. 31).

13. E. B. White, 1944, p. 266. Conversely, a decline in the popularity of hunting may be bemoaned as an omen of military decline (A. J. Butler, 1930, p. 27).

14. Xenophon, *Cynegeticus,* 5.14 (Marchant, p. 393).

15. Plato, *Laws,* 7 (E. Hamilton and H. Cairns, 1961, p. 1393). Cf. Vegetius, *De re militari,* 1.7, and Seneca, *On Providence,* 2: "It gives us pleasure . . . when a young man of steadfast courage meets a wild beast's charge with his hunting spear or faces a rushing lion without flinching, and the spectacle is the more pleasing in the degree that the hero is a man of position" (H. Shapiro and E. M. Curley, 1965, p. 82).

16. "In these myths," notes Joseph Fontenrose (1981, p. 254), "hunting has little or nothing to do with the food supply. We are told nothing about the eating of game animals . . . The only animals that enter the myth complex are those that kill the hunter and those into which he is transformed."

17. Xenophon, *Cynegeticus,* 1, 6 (Marchant, pp. 367, 407).

18. A few vestigial myths and usages suggest that Apollo may have been "the hunter-god of the wild wood" in prehistoric Greek religion (L. R. Farnell, 1914, p. 399). He was celebrated as an archer and was sometimes credited with the invention of hunting. His mysterious title Lykeios, which probably has something to do with *lykos,* the Greek word for "wolf," suggests ancient associations with wildness in its chaotic and threatening aspects. The adjective *lykeios* was also applied to Artemis (Pausanias, 2.31.4; P. Levi, 1971, vol. 1, p. 204). The similar title of Lykaios, given to Zeus in the rustic backwater of Arcadia, was associated with ritual lycanthropy, in which a participant nibbled at the entrails from a human sacrifice and was supposedly transformed into a wolf (Plato, *Republic,* 8 [E. Hamilton and H. Cairns, 1961, p. 794]; Pausanias, 6.8.2; 8.2.3–6; 8.38.7 [P. Levi, 1971, vol. 2, pp. 307, 372–373, 468]; J. G. Frazer, 1921, pp. 390–393). Robert Graves (1955, p. 141) surmised that the Arcadian shepherds practiced this werewolf ceremony "to discourage the wolves from preying on flocks and herds, by sending them a human king." If Apollo was originally a shepherd's god, then some such wolf-controlling ritual may underlie the epithet Lykeios. Cf. Euripides, *Alcestis,* 570 ff, where Apollo is depicted as a shepherd mastering and controlling wild beasts with his music (D. Grene and R. Lattimore, n.d., pp. 40–41).

19. Like Apollo, Artemis was an archer whose arrows were the cause of sudden, inexplicable death in mortals (e.g., *Odyssey,* 11.172; cf. *Iliad,* 1.46–52). As Apollo was identified with the sun, so Artemis was with the moon. She and Apollo were both invoked as guardians of roads (Callimachus, *Hymn to Artemis*). The poet Callimachus tells us how the infant Artemis sat in her father Zeus's lap and asked him to give her the same things her brother had: a multitude of titles, a bow and arrows, and the office of bringing light to the world (J. Banks, 1886, pp. 134–136).

20. *Iliad,* 21.409. Artemis plays an inglorious role in the *Iliad;* Hera thrashes her with her own quiver and sends her off bawling to tattle to her father, Zeus.

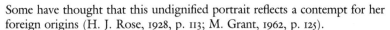

Some have thought that this undignified portrait reflects a contempt for her foreign origins (H. J. Rose, 1928, p. 113; M. Grant, 1962, p. 125).

21. T. Sargent, 1973, p. 76.
22. J. E. Fontenrose, 1981, pp. 13, 49–50, 58, 76–77, 133, 177, 187.
23. Catullus, *Carmina,* 34 (H. Gregory, 1956, p. 44).
24. Ovid, *Metamorphoses,* 3.200–203.
25. Artemis killed the hunter Orion for making sexual advances to her—or (in some accounts) for declaring that he would kill every wild beast on earth (Ovid, *Fasti,* 5.539–541 [J. G. Frazer, 1931, pp. 299–301]; cf. J. E. Fontenrose, 1981, pp. 13–14). Another hunter, Leukippos, disguised himself as a woman to join a troop of hunting maidens who, discovering the imposture as they bathed in a stream together, speared him to death (Pausanias, 8.20. 2; P. Levi, 1971, vol. 2, p. 419; cf. J. E. Fontenrose, 1981, p. 49). The virgin huntress Callisto was raped by Zeus disguised as Artemis. When the real Artemis saw Callisto bathing and noticed that the girl was pregnant, she angrily turned her into a bear (Ovid, *Metamorphoses,* 2.417 ff; F. J. Miller, 1925, pp. 88–94; cf. Apollodorus, *On the Gods,* 2.8.2; J. G. Frazer, 1921, vol. 1, pp. 394–396). A similar fate overtook Artemis' chaste protégée Erinoma, who was raped by the hunter Adonis and then changed by Artemis into a peahen. Artemis in turn caused Adonis to be killed by a boar while hunting. These myths and that of Actaeon share several motifs—the virgin huntress, the attempted rape, the discovery in the bath, the transformation—and they probably all stem from a single underlying prehistoric story, which has parallels in Lydian, Hindu, and Semitic mythology (J. E. Fontenrose, 1981, ch. 9).
26. Euripides, *Bacchae,* 734–747 (G. S. Kirk, 1970, p. 84).
27. E. R. Dodds, 1944, pp. xiv-xvii; 1951, pp. 276–278; M. Grant, 1962, p. 248; G. S. Kirk, 1970, pp. 41–42.
28. After being torn to bits by the Titans and restored to life by his grandmother Rhea, Dionysus was concealed from his enemies in the form of a kid or ram (Diodorus Siculus 3.62; Apollodorus, *On the Gods,* 3.4.3 [J. G. Frazer, 1921, vol. 1, pp. 320–321]; cf. I. M. Linforth, 1941, pp. 307 ff]. Dionysus was sometimes invoked or described as a horned beast or a horned human figure (M. Grant, 1962, p. 248; Euripides, *Bacchae,* 99–104, 920–922). Marcel Detienne (1979, p. 68 ff) advances a Lévi-Straussian structuralist argument against equating the sacrificial victim's *diasparagmos* with that of the god (the sacrificial animal was eaten raw, but the Titans cooked Dionysus).
29. Euripides, *The Cretans* (G. Murray, 1923, p. 324).
30. Euripides, *Bacchae,* 1060–1140; Theocritus, *Idylls,* 26 (A. Rist, 1978, pp. 197–198); Apollodorus, *On the Gods,* 3.1.2 (J. G. Frazer, 1921, vol. 1, p. 319). The myth of Pentheus is echoed by other stories about mortals who got involved with Dionysus and wound up killing their own sons in tragic endings involving hunting, madness, and *diasparagmos.* After driving Dionysus out of Thrace, King Lycurgus of Edonia went mad, mistook his son for a grapevine, and chopped him down with an ax. Lycurgus was eventually torn apart by wild horses (Apollodorus, *On the Gods,* 3.5.1; J. G. Frazer, 1921, vol. 1, pp. 326–

331). Driven mad as a punishment for rejecting Dionysus, Leucippe tore her son to pieces and ate him (Ovid, *Metamorphoses,* 4.1–41, 4.390–415). For daring to shield the infant Dionysus from her wrath, Hera afflicted King Athamas of Orchomenus with a madness that drove him to slay his son, thinking him a stag (Apollodorus, *On the Gods,* 3.4.3; J. G. Frazer, 1921, vol. 1, p. 319) or a lion (Ovid, *Metamorphoses,* 4.512–519).

31. Even the central myths of the two gods, the stories of Actaeon and Pentheus, are mirror images of each other. For looking at Artemis, Actaeon was turned into a beast and torn to bits; for *not* seeing Dionysus, Pentheus met the same fate—on the very spot "where once the hounds divided out Actaeon" (Euripides, *Bacchae,* 1291; G. S. Kirk, 1970, p. 129). One tradition has it that Euripides himself was torn to pieces by hunting dogs (G. Murray, 1946, p. 111).

32. E. R. Dodds, 1944, p. 176; G. S. Kirk, 1970, p. 96.

33. Euripides, *Bacchae,* 862–875 (G. Murray, 1904, p. 53; ellipses in original).

34. Skadi in Norse myth and Flidais in Irish legend are solitary huntresses that some have seen as vestigial Germanic and Celtic survivals from an Indo-European proto-Artemis (H. R. E. Davidson, 1964, p. 123; P. Mac Cana, 1970, p. 55). Baring-Gould (1914, vol. 12, pp. 545–547) argues that the medieval St. Ursula and her 11,000 virgins derive from a Germanic version of Artemis.

35. The Egyptian goddess Neith and the Canaanite goddess Anath are virgin huntresses associated with the bow (E. O. James, 1960, pp. 84, 103–106; C. H. Gordon, 1961; S. H. Hooke, 1963, p. 90). The Assyrians also depicted the love goddess Ishtar with a bow and revered her as, among other things, a goddess of the hunt. The Persian goddess Anahita, who resembles Ishtar in many respects, was worshipped as Mistress of the Animals in Lydia and identified with Artemis by Greek and Roman writers. Animals sacrificed to her were kept in enclosed parks and killed in a ritual hunt (F. Cumont, 1902, 1908). The similarity of the names Anahita, Anath, and Neith suggests that the three may have a common prehistoric source.

36. Shiva is Lord of the Animals and (in his manifestation as Rudra) the Wild Hunter and Divine Archer, whose arrow is the "belt" of the constellation Orion in Hindu star lore (S. Kramrisch, 1981). He and his consort lead "a kind of nomadic camping-out life" in the wilderness (R. N. Brown, 1961). In these respects, Shiva is reminiscent of Artemis. The deerskin is the sacred dress of the ascetic inhabitants of holy forests in Indian myth (e.g., *Ramayana,* 3.1), just as it is of the Bacchae and of Artemis (Euripides, *Bacchae,* 111, 137; Pausanias, 8.37.4).

37. For example, in the *Iliad* (1.225), where Achilles reviles Agamemnon by calling him "deer-hearted." Similarly, where Homer praises the goddess Hera as "ox-eyed" (*Iliad,* 1.551), we prefer to call a beautiful woman "doe-eyed"—an epithet that later European literature probably acquired via Islam from Eastern models like Urdu *mrignaini* and Nepalese *mirganaini* (J. Shakespear, 1834; T. C. Majupuria, 1977). Greek and Roman poets sometimes compared young girls to fawns (among other young animals) to emphasize their innocence and

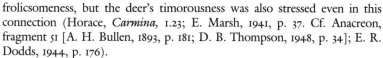

frolicsomeness, but the deer's timorousness was also stressed even in this connection (Horace, *Carmina*, 1.23; E. Marsh, 1941, p. 37. Cf. Anacreon, fragment 51 [A. H. Bullen, 1893, p. 181; D. B. Thompson, 1948, p. 34]; E. R. Dodds, 1944, p. 176).

38. Genesis 3.18. "Whether or not we find it practicable and desirable," concluded Karl Barth (1960, p. 208), "the diet assigned to men and beasts by God the Creator is vegetarian."

39. Ovid, *Metamorphoses*, 1.101–112.

40. Empedocles, *Fragments*, 405, 421 (M. C. Nahm, 1962, pp. 140–141). Cf. Plato, *Statesman*, 271e (E. Hamilton and H. Cairns, 1961, p. 1037). A favorite motif of Roman murals and mosaics was the Paradise of Animals, showing all sorts of birds and beasts living together in Empedoclean harmony (J. C. M. Toynbee, 1973, pp. 283–299). Some pagans looked forward to a future restoration of the Age of Gold the way Christians anticipated the restoration of the Earthly Paradise at the Second Coming. "The herds will not fear the mighty lions," wrote Virgil. "The timid deer will, in the age to come, drink beside the hounds" (*Eclogues*, 4.22, 8.27–28. Cf. Horace, *Epodes* 16.33).

41. Plutarch, *Moralia*, 352 (*Of Isis and Osiris;* F. C. Babbitt, 1936, p. 15); Porphyry, *De abstinentia*, 4 (E. Wynne-Tyson, 1965, pp. 154 ff); A. A. Bevan, 1916; E. R. Dodds, 1951, p. 149; W. K. C. Guthrie, 1952, pp. 194–198; D. A. Dombrowski, 1984.

42. Pausanias, 1.26.6 (P. Levi, 1971, vol. 1, p. 74).

43. Marcus Aurelius, *Meditations*, 6.23 (H. Shapiro and E. M. Curley, 1965, p. 136).

44. Aristotle, *Politics*, 1.5–6.

45. Plutarch, *Moralia*, 996a (*Of Eating the Flesh*, 1; H. Cherniss and W. C. Helmbold, 1957, p. 559).

46. Dio Cassius, 39.38.2–4.

47. Cicero, *Ad familiares*, 7.1.3 (W. G. Williams, 1929, vol. 2, p. 6).

48. J. Aymard, 1951, pp. 30 ff.

49. Plutarch, *Lives; Aemilius Paulus*, 6.5.

50. Sallust, *Catiline*, 4.1 (J. C. Rolfe, 1931, p. 10).

51. Varro, *Sat. Men.*, 161, 293–296, 361 (J. K. Anderson, 1961, p. 87).

52. *Odyssey*, 10.161–184 (R. Fitzgerald, 1963, p. 170).

53. *Aeneid*, 7.500–502 (A. Mandelbaum, 1961, p. 179).

54. *Aeneid*, 4.68–73.

55. Plutarch, *Moralia*, 959d-f (H. Cherniss and W. C. Helmbold, 1957, pp. 321–323).

56. Ibid., 985d-992e (pp. 492–553).

57. Pliny the Elder, *Natural History*, 10.63.83. Similar passages from Democritus, Diogenes, Philemon, Menander, Diodorus Siculus, and Ovid are marshaled by A. O. Lovejoy and G. Boas, 1935, pp. 389–420.

58. K. Bock, 1980, pp. 29–35.

59. The word was of course used in many different senses, then as now. Lovejoy and Boas (1935, pp. 447–456) distinguish 66 different meanings of the word "nature" (Latin *natura*, Greek *physis*), of which 44 were in use in classical

antiquity. Cf. C. S. Lewis, 1967, pp. 24–74, and Cicero, *De natura deorum,* 2.23 (H. Rackham, 1933, pp. 200 ff).

60. This notion had its genesis among the pre-Socratics and Sophists, and was generally accepted by Cynic, Stoic, and Epicurean philosophers (Epicurus, *Leading Doctrines,* 15, 25, and 29 [H. Shapiro and E. M. Curley, 1965, pp. 12–13]; Lucretius, *De rerum natura,* 5.1399–1435 [A. O. Lovejoy and G. Boas, 1935, p. 230]; Marcus Aurelius, *Meditations,* 4.51, 6.9, and 6.33 [Shapiro and Curley, pp. 131–138]; cf. Lovejoy and Boas, 1935, pp. 103–154); but some important thinkers dissented from it—especially Aristotle, who says that artifice may be needed to bring nature to its true end or full perfection (*Politics,* 1.1252b, 30 ff; *Physics,* 199a.17–20).

61. 1 Corinthians 11.3, 14.34–35; Ephesians 5.22–24, 6.5; Colossians 3.18–22, 4.1; 1 Peter 3.1; Augustine, *City of God,* 19.15–16 (W. M. Green, 1966, vol. 6, pp. 186–193); *Confessions,* 32 (W. J. Oates, 1948); Lactantius, *Epitome of the Divine Institutes,* 2 (W. Fletcher, 1871, vol. 2, p. 93). "As man is made for the sake of God, namely, that he may serve Him," say the medieval *Libri sententiarum,* "so is the world made for the sake of man, that it may serve him" (A. O. Lovejoy, 1936, p. 354). Cf. Albertus Magnus, *De animalibus,* 22.9 (J.J. Scanlan, 1987, p. 65).

62. This conclusion is implicit throughout early Christian thought (J. Gaffney, 1986), though as far as I know it first becomes explicit in Thomas Aquinas (1948, vol. 2, p. 505; *Summa theologica,* 1-2, Qcii, a.8).

63. Augustine, *On Original Sin,* 46 (W. J. Oates, 1948, vol. 1, p. 652).

64. T. Browne, *Religio medici,* 1.34 (N. J. Endicott, 1967, pp. 41–42).

65. Francis Bacon, *Wisdom of the Ancients,* 26 (J. Devey, n.d., pp. 395–396).

66. Cicero, *De natura deorum,* 2.53 (H. Rackham, 1933, p. 251); Xenophon, *Memorabilia,* 4.3 (E. C. Marchant, 1938, p. 303); Aristotle, *Politics,* 1.1256b.15 ff ; Augustine, *City of God,* 22.24 (W. M. Green, 1966, vol. 7, pp. 326–331).

67. The doctrine of man's innate depravity, wrote Wesley, is the "one grand fundamental difference between Christianity, considered as a system of doctrines, and the most refined Heathenism" (J. Wesley, 1958, vol. 6, p. 63).

68. Augustine, *On Nature and Grace,* 2 (W. J. Oates, 1948, vol. 1, pp. 522–523).

69. John Calvin, *Commentary upon the Book of Genesis,* 3.19 (J. King, 1847, vol. 1, p. 177). "As the *primum mobile* rolls all the celestial spheres along with it," wrote Calvin (ibid., 3.17; p. 173), "so the ruin of man drives headlong all those creatures which were formed for his sake, and had been made subject to him."

70. J. Donne, "The First Anniversarie," lines 196–200.

71. R. Hooker, *Of the Laws of Ecclesiastical Polity,* 1.9.1, 1.11.3 (C. Morris, 1954, vol. 1, pp. 185–186, 204).

72. E. M. W. Tillyard, 1944, p. 55.

73. C. S. Lewis, 1940, p. 129; J. Hick, 1977, p. 103.

74. See, for example, Augustine, *City of God,* 12.1, and *On Original Sin,* 46. Cf. Donne's sonnet, "If poisonous mineralls." Renaissance theologians, concludes Tillyard (1944, p. 80), "did not doubt that the world and its contents had

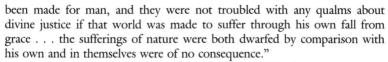

been made for man, and they were not troubled with any qualms about divine justice if that world was made to suffer through his own fall from grace . . . the sufferings of nature were both dwarfed by comparison with his own and in themselves were of no consequence."

75. Augustine, *On the Morals of the Catholic Church,* 22 (W. J. Oates, 1948, p. 337). Cf. 1 John 2.15–17.

76. H. McGraw et al., 1971, p. 300: cf. pp. 38, 121, 157, 332, 379.

77. J. Carlill, n.d., pp. 188–189.

78. "Nos quidquid illud significat faciamus et quam sit verum non laboremus." I take this sentence from T. H. White (1954, p. 245), who quotes it without any citation. I have not located the original source.

79. Augustine, *Freedom of the Will,* 2.69 (C. M. Sparrow, 1947, p. 143; J. Hick, 1977, p. 85).

80. John Donne, "The First Anniversarie," lines 161–166. Man, wrote the Renaissance theologian Marsilio Ficino, is "the vicar of God" and "the god of the Animals . . . [who] makes use of them all, rules them all, and instructs many of them" (J. L. Burroughs, 1944, p. 234).

81. C. S. Lewis, 1962, p. 138.

82. K. Thomas, 1983, p. 255. Cf. R. Nash, 1982, pp. 15–40.

4. The White Stag

EPIGRAPH: John Heath-Stubbs, "The Death of Digenes Akritas," in D. Hall et al. (eds.), 1957, pp. 111–112.

1. John the Baptist, the ragged herald of Christ's coming, is depicted in all four gospels as a holy anchorite "preaching in the wilderness of Judaea" (Mark 1.1–8, Matthew 3.1–12, Luke 3.1–18, 7.18–29, John 1.6–36). Even Jesus was called by the Spirit to spend forty days "with the wild beasts" in the wilderness (Mark 1.12–13).

2. In the tenth-century Arabic work *The Case of the Animals versus Man before the King of the Jinn,* the jackal argues that the moral superiority of animals over people is proved by the fact that the saintliest of humans quit human society and go off to dwell with the wild beasts (L. E. Goodman, 1978, pp. 164–165).

3. M. R. James, 1924. Although these stories remained apocryphal, the worshipping animals made their way into Christian tradition via the story of Christ's nativity. In Pseudo-Matthew, we already find the ox and the ass adoring the Christ Child (A. Roberts and J. Donaldson, 1870, p. 33). Creche scenes and Christmas cards today usually show oxen, asses, and sheep gathered around the manger in mute homage to the Holy Infant. Familiar Christmas carols (such as the twelfth-century French carol "The Friendly Beasts") even put words in the mouths of the worshipful animals.

4. This story motif is recorded as early as the second century A.D. in the *Golden Ass* of Apuleius (R. Graves, 1951, pp. 120–124). The motif recurs in modern folktales from all over Western Europe, including Italy ("Body-Without-

Soul," "Animal Speech," "Rosina in the Oven," and "Wormwood"; I. Calvino, 1980), Estonia ("The Forest-Father"; E. Mutt, 1930), Serbia ("The Golden Apple Tree"; E. L. Mijatovich, 1917), and various equivalents of the cited Grimm tales in other Germanic languages.

5. Asvaghosha, *Buddha-Karita,* 7.5–6 (E. B. Cowell, 1894, pp. 70–71). Cf. *Mahavagga,* 3 (T. W. Rhys Davids and H. Oldenberg, 1881, p. 80).

6. D. Bodde, 1961. This myth goes back at least to Chuang-Tze (L. Giles, 1906, p. 67; J. R. Ware, 1963, p. 63).

7. E. O. James, 1960, pp. 52, 105.

8. J. Campbell, 1969, ch. 7: W. La Barre, 1972, pp. 163 ff.

9. P. Mac Cana, 1970, p. 38.

10. Ibid., pp. 47–48; A. Ross, 1967, ch. 3.

11. *The Merry Wives of Windsor,* 4.4.26–32. It seems worth noting in this connection that English *h* in *Herne* is equivalent to Celtic *k* in *Kern-*(unnos).

12. A. Ross, 1967, p.165.

13. Of the saints tallied by H. Roeder (1955), 287 have animals as their conventional attributes in sacred iconography. Of these, 26 are symbolized by a deer. The only beast that symbolizes more saints (29) is the domestic cow.

14. L. Bieler, 1953, p. 69. The site of the altar for Patrick's church at Armagh was also pointed out to him by a roe and her fawn (S. Baring-Gould, 1914, vol. 3, p. 302).

15. K. Jackson, 1935, p. 4. These verses are attributed to the seventh-century St. Manchan of Liath.

16. J. G. O'Keeffe, 1931; J. Carney, 1955; E. Wäppling, 1984.

17. G. Murphy, 1956, p. 137.

18. S. Heaney, 1983, pp. 19–20.

19. See e.g. F. Goldin, 1973, pp. 105, 137–138, 191, 243, 421.

20. *Beowulf,* 20.

21. F. B. Gummere, 1907, p. 278.

22. E. E. Wardale, 1935, p. 101.

23. The Latin word *sylvaticus* has the secondary meanings "rustic, wild, savage, untamed." Cf. Greek *hylaios,* literally "woodsy," which has the secondary meaning "savage" (P. G. W. Glare, 1982; H. G. Liddell and R. Scott, 1894). The word *wild* in English and other Germanic languages also derives from a root meaning "forest" (German *Wald,* English *weald* or *wold*).

24. L. White Jr., 1962, pp. 39 ff.

25. C. Merchant, 1980, p. 48; F. Braudel, 1981, p. 33.

26. A. Dent, 1974.

27. D. Dalby, 1965, p. v. Cf. H. W. Eckardt, 1976, pp. 27–31.

28. I translate this passage from the text in M. H. Turk (1930), pp. 152–153.

29. E. P. Thompson, 1975, pp. 30–31; E. Hobusch, 1978, pp. 117–119.

30. Although the oldest surviving texts of the Robin Hood ballads and tales date to the mid fifteenth century, the Robin Hood legend is referred to in the B version of *Piers Plowman* (5.395), which was probably written in the late 1370s (W. W. Skeat, 1932).

31. M. Keen, 1961.

32. G. Tilander, 1956.

33. W. A. Baillie-Grohman and F. Baillie-Grohman, 1909; D. Dalby, 1965; B. Danielsson, 1977.

34. A. Dent, 1974.

35. G. Turbervile, 1576, pp. 97–98.

36. Ibid., p. 96.

37. M. Thiébaux, 1974, pp. 128–133; B. Danielsson, 1977.

38. G. Turbervile, 1576, pp. 127–135. Whatever the basis for this story may have been in fact, it became so widely repeated that it passed into the realm of folklore. The probably pseudonymous huntress "Dame Julians Barnes" wrote in her *Boke of Hunting* (ca. 1486) that the "corbyn bone" is "corbyn's fee, / At the death he will be" (G. Tilander, 1964). Turbervile is quoted almost word for word on this subject in the first scene of Ben Jonson's pastoral play *The Sad Shepherd:*

> He that undoes [the hart]
> Doth cleave the brisket bone, upon the spoon
> Of which a little gristle grows; you call it
> The raven's bone. Now o'er head sat a raven,
> On a sere bough, a grown great bird, and hoarse,
> Who, all the while the deer was breaking up,
> So croaked and cried for it, as all the huntsmen,
> Especially old Scathlock, thought it ominous.

39. C. E. Hare, 1949.

40. G. Turbervile, 1576, pp. 98–99, 237–238, 241, 245.

41. D. Dalby, 1965, p. xliii. This emphasis was apparently less sharp in Germany. As Dalby notes, the complimentary German term for a hunter, *Weidmann* (huntsman), has always been applied to both high and low participants in an organized hunt; but the English equivalent, *sportsman* (literally "one who amuses himself"), is applied exclusively to the hunt's genteel participants and not to the hunt servants.

42. Italics in the original.

43. J. Levron, 1974, pp. 126–127; J. Cronin, 1975, p. 17; F. Pinguet, 1978, p. 27. The king's tally has no doubt been inflated by various polite fictions. In some German principalities, all kills made on the prince's lands were attributed to the prince. This is why some histories of hunting credit Prince Johann Georg II of Saxony with killing 111,141 deer during the 24 years of his reign (1656–1680)—an impossible average of 13 deer a day (E. Hobusch, 1978, p. 8).

44. F. Remigereau, 1952.

45. F. J. Child, 1883–1898, vol. 3, p. 3.

46. D. Dalby, 1965, p. 239. The restriction of *tior* and *bestia* to female deer may have had an ambivalent connotation; stags were generally preferred as objects of the hunt, and the hind was also referred to contemptuously in medieval German usage as "whore" *(huore)* and "thing" *(dinc)* (ibid., p. 240). In

modern German, *Tier* means "hind" only in hunting jargon (W. Frevert, 1975); elsewhere it retains the more generalized meaning of "animal." Likewise, the modern French word *bête* retains the original sense of *bestia*, from which it and *biche* both derive via different dialectical forms.

47. C. D. Buck, 1949. Parallel semantic changes took place in the Indian subcontinent, where the Sanskrit word *mrga*, meaning "wild beast" in general, gave rise to words for "deer" and "hunting" in the descendant Indo-Aryan vernaculars of India and Pakistan (R. L. Turner, 1966).

48. D. Dalby, 1965, p. 47. In modern Dutch, the vernacular name for the red deer is *edelhert*, noble deer (B. Grzimek, 1969, vol. 13, p. 192).

49. *Iliad*, 1.225. Cf. Horace, *Carmina*, 1.23, and the Aesopian fable of the stag and fawn, "A Breed of Faint-Hearts."

50. G. Jones (ed.), 1977, p. 6.

51. Ibid., p. 26. The Welsh word *hyddgarw* (stag-hart) was used figuratively to mean "lord, patron, wise leader."

52. W. B. Lockwood, 1975, p. 131.

53. S. Heaney, 1983, p. 44. Heaney's phrase "royal blood" is not in the original Irish; cf. J. G. O'Keeffe, 1913, pp. 78–79.

54. *Julius Caesar*, 3.1.204–210.

55. Noble youths and beautiful maidens were conventionally compared to tame falcons, as John Skelton around 1495 compared Mistress Margaret Hussey: "merry Margaret, / This midsummer flower, / Gentle as falcon / Or hawk of the tower." ("Gentle" here has its original meaning of "well bred.") Falconry as a source of metaphor in medieval German literature is explored by D. Dalby, 1965, pp. xxix ff. The fox hunt furnished an allegory of the persecution of sin (M. Thiébaux, 1974, pp. 82–84). So did the hunting of the boar, an animal that stood in symbolic opposition to the Christian virtues embodied in the hunted stag (M. Thiébaux, 1968, p. 283).

56. C. Brown (ed.), 1932, p. 110. This simile has biblical sources in the conventional equation of Christ as Bridegroom of the Church with the male lover of the Song of Songs (who is likened to a roe or young hart), and in medieval interpretations of Psalm 22. This psalm, which is important to Christians because it contains the phrase "My God, why hast thou forsaken me?" that Jesus uttered on the cross, begins with the words "To the Chief Musician upon Aijeleth Shahar." The last two words can be interpreted as "the hind of the morning." This is probably the name of the tune to which the psalm was supposed to be sung (J. Calès, 1936, vol. I, pp. 262–263), but medieval and Renaissance exegetes took it as an appellation of Christ. "Christ," wrote Martin Luther, "is here called a hind . . . who is being hunted at morning" (E. Mülhaupt, 1959, vol. 1, pp. 291–292). In Luther's commentaries, the "panting hart" of Psalm 42 also becomes a hunted stag, and other interpreters have gone on to identify it as another symbol of the persecuted Christ (J. R. Harris, 1924, p. 17; cf. F. B. Meyer, 1950, p. 31; J. M. Neale and R. F. Littledale, 1884, vols. 1, pp. 289–290, and 2, pp. 57–58).

57. Shakespeare, *Troilus and Cressida*, 3.1. "Sore" here is both a metaphor and a

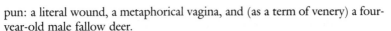

pun: a literal wound, a metaphorical vagina, and (as a term of venery) a four-year-old male fallow deer.

58. *Sophist,* 222d-e (E. Hamilton and H. Cairns, 1961, p. 965). Cf. J. Aymard, 1951, pp. 129–142.

59. The major medieval literary sources for the metaphor of the amorous chase are surveyed and summarized by D. Dalby, 1965 (pp. xxii-xxxi), and M. Thiébaux, 1974.

60. J. W. Hebel (ed.), 1931, vol. 1, p. 116.

61. M. Thiébaux, 1974, pp. 145–153.

62. Dafydd ap Gwilym, "Y Breuddwyd" (R. Bromwich, 1982, pp. 109–111).

63. *Die verfolgte Hindin:* M. Thiébaux, 1974, pp. 236–238.

64. Hadamar von Laber, *Der Jagd:* M. Thiébaux, 1974, pp. 185–228.

65. *Noli me tangere:* Touch me not.

66. P. F. Watson, 1979, pp. 91 ff.

67. K. Clark, 1980, pl. 77.

68. The closest things to uncanny quarry in classical literature are the Ceryneian hind and the Erymanthian boar that Heracles captured as part of his twelve labors; but even these have nothing of the supernatural or otherworldly about them.

69. M. Thiébaux, 1974, pp. 62–63.

70. The legend of St. Julian the Hospitaller, to whom a stag at bay prophesies that he will murder his parents, and who does so under the delusion that he is killing his wife and her lover (H. J. Thurston and D. Attwater, 1956), is of particular interest to the psychoanalytically minded.

71. K. Lindner, 1940, pp. 430–432. An alternative interpretation is that the Celtic and Indian forms of the stag motif have a common prehistoric source: see K. Lindner, 1937, pp. 365–367.

72. R. Bromwich, 1961.

73. M. Thiébaux, 1974, pp. 109 ff; E. M. Grimes, 1928, pp. 22–23, 83.

74. A. Gray, 1954, pp. 97–98.

75. L. C. Wimberly, 1928; M. Leach, 1955, p. 91.

76. F. J. Child, 1883–1898, vol. 1, p. 254.

77. Some North American tales and superstitions about white deer may stem from Native American rather than European tradition. Some Indians regarded white deer as supernatural tricksters that delighted in leading hunters to their doom (H. I. Smith, 1906).

78. This story was put into verse by Mark Van Doren (1941), who reported it told as historical fact in Illinois and Connecticut. Robinson Jeffers' (1916) poem "The Belled Doe" tells a similar tale from California.

79. C. H. Whedbee, 1966, pp. 24–25.

80. H. M. Wiltse, 1900; V. Randolph, 1947, p. 241. The feeling that it is wrong or unlucky to kill a white deer persists in the Appalachians today. The shooting of a white doe on the farm of my friend W. L. Hylander near Fries, Virginia, in the summer of 1988 aroused considerable indignation among the local people, many of whom are enthusiastic hunters themselves.

81. *Morte d'Arthur,* book 17, ch. 9 (E. Strachey, 1901, p. 399).
82. For instance, William Wordsworth's *The White Doe of Rylstone;* the ballad "The Wild Huntsman" by the so-called father of the German ballad, G. A. Bürger (L. Simonson, ed., 1868); Uhland's ballad "The White Stag" (L. Fränkel, 1893, p. 203); W. B. Yeats, "Mongan Laments the Change That Has Come upon Him and His Beloved"; T. S. Eliot , "Landscapes, III. Usk"; Ezra Pound, "The White Stag"; James Thurber, *The White Deer;* C. S. Lewis, *The Lion, the Witch and the Wardrobe.*

5. The Sobbing Deer

EPIGRAPH: *As You Like It,* 2.1.58–66.

1. There are no significant medieval sources of antihunting sentiment. Clergy of the Roman Catholic Church were forbidden to hunt, but only because hunting was regarded as a worldly amusement that distracts the pious soul from its contemplation of heavenly things. Ecclesiastical protests against the oppression of the poor by hunting-mad aristocrats began to show up as early as the ninth century (E. Hobusch, 1978, p. 74). In 1159, John of Salisbury offered a long condemnation of aristocratic hunting in his *Policraticus,* as oppressive to the common folk and destructive to the souls of the gentry. But John saw nothing wrong with hunting per se (J. B. Pike, 1938, p. 23) and he expressed no sympathy for the hunter's quarry. Thomas Gascoigne's *Liber Veritatum* condemned hunting in more modern terms, as "a pleasure that finds delight in seeing the gush of blood and the agonies of a dying animal" (J. E. T. Rogers, 1881, p. 224). Gascoigne's book, however, is not strictly medieval; it was written around 1457, only 21 years before Thomas More's birth. The Latin manuscript remained unpublished until 1881 and has never been translated into a vernacular language. Its influence was presumably negligible.
2. Erasmus, *Praise of Folly,* 1.18 (H. H. Hudson, 1941, pp. 53–54).
3. Erasmus wrote of More that "one of his amusements is in observing the forms, characters, and instincts of different animals. Accordingly there is scarcely any kind of bird that he does not keep about his residence, and the same of other animals not quite so common, as monkeys, foxes, ferrets, weasels and the like" (F. M. Nichols, 1962, pp. 387–401).
4. More, *Epigrammata,* 19 (L. Bradner and C. A. Lynch, 1953, p. 27).
5. More, *Utopia,* 2 (E. Surtz and J. Hexter, 1965, vol. 4, p. 170).
6. Ibid., pp. 151–152.
7. Montaigne, "Of Cruelty" (M. Frame, 1960, vol. 2, pp. 105–109).
8. *Julius Caesar,* 3.1.204, 255; *Macbeth,* 4.3; *As You Like It,* 2.1.
9. *Love's Labour's Lost,* 4.1.
10. *Titus Andronicus,* 2.1.
11. Ibid., 2.2.
12. Ibid., 3.1. "Unrecuring" (incurable).
13. Henry Howard, Earl of Surrey, "In Windsor Castle" (H. Gardner, 1972, p. 41).

"A force" (F. *parforce,* hunting on horseback, using dogs but no missile weapons).

14. E. H. Gombrich, 1961, p. 273; K. Clark, 1977, p. 107; F. Koreny, 1985, pp. 13–27.
15. Similar ambivalence toward the suffering of the lower orders is evident elsewhere in Dürer's art (A. Barton, 1991).
16. For example, in act 4 of Joseph Addison's 1713 play *Cato* (lines 32–37). In Marvell's "The Nymph Complaining for the Death of Her Faun" (B. K. Lewalski and A. J. Sabol, 1973, pp. 1085–1089) and Thomas Moore's poem "Come, rest in this bosom, my own stricken deer" (T. Moore, 1859, pp. 317–318), the wounded deer becomes a trope for lost maidenhead.
17. For instance, in Tennyson's *The Princess,* 5:

> Tut, you know them not, the girls . . . Look you, Sir!
> Man is the hunter; woman is his game:
> The sleek and shining creatures of the chase,
> We hunt them for the beauty of their skins;
> They love us for it, and we ride them down.

The confusion of sex with hunting is similarly lampooned in the old joke about the hunter who found a beautiful naked girl leaning against a tree in the woods. "I'm game," she murmured, so he shot her. Cf. Oliver Goldsmith, *She Stoops to Conquer,* 1.2; J. Thurber, *The White Deer;* Roy Lewis, 1960, p. 66. E. E. Cummings' (1928) poem "All in Green Went My Love Riding" features a neo-medieval erotic hunt with the poet as the hunted stag.

18. G. Tilander, 1967, p. 12.
19. G. Turbervile, 1576, pp. 136–137.
20. Ibid., pp. 139–140. "Mome" (fool).
21. Ibid., pp. 176–178. "Silly" (poor, wretched).
22. F. W. Nietzsche, *The Genealogy of Morals,* 2.6; S. Orwell and I. Angus, 1968, vol. 3, p. 281.
23. G. Turbervile, 1576, p. 125.
24. E. Hobusch, 1980, pp. 117–118.
25. R. Pace, *De Fructu qui ex Doctrina Percipitur* (F. Manley and R. S. Sylvester, 1967, p. 22).
26. Cervantes, *Don Quixote,* 2.9 (trans. W. Starkie, 1957, p. 331).
27. Montaigne, *Essays,* 2.12 ("Apology for Raimond Sebond"); D. M. Frame, 1960, pp. 130–168.
28. Ibid., pp. 130–131.
29. Xenophon, *Memorabilia,* 1.4.11; Plato, *Timaeus,* 90–92 (E. Hamilton and H. Cairns, 1961, pp. 1209–11); Ovid, *Metamorphoses,* 1.84–86 (F. J. Miller, 1925, pp. 8–9); Cicero, *De natura deorum,* 2.56 (H. Rackham, 1933, p. 256); Augustine, *City of God,* 22.24 (W. M. Green, 1966, vol. 7, p. 331); Lactantius, *Divine Institutes,* 2.10, 3.10, 7.8 (W. Fletcher, 1871, pp. 113, 159, 449).
30. D. M. Frame, 1960, pp. 165–168.
31. *De docta ignorantia,* 2.12 (G. Heron, 1954, p. 111).

32. The plurality of worlds was also argued by Montaigne (D. F. Frame, 1958, p. 390). From Cusa's time to the present, skeptical writers have postulated other worlds like ours to deflate human pretensions to special status in the universe (S. J. Dick, 1982; M. J. Crowe, 1986).

33. T. Browne, *Religio medici,* 1.22 (N. J. Endicott, 1967, p. 30).

34. M. Ficino, *Theologica platonica de immortalitate animorum,* 2.2 (J. L. Burroughs, 1944, p. 231). Renaissance humanism began in large part as a reaction by the Platonists of the Florentine Academy against the Averroists of the northern Italian universities, who denied human immortality and preached a naturalistic rationalism (J. H. Randall Jr., 1962, pp. 55–64; F. B. Artz, 1966, p. 29).

35. R. Adams, 1963, p. 85.

36. Gelli's horse denounces human beings as lustful, intemperate, and emotional creatures. Ulysses replies that although beasts act more temperately and sensibly than people, they do so through the compulsion of their nature rather than the operations of reason—they are not truly virtuous. All this sounds suspiciously like Houyhnhmns discussing Yahoos with Gulliver. The suspicion approaches certainty when Gelli's horse remarks that human poets are accustomed "to say the thing that is not" *(dire tal volta quello che non é),* the strained expression the Houyhnhmns invent to express the alien concept of lying that Gulliver brings to them. Robert Adams (1962, p. xlviii) thinks it unlikely that Swift lifted this phrase from Gelli because it did not occur in the then recent translation of *Circe* by Tom Brown; but Swift could have picked it up from the 1557 translation by Henry Iden ("Poets . . . say sometimes *that that is not*"). *Circe* is also thought to have influenced Montaigne (G. Boas, 1933, p. 28).

6. The Noise of Breaking Machinery

EPIGRAPH: George Starbuck, "Translations from the English" (1966, p. 28).

1. George Boas (1933, p. 52) argued that Montaigne was only indulging himself in a witty paradox when he put man on the same plane as the beasts. But Boas' own sources (pp. 67–68) show that Montaigne was taken quite seriously at the time.

2. N. Fontaine, 1736, vol. 2, p. 73.

3. The fourteenth-century scholar Jean Buridan, who developed the concept of the intrinsic impetus of a moving body, noted that his concept could explain the unending motion of the heavenly spheres without the need to postulate planetary intelligences (E. J. Dijksterhuis, 1959, p. 182). Nicholas of Oresme seems to have been the first to liken the resulting world mechanism to a clock (H. Butterfield, 1949, p. 8). Other theologians argued that God would not have simply put nature in motion and left it to run by itself, since that would have caused mortals to forget God's power and providence (John Calvin, *Institutes of the Christian Religion,* 1.16; J. B. Friedman, 1981, p. 3).

4. Aristotle, *Nicomachean Ethics,* 3.2. The Cartesian view of beasts was foreshad-

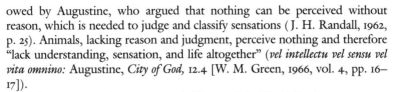

owed by Augustine, who argued that nothing can be perceived without reason, which is needed to judge and classify sensations (J. H. Randall, 1962, p. 25). Animals, lacking reason and judgment, perceive nothing and therefore "lack understanding, sensation, and life altogether" (*vel intellectu vel sensu vel vita omnino:* Augustine, *City of God,* 12.4 [W. M. Green, 1966, vol. 4, pp. 16–17]).

5. W. Ralegh (1964, vol. 2, pp. 29–30), *History of the World,* I.1.xi.

6. St. Bernard, *On Grace and Free Choice,* 1.2, 2.4 (D. O'Donovan, 1970, vol. 7, pp. 55–59).

7. H. Crew and A. de Salvio, 1914, pp. 245 ff.

8. F. Cajori, 1934, vol. 1, pp. xvii–xviii.

9. E. J. Dijksterhuis, 1959, pp. 310 ff.

10. E. Nordenskiöld, 1924, pp. 141 ff: F. J. Cole, 1949, pp. 270 ff. Experiments and interpretations of this sort go back to classical antiquity (C. Singer, 1957, pp. 32, 58), but they became much more frequent in the 1600s.

11. Descartes, *Méditations,* 2, 6; *Objections et réponses,* 2 (A. Bridoux, 1953, pp. 278, 330–331, 386).

12. Descartes, *Discours de la méthode,* 4; *Principles de la philosophie,* 2.1 (A. Bridoux, 1953, pp. 148–149, 152–153, 611–612).

13. Descartes, letter to Marquis of Newcastle, November 23, 1646 (A. Bridoux, 1953, pp. 1256–57): "Since the organs of [animals'] bodies are not very different from ours, it may be conjectured that there is attached to these organs some thoughts like those we experience in ourselves, though perhaps of a much less perfect kind. All I can say to this is that if they thought as we do, they would have an immortal soul like us. This is unlikely, because there is no reason to believe it of some animals without believing it of all, and many of them (oysters, sponges, etc.) are too imperfect for this to be credible."

14. Descartes, *Discours de la méthode,* 5 (A. Bridoux, 1953, pp. 165–166).

15. Ibid.

16. J. P. Mahaffy, 1901, p. 181.

17. M. Fontaine, 1736, vol. 2, pp. 52–53. Although Fontaine's testimony about vivisection at Port-Royal has been questioned, other sources exist (J. Rodman, 1986), and such practices are certainly in keeping with the view of animals as mindless automata that recurs throughout the writings of Descartes and his followers. The supposed indifference of Cartesians to the cruelties of vivisection was a favorite point of attack for Descartes' 17th-century critics (L. C. Rosenfield, 1941, pp. 86 ff).

18. Descartes, *Discours de la méthode,* 6 (A. Bridoux, 1953, p. 168).

19. F. Bacon, *Novum Organum,* aphorisms 59, 92 (B. Montagu, 1828, vol. 9, pp. 206, 282).

20. F. Bacon, *New Atlantis* (J. Devey, 1909, p. 297).

21. Descartes, *Les Passions de l'ame,* art. 34 (A. Bridoux, 1953, p. 712).

22. R. W. Church, 1931, pp. 23, 131.

23. J. Locke, 3rd letter to Bishop of Worcester (J. Locke, 1852, pp. 350–357). Cf. Voltaire, *Les Adorateurs ou les louanges de dieu* (L. C. Rosenfield, 1941, p. 131).

24. J. S. Slotkin, 1965, p. 197.

25. J. Wesley, *Sermons,* 2, 60 ("The General Deliverance"; Wesley, 1958, vol. 6, pp. 244, 252).

26. J. Locke, *Essay Concerning Human Understanding,* 2.10.10, 2.11.5–13, 2.27.8 (Locke, 1852, pp. 105–108, 209); J. Burnet, 1774, pp. 146–150; J. Wesley, 1958, vol. 6, pp. 241–252; E. Darwin, 1794, vol. 1, 16, 16.4–17.1 (pp. 263–264); R. E. Brantley, 1984; P. Quennell, 1968, p. 217; G. C. Bussey, 1912, pp. 29–32, 77–78; Voltaire, *Lettres philosophiques,* 13, and *Dictionnaire philosophique,* "Bêtes"; L. C. Rosenfield, 1941, pp. 149–153; J. S. Slotkin, 1965, pp. 179, 193, 204; A. Gode-von Aesch, 1941, pp. 57 ff.

27. A. Pope, *Essay on Man,* 1.207–226.

28. Plato, *Timaeus,* 40–41; A. O. Lovejoy, 1936, pp. 46 ff.

29. Ibid., p. 199. Cf. Pope, *Essay on Man,* 2.1–30.

30. D. Hume, "On Suicide," written ca. 1750 (R. Wollheim, 1963, p. 256).

31. A. Pope, *Essay on Man,* 3.21–26.

32. Ibid., 3.27–48.

33. This doctrine was elaborated in detail by Aquinas and is still the official teaching of the Roman Catholic Church (C. D. Niven, 1967, pp. 29 ff: P. Singer, 1990, pp. 193–197; J. Rachels, 1990, pp. 90–91).

34. J.-J. Rousseau, *Discours sur l'origine de l'inegalité parmi les hommes* (K. Weigand, 1955, p. 72); L. C. Rosenfield, 1941.

35. J. Bentham, 1780 (J. H. Burns and H. L. A. Hart, 1970, p. 283).

36. R. Boyle, *Of the Excellency and Grounds of the Corpuscular or Mechanical Philosophy* (Boyle, 1744, vol. 3, p. 450).

37. C. Harvie, 1984, p. 430. Cf. G. M. Trevelyan, 1942, vol. 3, p. 103. "Turn where you will," writes E. P. Thompson (1975, p. 263), "the rhetoric of 18th-century England is saturated with the notion of law."

38. I. Watts, 1707 (S. T. Porter, 1853, p. 140).

39. G. W. von Leibniz, *Abridgement of the Theodicy* (G. M. Duncan, 1908, p. 285).

40. A. Pope, *Essay on Man,* 1.289–294.

41. L. C. Rosenfield, 1941, p. 59. Some later Christian thinkers have adopted a similar line of reasoning (C. S. Lewis, 1940, p. 131–133; P. Teilhard de Chardin, 1969, p. 87; cf. A. R. Kingston, 1967, p. 486).

42. J. Wesley, *Sermons,* 2.60 ("The General Deliverance"), 1788 (Wesley, 1958, vol. 6, p. 251). Cf. D. Hume, *Dialogues concerning Natural Religion,* 10 (N. K. Smith, 1947, pp. 194–195).

43. K. V. Thomas, 1983, p. 182.

44. J. Wesley, 1958, vol. 6, pp. 249–251. Other Christian thinkers of the 17th and 18th centuries promulgated similar doctrines (K. V. Thomas, 1983, pp. 139–140).

45. T. R. Malthus, *Essay on the Principle of Population* (1798), 19 (G. Himmelfarb, 1960, p. 141).

46. A. Pope, 1777, vol. 4, p. 158 (*Guardian,* no. 61).

47. C. D. Niven, 1967, pp. 49 ff; S. Glubok, 1969, p. 189; S. Shesgreen, 1973, pls. 77–78; R. Darnton, 1984, pp. 75 ff, 90–91; K. V. Thomas, 1983, pp. 139–140; H. Ritvo, 1987, p. 155.

48. E. Hobusch, 1978, p. 152.
49. The flesh of animals subjected to pain or stress just before death has a lower lactic acid content than that of animals killed painlessly. Such "dark-cutting" meat has a distinctive flavor and texture, formerly prized but now regarded as unattractive (H. McGee, 1984, p. 96).
50. D. S. Landes, 1983, p. 228.
51. K. V. Thomas, 1983, pp. 157 ff.
52. C. D. Niven, 1967, p. 98.
53. Ibid., pp. 53–55; J. Wesley, 1958, vol. 6, pp. 247–248, 251–252. Be-kind-to-animals nursery rhymes of the "Mary had a little lamb" ilk originated around 1765 (I. Opie and P. Opie, 1952, p. 149), when the author of one of the first Mother Goose books tacked a moral tagline ("What a naughty boy was that / To try to drown poor pussy cat") onto the old jingle "Ding, dong, bell"— which was originally a mock dirge for a drowned cat.
54. J. Locke, *Thoughts on Education,* 116 (Locke, 1947, p. 305).
55. R. Bator, 1984a, pp. 134, 151–152, 154, 235–236, 274; 1984b, pp. 191, 361–362. The anonymous author of *The History of Little Goody Two-Shoes* (1766), whose heroine's name became a byword for this kind of juvenile moralizing, warned his readers that wicked children who "dare to torture and wantonly destroy God Almighty's creatures" could not count on attaining happiness in this life or Heaven in the next (R. Bator, 1984a, pp. 91–92).
56. In Newbery's kiddie-science book, *The Newtonian System of Philosophy Adapted to the Capacities of Young Gentlemen and Ladies* (1761), the practice of whipping pigs to death to tenderize their flesh is held up to detestation, and an experiment in which a live rat is placed in an evacuated glass bell is protested— and countenanced only on the understanding that the rat will be freed in return for his service to science, if he survives. He does and is released (R. Bator, 1984a, pp. 45, 68). For bull baiting, see Thomas Day's 1783 *The History of Sandford and Merton* (ibid., p. 165); for hunting, see H. Carpenter and M. Prichard, 1985, p. 24.
57. K. V. Thomas, 1983, pp. 162–165.
58. C. Fleury, *Moeurs des Israelites Anciens,* 2, chs. 2, 13 (A. Clarke, 1837, pp. 53, 126).
59. G. B. Hill, 1897, vol. 1, p. 288. Johnson, who often went fox hunting for exercise when a guest in the country, nevertheless once outraged a host by releasing a trapped hare (ibid., vol. 2, p. 397).
60. E. Hobusch, 1978, p. 149.
61. A. Pope, 1777, vol. 4, p. 160 (*Guardian,* no. 61). The Latin quotation comes from the description of the wounded stag in the *Aeneid* (7.501–502): "bleeding and suppliant-like with his complaint." The bizarre custom that Pope refers to was not unique to England. In Spain the noble ladies were seated atop a platform while hunted stags were driven underneath them and slaughtered (F. Braudel, 1981, p. 292).
62. K. V. Thomas, 1983, p. 294. "Many," wrote the Puritan minister Joseph Seccombe (1743), "have a great Aversion to those whose Trade it is to take away the Lives of the lower species of Creatures. A Butcher is (in their

apprehension) a mere Monster, and a Fisherman, a filthy Wretch." Cf. John Taylor's 1620 satire, "Jack-a-Lent" (J. Taylor, 1630, p. 116): "The cutthroat butchers, wanting throats to cut, / At Lent's approach their bloody shambles shut; / For forty days their tyranny doth cease, / And men and beasts take truce and live at peace."

63. "Physicians," wrote Swift in 1706, "ought not to give their Judgment of Religion, for the same Reason that Butchers are not admitted to be Jurors upon Life and Death" (R. Quintana, 1958, p. 418).
64. E. McCurdy, 1928, p. 78; K. V. Thomas, 1983, pp. 290 ff.
65. L. Ziff, 1959, pp. 13, 32.
66. J.-J. Rousseau, *Emile,* 1, 2 (B. Foxley, 1957, pp. 25–26, 118–120); Voltaire, *Dictionnaire philosophique,* "Viande"; A. Pope, 1777, vol. 4, p. 160 (*Guardian,* no. 61); *Essay on Man,* 3.65–68; K. V. Thomas, 1983, pp. 287–300; P. Singer, 1990, pp. 203, 210.
67. See e.g. the picture of the Indians of Carolina laid out by John Lawson in 1709 (H. T. Lefler, 1967). Cf. C. Fleury, *Moeurs des israelites anciens,* 2.2. Hunting, said Dr. Johnson, "was the labour of the savages of North America, but the amusement of the gentlemen of England" (G. B. Hill, 1897, vol. 2, p. 170). Some pointed to the supposed dependence of the Indians on hunting as a justification for taking their land away from them so that it could be put to productive (agricultural) use (R. F. Berkhofer Jr., 1978, pp. 120, 138).
68. T. Malthus, *Essay on the Principle of Population,* 3 (G. Himmelfarb, 1960, p. 18).
69. A. Pope, *Essay on Man,* 3.147–168.
70. J. Burnett, 1774, pp. 270–313, 367, 392–397, 416–420.
71. *Gulliver's Travels,* 4.1–2 (R. Quintana, 1958, pp. 181, 186).
72. M. P. Foster, 1961, pp. 7–73, 81–84; S. Orwell and I. Angus, 1968, pp. 205–223; R. Gravil, 1974, pp. 35 ff.
73. M. P. Foster, 1961, pp. 85–86.
74. Ibid; pp. 76–80.
75. Ibid., pp. 79–80.
76. *Gulliver's Travels,* 4.2 (R. Quintana, 1958, p. 186).

7. The Sorrows of Eohippus

EPIGRAPH: Arthur Conan Doyle, "The Adventure of the Cardboard Box."
1. J. G. Herder, *Menschengeschlechts,* 2.6 (B. Suphan, 1883, vol. 6, p. 253).
2. A. Kazin, 1946, p. 252. "Feeling is everything," proclaims Faust in Goethe's caricature of Romanticism (*Faust,* 1.3456).
3. R. W. Emerson, "Nature" (I. Edman, 1926, p. 400); "The Transcendentalist" (B. Atkinson, 1940, p. 89).
4. P. T. Holbach, *Système de la nature* (Y. Belaval, 1966, p. xxix).
5. W. Wordsworth, "The Tables Turned" (S. Gill, 1984, p. 131).
6. I. Babbitt, 1919, pp. 273–274; J. Canaday, 1959, pp. 115–116.
7. J. Addison, *Spectator,* 414 (W. L. Fleischauer, 1956, pp. 144–145).
8. D. Clifford, 1963, pp. 132–133. The concept of Eden itself probably derives

ultimately from this tradition of gardening. The word *paradise* comes from a Persian word meaning "walled garden," and the biblical Eden is described as a similar garden planted by God, who placed Adam in it as a gardener, "to dress it and to keep it" (Genesis 2.8–15).

9. A. Pope, *Moral Essays*, 4.113–118.
10. P. Quennell, 1968, p. 180.
11. J.-J. Rousseau, *Julie, ou La Nouvelle Héloïse*, 4.11 (R. Pomeau, 1960, pp. 453–468); I. Babbitt, 1919, p. 275; D. Clifford, 1963, p. 151; E. Hyams, 1971, p. 5.
12. J.-J. Rousseau, *Confessions*, 4 (J. Voisine, 1964, p. 195).
13. Burke, *On the Sublime and Beautiful*, 2. 2, 2. 5 (C. W. Eliot, 1909, pp. 49, 55).
14. J.-J. Rousseau, *Julie*, 4.11 (R. Pomeau, 1960, p. 462).
15. H. B. Forman and M. B. Forman, 1970, vol. 7, p. 129; J. Strachey, 1962, p. 11.
16. R. Wernaer, 1910, pp. 167–168.
17. R. W. Emerson, "Nature," 1 (B. Atkinson, 1940, p. 6).
18. Byron, *Childe Harold's Pilgrimage*, 3.72.
19. P. B. Shelley, "On the Medusa of Leonardo da Vinci in the Florentine Gallery" (C. Baker, 1951, p. 394).
20. H. D. Thoreau, *Walden*, 11 (L. Owens, 1906, vol. II, p. 243).
21. P. B. Shelley, *Adonais*, lines 382–387.
22. W. Wordsworth, *The Prelude*, 6.556–572 (S. Gill, 1894, p. 464).
23. F. W. Schelling, *Von der Weltseele* (M. Schröter, 1927, vol. 1, p. 418).
24. A. Tennyson, "The Higher Pantheism."
25. For example, in Schubert's songs "Jägers Abendlied," "Jägers Liebeslied," and "Der Alpenjäger," with respective texts by Goethe, Schober, and Mayrhofer; Robert Schumann's "Jägerlied" and "Jäger Wohlmut," and his settings of texts from H. Laube's *Jagdbrevier*; Brahms's "Der Jäger und sein Liebchen" and "Jägerlied"; Spohr's "Jagdlied"; and Weber's opera *Der Freischütz*.
26. L. Uhland, "Jägerlied" (L. Fränkel, 1893, pp. 31–32). Cf. "Der Jäger" and "Das Reh" (pp. 186–187, 202).
27. J. F. Cooper, *The Deerslayer*, ch. 16.
28. Ibid., ch. 2.
29. Ibid., ch. 25.
30. J. W. von Goethe and J. C. F. von Schiller, *Xenien*, "Die Weidtasche" (B. von Wiese, 1936, vol. 2, p. 145).
31. W. Blake, "Auguries of Innocence."
32. R. W. Emerson, "Forbearance."
33. H. D. Thoreau, *Walden*, 11 (L. Owens, 1906, vol. 2, pp. 235–236). Cf. Thoreau's *Journal* for February 21, 1861 (B. Torrey and F. H. Allen, 1906, vol. 14, pp. 315–319).
34. *Walden*, 11 (pp. 238–239).
35. P. B. Shelley, *Queen Mab*, notes, 8.
36. B. Alcott, *Journal*, February 5, 1839 (O. Shepard, 1938, p. 115). Alcott imposed a strictly meatless regimen on his family at their New England commune in the 1840s. In her 1876 book *Silver Pitchers* (G. F. Whicher, 1965, pp. 95–105), his grown daughter Louisa May Alcott recalled without affection the gray

vegetarian strictures of her childhood diet: "Unleavened bread, porridge, and water for breakfast; bread, vegetables, and water for dinner; bread, fruit, and water for supper was the bill of fare ordained by the elders. No teapot profaned that sacred stove, no gory steak cried aloud for vengeance from [my mother's] chaste gridiron."

37. W. Blake, "Jerusalem."
38. W. Blake, "Milton."
39. A. Kazin, 1946, p. 687.
40. P. B. Shelley, *Queen Mab,* 8 (C. Baker, 1951, pp. 8, 10). Cf. Shelley's "Ode to Liberty," lines 21–30.
41. A. Tennyson, *Maud,* 1.4.4.
42. L. Barber, 1980, pp. 71–82; A. Desmond, 1989, pp. 110–116.
43. J. F. Moore, 1899, pp. 133 ff.
44. W. Kirby, 1835, vol. 2, p. 525.
45. W. Paley, 1854, pp. 306, 308–310.
46. A. Tennyson, *In Memoriam A. H. H.,* 55–56.
47. R. Nisbet, 1980, pp. 118 ff.
48. L. Eiseley, 1958, p. 50.
49. J. C. Wieland, *Die Natur der Dinge,* 4. 399–402, 6. 7–12 (F. Homeyer, 1909, vol. 1, pp. 84, 117).
50. A. O. Lovejoy, 1936, p. 286.
51. E. Darwin, 1794, vol. 2, p. 247; J. B. Lamarck, *Philosophie zoologique,* 1, ch. 2 (H. Elliot, 1984, p. 55).
52. B. Disraeli, 1877, p. 109.
53. A. Desmond, 1989.
54. M. Millhauser, 1959, p. 122.
55. A. O. Lovejoy, 1959; J. Barzun, 1958, p. 54.
56. F. Darwin, 1896, vol. 2, p. 37.
57. G. B. Shaw, 1921, p. xlvi.
58. M. Ruse, 1979, pp. 239–241.
59. C. Darwin, 1859, ch. 4 (Modern Library ed., New York, 1936, p. 93).
60. Ibid., p. 373.
61. J. C. Greene, 1981, p. 74.
62. C. Darwin, 1871, ch. 21 (Modern Library ed., p. 919). Similar views were expressed by Malthus (G. Himmelfarb, 1960, p. 129).
63. P. Geddes, quoted in J. A. Thomson, 1910, p. 15.
64. As Andrew Carnegie put it after reading Darwin and Spencer: "Not only had I got rid of theology and the supernatural, but I had found the truth of evolution. 'All is well since all grows better' became my motto, my source of comfort" (J. C. Van Dyke, 1921, p. 339).
65. S. Persons, 1963, pp. 157, 166.
66. G. B. Shaw, 1921, pp. lxii–lxiii.
67. A. Gray, 1876, pp. 306–311.
68. G. Nakhnikian, 1958, pp. 18–20.
69. F. Darwin, 1896, vol. 2, p. 105. Per contra, Wallace (who wanted to preserve

some role for the supernatural in human evolution) concluded that the strggle for existence minimizes suffering and that "it is difficult even to imagine a system by which a greater balance of happiness could have been secured" (A. R. Wallace, 1889, p. 40; cf. G. Himmelfarb, 1959, p. 381).

70. T. H. Huxley, "The Struggle for Existence in Human Society," 1888 (A. Castell, 1948, pp. 60–61).

8. The Sick Animal

EPIGRAPH: F. W. Nietzsche, *Genealogy of Morals*, 3.13 (F. Golffing, 1956, p. 257).

1. C. Darwin, 1871, ch. 6 (Modern Library ed., New York, 1936, p. 521). Cf. A. R. Wallace, 1889, p. 467; E. Clodd, 1902, p. 23; J. C. Greene, 1981, pp. 102–105.

2. H. Ritvo, 1987, p. 254; J. M. MacKenzie, 1988, pp. 50–51, 158–160, 301–302.

3. W. S. Rainsford, 1909, pp. 19–45. The modern South African poet Roy Campbell, a great white hunter who might be described as a sort of Falangist Hemingway, boasted that he "never went out to hunt without bringing back *matumba*, which means offal or guts for the niggers to eat" (R. Campbell, 1934, p. 65).

4. H. Ritvo, 1987, p. 260; F. Russell, 1984, pp. 47–48.

5. F. Russell, 1984, p. 28.

6. H. L. Mencken, 1949, p. 308; J. M. MacKenzie, 1988, p. 45.

7. J. Turner, 1980, p. 140.

8. S. A. Sullivan, 1984, pp. 41 ff.

9. J. Rishel, 1981.

10. J. Canaday, 1962, p. 212.

11. R. Ormond, 1981, p. 22.

12. C. Day, 1948, p. 345.

13. The paintings and drawings I have in mind here are Courbet's *Le Cerf à l'eau, Le Hallali du cerf,* and *La Biche forcée dans la niege;* and Landseer's *Deer and Deerhounds in a Mountain Torrent, The Last Run of the Season, A Random Shot, Precious Trophies, Wounded Stag Swimming,* and *The Otter Speared.* Similar motifs and similar mixed feelings about the hunt pervade the work of Landseer's eighteenth-century precursor J.-B. Oudry, of whose paintings it was said that they would have persuaded Descartes himself that animals have souls (H. Opperman, 1983, p. 184).

14. R. Ormond, 1981, p. 17.

15. The Act of 1822 offered protection to calves, heifers, and steers but specifically excluded bulls, so as not to offend the fans of bull-baiting (C. D. Niven, 1967, p. 71; J. Turner, 1980, p. 40).

16. C. D. Niven, 1967, pp. 97–109; J. Turner, 1980, pp. 45–52.

17. J. Turner, 1980, pp. 36–37, 53–59; H. Ritvo, 1987, pp. 137–157.

18. M. T. Phillips and J. A. Sechzer, 1989, p. 3.

19. M. Foster, 1899, p. 204; J. M. D. Olmsted, 1938, pp. 95–96; C. Lansbury, 1985, p. 162.

20. H. Ritvo, 1987, p. 164.
21. C. Lansbury, 1985.
22. Ibid., p. 45.
23. C. D. Warner, 1878.
24. M. Twain, 1869, vol. 1, pp. 87–88, 268; 1871, vol. 1, pp. 154, 156.
25. F. Anderson, 1972, pp. 11–12.
26. M. Twain, 1897, vol. 1, pp. 80–88, 207–209.
27. Ibid., pp. 213–216.
28. Ibid., vol. 2, pp. 125–126.
29. M. Twain, 1904, pp. 30 ff: J. Smith, 1972, pp. 132–144.
30. M. Twain, 1962, pp. 222 ff. Cf. *The Mysterious Stranger* (M. Twain, 1916, pp. 192–200) and *What Is Man?* (M. Twain, 1917, pp. 76 ff).
31. M. Twain, 1894, p. 158.
32. T. H. Warren, 1971, pp. 91–96.
33. Ibid., pp. 522–523.
34. A. Schopenhauer, *Parerga und Paralipomena*, 12, "Nachträge zur Lehre vom Leiden der Welt" (J. Frauenstädt, 1922, vol. 6, p. 323; trans. T. B. Saunders, 1923, pp. 28–29).
35. Ibid. This is the same moral that Jeffers drew from his vision of the killer ape ("But we are what we are, and we might remember / Not to hate any person, for all are vicious"). Schopenhauer's influence on Jeffers has been analyzed at length by R. Squires (1956, pp. 41 ff).
36. Schopenhauer, *Parerga und Paralipomena*, 14, "Nachträge zur Lehre von der Bejahung und Verneinung des Willens zum Leben" (Frauenstädt, p. 343; Saunders, p. 26).
37. A. Schopenhauer, *Die Welt als Wille und Vorstellung*, 4 (I. Edman, 1928, pp. 35, 250).
38. "In the same way, evil presses upon an animal only with its own intrinsic weight; whereas fear and anticipation often make its burden ten times as heavy for us" (Schopenhauer, *Parerga und Paralipomena*, 14; Frauenstädt, p. 318).
39. Ibid. (Frauenstädt, p. 318; Saunders, pp. 25–26).
40. H. Huth, 1957, p. 135.
41. J. W. Krutch, 1950, p. 99.
42. H. Huth, 1957, pp. 142–143.
43. R. Nash, 1982, p. 113; H. Huth, 1957, p. 155.
44. *The Nation*, January 27, 1876, p. 66.
45. J. Burroughs, 1912, pp. 263–264, 271–272.
46. R. E. Nicholls, 1976.
47. S. Fox, 1981, p. 52.
48. R. H. Lutts, 1990, p. 29.
49. J. Burroughs, 1903, p. 305.
50. J. Burroughs, 1904, p. 515.
51. W. J. Long, 1903b.
52. R. H. Lutts, 1990, pp. 107–109.

53. R. Nash, 1982, pp. 150, 139.
54. P. R. Cutright, 1956, p. 000.
55. G. J. Stein, 1987; C. Brinton, 1965, ch. 7.
56. F. W. Nietzsche, *Genealogy of Morals*, 22 (F. Golffing, 1956, p. 226).
57. Ibid., 11 (Golffing, p. 174). Cf. *Die Wille zur Macht*, 1.98: "*Unfortunately*, man is no longer evil enough. Rousseau's opponents who say 'man is a beast of prey' are, unfortunately, wrong" (W. Kaufmann, 1967, p. 61).
58. In view of Nietzsche's loudly proclaimed contempt for pity and his supposed indifference to suffering, the incident that precipitated his final madness seems poignant and ironic. On June 3, 1888, as he was leaving his apartment in Turin, he saw an old cabhorse being savagely beaten by its driver. Nietzsche rushed to the horse, threw his arms protectively around the animal's neck, and collapsed in tears. He was taken home and put to bed. When he awoke, he perceived himself to be the crucified Dionysus, who had been resurrected from the dead to save the world. He spent most of the next twelve years in an asylum and died a hopeless madman in 1900 (E. F. Podach, 1931).
59. S. Freud, "Civilized Sexual Morality and Modern Nervousness" and *Civilization and Its Discontents* (S. Katz, 1947, p. 186; J. Strachey, 1962, ch. 4); C. Rycroft, 1972, pp. 20–21.
60. S. Freud, "The Most Prevalent Form of Degradation in Erotic Life" (S. Katz, 1947, pp. 216–217).
61. S. Freud, *Beyond the Pleasure Principle*, 6 (J. Strachey, 1950a); E. Fromm, 1973, pp. 439 ff; J. M. Dickinson, 1964.
62. S. Freud, *Civilization and Its Discontents* (J. Strachey, 1962, p. 92).
63. J. Huxley, 1948, pp. 21, 156. "Man's superiority over the other animals," wrote Norman Brown in summing up Freud, "is his capacity for neurosis" (N. O. Brown, 1959, p. 10).
64. E. Mendelson, 1977, p. 217. Cf. Auden's 1935 essay "Psychology and Art Today" (ibid., pp. 332–342).
65. S. Pope, 1925, p. 140.
66. Medieval tradition recognized the hare, the stag, the boar, and the wolf as the four proper "beasts of venery" (G. Tilander, 1964); other quarry were given lower status, as "beasts of the chase" or "vermin." The boar is not native to North America, and wolf hunting has rarely been practiced as a sport in the United States.
67. The symbolism of deer has also been influenced throughout the history of the English language by the homophones *deer/dear* and *hart/heart*. Both these puns are still alive and can be encountered in the mass media—for example, in the December 1983 promotional campaign that urged California radio audiences to "bring your dear and a little dough" to Las Vegas for Christmas, or in the news story about ranchers feeding starving deer that appeared on the CBS Evening News on February 29, 1984, under the teaser headline "Heart to Hart."
68. For instance, in Robert Frost's poems "Two Look at Two" and "The Most of It," in which human spiritual yearnings are answered by the sudden

273

appearance of deer carrying symbolic messages of love or despair. Similar cervine epiphanies occur in the works of Kenneth Patchen (1945) and Ted Hughes (1979, pp. 22–23).

69. Some examples in addition to those already noted: Cowper, *The Task* (3.108 ff); Shelley, *Epipsychidion* (272–275) and *Adonais* (xxxi–xxxiii); Tennyson, *The Princess,* 2 (T. H. Warren and F. Page, 1965, p. 164); John Davidson, "A Runnable Stag" (A. Turnbull, 1973, vol. 1, pp. 159–161); Edna St. Vincent Millay (1928),"The Buck in the Snow"; J. R. Harris, 1924, pp. 11–12, 17; E. Weismiller, 1936, pp. 78–79; and Andrew Wyeth's 1945 painting *Young Buck* (W. M. Corn, 1973, p. 26).

70. W. Kirby, 1835, vol. 2, p. 501.

71. K. Rexroth, "Deer" (Rexroth, 1956, p. 61).

72. E. Mendez, 1970; L. Erdrich, 1984, pp. 180 ff. For George Foreman's and George Bush's "awe" of deer and reluctance to hunt them, see *Time,* April 22, 1985, pp. 10–11, and *Newsweek,* January 8, 1989, p. 63.

73. J. Dickey, "Springer Mountain" (Dickey, 1964, p. 29).

74. CBS Evening News, July 17, 1982.

9. The Bambi Syndrome

EPIGRAPH: Fred Pfeil, 1986, p. 523.

1. Sources drawn on in describing Salten and his place in Viennese cultural life include K. Kraus, 1922; F. Salten, 1933; A. Werner, 1945; K. Riedmüller, 1949; A. Janik and S. Toulmin, 1973; C. E. Schorske, 1980; J. S. Jones, 1983; J. Rieckmann, 1985; S. Hampshire, 1991; and the collected letters of von Hofmannsthal (1937) and Schnitzler (T. Nickl and H. Schnitzler, 1964).

2. F. Salten, 1931, p. 124.

3. K. Riedmüller, 1949, p. 46.

4. G. Reiger, 1980, p. 16.

5. F. Salten, 1928, p. 78.

6. Ibid., p. 286.

7. J. Galsworthy, 1916.

8. *New York Times,* July 8, 1928, sec. 4, p. 5.

9. L. Mosley, 1985, p. 28.

10. *New York Times,* December 15, 1933, p. 5; January 24, 1939, p. 21.

11. G. Seldes, 1937, pp. 46–47.

12. S. Orwell and I. Angus, 1968, vol. 1, pp. 230–232.

13. F. S. Nugent, 1939.

14. A. I. Macy, *New York Times,* October 10, 1938, pt. 10, p. 9.

15. F. Thomas and O. Johnston, 1981, pp. 339–340.

16. Perce Pearce, transcript of sweatbox meeting, September 1, 1939; *Bambi* files, Disney Archives. All subsequent transcripts cited come from the Disney Archives.

17. S. Culhane, 1986, p. 142.

18. F. Thomas and O. Johnston, 1981, pp. 279–280.

19. The invention of the xeroxed cel in the 1950s and the subsequent replacement of the cel by computer-graphics technology have since provided better and cheaper solutions to the problem of multiple tracing errors.
20. Walt Disney, transcript of sweatbox meeting, March 10, 1941.
21. Perce Pearce, transcript of sweatbox meeting, September 1, 1939.
22. Larry Morey, transcript of meeting, March 19, 1940.
23. L. Maltin, 1980, pp. 280–281, 447; *Variety,* December 1, 1982. The obituary notice for the cartoon's director Hugh Harman in the *Los Angeles Times* (November 27, 1982) claims that he was nominated for a Nobel Peace Prize rather than an Academy Award.
24. It lacks a scene that was not eliminated from the story until September 9, 1939, but it retains a fox-hunt sequence that was dropped on November 22.
25. Undated, mimeographed draft continuity, headed "F#2—BAMBI," *Bambi* files, Disney Archives. This dialogue is adapted from Salten, but the subsequent twists of the knife—giving the last speech to Bambi's mother, having her killed in the following sequence, and making her hunters lure her baby in for the kill as well—are Disney innovations.
26. This line is so intolerably heavy with portent that it generated one of the few instances of Disney self-parody. In the Oscar-nominated 1955 Disney short *No Hunting,* Bambi and his mother appear briefly to watch a wave of trash discarded by hunters come down a stream—whereupon Mother murmurs in a husky contralto, "*Man* . . . is in the forest. Let's dig out."
27. Perce Pearce, transcript of story meeting, February 1, 1940.
28. Walt Disney, transcript of story meeting, June 20, 1940.
29. Story meeting, April 19, 1940.
30. The idea of having the movie end as it began came from consultant Sidney Franklin (O. Johnston and F. Thomas, 1990, p. 119) and was elaborated by Disney (Walt Disney, Leica meeting notes, December 18, 1939; Walt Disney, transcripts of story meetings, January 9 and June 21, 1940). The April Shower sequence in *Bambi* by itself forms an independent palindrome as elaborate as the one in *The Old Mill.*
31. "Whoever looks into the water," wrote Jung, "sees his own image, but behind it living creatures soon loom up; fishes, presumably, harmless dwellers of the deep—harmless, if only the lake were not haunted. They are water beings of a peculiar sort. Sometimes a nixie gets into the fisherman's net, a female, half-human fish . . . The nixie is an even more instinctive version of a magical feminine being whom I call the *anima* . . . An alluring nixie from the dim bygone is today called an 'erotic fantasy,' and she may complicate our psychic life in a most painful way. She comes upon us just as a nixie might; she sits on top of us like a succubus . . . and in general displays an unbearable independence that does not seem at all proper in a psychic content . . . She is full of snares and traps, in order that man should fall, should reach the earth, entangle himself there, and stay caught, so that life should be lived" (C. G. Jung, 1959, pp. 308–311).
32. Ibid., pp. 301 ff.

33. Transcripts of sweatbox meeting, September 1, 1939, and story meeting, March 13, 1940.
34. F. Salten, 1928, pp. 77, 80–81, 161–162.
35. G. Seldes, 1950, pp. 46–47.
36. "If this happens in one single night, I hope it won't leave one with the impression that IT HAPPENED ONE NIGHT," wrote one Disney staffer, referring to Paramount's 1934 bedroom comedy starring Clark Gable and Claudette Colbert.
37. Early Disney cartoons in fact derive much of their energy from a stream of Freudian imagery. As the animation historian Donald Crafton notes, the Disney silents were distinguished from their competitors precisely by "the overtly libidinous (but presumably innocent) content of the humor. Present audiences cannot help but be impressed by the extent to which phallic imagery informs the majority of gags" (D. Crafton, 1982, p. 294). This kind of symbolism persisted into the mid-1940s in Disney cartoons. The samba number in *The Three Caballeros,* in which a lustful Donald Duck dances with a beautiful, whip-wielding vaquerita amid a chorus line of rhythmically stiffening and sagging saguaros, prompted the *New Yorker*'s film critic to remark at the time that the sequence "would probably be considered suggestive in a less innocent medium" (February 10, 1945, p. 37). In *Bambi* the shot of the girl bunny laying Thumper's head in her lap and sending him into a paroxysm of thumping by toying with his rigid ears was criticized at the 1940 screening, and even today often raises snickers from adults in the audience.
38. C. Shows, 1980, p. 188.
39. Ibid., p. 117.
40. E. H. Hess, 1975.
41. This quote comes from an interview with Williams in the 1989 Disney promotional film, *It All Started with a Mouse.*
42. P. Kael, *New Yorker,* July 19, 1982, p. 16.
43. R. Ebert, *Durham* (N.C.) *Morning Herald,* July 15, 1988, *Friday* magazine, p. 4.
44. August 6, 1942, p. 6.
45. *New Republic,* June 29, 1942, p. 843.
46. See e.g. R. Stephenson, 1967; R. Schickel, 1968; G. Seldes, 1956; R. Benayoun, 1961.
47. R. J. Brown, 1942.
48. Ibid.
49. D. C. Peattie, 1942, pp. 266, 268.
50. Quoted in C. Amory, 1975, pp. 92–93. Similar criticisms of Disney have been urged by philosophers, naturalists, and biologists (B. Nietschmann, 1977; T. Williams, 1989a, b; R. H. Lutts, 1990, pp. 198 ff; M. Bekoff and D. Jamieson, 1991, p. 30; J. A. Fisher, 1991, p. 75).
51. *Durham* (N.C.) *Morning Herald,* January 16, 1983, p. 11b.
52. C. Amory, 1975, p. 150.
53. *Arizona Daily Star* (Tucson), December 16, 1985. Cf. B. R. Peterson, 1989,

pp. 25, 33–34. Some meat producers similarly blame Disney for trends toward vegetarianism (R. E. Taylor and R. Bogart, 1988, p. 553).

54. D. E. Petzal, 1988.

55. Paul Harvey news broadcast, July 19, 1982.

56. C. Amory, 1975, p. 136.

57. *Raleigh* (N.C.) *News and Observer,* September 24, 1986, p. 5c. Cf. C. J. Adams, 1991, p. 77.

58. G. Reiger, 1980, p. 16.

59. Some examples: in covering protests of tourist flights over Yosemite, CBS News assured viewers that the tour operators had "no intention of buzzing Bambi" (Evening News, March 20, 1984). In his syndicated column of August 3, 1985, Andy Rooney described his first encounter with a deer and reported, "This was Bambi in person" (*Arizona Daily Star,* p. A-10). A 1983 Associated Press story described a young Massachusetts girl's meeting with a French boy who had found a note she cast into the Atlantic in a bottle. Neither spoke the other's language. When she struggled to tell him something about a deer, he listened in mystification until the light suddenly dawned. "Ah, Bambi," he replied. "Je le sais" (*Durham* [N.C.] *Morning Herald,* September 1, 1983, p. 2a).

60. Van Lawick-Goodall and van Lawick-Goodall, 1973, p. 28.

61. B. R. Peterson, 1989, pp. 14, 33.

62. CNN broadcast, July 21, 1988. As deer in general have done since Shakespeare's time, Bambi also represents the archetypal innocent victim. After the Central Park rape and near-fatal beating of a young woman by a gang of teenagers in 1989, columnist Joanne Jacobs wrote, "The most critical element of this attack was that they were male. She was female. They were predators. She was Bambi." (*Newsweek,* May 15, 1989, p. 40.)

63. John Updike, writes a sardonic reviewer of his essays, looks at Doris Day "with eyes as dewed as Bambi's" (J. Wolcott, 1983, p. 66). "I'll give you doe eyes," gushes a cosmetics saleswoman to Miss Piggy in Jim Henson's movie *The Muppets Take Manhattan:* "Doe eyes are Bambi eyes." In Bill Watterson's comic strip *Calvin and Hobbes* for June 29, 1987, Calvin practices saying "Pleeeaase, Mom" with huge, mutely pleading eyes—until Hobbes comments, "I still don't think giving her 'Bambi eyes' is going to get you a flame thrower."

64. C. L. Brace informs me that the football player Lance Alworth, a former wide receiver for the San Diego Chargers, was nicknamed "Bambi" for his deerlike grace and leaping ability.

65. *U.S. News and World Report,* June 6, 1983, p. 54; R. Wolf, 1981, p. 61. During Watt's tenure, Bambi was in fact used as a symbol of nature by the U.S. Forest Service. Visitors to national parks in the Sierras in 1981 could drive past Forest Service posters that showed Bambi imploring them to help prevent forest fires—and then stop at an information center to buy a guide (Grater, 1978) imploring them not to treat mule deer as "a sort of true-life Bambi."

66. *Newsweek*, May 22, 1989, p. 72.
67. T. Williams, 1989a; N. Christensen, 1989.
68. J. G. Mitchell, 1980, pp. 15, 242.
69. J. G. Mitchell, 1982, p. 111.
70. Cutting continuities of *Nature's Half Acre* (1951) and *Secrets of Life* (1956), Disney Archives.
71. F. Butler, 1983.
72. R. K. MacDonald, 1982, chs. 5–6.
73. M. Blount, 1975, ch. 7; R. Bator, 1984b, pp. 263 ff; J. Cott, 1983, p. xviii.
74. C. Johnson, 1904, pp. 210–211.
75. B. Wishy, 1968, p. 53.
76. To get an unbiased sample, I tallied the 206 children's books merchandised by Scholastic Publications through their book clubs in American first-grade classrooms during the 1986–87 school year. I found that 106, or 51 percent of them, were stories about talking animals, mostly of the animal-burlesque subgenre, and an additional 5 percent were animal stories of other sorts.
77. The earliest stuffed animal I have found documented is a cloth elephant dated 1829, preserved in the Museum of the City of New York (K. M. McClinton, 1970).
78. I. McClintock and M. McClintock, 1961, pp. 357–358.
79. J. R. R. Tolkien, 1965, pp. 78, 82.
80. D. D. Pitts, 1974.
81. I am grateful to Kaye Brown for this insight. In 1990, when F. Warne & Co. changed the label of their infant-formula products from one showing a (white) mother and child to one sporting a Beatrix Potter picture of Peter Rabbit, the company's promotional literature explained that the animal characters "appeal to people of all ethnic backgrounds."

10. A Fatal Disease of Nature

EPIGRAPH: Robinson Jeffers, "The Beginning and the End" (1963, pp. 8–9).
1. A. Sedgwick, 1860; W. Hopkins, 1860; A. R. Wallace, 1869; G. D. Campbell (Lord Argyll), 1869; St. G. J. Mivart, 1871.
2. C. Darwin, 1871, ch. 2 (Modern Library ed., New York, p. 431).
3. Ibid., p. 434 (my italics).
4. M. Cartmill et al., 1986; P. J. Bowler, 1986, p. 151.
5. D. J. Morton, 1926, 1927, 1935; H. F. Osborn, 1927, 1929; F. W. Jones, 1929a, b; W. E. Le Gros Clark, 1934, pp. 138, 281; J. Fleagle and W. L. Jungers, 1982; P. J. Bowler, 1986.
6. G. E. Smith, 1924, p. 40.
7. H. F. Osborn, 1926, 1927. A. R. Wallace (1889, p. 459) offered a proper Darwinian argument to the same end: he reasoned that our terrestrial bipedalism could not have evolved in tropical forests, since most of the food in such forests is up in the trees and loss of climbing ability would have been correspondingly disadvantageous in foraging.

8. W. E. Le Gros Clark, 1934, p. 288. In this early version of his theories, Le Gros Clark described the primate evolutionary trends as orthogenetic—that is, produced by an inbuilt tendency to follow a predestined evolutionary path. After the triumph of the neo-Darwinian synthesis in the late 1930s, he reinterpreted those trends in selectionist terms, as adaptations for living in the trees (M. Cartmill, 1972, 1974, 1982; J. Fleagle and W. L. Jungers, 1982).

9. W. E. Le Gros Clark, 1959, p. 75.

10. C. Morris, 1890, p. 350. Cf. C. Morris, 1886, p. 503.

11. C. Morris, 1906, pp. 65, 119–125.

12. H. Campbell, 1913, pp. 1260, 1408; H. Campbell, 1904, p. 911.

13. H. Campbell, 1904, p. 911; 1913, p. 1408.

14. H. Campbell, 1904, p. 911. The subsequent history of this idea has been sketched by Wiktor Stoczkowski (1991).

15. H. Campbell, 1913, pp. 1334, 1409, 1410. Similar speculations on the evolutionary basis for man's intellectual superiority to women were offered by Darwin in chapter 19 of *The Descent of Man*.

16. H. Campbell, 1913, p. 1260.

17. H. Campbell, 1917, p. 469.

18. Ibid., pp. 433–434.

19. C. Read, 1914, p. 182.

20. C. Darwin, 1871, ch. 20 (Modern Library ed., pp. 895–896); S. Freud, *Totem and Taboo*, 5 (J. Strachey, 1950b, pp. 141 ff).

21. C. Read, 1920, pp. 34, 39, 48–49.

22. Ibid., p. 61; R. Hartmann, 1886, pp. 294–295.

23. C. Read, 1925, pp. 80–81.

24. Ibid., p. 38.

25. Morris' *Man and His Ancestor* came to the attention of Carveth Read after he had published his own book. He acknowledged Morris' priority in his second edition (1925, pp. vii-viii).

26. A. Hrdlicka, 1918.

27. A. Keith, 1948, p. 253.

28. M. Cartmill, 1983; P. Bowler, 1986, pp. 230–232; R. Lewin, 1987, p. 315.

29. The International Rules of Zoological Nomenclature (article VII, 26a and 29) provide that zoological names formed by compounding two existing names shall not include a hyphen and that family names shall be formed by adding the ending *-idae* (not *-adae*) to the name of some genus in the family (E. Mayr, 1969, p. 310). A new family comprising only the genus *Australopithecus* cannot be named "Homo-simiadae"; it would have to be named Australopithecidae. These rules were not yet formally codified in 1924, but they had the force of custom even then—which is presumably why Dart immediately corrected two of his three violations and tried to justify the third (R. A. Dart, 1925b) before giving up "Homo-simiadae" altogether.

30. Another possible source is a 1922 theological work by J. Y. Simpson (1922, p. 78), which expounded Read's version of the hunting hypothesis and dubbed the hypothetical protohominid *Homosimius*.

31. R. A. Dart, letter to M. Cartmill, June 16, 1983.
32. R. A. Dart, 1940. Dart nevertheless must have become aware of Read and Campbell when his old enemy Arthur Keith cited them as Dart's precursors in his 1948 book—which appeared the year before Dart's first publication attributing great hunting prowess to *Australopithecus* (R. A. Dart, 1949).
33. One important scientist, the paleontologist W. K. Gregory, did suggest in 1916 that man's origins had involved a shift to a hunting way of life. But the only trait that Gregory specifically pointed to as a "byproduct of the hunting habit" was human hairlessness, which he thought had originated when our ancestors started clothing themselves in the skins of their prey.
34. One early, much-reprinted source for this image of the caveman hunter is Langdon Smith's 1895 poem "Evolution," beginning, "When you were a Tadpole and I was a Fish, / In the Paleozoic time." By 1928, the image was a cliché parodied by Don Marquis in *Love Sonnets of a Cave Man* (p. 3).
35. H. G. Wells, 1922, vol. 1, p. 80. Wells quotes these words approvingly from W. G. Smith, 1894, p. 56. Similar conclusions about early hominids were presented by Frederick Engels in *The Origin of the Family* (1891) and by H. W. Van Loon in his popular grade-school text *The Story of Mankind* (1923).
36. W. W. Howells, 1946, p. 125.
37. P. J. Bowler, 1983.
38. E. Mayr, 1982, p. 549.
39. C. Read, 1925, p. viii.
40. H. S. Harrison, 1921. Read's own comment on the shift of scientific interest from Darwin to Mendel was razor-edged: "A well-disciplined pack follows only one quarry at a time" (C. Read, 1925, p. viii).
41. J. S. Huxley, 1942, p. 28.
42. S. L. Washburn, 1951b.
43. G. J. Romanes, 1889, p. 439.
44. E. Haeckel, 1902, p. 125; 1923, pp. 595 ff. Similar conclusions were propounded by Herbert Spencer (G. W. S. Stocking Jr., 1987, p. 141).
45. D. Gasman, 1971; G. J. Stein, 1986; R. Proctor, 1988; B. Müller-Hill, 1988.
46. E. Barkan, 1988; C. L. Brace, 1982.
47. E. A. Hooton, 1946, pp. 158–159.
48. T. H. Huxley, 1863, ch. 3.
49. M. Cartmill, 1990. Donna Haraway (1988) offers a very different interpretation of the "new physical anthropology" as a justification for capitalist exploitation of Third World peoples.
50. L. A. White, 1949, pp. 29, 35.
51. N. Chomsky, 1964; 1975, p. 53. Cf. E. H. Lenneberg, 1967.
52. For instance, M. Sahlins, 1976; K. E. Bock, 1980; D. Bickerton, 1990, ch. 8.
53. E. A. Hooton, 1946, p. 288.
54. W. W. Howells, 1946, p. 102.
55. W. E. Le Gros Clark, 1964, pp. 157–162.
56. S. L. Washburn, 1951a.
57. C. L. Brace, 1962, p. 3. Cf. W. W. Howells, 1959, p. 123.

58. A. E. Mann, 1972.
59. C. L. Brace, 1964, 1967; M. H. Wolpoff, 1971.
60. T. Hine, 1987.
61. P. Boyer, 1985, pp. 266–274.
62. H. E. Fosdick, 1946, pp. 23, 121.
63. S. Orwell and I. Angus, 1968, vol. 4, pp. 184–190. Orwell expressed the same feeling in other postwar essays and letters (pp. 9, 248, 387, 428, 451).
64. H. G. Wells, 1945, p. 1.
65. M. Bates, 1960, pp. 252–253.
66. John D. MacDonald elaborated this metaphor in a 1965 Travis McGee thriller (p. 37): "Imagine the great ship come from a far galaxy which inspects a thousand green planets and then comes to ours and, from on high, looks down at all the scabs, the buzzings, the electronic jabberings, the poisoned air and water, the fetid night glow. A little cave-dwelling virus mutated, slew the things which balanced the ecology, and turned the fair planet sick . . . I think they would be concerned. They would be glad to have caught it in time."
67. D. Macdonald, 1946; R. Jeffers, 1963, p. 15; R. Linton, 1956, p. 51.
68. Gary Snyder, "Mother Earth: Her Whales" (G. Snyder, 1974, p. 48). Cf. Kenneth Patchen, 1948, p. 93:

> Yours is the health of the pig which roots up
> The vines that would give him food;
> Ours is the sickness of the deer which is shot
> Because it is the activity of hunters to shoot him.

69. R. Rhodes, 1969, p. 198.
70. T. Hine, 1987, p. 133; J. J. Corn and B. Horrigan, 1984, p. 17.
71. H. G. Wells, 1945, p. 31.
72. T. H. White, 1977, pp. 40, 46, 166, 183.
73. C. E. Cartmill, 1942.
74. R. J. Healey and J. F. McComas, 1946.
75. P. Boyer, 1985, pp. 257–265.
76. K. Vonnegut Jr., 1975, pp. 97–98.
77. For example, Vonnegut's 1955 story, "Deer in the Works" (K. Vonnegut Jr., 1968) and the passage in *The Sirens of Titan* (1961, pp. 304–305, 312) where Chrono leaves humanity to join the bluebirds.
78. K. Vonnegut Jr., 1985, pp. 8–9.
79. Some other, more recent science-fiction movies also depict the hunter's thirst for blood as betokening a flaw in the whole human species. In John Carpenter's *Starman,* the half-divine alien hero is upset by the doe he sees tied to a truck fender in the parking lot outside a roadside diner. "It's a deer—a dead deer," explains his human companion Jenny:

Starman: Dead deer; why.
Jenny: People hunt them to eat for food.

> *Starman:* *(studying doe)* Do deer eat people.
> *Jenny:* No.
> *Starman:* Do people eat people.
> *Jenny:* Uh, no. Oh, of course not. What do you think we are?
> *Starman:* I think you are a very primitive species.
> *Hunter:* *(coming over angrily)* What are you, soft-hearted? Cry when you saw *Bambi?*
> *Starman:* Define "bambi."
> *Hunter:* Huh?
> *Jenny:* He doesn't understand. He's not from around here.

The alien sneaks back to the truck later and resurrects the dead doe, who bounds joyously off into the woods. The uncomprehending oafs whose prey the alien has restored to life then beat him to a pulp. Other science-fiction films depict nonhuman hominids as innocents free from the taint of hunting. In William Dear's *Harry and the Hendersons,* a proto-hominid Bigfoot trapped in a suburban hunter's home is portrayed as a sweet half-simian vegetarian, who grieves as he takes the hunter's mounted deer heads into the backyard and buries them. The film *Missing Link* shows the last robust australopithecine agonizing over—and rejecting as wrong—the possibility of making weapons to hunt and kill other animals.

80. A. Leopold, 1949, pp. 129–130; R. Nash, 1982, pp. 183, 192.
81. A. Leopold, 1949, pp. 203–204.
82. Ibid., p. 152.
83. Ibid., pp. 34, 166, 167, 176–187.
84. Ibid., pp. 153–154.
85. R. Carson, 1962, p. 262.
86. R. Nash, 1982, pp. 224–225.
87. "The Nature Conservancy's efforts to preserve biological diversity," proclaims its magazine for members, "are based first and foremost on the moral and spiritual imperatives that compel so many of the organization's members and staff," not on economic or prudential considerations (January-February 1991, p. 5).
88. S. Griffin, 1978, pp. 103–104; C. Merchant, 1980; B. DeVall and G. Sessions, 1985, pp. 13–14; T. Regan, 1991, chs. 5, 7.
89. For instance, O. Segerberg Jr., 1971, pp. 143–149; E. P. Walker, 1964, entry for *Homo;* J. Z. Young, 1971, pp. 631, 641; R. Jurmain et al., 1984, pp. 514–515; G. Richards, 1987, p. 316; E. L. Simons, 1989; J. Diamond, 1992.
90. D. Brower (ed.), 1965; B. DeVall and G. Sessions, 1985, pp. 101–102, 105–107.

11. The Spirit of the Beast

1. J. W. Krutch, 1929, p. 249.
2. For example, J. W. Krutch, 1956, p. 117.
3. J. W. Krutch, 1929, pp. 75–76.

4. C. S. Lewis, 1947, pp. 83, 88.

5. Ibid., pp. 89–90; cf. C. Merchant, 1980, pp. 290–295; R. Bleier, 1986, p. 16; M. Namenwirth, 1986, pp. 32–38.

6. C. Merchant, 1980, p. 291.

7. E. Mendelson, 1977, p. 298.

8. R. E. Egner and L. E. Denon, 1961, pp. 389–390.

9. L. Hogben, 1938, p. 952; D. R. Weiner, 1988, pp. 170, 207.

10. S. Orwell and I. Angus, 1968, vol. 2, p. 143.

11. B. Russell, 1945, p. 728.

12. W. H. Auden, 1945, p. 434.

13. The earliest example I know of is H. G. Wells's *The Island of Dr. Moreau* (1896). In C. S. Lewis' novel *That Hideous Strength* (1946), a revolt of the lab animals turns the tide of Armageddon. More recent versions of this motif occur in the popular films *E.T., Project X, The Dark Crystal, The Secret of NIMH,* and *Beethoven,* and in Richard Adams' 1978 bestseller *The Plague Dogs.*

14. C. S. Lewis, 1947, pp. 80–81.

15. S. Toulmin, 1984.

16. D. Struik, 1964, p. 111.

17. E. and M. Josephson, 1962, p. 27; R. Hughes, 1981, pp. 73 ff.

18. G. Lukacs, 1923, p. 136; J. Berger, 1980, p. 15; A. Elzinga and A. Jamison, 1981, p. 64.

19. D. R. Weiner, 1988, pp. 168–171, 234.

20. R. Waters, 1990; Raleigh (N.C.) *News and Observer,* August 18, 1991, p. 8j; M. Feshback and A. Friendly Jr., 1992.

21. For example, S. Lem, 1971, pp. 34–35, and 1983, opening monologue.

22. Of 244 Soviet children's books listed in the 1988 mail-order catalog of Imported Publications of Chicago, 110 (45 percent) were about animals, and 94 of them were talking-animal stories. In 1985, production of a live-action Soviet film version of *Bambi* came to an abrupt halt when two workers on the set killed and ate the two fawns that were the picture's stars. The culprits were sentenced to a total of ten years at hard labor and denounced in the press for inflicting "huge moral damage" on the legions of Soviet children waiting to see the movie (*Arizona Daily Star,* Tucson, February 7, 1985). A juvenile novel about the endangered huemul deer of the Andes, strikingly reminiscent of Salten's *Bambi,* was published in Castro's Cuba in 1976 (J. Murillo and A. M. Ramb, 1976).

23. *The Animals' Agenda,* June 1991, pp. 25–26.

24. Yu. Dmitriyev, 1984, p. 169.

25. Raleigh (N.C.) *News and Observer,* October 6, 1988, p. 7A.

26. M. Nesturkh, 1959, pp. 233–234, 244, 271–275; G. F. Debetz, 1961, pp. 145–147; E. E. Ruyle, 1977.

27. S. Zuckerman, 1991, p. 44.

28. M. Cartmill, 1990.

29. I. Pepperberg, 1990; E. S. Savage-Rumbaugh, 1986.

30. H. S. Terrace, 1983; H. S. Terrace et al., 1979; D. Bickerton, 1990, pp. 205 ff; S. Zuckerman, 1991.

31. B. Russell, 1945, pp. 726–727.
32. C. Darwin, 1871, ch. 3 ; B. E. Rollin, 1981; T. Regan, 1983; J. Rachels, 1990.

12. A View to a Death in the Morning

EPIGRAPH: José Ortega y Gasset, 1972, p. 54.

1. Lucretius, *De rerum natura,* 5.968, 1284 (W. H. D. Rouse, 1937, pp. 408, 430); M. C. Nahm, 1962, p. 65; J. Swift, *Gulliver's Travels,* 3.3 (R. Quintana, 1958, p. 134).
2. G. Ll. Isaac and D. C. Crader, 1981; K. Hill, 1982; D. R. Carrier, 1984; J. Tooby and I. DeVore, 1987, pp. 222–225; R. G. Klein, 1987, pp. 38–39; P. Shipman, 1987; S. McBrearty, 1989.
3. J. W. Krutch, 1956, pp. 147–148. The last sentence quoted identifies the hunter as a literally satanic figure, by putting into his mouth the words of Goethe's Mephistopheles: "Ich bin der Geist, der stets verneint" (*Faust,* 1.1338).
4. J. Williams, 1990.
5. *Animals,* March-April 1990, p. 25.
6. *U.S. News and World Report,* February 5, 1990, pp. 34, 31.
7. See e.g. the cartoons of Harvey Kurtzman (1959, "Decadence Degenerated," and *Trump,* January 1957, pp. 18–21); the newspaper comic strips *Bloom County* (B. Breathed, 1985, pp. 30–31) and *Judge Parker* (September 1989); the CBS sitcom *Silver Spoons* (February 18, 1984); and the controversial 1975 CBS Reports special, *The Guns of Autumn.* Examples in children's culture are too numerous to cite, but the egregious high-tech macho-lunatic hunter played by George C. Scott in the animated Disney film *The Rescuers Down Under* (1990) deserves special mention as a paradigm case. Many other films, from *Bless the Beasts and Children* (1971) to *Doc Hollywood* (1991), incorporate similar images of the hunter. In Michael Cimino's 1978 *The Deer Hunter,* the compulsive machismo of the deer hunt is linked to the Vietnam war. The film's Vietnam-veteran hero is abruptly redeemed when he goes hunting and is transfixed by the calm brown gaze of the Great Stag through his telescopic sights. Amid a swelling peal of liturgical music, he fires his rifle harmlessly into the air and shouts a promise to all of nature to study war no more.
8. T. Lehrer, 1954, p. 7.
9. H. Fontova, 1990. Cf. S. Ruggeri, 1990, p. 52.
10. R. Ruark, 1966, p. 47. Cf. F. C. Selous in C. Read, 1920, p. 41; E. Hemingway, 1953, p. 6; J. G. Mitchell, 1982, pp. 24 ff; S. A. Marks, 1991, p. 277. In 1987, the American Beef Industry Council ran a series of magazine ads suggesting that "people have a primal, instinctive craving" for hamburgers, and that anybody who does not cannot be trusted (*Newsweek,* February 9, 1987, p. 78).
11. T. McIntyre, 1988, p. 103.
12. J. G. Mitchell, 1982, p. 20; *Raleigh* (N.C.) *News and Observer,* July 26, 1988, p. 2a.
13. *U.S. News and World Report,* February 5, 1990, p. 34. In a recent Gallup poll,

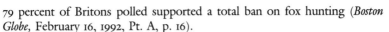

79 percent of Britons polled supported a total ban on fox hunting (*Boston Globe,* February 16, 1992, Pt. A, p. 16).

14. V. Geist, 1975, p. 153.

15. G. Mattis, 1980, pp. 151–153.

16. J. G. Mitchell, 1980, p. 46; cf. S. A. Marks, 1991, p. 226.

17. T. H. Watkins, 1980, p. 75.

18. Many writers on hunting obscure its consumptive character by describing it as a harvest or otherwise comparing it to agriculture. In hunting literature, the word "harvest" has become a favorite euphemism for "kill," a word that many hunters are strangely reluctant to use. For example, in Sam Fadala's popular treatise on *Successful Deer Hunting* (1983), the section describing how to kill deer reliably ("Where to Hit 'Em") entirely avoids the word "kill" and substitutes "hit," "drop," "take," "bring down"—and above all "harvest." "An arrow," writes Fadala (p. 88), "harvests game by the bleeding process." Cf. J. G. Mitchell, 1982, pp. 25–26, and the entry "harvest" in H. Rawson, 1981, p. 132.

19. F. Bonner, 1992.

20. *Reader's Digest,* November 1985, p. 19. Cf. G. Snyder, 1974, p. 98: "Don't shoot a deer if you don't know how . . . to use it all, with gratitude, right down to the sinew and hooves."

21. O. Wilde, *A Woman of No Importance,* act 1 (R. Ross, 1969, vol. 11, p. 23).

22. O. J. Murie, 1935; S. A. Marks, 1991, p. 45. See also the quotations under the entry "pot-hunter" in the *Oxford English Dictionary.* A similar disdain for economically motivated hunting persists among some rural Americans today (S. A. Marks, 1991, pp. 72, 175) and surfaces in fox hunters' arguments against fox trapping (Durham [N.C.] *Morning Herald,* January 22, 1984, p. 10C).

23. For instance, R. Baker, 1985, pp. 70–82; L. A. Dommer, 1989; J. Manuel, 1988, p. 4; L. L. Rue, III, 1978; G. Mattis, 1980, p. 189; J. Wilson, *Durham* (N.C.) *Morning Herald,* January 15, 1984, p. 11C.

24. J. Miller, 1956, p. 132; J. McPhee, 1977, pp. 303–304; T. Williams, 1981; N. L. Brownell, 1986; G. Mattis, 1980, p. 195.

25. S. A. Marks, 1991, pp. 63, 183–184, 218–219, 227.

26. R. Blount Jr., 1980, p. 207.

27. J. G. Mitchell, 1982, p. 20.

28. S. A. Marks, 1991, pp. 79, 198. In Marks's survey of hunters in rural Scotland County, North Carolina, 91 percent of the men interviewed—whites, blacks, and Lumbee Indians alike—agreed with the statement, "Hunting provides an opportunity for a boy to identify with the world of men, which is the most important influence of hunting on a boy" (p. 276).

29. M. M. H. Shastri, 1982, p. 84.

30. R. Wolkomir, 1985, p. 137.

31. J. G. Mitchell, 1982, p. 87; M. Clifton, 1990.

32. B. R. Peterson, 1989, p. 147.

33. E. Abbey, 1984, p. x.

34. "When one is hunting," insisted Ortega y Gassett, "the air has a different,

more exquisite feel as it glides over the skin or enters the lungs, the rocks acquire a more expressive physiognomy, the vegetation becomes loaded with meaning" (1972, p. 141).

35. J. G. Mitchell, 1982, p. 212.
36. *Durham* (N.C.) *Morning Herald,* November 11, 1990, p. B10.
37. V. Geist, 1975, p. 153.
38. *Raleigh* (N.C.) *News and Observer,* October 28, 1984, p. 14b.
39. J. C. Dunlap, *Newsweek,* March 7, 1983, pp. 12–14.
40. J. Ortega y Gasset, 1972, p. 59.
41. Ibid., p. 139. Some hunters feel that hunting narrows the gap between man and nature from the other direction; by bringing wild animals across the boundary into the human domain, the hunt "appropriates parts of the 'natural' universe and makes them a part of the 'human' world" (S. A. Marks, 1991, p. 7).
42. J. Wilson, *Durham* (N.C.) *Morning Herald,* January 15, 1984, p. 11C.
43. T. Regan, 1983, p. 362.
44. M. L. Knox, 1990, p. 59.
45. T. Nugent, *Harper's Magazine,* March 1989, p. 20.
46. For example, J. Berger, 1989. "Animals in their natural environment," insists one letter writer to the *Los Angeles Times* (December 15, 1982), are "always most humane. The act of a lion biting into the throat of a zebra is almost experienced as an act of love by a beast that nature provides with a state of euphoric shock. The house cat toys with the mouse, cruelly; but the house cat is not of nature but of man."
47. S. Orwell and I. Angus, 1968, vol. 1, p. 504.
48. F. Gummere, 1907, pp. 342–344.
49. J. Ortega y Gasset, 1972, p. 112.
50. S. Pope, 1925, p. 114.
51. H. Laube, *Jagdbrevier,* introduction (H. H. Houben, 1909, p. 11).
52. J. G. Mitchell, 1982, p. 140.
53. Cf. D. J. Jolma, 1992.
54. S. T. Warner, 1977, p. xv. White's sadistic ambivalence toward the suffering of animals is evident in the hanging of the bitch in "The Spaniel Earl" and the dialogue between the boy and the gamekeeper in "The Black Rabbit" (T. H. White, 1981, pp. 55–56, 133–138).
55. D. Scully, 1990, p. 109.
56. J. Ortega y Gasset, 1972, pp. 136–138. Italics in the original.
57. P. H. Gebhard et al., 1965, pp. 198, 204; D. E. H. Russell, 1975, p. 257 ff; C. J. Hursch, 1977, p. 43; D. Scully, 1990, pp. 128–129.
58. S. A. Marks, 1991, pp. 151–161.
59. S. Griffin, 1978, pp. 103–104; T. Regan, 1991, pp. 136–138; C. J. Adams, 1991, pp. 74, 122 ff.
60. "I have nothing against the killing of animals," wrote John Steinbeck (1962, p. 52). "Something has to kill them."
61. V. Bourjaily, 1984, p. 169.

62. This argument can be inverted to yield the reverse conclusion, that other forms of animal-killing cry out for suppression even more urgently than hunting. "Why," asks Peter Singer (1990, p. 231), "is the hunter who shoots a deer for venison subject to more criticism than the person who buys a ham at the supermarket? Overall, it is probably the intensively raised pig who has suffered more."

63. F. W. Nietzsche, *Geneaology of Morals* (F. Golffing, 1956, p. 208).

64. T. McIntyre, 1988, pp. 101–102.

Bibliography

Abbey, E., 1984. Foreword to V. Bourjaily, *The Unnatural Enemy*. University of Arizona Press, Tucson.

Adams, C. J., 1991. *The Sexual Politics of Meat: A Feminist-Vegetarian Critical Theory*. Continuum, New York.

Adams, R. (ed.), 1963. *The Circe of Signior Giovanni Battista Gelli*. Cornell University Press, Ithaca.

Adams, R., 1978. *The Plague Dogs*. Knopf, New York.

Amory, C., 1975. *Man Kind? Our Incredible War on Wildlife*. Dell, New York.

Anderson, F. (ed.), 1972. *A Pen Warmed-Up in Hell: Mark Twain in Protest*. Harper and Row, New York.

Anderson, J. K. 1985. *Hunting in the Ancient World*. University of California Press, Berkeley.

Ardrey, R., 1961. *African Genesis: A Personal Investigation into the Animal Origins and Nature of Man*. Atheneum, New York. 1963 reprint, Dell, New York.

——— 1976. *The Hunting Hypothesis: A Personal Conclusion Concerning the Evolutionary Nature of Man*. Atheneum, New York.

Artz, F. B., 1966. *Renaissance Humanism, 1300–1550*. Kent State University Press, Kent, Ohio.

Atkinson, B. (ed.), 1940. *The Complete Essays and Other Writings of Ralph Waldo Emerson*. Modern Library, New York.

Auden, W. H., 1945. *The Collected Poems of W. H. Auden*. Random House, New York.

Aymard, J., 1951. *Essai sur les chasses romains des origines à la fin du siècle des Antonins*. Boccard, Paris.

Babbitt, F. C. (ed. and trans.), 1932. *Plutarch: Moralia*, vol. 5. Harvard University Press, Cambridge.

Babbitt, I., 1919. *Rousseau and Romanticism*. Houghton Mifflin, Boston.

Baillie-Grohman, W. A., and F. Baillie-Grohman (eds.), 1909. *The Master of Game*. Duffield, New York.

Banks, J. (trans.), 1886. *The Works of Hesiod, Callimachus, and Theognis*. George Bell, London.

Baker, C. (ed.), 1951. *The Selected Poetry and Prose of Shelley.* Modern Library, New York.

Baker, R., 1985. *The American Hunting Myth.* Vantage, New York.

Barber, L., 1980. *The Heyday of Natural History, 1820–1870.* Doubleday, Garden City.

Baring-Gould, S., 1914. *The Lives of the Saints.* John Grant, Edinburgh.

Barkan, E., 1988. "Mobilizing Scientists against Nazi Racism, 1933–1939." In G. W. Stocking (ed.), *Bones, Bodies, Behavior: Essays on Biological Anthropology.* University of Wisconsin Press, Madison, pp. 180–205.

Barnett, S. A., 1980. "Biological Determinism and the Tasmanian Native Hen." In M. F. A. Montagu (ed.), *Sociobiology Examined.* Oxford University Press, New York, pp. 135–157.

Barth, K., 1960. *Church Dogmatics,* vol. 3, pt. I. Clark, Edinburgh.

Bartholomew, G. A., and J. B. Birdsell, 1953. "Ecology and the Protohominids." *American Anthropologist,* 55:481–498.

Barton, A., 1991. "Perils of Historicism." *New York Review of Books,* March 28, pp. 53–56.

Barzun, J., 1958. *Darwin, Marx, Wagner: Critique of a Heritage.* 2nd ed. Doubleday, Garden City.

Bates, M., 1960. *The Forest and the Sea: A Look at the Ecology of Nature and the Economy of Man.* 1965 reprint, Vintage, New York.

Bator, R. (ed.), 1984a. *Masterworks of Children's Literature,* vol. 3. Chelsea House, New York.

———— 1984b. *Masterworks of Children's Literature,* vol. 4. Chelsea House, New York.

Bauer, E., 1983. *Deer in Their World.* Outdoor Life, New York.

Bekoff, M., and D. Jamieson, 1991. "Reflective Ethology, Applied Philosophy, and the Moral Status of Animals." *Perspectives in Ethology,* 9:1–47.

Belaval, Y. (ed.), 1966. *Paul-Henry Th. d'Holbach: Système de la nature.* Georg Olm, Hildesheim (Germany).

Benayoun, R., 1961. *Le Dessin animé après Walt Disney.* J.-J. Pauvert, Paris.

Berger, J., 1980. *About Looking.* Pantheon, New York.

———— 1989. "Muck and Its Entanglements." *Harper's Magazine* (May), pp. 60–61.

Berkhofer, R. F., Jr., 1978. *The White Man's Indian: Images of the American Indian from Columbus to the Present.* Knopf, New York.

Bernal, J. D., 1965. *Science in History.* 3rd ed. MIT Press, Cambridge.

Bickerton, D., 1990. *Language and Species.* University of Chicago Press, Chicago.

Bieler, L. (ed.), 1953. *The Works of St. Patrick.* Newman Press, Westminster, Maryland.

Birdsell, J. B., 1975. *Human Evolution: An Introduction to the New Physical Anthropology.* 2nd ed. Rand McNally, Chicago.

Bleier, R., 1986. Introduction. In R. Bleier (ed.), *Feminist Approaches to Science,* Pergamon, New York, pp. 1–17.

Blount, M., 1975. *Animal Land: The Creatures of Children's Fiction*. Morrow, New York.

Blount, R., Jr., 1980. *Crackers: This Whole Many-Angled Thing of Jimmy, More Carters, Ominous Little Animals, Sad-Singing Women, My Daddy and Me*. Knopf, New York.

Boas, G., 1933. *The Happy Beast in French Thought of the Seventeenth Century*. Johns Hopkins University Press, Baltimore. 1966 reprint, Octagon, New York.

Bock, K. E., 1980. *Human Nature and History: A Response to Sociobiology*. Columbia University Press, New York.

Bodde, D., 1961. "Myths of Ancient China." In S. N. Kramer (ed.), *Mythologies of the Ancient World*, Doubleday, Garden City, pp. 367–408.

Boesch, C., and H. Boesch, 1989. "Hunting Behavior of Wild Chimpanzees in the Taï National Park." *American Journal of Physical Anthropology*, 78:547–573.

Bonner, F., 1992. "Ethics Afield: Let's Police Our Own Ranks Lest We Become Our Own Worst Enemy." *Carolina Adventure*, Raleigh, N.C., 7 (February), pp. 4–5.

Boulding, K. E., 1967. "Am I a Man or a Mouse—or Both?" *War/Peace Report*, March 1967, pp. 14–17. 1968 reprint in M. F. A. Montagu (ed.), *Man and Aggression*. Oxford University Press, New York, pp. 83–90.

Bourjaily, V., 1984. *The Unnatural Enemy*. University of Arizona Press, Tucson.

Bowler, P. J., 1983. *The Eclipse of Darwinism: Anti-Darwinian Evolution Theories in the Decades Around 1900*. Johns Hopkins University Press, Baltimore.

——— 1986. *Theories of Human Evolution: A Century of Debate, 1844–1944*. Johns Hopkins University Press, Baltimore.

Boyer, P., 1985. *By the Bomb's Early Light: American Thought and Culture at the Dawn of the Atomic Age*. Pantheon, New York.

Boyle, R., 1744. *Works*. A. Millar, London.

Brace, C. L., 1962. "The Fate of the 'Classic' Neanderthals: A Consideration of Hominid Catastrophism." *Current Anthropology*, 5:3–43.

——— 1971. Review of *The Social Contract*, by R. Ardrey. *American Scientist*, May 1971, pp. 376–377.

——— 1978. Review of *The Hunting Hypothesis*, by R. Ardrey. *American Anthropologist*, 80:172–173.

——— 1982. "The Roots of the Race Concept in American Physical Anthropology." In F. Spencer (ed.), *A History of American Physical Anthropology, 1930–1980*. Academic Press, New York, pp. 11–29.

——— and J. Metress (eds.), 1973. *Man in Evolutionary Perspective*. Wiley, New York.

Bradner, L., and C. A. Lynch (eds.), 1953. *The Latin Epigrams of Thomas More*. University of Chicago Press, Chicago.

Brain, C. K., 1970. "New Finds at the Swartkrans Australopithecine Site." *Nature*, 225:1112–19.

——— 1981. *The Hunters or the Hunted? An Introduction to African Cave Taphonomy*. University of Chicago Press, Chicago.

Brantley, R. E., 1984. *Locke, Wesley, and the Method of Romanticism.* University Presses of Florida, Gainesville.

Braudel, F., 1981. "The Structure of Everyday Life." *Civilization and Capitalism, 15th–18th Century,* vol. 1. S. Reynolds, trans. Harper and Row, New York.

Breathed, B., 1985. *Penguin Dreams and Stranger Things.* Little, Brown, Boston.

Bridoux, A. (ed.), 1953. *Oeuvres et lettres de Descartes.* Gallimard, Dijon.

Brinton, C., 1965. *Nietzsche.* Rev. ed. Harper and Row, New York.

Bromwich, R., 1961. "Celtic Dynastic Themes and the Breton Lays." *Etudes celtiques,* 9:439–474.

——— (ed.), 1982. *Dafydd ap Gwilym: A Selection of Poems.* Gomer Press, Llandysul, Dyfed.

Broom, R., 1949. "The Ape-Men." *Scientific American,* 181 (November), pp. 20–24.

Brower, D. (ed.), 1965. *Not Man Apart.* Sierra Club/Ballantine, New York.

Brown, C. (ed.), 1932. *English Lyrics of the XIIIth Century.* Oxford University Press, London.

Brown, N. O., 1959. *Life Against Death: The Psychoanalytic Meaning of History.* Routledge and Kegan Paul, London.

Brown, R. J., 1942. "Outdoor Life Condemns Walt Disney's Film 'Bambi' as Insult to American Sportsmen." *Outdoor Life* (September), pp. 17, 66.

Brownell, N. L., 1986. "The Coyotes Are Killing the Deer." *Deer and Deer Hunting* (October), pp. 82–90.

Brues, A., 1960. "The Spearman and the Archer: An Essay on Selection in Body Build." *American Anthropologist,* 61:457–469.

Buck, C. D., 1949. *A Dictionary of Selected Synonyms in the Principal Indo-European Languages: A Contribution to the History of Ideas.* University of Chicago Press, Chicago.

Buettner-Janusch, J., 1973. *Physical Anthropology: A Perspective.* Wiley, New York.

Bullen, A. H. (ed.), 1893. *Anacreon: With Thomas Staley's Translation.* Lawrence and Bullen, London.

Burnett, James, 1774. *Of the Origin and Progress of Language.* 2nd ed. J. Balfour, Edinburgh. 1973 facsimile ed., AMS Press, New York.

Burns, J. H., and H. L. A. Hart (eds.), 1970. *An Introduction to the Principles of Morals and Legislation,* by Jeremy Bentham. Athlone, London.

Burroughs, J., 1903. "Real and Sham Natural History." *Atlantic Monthly,* 91:298–309.

——— 1904. "Current Misconceptions in Natural History." *Century Magazine,* 67:509–517.

——— 1912. *Time and Change.* Houghton Mifflin, Boston.

Burroughs, J. L. (trans.), 1944. "Marsilio Ficino, *Platonic Theology.*" *Journal of the History of Ideas,* 5:227–239.

Bussey, G. C. (trans. and ed.), 1912. *Man a Machine,* by Julien Offray de La Mettrie. Open Court, Chicago.

Butler, A. J., 1930. *Sport in Classic Times.* Dutton, New York.

Butler, F., 1983. "Children's Literature from the Late Sixteenth to the Early

Eighteenth Century." In F. Butler (ed.), *Masterworks of Children's Literature.* Chelsea House, New York, vol. 1, pp. xxi–xxxiii.

Butterfield, H., 1949. *The Origins of Modern Science, 1300–1800.* Bell, London.

Cajori, F. (ed.), 1934. *Sir Isaac Newton's Mechanical Principles of Natural Philosophy and His System of the World.* University of California Press, Berkeley.

Calès, J., 1936. *Le Livre des Psaumes, traduit et commenté.* Gabriel Beauchesne, Paris.

Calvino, I., 1980. *Italian Folktales.* Trans. G. Martin. Harcourt Brace Jovanovich, New York.

Campbell, B. G., 1966. *Human Evolution: An Introduction to Man's Adaptations.* Aldine, Chicago.

——— 1972. "Man for All Seasons." In B. G. Campbell (ed.), *Sexual Selection and the Descent of Man, 1871–1971.* Aldine, Chicago, pp. 40–58.

Campbell, G. D. (Lord Argyll), 1869. *Primaeval Man: An Examination of Some Recent Speculations.* 1884 reprint, J. B. Alden, New York.

Campbell, H., 1904. "The Evolution of Man's Diet." *Lancet,* pp. 781–784, 848–851, 909–912, 967–969, 1097–99, 1234–37, 1368–70, 1519–22, 1667–70.

——— 1913. "Man's Mental Evolution, Past and Future." *Lancet,* pp. 1260–62, 1333–35, 1408–10, 1473–76.

——— 1917. "The Biological Aspects of Warfare." *Lancet,* pp. 433–435, 469–471, 505–508.

——— 1921. "Man's Evolution from the Anthropoid." *Lancet* (2), p. 629.

Campbell, J., 1969. *The Masks of God: Primitive Mythology.* 1976 reprint, Penguin, New York.

Campbell, R., 1934. *Broken Record.* Boriswood, London.

Canaday, J., 1959. *Mainstreams of Modern Art.* Simon and Schuster, New York.

——— 1962. *Embattled Critic: Views on Modern Art.* Farrar, Straus and Cudahy, New York.

Carlill, J., n.d. "Physiologus." In W. Rose (ed.), *The Epic of the Beast.* Routledge, London, pp. 153–250.

Carney, J., 1955. *Studies in Irish Literature and History.* Dublin Institute for Advanced Studies, Dublin.

Carpenter, H., and M. Prichard, 1985. *The Oxford Companion to Children's Literature.* Oxford University Press, Oxford.

Carrier, D. R., 1984. "The Energetic Paradox of Human Running and Hominid Evolution." *Current Anthropology,* 25:483–495.

Carson, R., 1962. *Silent Spring.* Houghton Mifflin, Boston.

Cartmill, C. E., 1942. "The Link." *Astounding Science Fiction* (August), pp. 84–91. 1979 reprint in M. H. Greenberg, J. Olander, and R. Silverberg (eds.), *Dawn of Time: Prehistory through Science Fiction.* Elsevier/Nelson, New York, pp. 100–114.

Cartmill, M., 1972. "Arboreal Adaptations and the Origin of the Order Primates." In R. H. Tuttle (ed.), *The Functional and Evolutionary Biology of Primates.* Aldine, Chicago, pp. 97–122.

——— 1974. "Rethinking Primate Origins." *Science,* 184:436–443.

——— 1982. "Basic Primatology and Prosimian Evolution." In F. Spencer (ed.), *A History of American Physical Anthropology, 1930–1980.* Academic Press, New York, pp. 147–186.

——— 1983. "Four Legs Good, Two Legs Bad: Man's Place (If Any) in Nature." *Natural History,* 92(1):64–79.

——— 1990. "Human Uniqueness and Theoretical Content in Paleoanthropology." *International Journal of Primatology,* 11:173–192.

——— D. Pilbeam, and G. Ll. Isaac, 1986. "One Hundred Years of Paleoanthropology." *American Scientist,* 74:410–420.

Castell, A. (ed.), 1948. *Selections from the Essays of T. H. Huxley.* Appleton-Century-Crofts, New York.

Chance, M. R. A., and C. J. Jolly, 1970. *Social Groups of Monkeys, Apes and Men.* Dutton, New York.

Chand, M., 1982. Introduction. In M. M. H. Shastri (ed.), *Śyainika Sāstram: The Art of Hunting in Ancient India.* Eastern Book Linkers, Delhi, pp. 13–64.

Chavaillon, J., 1976. "Evidence for the Technical Practices of Early Pleistocene Hominids, Shungura Formation, Lower Omo Valley, Ethiopia." In Y. Coppens, F. C. Howell, G. Ll. Isaac, and R. E. F. Leakey (eds.), *Earliest Man and Environments in the Lake Rudolf Basin.* University of Chicago Press, Chicago, pp. 565–573.

Cherniss, H. and W. C. Helmbold (eds.), 1957. *Plutarch: Moralia,* vol. 12. Harvard University Press, Cambridge.

Child, F. J. (ed.), 1883–1898. *English and Scottish Popular Ballads,* vols. 1–5. Houghton, Boston.

Chomsky, N., 1964. *Language and Mind.* Harcourt, Brace and World, New York.

——— 1975. *Reflections on Language.* Random House, New York.

Christensen, N., 1989. "Rethinking Forest Fire." *Duke Chronicle Report* (Durham, N.C.), January 24, pp. 3–7.

Church, R. W., 1931. *A Study in the Philosophy of Malebranche.* Allen and Unwin, London.

Clark, G., and S. Piggott, 1967. *Prehistoric Societies.* Allen and Unwin, London.

Clark, K., 1977. *Animals and Men: Their Relationship as Reflected in Western Art from Prehistory to the Present Day.* Morrow, New York.

——— 1980. *Feminine Beauty.* Weidenfield and Nicolson, London.

Clarke, A., (ed.), 1837. *Manners of the Ancient Israelites . . . with a Short Account of the Ancient and Modern Samaritans, written originally in French by Claude Fleury.* Mason and Lane, New York.

Clifford, D., 1963. *A History of Garden Design.* Praeger, New York.

Clifton, M., 1990. "Killing the Female: The Psychology of the Hunt." *The Animals' Agenda* (September), pp. 26–57.

Clodd, E., 1902. *Thomas Henry Huxley.* Blackwood, Edinburgh.

Cohen, D., 1975. *Human Nature Animal Nature: The Biology of Human Behavior.* McGraw-Hill, New York.

Cole, F. J., 1949. *A History of Comparative Anatomy from Aristotle to the Eighteenth Century.* Macmillan, New York. 1975 reprint, Dover, New York.

Coleman, R. (ed.), 1977. *Vergil: Eclogues*. Cambridge University Press, Cambridge.

Commoner, B., 1971. *The Closing Circle: Nature, Man, and Technology*. Knopf, New York.

Coon, C., 1962. *The Origin of Races*. Knopf, New York.

Corn, J., J., and B. Horrigan, 1984. *Yesterday's Tomorrows: Past Visions of the American Future*. Summit, New York.

Corn, W. M., 1973. *The Art of Andrew Wyeth*. New York Graphic Society, Boston.

Cott, J. (ed.), 1983. *Masterworks of Children's Literature*, vol. 7. Chelsea House, New York.

Cowell, E. B. (ed.), 1894. *Buddhist Mahayana Texts, Part I*. Oxford University Press, Oxford. 1965 reprint, Motilal Barnasidass, Delhi.

Crafton, D., 1982. *Before Mickey: The Animated Film, 1898–1928*. MIT Press, Cambridge.

Crew, H., and A. de Salvio (eds.), 1914. *Dialogues Concerning Two New Sciences*, by Galileo Galilei. Macmillan, New York.

Cronin, V., 1975. *Louis and Antoinette*. Morrow, New York.

Crowe, M. J., 1986. *The Extraterrestrial Life Debate, 1750–1900: The Idea of a Plurality of Worlds from Kant to Lowell*. Cambridge University Press, Cambridge.

Culhane, S., 1986. *Talking Animals and Other People*. St. Martin's, New York.

Cummings, E. E., 1928. *Tulips and Chimneys*. Thomas Seltzer, New York.

Cumont, F., 1902. *The Mysteries of Mithra*. T. J. McCormack, trans. 1956 reprint, Dover, New York.

Cumont, F., 1908. Anahita. In J. Hastings (ed.), *Encyclopedia of Religion and Ethics*, Scribner's, New York, vol. 1, pp. 414–415.

Cutright, P. R., 1956. *Theodore Roosevelt, the Naturalist*. Harper, New York.

Dalby, D. 1965. *Lexicon of the Mediaeval German Hunt*. Walter de Gruyter, Berlin.

Danielsson, B. (ed.), 1977. "William Twiti's The Art of Hunting." *Stockholm Studies in English*, 37:1–116.

Darnton, R., 1984. *The Great Cat Massacre and Other Episodes in French Cultural History*. Basic Books, New York.

Dart, R. A., 1925a. "Australopithecus Africanus: The Man-Ape of South Africa." *Nature*, 115:195–199.

—— 1925b. "The Word 'Australopithecus' and Others." *Nature*, 115:875.

—— 1926. "Taungs and Its Significance." *Natural History*, 26:315–327.

—— 1940. "The Status of *Australopithecus*." *American Journal of Physical Anthropology*, 26:167–186.

—— 1948. "A (?) Promethean *Australopithecus* from Makapansgat Valley." *Nature*, 162:375–376.

—— 1949. "The Predatory Implemental Technique of *Australopithecus*." *American Journal of Physical Anthropology*, n.s. 7:1–38.

—— 1953. "The Predatory Transition from Ape to Man." *International Anthropological and Linguistic Review*, 1:201–217.

—— 1955. "Cultural Status of the South African Man-Apes." *Annual Report of the Smithsonian Institution*, 1955:317–338.

—— 1957a. "The Makapansgat Australopithecine Osteodontokeratic Culture." In J. D. Clark (ed.), *Third Pan-African Congress on Prehistory.* Chatto and Windus, London, pp. 161–171.

—— 1957b. "The Osteodontokeratic Culture of *Australopithecus prometheus.*" *Transvaal Museum Memoirs,* 10:1–105.

—— and Craig, D., 1959. *Adventures with the Missing Link.* Harper, New York. 1961 reprint, Viking, New York.

Darwin, C., 1859. *The Origin of Species by Means of Natural Selection: or, The Preservation of Favoured Races in the Struggle for Life.* Modern Library reprint (4th ed.), New York, 1936.

—— 1871. *The Descent of Man and Selection in Relation to Sex.* John Murray, London. Modern Library reprint, New York, 1936.

Darwin, E., 1801. *Zoonomia; or, The Laws of Organic Life.* 3rd ed. J. Johnson, London.

Darwin, F. (ed.), 1896. *The Life and Letters of Charles Darwin.* D. Appleton, New York.

Davidson, H. R. E., 1964. *Gods and Myths of Northern Europe.* Penguin, Harmondsworth.

Day, C., 1948. *The Best of Clarence Day.* Knopf, New York.

Debetz, G. F., 1961. "The Social Life of Early Paleolithic Man as Seen Through the Work of the Soviet Anthropologists." In S. L. Washburn (ed.), *Social Life of Early Man.* Aldine, Chicago, pp. 137–149.

Dent, A., 1974. *Lost Beasts of Britain.* Harrap, London.

Desmond, A. J., 1989. *The Politics of Evolution: Morphology, Medicine, and Reform in Radical London.* University of Chicago Press, Chicago.

Detienne, M., 1979. *Dionysos Slain.* M. Muellner and L. Muellner, trans. Johns Hopkins University Press, Baltimore.

DeVall, B., and G. Sessions, 1985. *Deep Ecology.* Gibbs M. Smith, Layton, Utah.

Devey, J. (ed. and trans.), n.d. *Bacon's Essays and Wisdom of the Ancients.* T. Nelson, London.

—— (ed.), 1909. *The Moral and Historical Works of Lord Bacon.* George Bell, London.

DeVore, I., 1964. "The Evolution of Social Life." In S. Tax (ed.), *Horizons of Anthropology.* Aldine, Chicago, pp. 25–36.

Diamond, J., 1992. *The Third Chimpanzee: The Evolution and Future of the Human Animal.* Harper Collins, New York.

Dick, S. J., 1982. *Plurality of Worlds: The Origins of the Extraterrestrial Life Debate from Democritus to Kant.* Cambridge University Press, Cambridge.

Dickey, J., 1964. *Helmets.* Wesleyan University Press, Middletown.

Dickinson, J. M., 1964. "Aggression and the Status of Evil in Man: A Critical Analysis of Sigmund Freud's Assumptions from the Theological Perspective of Reinhold Niebuhr." Dissertation, Boston University.

Dijksterhuis, E. J., 1959. *The Mechanization of the World Picture.* Meulenhoff, Amsterdam. 1986 English trans., Princeton University Press, Princeton.

Disraeli, B., 1877. *Tancred, or The New Crusade.* Longmans, Green, London.

Dmitriyev, Yu., 1983. *Man and Animals.* 1984 English trans., Raduga, Moscow.

Dobzhansky, T., 1962. *Mankind Evolving: The Evolution of the Human Species.* Yale University Press, New Haven.

Dodds, E. R. (ed.), 1944. *Euripides: Bacchae.* Oxford University Press, Oxford.

—— 1951. *The Greeks and the Irrational.* University of California Press, Berkeley.

Dombrowski, D. A., 1984. *The Philosophy of Vegetarianism.* University of Massachusetts Press, Amherst.

Dommer, L. A., 1989. "A Hunter's Delusions: Saving the Deer from Starvation." *Animals' Voice* (April), pp. 82–84.

Duncan, G. M. (ed.), 1908. *The Philosophical Works of Leibnitz.* Tuttle, Morehouse and Taylor, New Haven.

Eckardt, H. W., 1976. *Herrschaftliche Jagd, bäuerliche Not und bürgerliche Kritik: Zur Geschichte der fürstlichen und adligen Jagdprivilegien, vornehmlich im südwestdeutschen Raum.* Vandenhoeck and Ruprecht, Göttingen.

Edman, I. (ed.), 1926. *Essays by Ralph Waldo Emerson.* Crowell, New York.

—— (ed.), 1928. *The Philosophy of Schopenhauer.* Modern Library, New York.

Egner, R. E., and L. E. Denon (eds.), 1961. *The Basic Writings of Bertrand Russell.* Simon and Schuster, New York.

Eiseley, L., 1958. *Darwin's Century.* Anchor Books, Garden City.

Eldredge, N., and I. Tattersall, 1982. *The Myths of Human Evolution.* Columbia University Press, New York.

Eliot, C. W. (ed.), 1909. *On Taste; On the Sublime and Beautiful; Reflections on the French Revolution; A Letter to a Noble Lord,* by Edmund Burke. Harvard Classics, vol. 24. Collier, New York.

Elliot, H. (trans.), 1984. *Zoological Philosophy: An Exposition with Regard to the Natural History of Animals,* by J. B. Lamarck. University of Chicago Press, Chicago.

Elzinga, A., and A. Jamison, 1981. *Cultural Components in the Scientific Attitude to Nature: Eastern and Western Modes.* Research Policy Institute, University of Lund, Sweden.

Endicott, N. J. (ed.), 1967. *The Prose of Sir Thomas Browne.* Doubleday, Garden City.

Engels, F., 1891. *The Origin of the Family, Private Property, and the State.* 4th ed. E. Untermann, trans. C. H. Kerr, Chicago, 1902.

Erdrich, L., 1984. *Love Medicine: A Novel.* Holt, Rinehart, and Winston, New York.

Etkin, W., 1954. "Social Behavior and the Evolution of Man's Mental Faculties." *American Naturalist,* 88:129–142.

Everson, W., 1977. Foreword. In R. Jeffers, *The Double Axe and Other Poems, Including Eleven Suppressed Poems.* Liveright, New York, pp. vii–xix.

Fadala, S., 1983. *Successful Deer Hunting.* DBI Books, Northfield, Illinois.

Farnell, L. R., 1914. "Greek Religion." In J. Hastings (ed.), *Encyclopaedia of Religion and Ethics,* Scribner's, New York, vol. 6, pp. 392–425.

Feshback, M., and A. Friendly, 1992. *Ecocide in the USSR: The Looming Disaster in Soviet Health and Environment.* Basic Books, New York.

Fisher, J. A., 1991. "Disambiguating Anthropomorphism: An Interdisciplinary Review." *Perspectives in Ethology,* 9:49–85.

Fitzgerald, R. (trans.), 1961. *Homer: The Odyssey.* Doubleday, Garden City. 1963 Anchor Books ed.

Fleagle, J. G., and W. L. Jungers, 1982. "Fifty Years of Higher Primate Phylogeny." In F. Spencer (ed.), *A History of American Physical Anthropology, 1930–1980.* Academic Press, New York, pp. 187–230.

Fleischauer, W. L. (ed.), 1956. *Joseph Addison and Richard Steele: Selected Essays from the Tatler and the Spectator.* Henry Regnery, Chicago.

Fletcher, W. (ed.), 1871. *The Works of Lactantius.* Clark, Edinburgh.

Fontaine, N., 1736. *Memoires pour servir a l'histoire de Port-Royal,* Utrecht, "Aux dépens de la Compagnie." 1970 facsimile reprint, Slatkine Reprints, Geneva.

Fontenrose, J. E., 1981. "Orion: The Myth of the Hunter and the Huntress." *University of. California Publications in Classical Studies,* 23:i–xii, 1–315.

Fontova, H., 1990. "Why We Hunt." *Sierra* (November/December), pp. 54–55.

Forman, H. B., and M. B. Forman (eds.), 1970. *The Poetical Works and Other Writings of John Keats.* Phaeton, New York.

Fosdick, H. E., 1946. *On Being Fit to Live With: Sermons on Post-War Christianity.* Harper, New York.

Foster, M., 1899. *Claude Bernard.* Longmans, Green, New York.

Foster, M. P. (ed.), 1961. *A Casebook on Gulliver among the Houyhnhmns.* Crowell, New York.

Fox, S., 1981. *John Muir and His Legacy: The American Conservationist Movement.* Little, Brown, Boston.

Foxley, B. (trans.), 1957. *Emile,* by Jean-Jacques Rousseau. Dent, London.

Frame, D. M., (ed.) 1958. *The Complete Works of Montaigne.* Stanford University Press, Stanford.

—— (trans.), 1960. *The Complete Essays of Montaigne.* Anchor Books, Garden City.

Fränkel, L. (ed.), 1893. *Uhlands Werke.* Bibliographisches Institut, Leipzig.

Frauenstädt, J. (ed.), 1922. *Arthur Schopenhauer's sämmtliche Werke.* 2nd ed. Brockhaus, Leipzig.

Frazer, J. G., (ed.) 1921. *Apollodorus: The Library.* Harvard University Press, Cambridge.

—— (ed.), 1989. *Ovid's Fasti.* 2nd ed. Harvard University Press, Cambridge.

Frevert, W., 1975. *Wörterbuch der Jägerei.* 4th ed. Paul Parey, Hamburg.

Friedman, J. B., 1981. *The Monstrous Races in Medieval Art and Thought.* Harvard University Press, Cambridge.

Gaffney, J., 1986. "The Relevance of Animal Experimentation to Roman Catholic Ethical Methodology." In T. Regan (ed.), *Animal Sacrifices: Religious Perspectives on the Use of Animals in Science.* Temple University Press, Philadelphia, pp. 149–170.

Galsworthy, J., 1916. *A Sheaf.* Scribner's, New York.

Gardner, M. (ed.), 1965. *The Annotated Ancient Mariner.* World, Cleveland.

Gasman, D., 1971. *The Scientific Origins of National Socialism: Social Darwinism in Ernst Haeckel and the German Monist Leagu*e. MacDonald, London.

Gebhard, P. H., J., H. Gagnon, W. B. Pomeroy, and C. V. Christenson, 1965. *Sex Offenders: An Analysis of Types.* Harper and Row, New York.

Geist, V., 1975. *Mountain Sheep and Man in the Northern Wilds.* Cornell University Press, Ithaca.

Giles, L. (ed.), 1906. *Musings of a Chinese Mystic: Selections from the Philosophy of Chuang Tzu.* John Murray, London.

Gill, S. (ed.), 1984. *William Wordsworth.* Oxford University Press, Oxford.

Glacken, C. J., 1967. *Traces on the Rhodian Shore: Nature and Culture in Western Thought from Ancient Times to the End of the Eighteenth Century.* University of California Press, Berkeley.

Glubok, S. (ed.), 1969. *Home and Child Life in Colonial Days.* Macmillan, New York.

Gode-von Aesch, A. 1941. *Natural Science in German Romanticism.* Columbia University Press, New York.

Gohdes, C. (ed.), 1967. *Hunting in the Old South.* Louisiana State University Press, Baton Rouge.

Goldin, F. (ed.), 1973. *Lyrics of the Troubadours and Trouvères.* Doubleday, Garden City.

Golding, W., 1954. *Lord of the Flies.* Putnam, New York.

―――― 1955. *The Inheritors.* Harcourt, Brace and World, New York.

―――― 1966. *The Hot Gates.* Harcourt, Brace and World, New York. 1967 reprint, Pocket Books, New York.

Golffing, F. (trans.), 1956. *The Birth of Tragedy and the Genealogy of Morals,* by Friedrich Nietzsche. Doubleday, Garden City.

Gombrich, E. H., 1961. *Art and Illusion: A Study in the Psychology of Pictorial Representation.* Princeton University Press, Princeton.

Goodall, J., 1986. *The Chimpanzees of Gombe: Patterns of Behavior.* Harvard University Press, Cambridge.

Goodman, L. E. (ed.), 1978. *The Case of the Animals versus Man before the King of the Jinn.* Twayne, Boston.

Gordon, C. H., 1981. "Canaanite Mythology." In S. N. Kramer (ed.), *The Mythologies of the Ancient World,* Doubleday, Garden City, pp. 181–218.

Grant, M., 1962. *Myths of the Greeks and Romans.* World, New York. Undated reprint, New American Library, New York.

Grater, R. K., 1978. *Discovering Sierra Mammals.* Yosemite Natural History Association, Yosemite National Park, California.

Graves, R. (trans.), 1951. *The Golden Ass of Apuleius.* Farrar, Straus, and Young, New York. 1954 reprint, Pocket Books, New York.

Graves, R., 1955. *Greek Myths.* Cassell, London.

Gravil, R. (ed.), 1974. *Gulliver's Travels: A Casebook.* Macmillan, London.

Gray, A., 1876. *Darwiniana: Essays and Reviews Pertaining to Darwinism.* D. Appleton, New York. 1963 reprint, Harvard University Press, Cambridge.

Gray, A., 1954. *Four-and-Forty: A Selection of Danish Ballads Presented in Scots.* University of Edinburgh Press, Edinburgh.

Green, W. M. (ed. and trans.), 1966. *Saint Augustine: The City of God against the Pagans.* Harvard University Press, Cambridge.

Greene, J. C., 1981. *Science, Ideology, and World View: Essays in the History of Evolutionary Ideas.* University of California Press, Berkeley.

Gregory, H., 1956. *The Poems of Catullus.* Grove, New York.

Gregory, W. K., 1916. "Studies on the Evolution of the Primates." *Bulletin of the American Museum of Natural History,* 35:336–344.

Gregory, W. K., and M. Hellman, 1939. "South African Fossil Man-Apes and the Origin of the Human Dentition." *Journal of the American Dental Association,* 26:558–564.

Grene, D., 1942. *Three Greek Tragedies in Translation.* University of Chicago Press, Chicago.

——— and R. Lattimore (eds.), n.d. *Euripides, I.* Modern Library, New York.

Griffin, S., 1978. *Woman and Nature: The Roaring Inside Her.* Harper and Row, New York.

Grimes, E. M. (ed.), 1928. *The Lays of Desiré, Graelent and Melion.* Institute of French Studies, New York.

Grzimek, B. (ed.), 1969. *Het Leven der Dieren.* Het Spectrum, Utrecht.

Gummere, F., 1907. *The Popular Ballad.* 1957 reprint, Dover, New York.

Guthrie, W. K. C., 1952. *Orpheus and Greek Religion: A Study of the Orphic Movement.* 2d ed. Methuen, London.

Haeckel, E., 1902. *The Riddle of the Universe at the Close of the Nineteenth Century.* J. McCabe, trans. Harper, New York.

Haeckel, E., 1923. *Natürliche Schöpfungs-Geschichte: Gemeinverständliche wissenschaftliche Vorträge über die Entwickelungslehre.* 12th ed. Walter de Gruyter, Berlin.

Haight, A. D., 1939. *The Biography of a Sportsman.* Crowell, New York.

Hall, D., R. Pack, and L. Simpson (eds.), 1957. *The New Poets of England and America.* World, Cleveland.

Hallock, C., 1860. "Wild Cattle Hunting on Green Island." *Harper's Magazine* (July), pp. 220–224.

Hamilton, E., and H. Cairns (eds.), 1961. *Plato: The Collected Dialogues.* Pantheon, New York.

Hampshire, S., 1991. "'A Wonderful Life.'" *New York Review of Books,* January 31, pp. 3–6.

Haraway, D. J., 1988. "Remodelling the Human Way of Life: Sherwood Washburn and the New Physical Anthropology, 1950–1980." In G. Stocking (ed.), *Bones, Bodies, Behavior: Essays on Biological Anthropology.* University of Wisconsin Press, Madison, pp. 206–259.

——— 1989. *Primate Visions: Gender, Race, and Nature in the World of Modern Science.* Routledge, New York.

Hare, C. E., 1949. *The Language of Field Sports.* 4th ed. Country Life, London.

Harris, J. R., 1924. *As Pants the Hart, and Other Devotional Addresses.* Hodder and Stroughton, London.

Harrison, H. S., 1921. Review of *The Origin of Man and of His Superstitions,* by Carveth Read. *Man,* 21:142–143.

Harrison, R. J., and W. Montagna, 1969. *Man.* Appleton-Century-Crofts, New York.

Hartmann, R., 1886. *Anthropoid Apes.* D. Appleton, New York.

Harvie, C., 1984. "Revolution and the Rule of Law." In K. O. Morgan (ed.), *The Oxford Illustrated History of Britain.* Oxford University Press, Oxford, pp. 419–462.

Healey, R. J., and J. F. McComas (eds.), 1946. *Adventures in Time and Space.* Random House, New York.

Heaney, S., 1983. *Sweeney Astray.* Farrar Straus Giroux, New York.

Hemingway, E., 1953. Foreword to F. Sommer, *Man and Beast in Africa,* Herbert Jenkins, London, pp. 5–7.

Heron, G. (trans.), 1954. *Of Learned Ignorance,* by Nicolas Cusanus. Routledge and Kegan Paul, London.

Hess, E. H., 1975. "The Role of Pupil Size in Communication." *Scientific American,* 233 (May), pp. 110–119.

Hick, J., 1977. *Evil and the God of Love.* Rev. ed. Harper and Row, New York.

Hill, G. B. (ed.), 1897. *Johnsonian Miscellanies.* Harper, New York.

Hill, K., 1982. "Hunting and Human Evolution." *Journal of Human Evolution,* 11:521–544.

Himmelfarb, G., 1959. *Darwin and the Darwinian Revolution.* Doubleday, Garden City.

Himmelfarb, G. (ed.), 1960. *On Population: Thomas Robert Malthus.* Modern Library, New York.

Hine, T., 1987. *Populuxe.* Knopf, New York.

Hobusch, E., 1978. *Von den edlen Kunst des Jägens: Eine Kulturgeschichte der Jagd und der Hege der Tierwelt.* Pinguin, Innsbruck.

Hockett, C. F., and R. Ascher, 1964. "The Human Revolution." *Current Anthropology,* 5:135–147.

Hofmannsthal, H. von, 1937. *Briefe.* Bermann-Fischer, Vienna.

Hogben, L., 1938. *Science for the Citizen.* Knopf, New York.

Holloway, R. L., Jr., 1967. Review of *The Territorial Imperative,* by R. Ardrey. *Political Science Quarterly,* 82:630–632.

——— 1968. "The Human Brain in Evolutionary Perspective." In M. H. Fried (ed.), *Readings in Anthropology.* 2nd ed. Crowell, New York, vol. 1, pp. 215–223.

Homeyer, F. (ed.), 1909. *Wielands gesammelte Schriften. Erste Abteilung: Werke.* Weidmannsche, Berlin.

Hooton, E. A., 1946. *Up from the Ape.* Macmillan, New York.

Hopkins, W., 1860. "Physical Theories of the Origin of Life." *Fraser's Magazine,* 61:739–752; 62:74–90.

Houben, H. H. (ed.), 1909. *Heinrich Laubes gesammelten Werke,* vol. 42. Max Hesse, Leipzig.

Howell, F. C., 1963. "Early Phases in the Emergence of Man." *Proceedings, 16th International Congress of Zoology,* 4:80–87.

——— 1964. "The Hominization Process." In S. Tax (ed.), *Horizons of Anthropology.* Aldine, Chicago, pp. 49–59.

——— 1967. "Recent Advances in Human Evolutionary Studies." *Quarterly Review of Biology,* 42:471–513.

——— 1973. *Early Man.* Time-Life, New York.

Howells, W. W., 1946. *Mankind So Far*. Doubleday, Garden City.
——— 1959. *Mankind in the Making*. Doubleday, Garden City.
Hrdlička, A., 1918. Review of H. Campbell, "The Biological Aspects of Warfare." *American Journal of Physical Anthropology*, 1:464–465.
Hudson, H. H. (trans.), 1941. *The Praise of Folly*, by Desiderius Erasmus. Princeton University Press, Princeton.
Hughes, R., 1981. *The Shock of the New*. Knopf, New York.
Hughes, T., 1979. *Moortown*. Harper and Row, New York.
Hull, D. B., 1964. *Hounds and Hunting in Ancient Greece*. University of Chicago Press, Chicago.
Hursch, C. J., 1977. *The Trouble with Rape*. Nelson-Hall, Chicago.
Huth, H., 1957. *Nature and the American: Three Centuries of Changing Attitudes*. University of California Press, Berkeley.
Huxley, J. S., 1942. *Evolution: The Modern Synthesis*. Allen and Unwin, London.
——— 1948. *Man in the Modern World*. New American Library, New York.
Huxley, T. H., 1863. *Evidence as to Man's Place in Nature*. Williams and Norgate, London. 1899 reprint in T. H. Huxley, *Man's Place in Nature and Other Anthropological Essays*. Appleton, New York.
Hyams, E., 1971. *Capability Brown and Humphry Repton*. Scribner's, New York.
Isaac, G. Ll., 1976. "Plio-Pleistocene Artifact Assemblages from East Rudolf, Kenya." In Y. Coppens, F. C. Howell, G. Ll. Isaac, and R. E. F. Leakey (eds.), *Earliest Man and Environments in the Lake Rudolf Basin*. University of Chicago Press, Chicago, pp. 552–564.
Isaac, G. Ll., 1978. "The Food-Sharing Behavior of Protohuman Hominids." *Scientific American*, 238 (April), pp. 90–108.
Isaac, G. Ll., and D. C. Crader, 1981. "To What Extent Were Early Hominids Carnivorous? An Archaeological Perspective." In R. S. O. Harding and G. Teleki (eds.), *Omnivorous Primates: Gathering and Hunting in Human Evolution*. Columbia University Press, New York, pp. 37–103.
James, E. O., 1960. *The Ancient Gods: The History and Diffusion of Religion in the Ancient Near East and Eastern Mediterranean*. 1964 reprint, Capricorn, New York.
James, M. R. (trans.), 1924. *The Apocryphal New Testament*. Oxford University Press, Oxford.
Janik, A., and S. Toulmin, 1973. *Wittgenstein's Vienna*. Simon and Schuster, New York.
Jeffers, R., 1916. *Californians*. Macmillan, New York.
——— 1948. *The Double Axe and Other Poems*. Random House, New York. 1977 reprint, Liveright, New York.
——— 1963. *The Beginning and the End and Other Poems*. Random House, New York.
Johanson, D. C., and M. A. Edey, 1981. *Lucy: The Beginnings of Humankind*. Simon and Schuster, New York.
Johnson, C., 1904. *Old-Time Schools and Schoolbooks*. Macmillan, New York. 1963 reprint, Dover, New York.

Johnston, O., and F. Thomas, 1990. *Walt Disney's Bambi: The Story and the Film.* Stewart, Tabori, and Chang, New York.

Jolly, C. J., 1970. "The Seed-Eaters: A New Model of Hominid Differentiation Based on a Baboon Analogy." *Man* (n.s.), 5:5–27.

Jolma, D. J., 1992. "Why They Quit: Thoughts from Ex-Hunters." *The Animals' Agenda* (July-August), pp. 38–40.

Jones, F. W., 1929a. *Man's Place among the Mammals.* Arnold, London.

————— 1929b. "Some Landmarks in the Phylogeny of the Primates." *Human Biology,* 1:214–228.

Jones, G. (ed.), 1977. *The Oxford Book of Welsh Verse in English.* Oxford University Press, Oxford.

Jones, J. S., 1983. *Hitler in Vienna, 1907–1913.* Stein and Day, New York.

Josephson, E., and M. Josephson, 1962. Introduction. In E. Josephson and M. Josephson (eds.), *Man Alone: Alienation in Modern Society.* Dell, New York, pp. 9–53.

Jung, C. G., 1959. *The Basic Writings of C. G. Jung.* V. S. de Laszlo, ed. Modern Library, New York.

Jurmain, R., H. Nelson, and W. A. Turnbaugh, 1984. *Understanding Physical Anthropology and Archaeology.* 2nd ed. West, St. Paul.

Katz, S. (ed.), 1947. *Freud: On War, Sex, and Neurosis.* Arts and Science Press, New York.

Kaufman, W. (ed. and trans.), 1967. *The Will to Power,* by Friedrich Nietzsche. Random House, New York.

Kazin, A. (ed.), 1942. *The Portable Blake.* Viking, New York.

Keen, M., 1961. *The Outlaws of Medieval Legend.* Routledge and Kegan Paul, London.

Keith, A., 1948. *A New Theory of Human Evolution.* Watts, London.

Kenny, A. (ed.), 1970. *Descartes: Philosophical Letters.* Oxford University Press, Oxford.

Keynes, G. (ed.), 1966. *Blake: Complete Writings.* Oxford University Press, Oxford.

King, J. (ed. and trans.), 1847. *Commentaries upon the First Book of Moses Called Genesis,* by John Calvin. 1948 reprint, W. B. Eerdmans, Grand Rapids.

Kingston, A. R., 1967. "Theodicy and Animal Welfare." *Theology,* 70:482–488.

Kinney, J., 1988. *Walt Disney and Assorted Other Characters: An Unauthorized Account of the Early Years at Disney's.* Harmony, New York.

Kirby, W., 1835. *The Bridgewater Treatises on the Power, Wisdom, and Goodness of God as Manifested in the Creation, VII. On the History, Habits, and Instincts of Animals.* William Pickering, London.

Kirk, G. S. (ed. and trans.), 1970. *Euripides: The Bacchae.* Prentice-Hall, Englewood Cliffs.

Klein, R. G., 1987. "Reconstructing How Early People Exploited Animals: Problems and Prospects." In M. H. Nitecki and D. V. Nitecki (eds.), *The Evolution of Human Hunting.* Plenum, New York, pp. 11–45.

Knox, M. L., 1990. "In the Heat of the Hunt." *Sierra* (November-December), pp. 48–59.

Koreny, F., 1985. *Albrecht Dürer and the Animal and Plant Studies of the Renaissance.* 1988 English trans., Little, Brown, Boston.

Kramrisch, S., 1981. *The Presence of Śiva.* Princeton University Press, Princeton.

Kraus, K., 1922. *The Last Days of Mankind.* 1974 English trans. by A. Gode and S. E. Wright. Ungar, New York.

Krutch, J. W., 1929. *The Modern Temper: A Study and a Confession.* Harcourt, Brace, New York.

——— (ed.), 1955. *Great American Nature Writing.* William Sloane, n.p.

——— 1956. *The Great Chain of Life.* Houghton Mifflin, Boston.

Kurtzman, H., 1959. *Harvey Kurtzman's Jungle Book.* Ballantine, New York.

La Barre, W., 1954. *The Human Animal.* University of Chicago Press, Chicago.

——— 1964. "Comment on Hockett and Ascher." *Current Anthropology,* 5:147–150.

——— 1972. *The Ghost Dance: Origins of Religion.* Dell, New York.

Landes, D. S., 1983. *Revolution in Time: Clocks and the Making of the Modern World.* Harvard University Press, Cambridge.

Lansbury, C., 1985. *The Old Brown Dog: Women, Workers, and Vivisection in Edwardian England.* University of Wisconsin Press, Madison.

Lattimore, R. (trans.), 1951. *The Iliad of Homer.* University of Chicago Press, Chicago.

Laughlin, W. S., 1968. "Hunting: An Integrating Biobehavior System and Its Evolutionary Importance." In R. B. Lee and I. DeVore (eds.), *Man the Hunter.* Aldine, Chicago, pp. 304–320.

Leach, E., 1966. "Don't Say 'Boo' to a Goose." *New York Review of Books,* December 15, pp. 8–12.

Leach, M. (ed.), 1955. *The Ballad Book.* Harper, New York. Undated reprint, A. S. Barnes, New York.

Leakey, R. E., and R. Lewin, 1977. *Origins.* Dutton, New York.

Lee, R. B., 1968. "What Hunters Do for a Living, or, How to Make Out on Scarce Resources." In R. B. Lee and I. DeVore (eds.), *Man the Hunter.* Aldine, Chicago, pp. 30–48.

Lefler, H. T. (ed.), 1967. *A New Voyage to Carolina,* by John Lawson. University of North Carolina Press, Chapel Hill.

Le Gros Clark, W. E., 1934. *Early Fore-Runners of Man.* Balliere, London.

——— 1959. *History of the Primates: An Introduction to the Study of Fossil Man.* University of Chicago Press, Chicago.

——— 1964. *The Fossil Evidence for Human Evolution: An Introduction to the Study of Paleoanthropology.* 2nd ed. University of Chicago Press, Chicago.

——— 1967. *Man-Apes or Ape-Men? The Story of Discoveries in Africa.* Holt, Rinehart and Winston, New York.

Lehrer, T., 1954. *The Tom Lehrer Songbook.* Crown, New York.

Lem, S., 1971. *The Star Diaries* (M. Kandel, trans.). Avon, New York.

——— 1983. *His Master's Voice.* Harcourt Brace Jovanovich, New York.

Lenneberg, E. H., 1967. *Biological Foundations of Language.* Wiley, New York.

Leopold, A., 1949. *A Sand County Almanac and Sketches Here and There.* Oxford University Press, New York.

Levi, P. (trans.), 1971. *Pausanias: Guide to Greece*. Penguin, Harmondsworth.

Levron, J., 1974. *Louis XV: L'homme et le roi*. Librairie Académique Perrin, Paris.

Lewin, R., 1987. *Bones of Contention*. Simon and Schuster, New York.

Lewis, C. S., 1946. *That Hideous Strength: A Modern Fairy-Tale for Grown-Ups*. 1965 reprint, Macmillan, New York.

———— 1947. *The Abolition of Man*. 1962 reprint, Collier, New York.

———— 1962. *The Problem of Pain*. Macmillan, New York.

———— 1964. *The Discarded Image*. Cambridge University Press, Cambridge.

———— 1967. *Studies in Words*. Cambridge University Press, Cambridge.

Lewis, R., 1960. *What We Did to Father*. 1964 reprint, *The Evolution Man*. Penguin, Harmondsworth.

Liddell, H. G., and R. Scott, 1897. *A Greek-English Lexicon*. Harper, New York.

Lindner, K., 1937. *Die Jagd der Vorzeit*. W. de Gruyter, Berlin.

———— 1940. *Die Jagd im frühen Mittelalter*. W. de Gruyter, Berlin.

Lindsay, A. D. (ed.), 1901. *Hobbes' Leviathan*. J. M. Dent, London.

Linforth, I. M., 1941. *The Arts of Orpheus*. University of California Press, Berkeley.

Linton, R., 1956. *The Tree of Culture*. Knopf, New York.

Linton, S., 1971. "Woman the Gatherer: Male Bias in Anthropology." In S. E. Jacobs (ed.), *Women in Cross-Cultural Perspective: A Preliminary Sourcebook*. University of Illinois Department of Urban and Regional Planning, Champaign, pp. 9–21.

Linzey, A., 1976. *Animal Rights: A Christian Assessment of Man's Treatment of Animals*. SCM Press, London.

Livingstone, F. B., 1962. "Reconstructing Man's Pliocene Pongid Ancestor." *American Anthropologist*, 64:301–305.

Locke, J., 1852. *An Essay Concerning Human Understanding and A Treatise on the Conduct of the Understanding*. Troutman and Hayes, Philadelphia.

Locke, J., 1947. *On Politics and Education*. Walter J. Black, Roslyn, New York.

Lockwood, W. B., 1975. *Languages of the British Isles Past and Present*. Deutsch, London.

Long, W. J., 1903. "The Modern School of Nature-Study and Its Critics." *North American Review*, 176:688–698.

Lonsdale, S., 1981. *Animals and the Origins of Dance*. Thames and Hudson, London.

Lorenz, K., 1963. *Das sogenannte Böse. Zur Naturgeschichte der Aggression*. G. Borotha-Schoeler, Vienna. 1966 trans. *(On Aggression)* by M. K. Wilson. Harcourt, Brace and World, New York.

Lovejoy, A. O., 1936. *The Great Chain of Being: A Study of the History of an Idea*. Harvard University Press, Cambridge.

———— 1959. "The Argument for Organic Evolution before the *Origin of Species, 1830–1858*." In B. Glass, O. Temkin, and W. L. Strauss, Jr. (eds.), *Forerunners of Darwinism, 1745–1859*. Johns Hopkins University Press, Baltimore, pp. 356–414.

———— and G. Boas, 1935. *Primitivism and Related Ideas in Antiquity*. Johns Hopkins University Press, Baltimore.

Lovejoy, C. O. 1981. "The Origin of Man." *Science*, 211:341–350.

Lukács, G., 1923. *History and Class Consciousness: Studies in Marxist Dialectics.* 1971 English trans. MIT Press, Cambridge.

Lutts, R. H., 1990. *The Nature Fakers: Wildlife, Science, and Sentiment.* Fulcrum Publishing, Golden, Colorado.

Mac Cana, P., 1970. *Celtic Mythology.* Hamlyn, London.

Macdonald, D., 1946. "The Root is Man." *Politics* (1946), pp. 149–150, 194–214.

MacDonald, J. D., 1965. *A Deadly Shade of Gold.* Fawcett Gold Medal, New York.

MacDonald, R. K., 1982. *Literature for Children in England and America from 1646 to 1774.* Whitston, Troy, New York.

MacKenzie, J. M., 1988. *The Empire of Nature: Hunting, Conservation and British Imperialism.* Manchester University Press, Manchester.

Mahaffy, J. P., 1901. *Descartes.* Blackwood, Edinburgh.

Majupuria, T. C., 1977. *Sacred and Symbolic Animals of Nepal.* Sakayogi Prakashan, Tripureswar, Katmandu, Nepal.

Maltin, L., 1980. *Of Mice and Magic: A History of American Animated Cartoons.* New American Library, New York.

——— 1984. *The Disney Films.* Rev. ed. Crown, New York.

Mandelbaum, A. (trans.), 1961. *The Aeneid of Virgil.* Bantam, New York.

Manley, F., and R. S. Sylvester (eds.), 1967. *De Fructu qui ex Doctrina Percipitur,* by Richard Pace. Ungar, New York.

Mann, A. E., 1972. "Hominid and Cultural Origins." *Man,* 7:379–386.

Manuel, J., 1988. "The Deer Hunt." *Leader Magazine,* Raleigh (N.C.), October 20, pp. 3–7.

Marchant, E. C. (ed.), 1938. *Xenophon: Memorabilia and Oeconomicus.* Harvard University Press, Cambridge.

——— 1968. *Xenophon: Scripta Minora.* Harvard University Press, Cambridge.

Marks, S. A., 1991. *Southern Hunting in Black and White: Nature, History, and Ritual in a Carolina Community.* Princeton University Press, Princeton.

Marquis, D., 1928. *Love Sonnets of a Cave Man and Other Verses.* Doubleday, Doran, Garden City.

Marsh, E. (trans.), 1941. *The Odes of Horace.* Macmillan, London.

Marsh, G. P., 1864. *Man and Nature: or, Physical Geography as Modified by Human Action.* Scribner's, New York. 1965 reprint (D. Lowenthal, ed.), Harvard University Press, Cambridge.

Mattis, G., 1980. *Whitetail: Fundamentals and Fine Points for the Hunter.* Van Nostrand Reinhold, New York.

Mayr, E., 1962. *The Growth of Biological Thought: Diversity, Evolution, and Inheritance.* Harvard University Press, Cambridge.

——— 1969. *Principles of Systematic Zoology.* McGraw-Hill, New York.

McBrearty, S., 1989. "Cutlery and Carnivory." *Journal of Human Evolution,* 18:277–282.

McClintock, I., and M. McClintock, 1961. *Toys in America.* Public Affairs Press, Washington, D.C.

McClinton, K. M., 1970. *Antiques of American Childhood.* Clarkson N. Potter, New York.

McCurdy, E., 1928. *The Mind of Leonardo da Vinci.* Dodd, Mead, New York.

McGee, H., 1984. *On Food and Cooking: The Science and Lore of the Kitchen.* Scribner's, New York.

McGraw, H., et al. (eds.), 1971. *Original Sacred Harp,* Denson Revision. Sacred Harp, Bremen, Georgia.

McIntyre, T., 1988. *The Way of the Hunter: The Art and the Spirit of Modern Hunting.* Dutton, New York.

McPhee, J., 1977. *Coming into the Country.* 1979 reprint, Bantam, New York.

Mencken, H. L., 1949. *A Mencken Chrestomathy.* Knopf, New York.

Mendelson, E. (ed.), 1977. *The English Auden: Poems, Essays, and Dramatic Writings, 1927–1939.* Random House, New York.

Merchant, C., 1980. *The Death of Nature: Women, Ecology, and the Scientific Revolution.* Harper and Row, New York.

Meyer, F. B., 1950. *F. B. Meyer on the Psalms.* Zondervan, Grand Rapids.

Mijatovich, E., 1917. *Serbian Fairy Tales.* Heinemann, London.

Millay, E. St. V., 1928. *The Buck in the Snow, and Other Poems.* Harper, New York.

Miller, F. J. (ed.), 1925. *Ovid: Metamorphoses.* Putnam, New York.

Miller, J. (ed.), 1956. *Arizona, the Grand Canyon State.* Hastings House, New York.

Millhauser, M., 1959. *Just Before Darwin: Robert Chambers and* Vestiges. Wesleyan University Press, Middletown.

Mitchell, J. G., 1980. *The Hunt.* Knopf, New York.

———— 1982. "Our Wily White-Tailed Deer: Elegant but Perplexing Neighbors." *Smithsonian* (November), pp. 111–118.

Mivart, St. G. J., 1871. "Darwin's Descent of Man." *Quarterly Review,* 131:47–90.

Montagu, B. (ed.), 1828. *The Works of Francis Bacon.* William Pickering, London.

Montagu, M. F. A., 1968a. Introduction. In M. F. A. Montagu (ed.), *Man and Aggression.* Oxford University Press, New York, pp. vii–xiv.

———— 1968b. "The New Litany of 'Innate Depravity,' or Original Sin Revisited." In M. F. A. Montagu (ed.), *Man and Aggression.* Oxford University Press, New York, pp. 3–17.

———— 1978. "Is Man Innately Aggressive?" In R. K. Morris and M. W. Fox (eds.), *On the Fifth Day: Animal Rights and Human Ethics,* Acropolis Books, Washington, D.C., pp. 93–110.

Moore, J. F. (ed.), 1899. *Thoughts Regarding the Future State of Animals.* Warren, Winchester, U.K.

Moore, T., 1859. *Poetical Works.* Phillips, Sampson, Boston.

Morris, C., 1886. "The Making of Man." *American Naturalist,* 20:493–504.

———— 1890. "From Brute to Man." *American Naturalist,* 24:341–350.

———— 1906. *Man and His Ancestor: A Study in Evolution.* 2nd ed. Macmillan, New York.

———— (ed.), 1965. *Of the Laws of Ecclesiastical Polity.* E. P. Dutton, New York.

Morris, D., 1967. *The Naked Ape: A Zoologist's Study of the Human Animal.* Cape, London.

——— 1978. Introduction. In P. Whitefield, *The Hunters*. Simon and Schuster, New York, pp. 6–7.

Morton, D. J., 1926. "Evolution of Man's Erect Posture." *Journal of Morphology and Physiology*, 43:147–179.

——— 1927. "Human Origin: Correlation of Previous Studies of Primate Feet and Posture with Other Morphologic Evidence." *American Journal of Physical Anthropology*, 10:173–203.

——— 1935. *The Human Foot: Its Evolution, Physiology and Functional Disorders*. Columbia University Press, New York.

Mosley, L., 1985. *Disney's World*. Stein and Day, New York.

Mülhaupt, D. (ed.), 1959. *D Martin Luthers Psalmen-Auslegung*. Vandenhoek und Ruprecht, Göttingen.

Müller-Hill, B., 1988. *Murderous Science: Elimination by Scientific Selection of Jews, Gypsies, and Others, Germany, 1933–1945*. G. R. Fraser, trans. Oxford University Press, New York.

Murie, O. J., 1935. "The Elk of Jackson Hole." *Natural History* (March), pp. 237–247.

Murillo, J., and A. M. Ramb, 1976. *Renanco y los ultimos huemules*. Casa de las Américas, Havana.

Murphy, G. (ed.), 1956. *Early Irish Lyrics, Eighth to Twelfth Century*. Oxford University Press, New York.

Murray, G. (trans.), 1904. *The Bacchae of Euripides*. Allen and Unwin, London.

——— 1923. *Euripides*. Longmans, Green, New York.

——— 1946. *Euripides and His Age*. 2nd ed. Oxford University Press, London.

Mutt, E. (ed.), 1930. *Fairy Tales from Baltic Shores*. Penn, Philadelphia.

Nahm, M. C. (ed.), 1962. *Selections from Early Greek Philosophy*. Appleton-Century-Crofts, New York.

Namenwirth, M., 1986. "Science Seen through a Feminist Prism." In R. Bleier (ed.), *Feminist Approaches to Science*. Pergamon, New York, pp. 18–41.

Nash, R., 1982. *Wilderness and the American Mind*. 3rd ed. Yale University Press, New Haven.

Neale, J. M., and R. F. Littledale, 1884. *A Commentary on the Psalms: from Primitive and Medieval Writers; and from the Various Office-Books and Hymns of the Roman, Mozarabic, Ambrosian, Gallician, Greek, Coptic, Armenian, and Syriac Rites*. Pott, New York.

Nesturkh, M., 1959. *The Origin of Man*. Foreign Languages Publishing House, Moscow.

Nicholls, R. E., 1976. "John Muir." In J. Muir (ed.), *West of the Rocky Mountains*. 1976 reprint. Running Press, Philadelphia, p. iv.

Nichols, F. M. (ed.), 1962. *The Epistles of Erasmus*. Russell, New York.

Nickl, T., and H. Schnitzler (eds.), 1964. *Briefwechsel von Hugo von Hofmannsthal und Arthur Schnitzler*. Fischer, Stuttgart.

Nietschmann, B., 1977. "The Bambi Factor." *Natural History* (August-September), pp. 84–87.

Nisbet, R., 1980. *History of the Idea of Progress*. Basic Books, New York.

Nitecki, M. H., and D. V. Nitecki (eds.), 1987. *The Evolution of Human Hunting.* Plenum, New York.

Niven, C. D., 1967. *History of the Humane Movement.* Transatlantic Arts, New York.

Nolte, W. H., 1978. *Rock and Hawk: Robinson Jeffers and the Romantic Agony.* University of Georgia Press, Athens.

Nordenskiöld, E., 1924. *The History of Biology.* Björck and Börjesson, Stockholm. 1928 English trans. by L. B. Eyre. Knopf, New York; 1952 reprint, Tudor, New York.

Nugent, F. S., 1939. "Disney Is Now Art—But He Wonders." *New York Times Magazine,* February 26, pp. 4–5.

Oakley, K. P., 1951. "A Definition of Man." *Science News,* 20:69–81.

——— 1954. "Skill as a Human Possession." In C. J. Singer, E. J. Holmyard, and A. R. Hall (eds.), *A History of Technology.* Oxford University Press, Oxford, vol. 1, pp. 1–37.

——— 1959. "Tools Makyth Man." *Smithsonian Reports,* 1958:431–456.

——— 1961. "On Man's Use of Fire, with Comments on Tool-Making and Hunting." In S. L. Washburn (ed.), *Social Life of Early Man.* Aldine, Chicago, pp. 176–193.

Oates, W. J. (ed.), 1948. *Basic Writings of Saint Augustine.* Modern Library, New York.

O'Donovan, D. (trans.), 1970. *The Works of Bernard of Clairvaux.* Cistercian, Kalamazoo.

O'Keeffe, J. G. (ed.), 1913. *Buile Suibhne: Being The Adventures of Suibhne Geilt. A Middle-Irish Romance.* D. Nutt, London.

Olmsted, J. M. D., 1938. *Claude Bernard, Physiologist.* Harper, New York.

Opie, I., and P. Opie, 1952. *The Oxford Dictionary of Nursery Rhymes.* Oxford University Press, Oxford.

Opperman, H., 1983. *J.-B. Oudry.* Kimbell Art Museum, Fort Worth.

Ormond, R., 1981. *Sir Edwin Landseer.* Philadelphia Museum of Art, Philadelphia.

Ortega y Gasset, J., 1972. *Meditations on Hunting.* H. B. Wescott, trans. Scribner's, New York.

Orwell, S., and I. Angus (eds.), 1968. *The Collected Essays, Journalism, and Letters of George Orwell.* Harcourt Brace Jovanovich, New York.

Osborn, H. F., 1926. "Why Central Asia?" *Natural History,* 26:263–269.

Osborn, H. F., 1927. "Recent Discoveries Relating to the Origin and Antiquity of Man." *Science,* 65:481–488.

Osborn, H. F., 1929. "Is the Ape-Man a Myth?" *Human Biology,* 1:4–9.

Paley, W., 1802. *Natural Theology.* 1854 reprint, American Tract Society, New York.

Patchen, K., 1945. *Memoirs of a Shy Pornographer.* New Directions, New York. 1958 reprint, City Lights Books, San Francisco.

——— 1948. *Cloth of the Tempest.* New Directions, New York.

Paton, A., 1964. *Hofmeyr.* Oxford University Press, Cape Town.

Paton, L. B., 1915. "Ishtar." In J. Hastings (ed.), *Encyclopedia of Religion and Ethics,* Scribner's, New York, vol. 7, pp. 428–434.

Peattie, D. C., 1942. "The Nature of Things." *Audubon Magazine,* 44:266–271.

Pepperberg, I., 1990. "Conceptual Abilities of Some Nonprimate Species, with an Emphasis on an African Grey Parrot." In S. T. Parker and K. R. Gibson (eds.), *"Language" and Intelligence in Monkeys and Apes: Comparative Developmental Perspectives.* Cambridge University Press, Cambridge, pp. 469–507.

Perper, T., and C. Schrire, 1977. "The Nimrod Connection: Myth and Science in the Hunting Model." In M. R. Kare and O. Maller (eds.), *The Chemical Senses and Nutrition.* Academic Press, New York, pp. 447–459.

Persons, S. (ed.), 1963. *Social Darwinism: Selected Essays of William Graham Sumner.* Prentice-Hall, Englewood Cliffs.

Peterson, B. R., 1989. *Buck Peterson's Complete Guide to Deer Hunting.* Ten Speed Press, Berkeley.

Petzal, D. E., 1988. "Rambo Comes to England, and Other Bad News." *Field and Stream* (May), pp. 28–29.

Pfeil, F., 1986. "Policiers Noirs." *The Nation,* 243:523–525.

Pfeiffer, J., 1969. *The Emergence of Man.* Harper, New York.

———— 1971. "Man the Hunter." *Horizon,* 13:28–33.

Phillips, M. T., and J. A. Sechzer, 1989. *Animal Research and Ethical Conflict.* Springer, New York.

Pike, J. B. (ed. and trans.), 1938. *Frivolities of Courtiers and Footprints of Philosophers. Being a Translation of the First, Second, and Third Books and Selections from the Seventh and Eighth Books of the Policraticus of John of Salisbury.* University of Minnesota Press, Minneapolis.

Pilbeam, D., 1972. *The Ascent of Man: An Introduction to Human Evolution.* Macmillan, New York.

Pinguet, F., 1978. "La vénerie et sa musique." *Revue musicale,* 310/311:1–123.

Pitts, D. D., 1974. "Discerning the Animal of the Thousand Faces." *Children's Literature,* 3:169–172.

Podach, E. F., 1931. *The Madness of Nietzsche.* Putnam, London.

Poirier, F., 1973. *Fossil Man: An Evolutionary Journey.* Mosby, St. Louis.

Pomeau, R. (ed.), 1960. *Julie, ou la Nouvelle Hèloïse: Lettres de deux amants habitants d'une petite ville au pied des Alpes.* Garniere, Paris.

Pope, S., 1925. *Hunting with the Bow and Arrow.* Putnam, New York.

Popper, K., 1957. *The Poverty of Historicism.* 1964 reprint, Harper and Row, New York.

Porter, S. T. (ed.), 1853. *A Selection of Hymns, Chiefly Watts's, for Use in Public Christian Worship.* John Nielson, Glasgow.

Prishvin, M. M., 1936. *Jen Sheng: The Root of Life.* Putnam, New York.

Proctor, R., 1988. "From *Anthropologie* to *Rassenkunde* in the German Anthropological Tradition." In G. W. Stocking (ed.), *Bones, Bodies, Behavior: Essays on Biological Anthropology.* University of Wisconsin Press, Madison, pp. 138–179.

Quennell, P. 1968. *Alexander Pope: The Education of Genius, 1688–1728.* Stein and Day, New York.

Quintana, R. (ed.), 1958. *Gulliver's Travels and Other Writings by Jonathan Swift.* Modern Library, New York.

Rachels, J., 1990. *Created from Animals: The Moral Implications of Darwinism.* Oxford University Press, Oxford.

Rackham, H. (ed. and trans.), 1933. *Cicero: De natura deorum and Academica.* Harvard University Press, Cambridge.

Rainsford, W. S., 1909. *The Land of the Lion.* Doubleday, Page, New York.

Ralegh, W., 1964. *The Works of Sir Walter Ralegh.* Burt Franklin, New York.

Randall, J. H., Jr., 1962. *The Career of Philosophy from the Middle Ages to the Enlightenment.* Columbia University Press, New York.

Randolph, V., 1947. *Ozark Superstitions.* Columbia University Press, New York.

Rawson, H. 1981. *A Dictionary of Euphemisms.* Crown, New York.

Read, C., 1914. "On the Differentiation of Man from the Anthropoids." *Man,* 14:181–186.

———— 1920. *The Origin of Man and of His Superstitions.* Cambridge University Press, Cambridge.

———— 1925. *The Origin of Man.* Cambridge University Press, Cambridge.

Reader, J., 1988. *Missing Links: The Hunt for Earliest Man.* Penguin, London.

Regan, T., 1983. *The Case for Animal Rights.* University of California Press, Berkeley.

———— 1991. *The Thee Generation: Essays on the Coming Revolution.* Temple University Press, Philadelphia.

Reiger, G., 1980. "The Truth about Bambi." *Field and Stream* (March), pp. 12–17.

Remigereau, F., 1952. "Jacques du Fouilloux et sa Traité de la Vénerie." *Publications de la Faculté des Lettres de la Université de Strasbourg,* 117:1–191.

Rexroth, K., 1956. *In Defense of the Earth.* New Directions, Norfolk.

Rhodes, R., 1969. "Death All Day in Kansas." *Esquire* (November), pp. 146–198.

Rhys Davids, T. S., and H. Oldenberg (ed. and trans.), 1881. *Vinaya Texts.* Oxford University Press, Oxford. 1965 reprint, Motilal Barnasidass, Delhi.

Richards, G., 1987. *Human Evolution: An Introduction for the Behavioural Sciences.* Routledge and Kegan Paul, London.

Rieckmann, J., 1985. *Aufbruch in die Moderne: Die Anfänge des jungen Wien. Osterreichische Literatur und Kritik in Fin de Siècle.* Athenäum, Königstein.

Riedmüller, K., 1949. "Felix Salten als Mensch, Dichter und Kritiker." Dissertation, University of Vienna.

Rishel, J., 1981. "Landseer and the Continent: The Artist in International Perspective." In R. Ormond, *Sir Edwin Landseer.* Philadelphia Museum of Art, Philadelphia, pp. 25–40.

Rist, A. (ed. and trans.), 1978. *The Poems of Theocritus.* University of North Carolina Press, Chapel Hill.

Ritvo, H., 1987. *The Animal Estate: The English and Other Creatures in the Victorian Age.* Harvard University Press, Cambridge.

Robert, C. (ed.), 1963. *Eratosthenis Catasterismorum Reliquae.* Weidmann, Berlin.

Roberts, A., and J. Donaldson (eds.), 1870. *Ante-Nicene Christian Writings: Translations of the Writings of the Fathers down to A.D. 325.* Clark, Edinburgh.

Robinson, J. T., 1961. "The Australopithecines and Their Bearing on the Origin of Man and of Stone Tool-Making." *South African Journal of Science,* 57:3–13.

——— 1962. "The Origins and Adaptive Radiation of the Australopithecines." In G. Kurth (ed.), *Evolution und Hominization.* Fischer, Stuttgart, pp. 120–140.

——— 1963. "Adaptive Radiation in the Australopithecines and the Origin of Man." In F. C. Howell and F. Bourlière (eds.), *African Ecology and Human Evolution.* Aldine, Chicago, pp. 385–416.

Rodman, J., 1986. "The Dolphin Papers." In D. Halpern (ed.), *On Nature.* North Point Press, Berkeley, pp. 252–280.

Roeder, H. 1955. *Saints and Their Attributes, with a Guide to Localities and Patronage.* Longmans, Green, London.

Rogers, J. E. T. (ed.), 1881. *Loci e Libro Veritatum: Passages Selected from Gascoigne's Theological Dictionary Illustrating the Condition of Church and State, 1403–1458.* Oxford University Press, Oxford.

Rolfe, J. C. (ed.), 1931. *Sallust.* Harvard University Press, Cambridge.

Rollin, B. E., 1981. *Animal Rights and Human Morality.* Prometheus Books, Buffalo.

Roosevelt, T., 1893. *The Wilderness Hunter: An Account of the Big Game of the United States and Its Chase with Horse, Hound, and Rifle.* Putnam, New York.

Rose, H. J., 1928. *A Handbook of Greek Mythology.* Methuen, London.

Rosenfield, L. C., 1941. *From Beast-Machine to Man-Machine: Animal Soul in French Letters from Descartes to La Mettrie.* Oxford University Press, New York.

Ross, A., 1967. *Pagan Celtic Britain: Studies in Iconography and Tradition.* Routledge and Kegan Paul, London.

——— 1986. *The Pagan Celts.* Barnes and Noble, Totowa.

Ross, R. (ed.), 1969. *The Works of Oscar Wilde.* Dawsons of Pall Mall, London.

Rouse, W. H. D. (trans.), 1937. *Lucretius: De rerum natura.* 3rd ed. Harvard University Press, Cambridge.

Ruark, R., 1966. *Use Enough Gun.* New American Library, New York.

Rue, L. L., III, 1978. *The Deer of North America.* Times-Mirror, Los Angeles.

Ruggeri, S., 1990. "Why I Don't Hunt." *Sierra* (December), pp. 52–53.

Ruse, M., 1979. *The Darwinian Revolution: Science Red in Tooth and Claw.* University of Chicago Press, Chicago.

Russell, B., 1945. *A History of Western Philosophy.* Simon and Schuster, New York.

Russell, D. E. H., 1975. *The Politics of Rape.* Stein and Day, New York.

Russell, F., 1984. *The Hunting Animal.* Hutchinson, London.

Ruyle, E. E., 1977. "Labor, People, Culture: A Labor Theory of Human Origins." *Yearbook of Physical Anthropology,* 20:136–163.

Rycroft, C., 1972. *Wilhelm Reich.* Viking, New York.

Sabbag, G. E., 1986. "Unfair Game: Hunters Draw Lots to Shoot at Bison That Wander Outside Yellowstone." *National Parks* (May-June), pp. 14–15.

Sahlins, M., 1976. *The Use and Abuse of Biology.* University of Michagan Press, Ann Arbor.

Salten, F., 1928. *Bambi: A Life in the Woods.* W. Chambers, transl. Simon and Schuster, New York.

———— 1931. *Fünf Minuten Amerika.* Paul Zsolnay, Vienna.

———— 1933. "Aus den Anfängen: Erinnerungsskizzen." *Jahrbuch deutscher Bibliophilen,* 18/19:31–46.

Sargent, T. (ed. and trans.), 1973. *The Homeric Hymns: A Verse Translation.* Norton, New York.

Saunders, T. B. (ed. and trans.), 1923. *Studies in Pessimism, a Series of Essays by Arthur Schopenhauer.* Allen and Unwin, London.

Savage-Rumbaugh, E. S., 1986. *Ape Language: From Conditioned Response to Symbol.* Columbia University Press, New York.

Scanlan, J. J. (ed. and trans.), 1987. *Albert the Great: Man and the Beasts (De animalibus,* books 22–26). Medieval and Renaissance Texts and Studies, Binghamton.

Schaller, G. B., 1972a. "Are You Running with Me, Hominid?" *Natural History* (March), pp. 60–68.

Schaller, G. B., 1972b. *The Serengeti Lion.* University of Chicago Press, Chicago.

Schickel, R., 1968. *The Disney Version.* Avon, New York.

Schorske, C. E., 1980. *Fin-de-siècle Vienna: Politics and Culture.* Knopf, New York.

Schröter, M. (ed.), 1927. *Schellings Werke.* Beck und Oldenbourg, Munich.

Scully, D., 1990. *Understanding Sexual Violence: A Study of Convicted Rapists.* Unwin Hyman, Boston.

Seccombe, J., 1743. *A Discourse Utter'd in Part at Ammauskeeg-Falls in the Fishing-Season.* 1971 reprint, Barre Publishers, Barre.

Sedgwick, A., 1860. "Objections to Mr. Darwin's Theory of the Origin of Species." *The Spectator,* March 24, pp. 285–286.

Segerberg, O., Jr., 1971. *Where Have All the Flowers, Fishes, Birds, Trees, Water, and Air Gone? What Ecology Is All About.* McKay, New York.

Seldes, G., 1937. *The Movies Come from America.* Scribner's, New York.

———— 1950. *The Big Audience.* Viking, New York.

———— 1956. *The Public Arts.* Simon and Schuster, New York.

Seton, E. T., 1898. *Wild Animals I Have Known.* Scribner's, New York.

———— 1901. *Lives of the Hunted.* Scribner's, New York.

Shakespear, J., 1934. *Urdu-English and English-Urdu Dictionary.* 1980 reprint, Sang-e-Meel, Lahore.

Shapiro, H., and E. M. Curley, 1965. *Hellenistic Philosophy.* Modern Library, New York.

Shastri, M. M. H. (ed.), 1982. *Śyainika Sāstram: The Art of Hunting in Ancient India.* Eastern Book Linkers, Delhi.

Shaw, G. B., 1921. *Back to Methuselah: A Metabiological Pentateuch.* Brentano's, New York.

Shawcross, J. T. (ed.), 1967. *The Complete Poetry of John Donne.* Doubleday, Garden City.

Shepard, O. (ed.), 1938. *The Journals of Bronson Alcott.* Little, Brown, Boston.

Sherrington, C., 1941. *Man on His Nature.* Cambridge University Press, Cambridge.

Shesgreen, S., 1973. *Engravings by Hogarth.* Dover, New York.

Shipman, P., 1986. "Scavenging or Hunting in Early Hominids: Theoretical Framework and Tests." *American Anthropologist,* 88:27–43.

——— 1987. "Why Did the Human Lineage Survive?" *Discover* (April), pp. 60–64.

Shows, C., 1980. *Walt: Backstage Adventures with Walt Disney.* Communication Creativity, La Jolla.

Simonson, L. (ed.), 1868. *The German Ballad Book.* Leypoldt and Holt, New York.

Simpson, J. Y., 1922. *Man and the Attainment of Immortality.* Doran, New York.

Singer, C., 1957. *A Short History of Anatomy and Physiology from the Greeks to Harvey.* 2nd ed. Dover, New York.

Singer, P., 1990. *Animal Liberation.* 2nd ed. Avon, New York.

Skeat, W. W. (ed.), 1932. *Piers the Plowman,* by William Langland. 10th ed. Oxford University Press, Oxford.

Slotkin, J. S. (ed.), 1965. "Readings in Early Anthropology." *Viking Fund Publications in Anthropology,* 40:1–530.

Smith, G. E., 1924. *The Evolution of Man.* Oxford University Press, Oxford.

Smith, H. I., 1906. "Some Ojibwa Myths and Traditions." *Journal of American Folklore,* 19:215–230.

Smith, J. (ed.), 1972. *Mark Twain on Man and Beast.* Lawrence Hill, New York.

Smith, N. K. (ed.), 1947. *Dialogues Concerning Natural Religion,* by David Hume. Bobbs-Merrill, Indianapolis.

Smith, W. G., 1894. *Man, the Primeval Savage: His Haunts and Relics from the Hill-tops of Bedfordshire to Blackwall.* E. Stanford, London.

Snyder, G., 1974. *Turtle Island.* New Directions, New York.

Sparrow, C. M. (ed.), 1947. *S. Aurelii Augustine: De libero arbitrio voluntatis.* University of Virginia Press, Charlottesville.

Speth, J. D., and D. D. Davis, 1976. "Seasonal Variability in Early Hominid Predation." *Science,* 192:441–445.

Spuhler, J. N., 1959. "Somatic Paths to Culture." *Human Biology,* 31:1–13.

Squires, R., 1956. *The Loyalties of Robinson Jeffers.* University of Michigan Press, Ann Arbor.

Starbuck, G., 1966. *White Paper.* Little, Brown, Boston.

Starkie, W. (ed. and trans.), 1957. *Don Quixote of La Mancha,* by Miguel de Cervantes Saavedra. New American Library, New York.

Stein, G. J., 1986. "The Biological Bases of Ethnocentrism, Racism and Nationalism in National Socialism." In V. Reynolds, V. Falger, and I. Vine (eds.), *The Sociobiology of Ethnocentrism,* University of Georgia Press, Athens, pp. 250–267.

Steinbeck, J., 1962. *Travels with Charley in Search of America.* Viking, New York.

Stephenson, R., 1967. *Animation in the Cinema.* Zwemmer, London.

Stocking, G. W. S., Jr., 1987. *Victorian Anthropology.* Free Press, New York.

Stoczkowski, W., 1991. "De l'origine de la division sexualle du travail: quelques fossiles vivants de l'imaginaire." *Les nouvelles de l'archaeologie,* 44:15–18.

Strachey, J. (ed. and trans.), 1950a. *Beyond the Pleasure Principle,* by Sigmund Freud. Liveright, New York.

———— 1950b. *Totem and Taboo,* by Sigmund Freud. Norton, New York.

———— 1962. *Civilization and Its Discontents,* by Sigmund Freud. Norton, New York.

Struik, D. (ed.), 1964. *The Economic and Philosophical Manuscripts of 1844,* by Karl Marx. Trans. M. Milligan. International, New York.

Sullivan, S. A., 1984. *The Dutch Gamepiece.* Rowman and Allenheld, Totowa.

Suphan, B. (ed.), 1883. *Herders sämmtliche Werke.* Weidmannsche, Berlin.

Surtz, E., and J. H. Hexter (eds.), 1965. *The Complete Works of St. Thomas More.* Yale University Press, New Haven.

Swedenberg, H. T., Jr. (ed.), 1969. *The Works of John Donne.* University of California Press, Berkeley.

Tanner, N. M., 1981. *On Becoming Human.* Cambridge University Press, Cambridge.

Tanner, N. M., and A. L. Zihlman, 1976. "Women in Evolution. Part I: Innovation and Selection in Human Origins." *Signs,* 1:585–608.

Tattersall, I., 1970. *Man's Ancestors: An Introduction to Primate and Human Evolution.* Murray, London.

Taylor, J., 1630. *All the Workes of J. Taylor the Water Poet: Beeing sixty and three in number.* J. Boler, London.

Taylor, R. E., and R. Bogart, 1988. *Scientific Farm Animal Production: An Introduction to Animal Science.* 3rd ed. Macmillan, New York.

Teilhard de Chardin, P., 1969. *Human Energy.* Collins, London.

Teleki, G., 1973. *The Predatory Behavior of Wild Chimpanzees.* Bucknell University Press, Lewisburg.

———— 1981. "The Omnivorous Diet and Eclectic Feeding Habits of Chimpanzees in Gombe National Park, Tanzania." In R. S. O. Harding and G. Teleki (eds.), *Omnivorous Primates: Gathering and Hunting in Human Evolution,* Columbia University Press, New York, pp. 303–343.

Terrace, H. S., 1983. "Apes Who 'Talk': Language or Projection of Language by Their Teachers?" In J. de Luce and H. T. Wilder, *Language in Primates: Perspectives and Implications,* Springer, New York, pp. 19–42.

Terrace, H. S., L. A. Pettito, R. J. Sanders, and T. G. Bever, 1979. Can an ape create a sentence? *Science,* 206:891–900.

Thiébaux, M., 1969. "The Mouth of the Boar as a Symbol in Medieval Literature." *Romance Philology,* 22:281–299.

———— 1974. *The Stag of Love: The Chase in Medieval Literature.* Cornell University Press, Ithaca.

Thomas, F., and O. Johnston, 1981. *Disney Animation: The Illusion of Life.* Abbeville Press, New York.

Thomas, K., 1983. *Man and the Natural World: A History of the Modern Sensibility.* Pantheon, New York.

Thompson, D. B., 1948. *Swans and Amber.* University of Toronto Press, Toronto.

Thompson, E. P., 1975. *Whigs and Hunters: The Origin of the Black Act.* Pantheon, New York.

Thomson, J. A., 1910. "Darwin's Predecessors." In A. C. Seward (ed.), *Darwin and Modern Science*. Cambridge University Press, Cambridge, pp. 3–17.

Thurston, H. J., and D. Attwater (eds.), 1956. *Butler's Lives of the Saints*. Burns and Oates, London.

Tilander, G., 1956. "Guicennas. De Arte Bersandi. Le plus ancient traité de chasse de l'occident." *Cynegetica* (Uppsala), 3:1–32.

——— (ed.), 1964. *The Boke of Hunting*. E. G. Johansson, Karlshamn.

——— 1967. "Jacques du Fouilloux: *La Vénerie* et *L'Adolescence*." *Cynegetica* (Uppsala), 16:1–330.

Tillyard, E. M. W., 1944. *The Elizabethan World Picture*. Macmillan, New York.

Tobias, P. V., 1965. "Early Man in East Africa." *Science*, 149:22–33.

——— 1984. *Dart, Taung, and the 'Missing Link.'* Witwatersrand University Press, Johannesburg.

Tolkien, J. R. R., 1965. *Tree and Leaf*. Houghton Mifflin, Boston.

Tooby, J., and I. DeVore, 1987. "The Reconstruction of Hominid Behavioral Evolution through Strategic Modeling." In W. G. Kinzey (ed.), *The Evolution of Human Behavior: Primate Models*. State University of New York Press, Albany, pp. 183–237.

Torrey, B., and F. H. Allen (eds.), 1906. *The Journal of Henry D. Thoreau*. Houghton Mifflin, Boston.

Toulmin, S., 1984. "The New Philosophy of Science and the 'Paranormal.'" *Skeptical Inquirer*, 9 (1):48–55.

Toynbee, J. M. C., 1973. *Animals in Roman Life and Art*. Cornell University Press, Ithaca.

Trevelyan, G. M., 1942. *English Social History*. Longmans, Green, London. 1964 reprint, Penguin, Harmondsworth.

Turbervile, G., 1576. *The Noble Arte of Venerie or Hunting: wherein is handled and set out the Vertues, Nature, and Properties of fivetene sundrie Chaces togither, with the order and maner how to Hunte and kill every one of them*. 1908 reprint, Oxford University Press, Oxford.

Turk, M. H. (ed.), 1930. *An Anglo-Saxon Reader*. Scribner's, New York.

Turnbull, A. (ed.), 1973. *The Poems of John Davidson*. Scottish Academic Press, Edinburgh.

Turner, J., 1980. *Reckoning with the Beast: Animals, Pain, and Humanity in the Victorian Mind*. Johns Hopkins University Press, Baltimore.

Turner, R. L., 1966. *A Comparative Dictionary of the Indo-Aryan Languages*. Oxford University Press, Oxford.

Twain, M., 1869. *The Innocents Abroad*. 1913 ed. Harper, New York.

——— 1871. *Roughing It*. 1913 ed. Harper, New York.

——— 1894. *Pudd'nhead Wilson and Those Extraordinary Twins*. 1913 ed. Harper, New York.

——— 1897. *Following the Equator*. 1913 ed. Harper, New York.

——— 1916. *The Mysterious Stranger and Other Stories*. Harper, New York. 1962 reprint, New American Library, New York.

——— 1917. *What Is Man?* Harper, New York.

——— 1962. *Letters from the Earth*. Harper and Row, New York.

Van Doren, M., 1941. *The Mayfield Deer*. Holt, New York.

Van Dyke, J. C. (ed.), 1921. *The Autobiography of Andrew Carnegie*. Houghton Mifflin, Boston.

Van Lawick-Goodall, J., and H. van Lawick-Goodall, 1973. *Innocent Killers*. Ballantine, New York.

Voisine, J. (ed.), 1964. *Jean-Jacques Rousseau: Les Confessions*. Garnier, Paris.

Vonnegut, K., Jr., 1961. *The Sirens of Titan*. Houghton Mifflin, Boston.

—— 1968. *Canary in a Cat House*. Fawcett Gold Medal, Greenwich.

—— 1975. *Wampeters Foma and Granfaloons*. Dell, New York.

—— 1985. *Galápagos*. Delacorte/Seymour Lawrence, New York. 1988 ed., Dell, New York.

Walford, E. (ed.), 1910. *The Politics and Economics of Aristotle*. Bell, London.

Walker, A., 1976. "The Hunter Hunted." *Natural History* (May), pp. 76–81.

—— and R. E. F. Leakey, 1978. "The Hominids of East Turkana." *Scientific American,* 239 (August), pp. 54–66.

Walker, E. P., 1964. *Mammals of the World*. Johns Hopkins University Press, Baltimore.

Wallace, A. R., 1869. Review of C. Lyell, *Principles of Geology and Elements of Geology. Quarterly Review,* 126:359–394.

—— 1889. *Darwinism*. Macmillan, London.

Wallace, J. A., 1975. "Dietary Adaptations of *Australopithecus* and Early *Homo*." In R. H. Tuttle (ed.), *Paleoanthropology, Morphology, and Paleoecology*. Mouton, The Hague, pp. 203–223.

Wäppling, E., 1984. "Four Irish Legendary Figures in *At Swim-Two-Birds*." *Acta Universitatis Upsaliensis,* 56:1–109.

Wardale, E. E., 1935. *Chapters on Old English Literature*. Kegan Paul, Trench, Trubner, London.

Ware, J. R. (trans.), 1963. *The Sayings of Chuang Chou*. Mentor, New York.

Warner, C. D., 1878. "A-Hunting of the Deer." *Atlantic Monthly* (April), pp. 522–529.

Warner, S. T., 1977. Introduction to T. H. White, *The Book of Merlyn*. Berkeley, New York, 1978, pp. ix–xxvi.

Warren, T. H., and F. Page (eds.), 1965. *Tennyson: Poems and Plays*. Oxford University Press, Oxford.

Washburn, S. L., 1951a. "The Analysis of Primate Evolution with Particular Reference to the Origin of Man." *Symposia on Quantitative Biology,* 15:67–77.

—— 1951b. "The New Physical Anthropology." *Transactions of the New York Academy of Sciences* (series 2), 13:298–304.

—— 1960. "Tools and Human Evolution." *Scientific American,* 203 (September), pp. 63–75.

—— and V. Avis, 1958. "Evolution of Human Behavior." In A. Roe and G. G. Simpson (eds.), *Behavior and Evolution*. Yale University Press, New Haven, pp. 421–436.

—— and I. DeVore, 1961. "Social Behavior of Baboons and Early Man." In S. L. Washburn (ed.), *Social Life of Early Man*. Aldine, Chicago, pp. 91–105.

—— and R. S. O. Harding, 1975. "Evolution and Human Nature." In S. Arieti (ed.), *American Handbook of Psychiatry*. Basic Books, New York, vol. 6, pp. 3–13.

——— and C. S. Lancaster, 1968. "The Evolution of Hunting." In R. B. Lee and I. DeVore (eds.), *Man the Hunter*. Aldine, Chicago, pp. 293–303.

Waters, R., 1990. "A New Dawn in Bohemia?" *Sierra* (May/June), pp. 34–40.

Watkins, T. H., 1980. "The Thin Green Line." *Audubon* (September), pp. 68–87.

Watson, P. F., 1979. *The Garden of Love in Tuscan Art of the Early Renaissance*. Art Alliance Press, Philadelphia.

Weigand, K. (ed.), 1955. *Rousseau: Discourses*. Felix Meiner, Hamburg.

Weiner, D. R., 1988. *Models of Nature: Ecology, Conservation, and Cultural Revolution in Soviet Russia*. Indiana University Press, Bloomington.

Weismiller, E., 1936. *The Deer Come Down*. Yale University Press, New Haven.

Wells, H. G., 1922. *The Outline of History: Being a Plain History of Life and Mankind*. 4th edition. 1925 reprint, Collier, New York.

Wernaer, R., 1910. *Romanticism and the Romantic School in Germany*. D. Appleton, New York.

Werner, A., 1945. "The Author of 'Bambi.'" *Saturday Review of Literature*, November 3, pp. 17–18.

Wesley, J., 1958. *The Works of John Wesley*. Zondervan, Grand Rapids.

Whedbee, C. H., 1966. *Legends of the Outer Banks and Tar Heel Tidewater*. John F. Blair, Winston-Salem.

Whicher, G. F. (ed.), 1965. *The Transcendentalist Revolt against Materialism*. Heath, Boston.

Whisker, J. B., 1981. *The Right to Hunt*. North River Press, n.p.

White, E. B., 1944. *One Man's Meat*. Harper, New York.

White, L. A., 1949. *The Science of Culture: A Study of Man and Civilization*. Grove, New York.

White, L., Jr., 1962. *Medieval Technology and Social Change*. Oxford University Press, London.

White, T. H., 1954. *The Book of Beasts*. Jonathan Cape, London.

——— 1977. *The Book of Merlyn*. University of Texas Press, Austin. 1978 ed., Berkeley, New York.

——— 1981. *The Maharajah and Other Stories*. Putman, New York.

Wiese, B. von (ed.), 1936. *Schillers Werke*. Bibliographisches Institut, Leipzig.

Wilbur, R., 1963. *The Poems of Richard Wilbur*. Harcourt, Brace, and World, New York.

Wille, F. (ed.), 1986. *Flavius Renatus Vegetius: Epitoma Rei Militaris (Das gesamte Kriegswesen)*. Verlag Sauerländer, Aarau.

Williams, W. G. (ed.), 1929. *Cicero: The Letters to His Friends*. Harvard University Press, Cambridge.

Williams, J., 1990. "The Killing Game." *Esquire* (October), pp. 113–128.

Williams, T., 1981. "'The Worst Predatator in Maine.'" *Audubon* (March), pp. 36–41.

——— 1989a. "The Incineration of Yellowstone." *Audubon* (January), pp. 38–85.

——— 1989b. "Circus Whales." *Audubon* (February), pp. 16–23.

Wiltse, H. M., 1900. "In the Southern Field of Folk-Lore." *Journal of American Folklore,* 13:209–212.

Wimberly, L. C., 1928. *Folklore in the English and Scottish Ballads.* University of Chicago Press, Chicago.

Wishy, B., 1968. *The Child and the Republic: The Dawn of Modern American Child Culture.* University of Pennsylvania Press, Philadelphia.

Wolberg, D. L., 1970. "The Hypothesized Osteodontokeratic Culture of the Australopithecinae: A Look at the Evidence and the Opinions." *Current Anthropology,* 11:23–37.

Wolcott, J., 1983. "The Prince of Finesse." *Harper's* (September), pp. 63–66.

Wolf, R., 1981. "God, James Watt, and the Public Land." *Audubon* (March), pp. 58–65.

Wolkomir, R., 1985. "High-Tech Materials Blaze Urban Trail for Outdoorsy Duds." *Smithsonian* (January), pp. 122–137.

Wollheim, R. (ed.), 1963. *David Hume on Religion.* World, Cleveland.

Wynne-Tyson, E. (ed. and trans.), 1965. *Porphyry: On Abstinence from Animal Food.* Barnes and Noble, New York.

Young, J. Z., 1971. *An Introduction to the Study of Man.* Oxford University Press, New York.

Ziff, L. (ed.), 1959. *Benjamin Franklin's Autobiography and Selected Writings.* Holt, Rinehart and Winston, New York.

Zuckerman, S., 1991. "Apes R Not Us." *New York Review of Books,* May 30, pp. 43–49.

Acknowledgments

Many people have contributed to this book in more ways than I can recount here. I owe special thanks to my colleagues at Duke University for their understanding support and to the John Simon Guggenheim Memorial Foundation for the provision of a Guggenheim Fellowship that afforded me a year of free time to study and think about the issues addressed here. I am grateful to R. D. Martin, John Pfeiffer, David Pilbeam, B. J. Williams, Peter Winkler, and Dorothea Cook for all their interest and encouragement; to C. Loring Brace, Weston La Barre, Charles Leslie, Pat Shipman, and the late John Buettner-Janusch for many useful ideas and criticisms; and to Cleveland Amory, Michael Corcoran, W. L. Hylander, Judi Klein-Dial, Bill Taylor, Phillip Tobias, and the late Raymond Dart for helping me answer questions and locate sources.

I am particularly thankful for the help I have received from the people at Harvard University Press. I am indebted to Michael G. Fisher for his support and advice, to A. J. Sullivan for his invaluable help in securing illustrations, and to my editor Joyce Backman for all the thoughtful and sympathetic effort that she put into guiding me and my book through the process of publication. Special thanks are due to Howard Boyer, whose sustaining enthusiasm for this project saw me through difficult times at the beginning and helped bring me through to the end. The research for Chapter 9 was made possible by the generous assistance of David Smith and the rest of the staff at the Walt Disney Archives.

The following have granted permission to reprint quoted material:

HARCOURT BRACE JOVANOVICH, INC.
Lines from Richard Wilbur, "Castles and Distances," in *The Poems of Richard Wilbur*, © 1963 by Richard Wilbur

FARRAR, STRAUS & GIROUX, INC.
Excerpts from Seamus Heaney, *Sweeney Astray*, © 1983 by Seamus Heaney

TOM LEHRER
Too Many Songs by Tom Lehrer (Pantheon, 1981), © 1953, renewed, by Tom Lehrer

LITTLE, BROWN AND COMPANY
George Starbuck, "Translations from the English," from *White Paper*, © 1965 by
  George Starbuck; first appeared in the *Atlantic*

NEW DIRECTIONS PUBLISHING CORP.
Lines from Kenneth Patchen, *Cloth of the Tempest* (1948)
Lines from Kenneth Rexroth, *In Defense of the Earth* (1956)

RANDOM HOUSE, INC.
W. H. Auden, "Fugal-Chorus," from *Collected Poems*, ed. Edward Mendelson,
  © 1944 by W. H. Auden
Lines from *The English Auden*, ed. Edward Mendelson, © 1977 by Edward Mendelson, William Meredith, and Monroe K. Spears, Executors of the Estate of
  W. H. Auden; published in London by Faber and Faber, Ltd.
Robert Fitzgerald, trans., *The Odyssey* by Homer, © 1961, 1963 by Robert Fitzgerald, renewed 1989 by Benedict R. C. Fitzgerald; published by Vintage Books,
  a Division of Random House, Inc.
Robinson Jeffers, "The Beginning and the End," from *The Beginning and the End
  and Other Poems*, © 1963 by Garth Jeffers and Donnan Jeffers; "Original Sin,"
  from *Selected Poems*, © 1948 by Robinson Jeffers

UNIVERSITY PRESS OF NEW ENGLAND
James Dickey, "Springer Mountain," from *Helmets*, © 1962 by James Dickey;
  published by Wesleyan University Press

WALT DISNEY PRODUCTIONS
For access to their Archives in reference to *Bambi*

LIVERIGHT PUBLISHING CORP.
Robinson Jeffers, "The King of the Beasts," from *The Double Axe and Other
  Poems*, © 1977 by Liveright Publishing Corporation, © 1948 and renewed
  © 1975 by Donnan Call Jeffers and Garth Jeffers

STANFORD UNIVERSITY PRESS
Robinson Jeffers, "Orca," from *The Collected Poetry of Robinson Jeffers, Vol. III
  (1939–1962)*, © 1995 by the Board of Trustees of the Leland Stanford Junior
  University

Index